GIFTS OF THE GODS

FOODS AND NATIONS is a new series from Reaktion that explores the history – and geography – of food. Books in the series reveal the hidden history behind the food eaten today in different countries and regions of the world, telling the story of how food production and consumption developed, and how they were influenced by the culinary practices of other places and peoples. Each book in the Foods and Nations series offers fascinating insights into the distinct flavours of a country and its culture.

Already published

Al Dente: A History of Food in Italy
Fabio Parasecoli

Beyond Bratwurst: A History of Food in Germany
Ursula Heinzelmann

Feasts and Fasts: A History of Food in India
Colleen Taylor Sen

Gifts of the Gods: A History of Food in Greece
Andrew and Rachel Dalby

Rice and Baguette: A History of Food in Vietnam
Vu Hong Lien

A Rich and Fertile Land: A History of Food in America
Bruce Kraig

Gifts of
the Gods

A History of Food
in Greece

ANDREW AND RACHEL DALBY

REAKTION BOOKS

To Maureen and Kosta

Published by Reaktion Books Ltd
Unit 32, Waterside
44–48 Wharf Road
London N1 7UX, UK
www.reaktionbooks.co.uk

First published 2017
Copyright © Andrew Dalby and Rachel Dalby 2017

Printed and bound in China by 1010 Printing International Ltd

A catalogue record for this book is available from the British Library

ISBN 978 1 78023 854 8

CONTENTS

PROLOGUE

This is the story of the foods of Greece and how people have enjoyed them. It begins in prehistory. No one can say when it was, in that long period, that Greek-speakers first arrived in the country; it turns out to be easier to pin down the time when people in Greece began to taste olive oil, wine and fine fish. In classical Greece the world's oldest tradition of local food and wine specialities developed. Roman Greece, though an insignificant province in wealth and population, was celebrated throughout the Roman Empire for its honey and mountain herbs. Byzantine Greece, heartland of an empire, gave medieval Europe its legendary sweet wines. Greece under Turkish rule, a backwater once more, fed the great Greek cities of Constantinople and Smyrna and was the source of a world diaspora. Modern Greece, a nation state, has the most varied landscapes of Europe; its good foods and wines, as local and individual as ever, draw their quality directly from those lands and seas. The ways of dining and festivity have always been unique to Greece and they still are; with luck they always will be.

What politics preceded the Minoan and Mycenaean palaces is unknown. Those palaces collapsed, whether destroyed by some outside force or by their own weight, and since then the political geography has been forever changing. Classical Greece was an admirable, uneasy world of independent 'cities', some no larger than villages, often at war with one another, always under threat from larger cities that were bullies and from empires that were even bigger bullies. Persia was the first of those, and then Macedon, and the Hellenistic monarchies that followed Alexander, and then Rome, the biggest of all. Greece stayed quiet under Roman rule, and taught civilization and cookery to Rome, but can't be said to have prospered.

Greek food and wine at a taverna in Kambi, Zakynthos.

As the Roman Empire shrank and became Byzantine, with its capital at Greek Constantinople, Greece became the home farm, but still prospered less than it might. Empires are not good for Greece, but they fall. The Ottoman Empire that followed the Byzantine – ruled still from Constantinople – wasn't the best of them: it also fell. Modern Greece, independent from 1832, increasing in territory until 1947, when Italy had to give up the Dodecanese, has had its ups and downs. These days Greece may feel like a colony again, in thrall to its tourists, in debt to northern Europe, from where most of its tourists come; but the new and shapeless empire to which it currently belongs will surely fall as the others did.

As told here, the story begins (Chapter One) with the landscape of Greece and the animal and plant foods that people have found there from prehistory to our own time. The recorded history of food, cookery and gastronomy is then traced: classical (Chapter Two), Roman and early Byzantine (Chapter Three), medieval and Ottoman (Chapter Four). We look at the food traditions of the Greeks who live beyond Greek frontiers (Chapter Five), we return to explore local foods of the regions and islands of Greece (Chapter Six), and finally we survey the modern food traditions of the country as a whole (Chapter Seven). In a brief epilogue Greek food is explicitly placed in a wider context – that of conviviality. This structure brings out the unique contributions of Greece to the world of food. The country's remarkable landscape and microclimates led to a flowering of local produce and local gastronomy long before such ideas were thought of anywhere else in the world. Its status as a centre of travel and trade required a special openness to the outside world, and that openness enlivens Greek hospitality to this day. In this shared exploration the historical text is mostly Andrew's, the recipe texts and many of the photographs are Rachel's. Should our spelling of Greek place names be consistent? It isn't always: Rachel begins from Paros now and Andrew begins from the *Odyssey* 2,700 years ago.

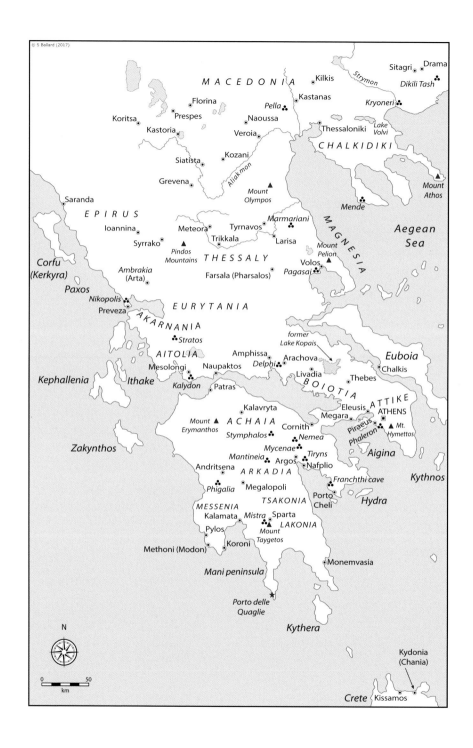

© S Ballard (2017)

M A C E D O N I A

Sitagri • Drama

Kilkis

Strymon

Dikili Tash

Florina • Kastanas

Pella • Kryoneri

Koritsa • Prespes • Naoussa

Kastoria • Veroia • Thessaloniki • *Lake Volvi*

Siatista • Kozani *C H A L K I D I K I*

Grevena • *Mount Olympos* • Mount Athos

Aliakmon *Mende*

Saranda

E P I R U S • *Marmariani*

Ioannina • Meteora • Tyrnavos • Aegean Sea

Syrrako • Trikkala • Larisa *M A G N E S I A*

Corfu (Kerkyra) • *Pindos Mountains* • *T H E S S A L Y* • Mount Pelion

Paxos • *Ambrakia (Arta)* • Farsala (Pharsalos) • Volos • *Pagasai*

Nikopolis • *E U R Y T A N I A*

Preveza • *A K A R N A N I A*

Stratos • *former Lake Kopais*

A I T O L I A • Amphissa • Arachova

Mesolongi • Naupaktos • *Delphi* • Livadia • Thebes • Euboia

Kephallenia • Ithake • *Kalydon* • Patras • *B O I O T I A* • Chalkis

Kalavryta • *A T T I K E*

A C H A I A • Eleusis • ATHENS

Mount Erymanthos • Cornith • Megara • Piraeus • *Mt. Hymettos*

Zakynthos • *Stymphalos* • Nemea • *Phaleron*

Mycenae • Tiryns • Aigina

Andritsena • *Mantineia* • Argos • Nafplio

A R K A D I A • *Franchthi cave* • Kythnos

Phigalia • Megalopoli • Porto Cheli • Hydra

T S A K O N I A

M E S S E N I A • *Mistra* • Sparta

Kalamata • *L A K O N I A*

Pylos • *Mount Taygetos*

Methoni (Modon) • Koroni • Monemvasia

Mani peninsula

Porto delle Quaglie

N

Kythera

Kydonia (Chania)

0 — 50 km

Crete • Kissamos

© S Ballard (2017)

T H R A C E

Sitagri Drama
Dikili Tash Porto Lago
Kryoneri Maroneia

Bosporos
Pera (Galata)
Constantinople
(Istanbul)
Propontis

Thasos

Hellespont
(Dardanelles)
Abydos

Triglia
(Mudanya)

Lemnos

Tenedos

Sporades *Gioura*
Methymna
Lesbos *Thermi*
Eresos Mytilene
Pergamon

Aegean Sea Plomari

Skyros

Euboia *Psara*

Smyrna (İzmir)

Erythrai

L Y D I A

ATHENS Karystos
Andros *Samos* Phygela
Aigina *Tinos* *Ikaria*
Syros *Mykonos* Iasos
Kythnos *Delos*
Hydra *Paros* *Naxos*
Siphnos *Kalymnos* *Kos*

Melos *Ios*
Therasia *Anafi*
Thera *Dodecanese*
(Santorini) *Rhodes*

Kydonia
(Chania) *Karpathos*

Kissamos *Crete* *Kasos*
Rethymno Knossos N
Samaria gorge Archanes *PEZA*
Phaistos Ierapetra
Myrtos

0   50
km

ONE

Origins

A land where steep mountains, low-lying plains, islands and seas are intimately mixed. The mountains are darkly wooded with slow-maturing oak, terebinth and linden. The foothills and plains, relatively waterless, consist largely of open woodland of the same three species with some juniper towards the south. There is wild pear, wild plum, almond, hawthorn, cornel, danewort, rose and bramble, but the pear and plum trees are as spiny as the hawthorns and their fruits not as sweet as they sound. Open hillsides are aromatic with thyme and sage and mountain savory. There are other herbs to be found with skill and a good nose, fennel, anise, perhaps coriander; there are pulse seeds – vetches, lentils, lupins and grass peas – but not the beans most familiar to us and not all of them to be thoughtlessly eaten. The lowlands are grassed. The oats repay attention, and there are worthwhile greens and roots of dandelion and carrot kinds, although, like the pulses, these need to be carefully chosen. In season there are young shoots, wild asparagus and the like, that are very good to eat. The open country is grazed by wild ass, red deer and roe deer. There are hares, foxes and wild pigs. There are squirrels and various smaller animals, pigeons and many other birds. In the northern mountains are ibex and chamois, which migrate seasonally between highlands and valleys. The juiciest inhabitants of the wetlands, not counting ducks, are worms, slugs and snails. There are shellfish, shrimps and many small fish species in shallow waters, some larger fish in the rivers and more of these hovering, tantalizingly, not far from the shore in open sea.

First of all a very mountainous mainland peninsula, extending towards the south and the sun from a larger, almost equally mountainous, northerly continental mass. The high backbone lies westwards; towards the east the highlands descend to a series of low-lying plains separated by narrower mountain chains. East of the mainland there is a wide, sometimes stormy, moderately deep sea. It has a single, large, relatively low-lying island at its centre – call it 'Cycladia' – with many smaller islands and, to the south, serving to divide this sea from its much vaster parent, a long, narrow and extremely mountainous island that we can't call anything but Crete. Thus it is not quite an inland sea. At times it is closed off entirely to the north; at other periods a narrow strait flows in from the northeast, making a link with a more distant, more northerly, very deep, ice-fed sea. The northern and eastern coasts, to either side of this intermittent strait, offer wider, steppe-like plains, traversed by a series of large rivers.

There are fierce animals in the mountains to the north, both lions and bears, but not many of them. The dwarf hippopotami, dwarf elephants and native deer of Crete have not held on this long: they are extinct. In any case, taken as a proportion of the available whole, any such rarities would offer little food value.

There are very few humans but a fair number of inviting caves, some of which, as is evident from skulls and skeletons, were already inhabited by humans (Neanderthals or their relatives) in the distant past.

This is Greece at 15,000 BC, towards the end of the Paleolithic period. The almost-inland sea is the Aegean, and the big island of Cycladia may, for all we know, have lived on in popular memory long enough to become the Atlantis of Greek myth.[1] The ice fields in the northern hemisphere were at their widest, the weather was coldest and the sea level was at least 100 metres lower than today. Greece of seventeen thousand years ago was a beautiful country, even if its few adventurous inhabitants did not see it as such. Our appreciation of landscape began to develop far later than our admiration for a well-shaped human or for an animal worth hunting. It is not fully developed yet, to judge by the plastic and concrete with which we have littered the modern coastlines of Greece.

STONE AGE

The humans of Greece, seventeen thousand years ago, gathered and hunted their daily subsistence. They had to live close to sources of food. In the high mountains they watched the seasonal movements of ibex and chamois. They used rock shelters – overhanging cliffs, not as welcoming as caves – at strategic points where they could prey on the migrating herds. In the lowlands, although nearly all foods were seasonal, something at least could be found almost all through the year. Caves were good places to live: they offered shelter from cold and storm.

Mackerel

Eleven thousand years ago mackerel were among the delicacies caught with bone fish-hooks by the people who used the Cave of the Cyclops on Gioura in the Sporades.

Sun-dried mackerel (*pariani gouna*) as described here is a speciality of Paros, although Chios has a similar dish. Sun-drying, an ancient technique for preserving food, is extremely efficient in such a dry and sun-drenched country (admittedly not all readers will be able to do it this way). The method was given to us by Manolis, the grill-chef at Kolymbithres restaurant near Naoussa on Paros.

To prepare *gouna* you will need roughly one fresh medium mackerel for every two people eating. Clean and gut the fish, remove the head, then butterfly each one so that it is open like a book but still attached along one side. Remove the bones and clean well inside. Place in a shallow dish and splash liberally with white wine, salt, pepper and plenty of dried oregano. The idea is to wet the fish but not to marinate it in wine; the oregano should be enough to virtually cover the surface, which sounds a lot, but the flavours in this dish are strong.

Place the fish on a rack — say a biscuit-cooling wire rack — and leave outside under a hot summer sun, covered with fine

Those lowland plains are now largely under water; their evidence is inaccessible to us or washed away. This is why Franchthi cave, halfway up a coastal hill near Porto Cheli, is so important. It was on the edge of a lowland plain — but it has never been flooded. Time and again new groups of people have discovered it and decided to live in it. Its history as a human settlement is longer than that of any other place in Greece, and through most of that history we know what the inhabitants of Franchthi cave chose to eat. From the rock shelter of Klithi in northern Epiros, used in spring and autumn, to Franchthi, which was probably inhabited all year round, we can observe the most distant origins of the Greek cuisine of today.

At Franchthi about 12,000 BC red deer and wild ass were the occasional highlights in a regular diet of wild lentils, vetch, almonds, acorns, wild pears and terebinth fruits (smaller than pistachios but equally

gauze to keep the flies away, for two to three hours. Turn once and leave for another few hours. The length of time is a matter of taste: the longer the fish is dried, the stronger and drier it will be. Some leave it drying for several days.

When you are ready to eat, simply grill the *gouna* over charcoal (or on a grill pan) and eat with a good amount of lemon juice squeezed over. A plate of summer tomatoes, or a shredded cabbage and carrot salad dressed with oil and lemon, would go well with it.

Two of the most familiar fresh fish of Greece, on sale at Athens Central Market: gilthead bream, Greek *tsipoura*, and red mullet, Greek *barbouni*.

nourishing), to which the usual relishes were shellfish and inshore fish. A thousand years later someone around Franchthi was becoming more adventurous: sharp slivers of the natural volcanic glass obsidian were being used as knives to cut up animal meat – the first Greek kitchenware – and this obsidian came from out in the Aegean, from Melos, which was always an island even when the sea was at its lowest. No one could have discovered obsidian except by canoeing around Melos and noting the unusual colour of two shiny rock faces, and no one could have got it from Melos to Franchthi without several days of island-hopping and a very long walk.

If people in Greece were making journeys of that kind, surely they also tried to catch deep-water fish? Sure enough, there is evidence that they did: not at Franchthi, as it happens, but further north, in the Cave of the Cyclops on what is now the tiny island of Gioura in the Sporades. It was a larger island then, but the cave was already close to the sea. By 9,000 BC the people who lived there were making bone fish-hooks. Then, as now, the Aegean was notable for the variety of fish it offered. Those fish-hooks caught bream, mackerel and grouper along with some hake, grey mullet, rascasse and moray – a dangerous opponent, this last, as Lawrence Durrell discovered on the shore of Corfu in 1937, where at the cry of '*Zmyrna!*' a moray eel was speared, but 'it took three of them to lug it on to the rock, and for a quarter of an hour on dry land it fought savagely, with two tridents piercing its brain . . . I can hear the dry snapping of its jaws . . . it had the ferocity and determination of Satan'. Supper for the Durrells that evening was moray and red sauce.[2]

Back to the Cave of the Cyclops, where people were also experimenting with the keeping and breeding of pigs. Franchthi, meanwhile, was eating a range of animals and birds and enjoying a sudden wealth of snails, with wild oats and wild barley on the side. Then a new group appeared who had as their main purpose in life the catching of tuna, as we know from the tuna backbones they discarded. Tuna, like moray, is no easy catch. They are big, fierce fish and they travel in large shoals well away from the shore. These days they pass through Greek waters twice a year on their remarkable migration from the Black Sea to the Atlantic and back. They evidently started doing so soon after 8000 BC – which could well be when the Bosporus and Dardanelles, linking the Black Sea and the Aegean, first came into existence – and Greece's love affair with tuna, fresh, pickled, dry-salted and dried, began. Far in the future Greeks would found

Tuna are not all so very big and fierce.

Hunting scene from early Minoan funerary chest.

a series of colonies along the migration route: Byzantion (Constantinople, Istanbul) would be the greatest of those colonies.

Then came a change: so big a change that it has been called the 'Neolithic revolution'. It spread from the east towards the west and first touched Greece shortly after 7000 BC. There were new plant and animal foods, and they were not being hunted but farmed. People were spending their days differently, perhaps more monotonously, but with reliable harvests brought by farming there were soon more settlements. Population began to grow, and the very appearance of the Greek landscape changed as farmers planted fields of barley and emmer wheat, lentils, peas, soon afterwards broad beans and chickpeas; as they kept pigs, sheep, goats and cattle. Those new species have been central to Greek food ever since.

Some of the new ideas had been tried locally, but these domesticated breeds and varieties were new to Greece, introduced from Anatolia or the Near East. Local varieties, wild lentils and peas, wild barley and wild pigs became ever more marginal, as did the ibexes and chamois of the northern mountains.

The change was probably brought by migrating peoples. This is certainly the way it was with Crete, because until this moment Crete had no known human inhabitants. Then, at a date close to 6950 BC, a first settlement appeared at the very site of Knossos. These migrants grew barley and emmer and something very like durum wheat. They kept sheep, goats, pigs and cows, and they must have brought the barley, both kinds of wheat and all four animal species with them to Crete by sea.

In this way Knossos, target of an ancient and astonishingly bold act of colonization, became one of the first areas outside the Near East where village farming was practised. The Cretan mountains are visible from a great distance, and the original journey would have required several days at sea. Knossos lived and grew. Lying at the northern edge of one of the largest arable areas on Crete, its lands are ploughable and fertile, with a stream immediately below the site and a perennial spring close by. The colonists knew just what they were doing. But no one now knows where they came from or why they chose Crete.

Crete can tell us how and when cheese began to be made in the region. In the years following 4000 BC there was a major increase in the number of settlements on the island, and the striking thing is their location. Crete is largely not arable land, and these new sites would have been almost useless except as bases for herding animals – cattle, sheep and goats – in the high plateaux in summer, where there was certainly no great number of consumers of meat. So the new herds and flocks must have been wanted for wool, skins and milk, and at such a distance from potential consumers the milk could be useful only if made into cheese. Other kinds of evidence for cheese on Crete also exist, though from later periods: cheese-strainers (they might be something else, but no one can suggest *what* else) and images of men leading goats and carrying churns. Cheese is easily stored if it has been well made. Almost on its own, harvested from wide stretches of land that

An olive tree, several hundred years old and still flourishing, in a grove beside the church of Agios Georgios at Chalki on Naxos.

previously offered little or no food, it surely allowed the human population of the island to grow steadily. As far as the Aegean is concerned, Crete may well have 'invented' cheese, but the idea spread. Finds of cheese-strainers show that cheese was being made in Thessaly by 3000 BC and on Melos and several Cycladic islands soon after 2000 BC. But Crete has never ceased to be a producer of fine cheese on a large scale.

There's more from Crete. Palynologists – who work on pollen found in layers of archaeological sediment – can show that even before 5000 BC, very early in the Neolithic history of Crete, while native oak and pine remained the principal forest trees, a third species, olive, was more noticeably flourishing. This is still wild olive, not a true cultivated variety, but the human population of Crete must have been encouraging it.[3] Sure enough, at 3000 BC or soon after, at Myrtos on the southeastern coast of Crete, at a large farm or small palace, the local economy included not only barley and durum wheat, goats, sheep, pigs and cattle, but wine (we'll come back to the wine), and also plenty of olives. There is no olive mill or olive press at the Myrtos site, but there are troughs – presumably used to extract oil from olive pulp – and storage jars: 'When burnt earth samples from the store jars in Room 22 were immersed in water in flotation tests for grain the mixture appeared distinctly greasy with an oil-like film. It is most probable that these jars contained oil.'[4] There is even olive-wood charcoal: the favoured fuel at Myrtos was olive prunings, which could only have come from mature, regularly tended olive trees. Myrtos foreshadows the fully developed Minoan civilization and the great palaces of Knossos and Phaistos, whose stores and cellars were filled with grain, olive oil and wine.

Along the north coast of the Aegean, in modern Thrace and Macedonia, the story is different. From the Neolithic revolution onwards the number of settlements steadily grows, and the food question here has attracted the attention of Tania Valamoti of Thessaloniki University, who has teased out the evidence from several northern sites. The selection of staple foods is different from that on Crete. The cereals were emmer, barley and einkorn, and the favourite was the simplest wheat species, einkorn, the one that was never grown on Crete. The pulses were lentils – popular even now – with grass peas and bitter vetch; the last two are poisonous until soaked. Oil was important from the beginning, but in northern Greece olives were not yet known and the oil plants were flax and occasionally gold-of-pleasure (*Camelina sativa*). Flax offers fibre and chewable seeds as well as linseed oil, but this, very different from olive oil, is useless to store: it quickly goes rancid. People gathered blackberries, wild pears, acorns, terebinth fruits, grapes and figs.

Not just seeds but whole dried figs have been found at two Neolithic sites, one of which is Dikili Tash, close to classical Philippi. Wild figs are so commonly found near cultivated land that they seem to be a native species. In reality the wild figs, like the cultivated ones, have been deliberately planted. Fig producers need wild figs close at hand, as this eighteenth-century description of Chios explains:

> They collect about May or June a number of wild figs, and fasten them to the branches of domestic fig trees, that the small fly bred in these figs may settle on the domestic, and deposit their eggs in them, by which means they ripen much better than they otherwise would.[5]

Nearly right. The fig wasp, which breeds in the wild fruit, is the only insect capable of pollinating figs, and most cultivated varieties do not ripen their fruit unless pollinated. Those who first planted figs in California lost many years of fruit production because they ignored this ancient wisdom, which must have been perfectly well known to those who, soon after the Neolithic revolution, introduced figs from western Asia to Greece.

Fresh figs are a luxury, but, wherever the late summer is hot and dry enough to dry figs under the sun, drying is by far the best way to use them: dried figs, whether eaten whole or used in cuisine, are a rich source of sugar and they store extremely well (as was evident from the find of whole dried figs at Dikili Tash). They are also unbeatable as an aid to digestion: it is no surprise that fig seeds and grape pips were found in the drain below a latrine at the Bronze Age site of Akrotiri on Thera (Santorini).

An even more exciting find from Neolithic northern Greece comes from the same site of Dikili Tash: grape pressings, compressed pips and skins, dated to somewhere before 4000 BC. The fruits are wild – at least, the pips are indistinguishable in size and shape from those of wild grapes – but the juice must have been sweet enough to be worth pressing, and, once pressed, wild yeast, always present on grape skins, would have ensured that it was fermented. So the aim must have been to make wine.

The cradle of wine is not Greece, nor anywhere in Europe, but the mountainous country south of the Caucasus. Storage jars containing wine residues found at Shulaveri in Georgia have been dated to about 6000 BC, and what is unmistakably a winery, with the remains of a press as well as storage jars, from a cave at Areni in Armenia, dates from just before 4000 BC – the same period as Dikili Tash. But wild grapes were native to Greece too, and there is no sign that cultivated grape varieties were transmitted from the Caucasus to Greece. The grapes found at Dikili Tash, and the long sequence of grape pips from the nearby site of Sitagri, dated roughly from 4500 to 2500 BC, are stages in the development of cultivated varieties from local wild grapes. The size of the pips gradually increased: how could this happen unless people were selecting and propagating vines that produced bigger fruit? How could it be that the classical Greek philosopher Demokritos was able to claim that the varieties of vine were 'uncountable and infinite'? – and that was in the fourth century BC. It was exactly at that period that the Crimean vineyards of the Greek colony of Chersonesus Taurica were developed, and, sure enough, those Crimean vines were not carried there from Greece but tamed from local wild vines. Wherever the vine was native, many varieties have gradually emerged from the wild stock with human help, and have been propagated by cuttings. Within that age-long process it is impossible to identify any single moment at which wild becomes domesticated.

Winemaking skills are mainly developed and passed on locally. The natural fermentation results in a pleasant and intoxicating beverage, but that is only the beginning of the story. Skilful manipulation of the fermentation process and careful storage of the resulting wine make a vast difference to its eventual quality. A lot depends on local conditions. So although Dikili Tash is far distant from the origin of winemaking, it belongs to a very early chapter and gives northern Greece unexpected prominence in the story.

In this way olives and vines, which, more than any other crops, give the landscape of Greece its unique character, first appeared on the regional scene. They were soon to spread. At Thermi on Lesbos, for example, olive wood was being used in the period 2700–2350 BC, and vine wood is recognized even earlier, from 2900 to 2700 BC: the vine concerned was (as at Dikili Tash) 'probably a native type, entering early into cultivation'.[6]

BRONZE AGE

The second revolution in this story took as long to happen as the first: it is the collapse of the Cycladic, Minoan and Mycenaean civilizations of later prehistoric Greece. Art historians focus on their flowering, not their collapse, but there is no practical difference. We know about these cultures, their food as well as their art, because they fell.

They fell three times. The first catastrophe was the great volcanic eruption of Thera (Santorini) in the late seventeenth century BC, probably 1629 or 1627 BC. It buried at least two towns under volcanic ash, and caused a tsunami that devastated nearby islands and the north coast of Crete. The second event, around 1450 BC, was the conquest of Minoan Crete by the Mycenaeans of mainland Greece. The third was the violent eradication of the Mycenaean culture itself by some cause or causes unknown; the Mycenaean palaces were destroyed by fire around 1200 BC and were not rebuilt. Each of the three catastrophes consigned whole towns to destruction, their art, their equipment, their stores, their records – a destruction that left rich remains for modern archaeologists to find.

If art tells the truth, the Minoans were a peaceful people with bull-leaping acrobats and bare-breasted priestesses. Their language, written in Linear A script on clay tablets, has not been deciphered. The most obvious assumption, and probably the true one, is that their civilization was the direct continuation and final flowering of the Neolithic culture that had been brought to Crete around 6950 BC. They were conquered by the warlike Mycenaeans, who spoke Greek, fought with spears, copied the clay tablets idea from the Minoans and kept their records in Linear B script. The most obvious assumption about them, though it is currently accepted by only a minority of archaeologists, is that they were direct descendants of the Neolithic peoples of southern and central Greece.

The Minoans are at the centre of this story. Their deep-rooted culture continued to flourish through natural catastrophes and violent conquest. It influenced the people of the Aegean islands very deeply, and eventually it was largely adopted by the Mycenaean conquerors. The Mycenaeans are also central because, unlike all other peoples so far mentioned, they wrote a language that we can read (up to a point). Minoan art and Mycenaean texts add perspectives to our understanding of Bronze Age food sources, perspectives that are not available for earlier periods. There is still more: the *Iliad* and *Odyssey*, composed and written down several centuries after the Mycenaean collapse, depend on an oral tradition that preserved many details of that earlier world. We cannot start from them, however, because we would have no way to tell which details are really Mycenaean. Contemporary evidence is essential, and that is why archaeology retains first place.

A French geologist, Ferdinand Fouqué, while investigating the Santorini volcano in the 1860s, happened on the remains of two ancient towns buried under volcanic ash, one at Akrotiri on the main island of Thera, another on the small island of Therasia. He guessed a date of 2000 BC for the great eruption that had destroyed them. Archaeology was still in its infancy, but the finding of storerooms still containing food that had been abandoned nearly four millennia ago was a gift to any scientific observer.

Lathyrus clymenum, known in Greece as *arakas* or *fava Santorinis*, a Mediterranean wild legume but cultivated for at least 3,500 years on the islands of Santorini, Anafi and Karpathos.

Fouqué found large quantities of stored barley, lentils, chickpeas and 'a kind of pea still cultivated on the island, known locally as *arakas*' (we'll return to that). He identified the bones of sheep, horses, donkeys, dogs, cats and goats, including three whole skeletons of animals that were in their shed when the eruption struck. He observed the abundance of carbonized olive wood and mastic wood (*Pistacia lentiscus*), reasoning that Thera was more tree-covered before the eruption than it is today. He noted the absence of wheat and of cattle, evidently unsuitable for Thera then as now, and, more surprisingly, the absence of vines and grapes. He found flour mills and an olive mill of a primitive type, and his workmen showed him how to use it. A local informant even discovered, in a storage jar, a 'paste-like substance' that they guessed must have been cheese, though neither of them tasted it.[7]

Thanks to Fouqué's observation, confirmed from more recent finds at Akrotiri by Glynis Jones and Anaya Sarpaki, there is no doubt that at least one uniquely Cycladic food was already cultivated before the Santorini eruption. A grass-pea species, *Lathyrus clymenum*, locally called *arakas*, and known as a wild plant in some other parts of the Mediterranean region, was stored in jars in such large quantities that it could not possibly have been gathered from the wild. Fouqué and his two successors knew enough about local foods to see that this same species, unnoticed by almost everyone else, is still grown on Thera and the neighbouring islands of Anafi and Karpathos. Presumably it has been cultivated through the whole intervening period. Under its best-known name, *fava Santorinis*, this prehistoric survival has now suddenly become a fashionable and expensive food, offered to the gastronomically aware in tavernas across Greece.[8]

There is as yet no sign that wine was made on Santorini, as it certainly has been – to very good effect – ever since classical times, but the whole geography of this violently volcanic island group has changed so drastically that, after all, we cannot be sure: much evidence of human activity may have been completely destroyed, and, as Fouqué already knew, much may now lie deeply submerged. Elsewhere in the Minoan and Mycenaean worlds wine and olive oil were, one may say, equally important. How important, though? Everyone wants to know this, because wine and olive oil have been so essential to Greek and Mediterranean food culture in later times. But there is no consensus. Colin Renfrew, excavator at Melos, Sitagri and elsewhere, in *The Emergence of Civilisation: The Cyclades and the Aegean in the Third Millennium BC* (1972) stated his theory that Aegean Bronze Age culture developed locally, based on three food sources, grain, wine and olives, and that the latter two were brought into cultivation. Some say that Renfrew is wrong – the growing of vines and olives did not happen in the Aegean until later – but we can ignore them. The finds of charcoal

Olive oil workshop from the early Byzantine city of Sergilla in Syria, soon to succumb to Islamic conquest.

from olive pruning and vine pruning, from early Minoan Myrtos and early Bronze Age Lesbos, show that both species were already tended, encouraged and therefore plentiful. In the same year in which Renfrew published *The Emergence of Civilisation*, Peter Warren, excavator of Myrtos, claimed: 'Olive growing and viticulture were new in this period and the realization of their potential gave a wholly new pattern to life and an impetus to progress.'[9] Myrtos is at the very southern edge of the Aegean world; wine was perhaps new there, but we now know that at Dikili Tash, in the far north, it was familiar even earlier.

Later, supplies of wine and oil – especially oil – are listed on Mycenaean Linear B tablets, often in very large quantities. Big storerooms for wine and oil have been excavated, notably at the palace of Pylos in the Peloponnese. It's relevant here that the *Odyssey*, in describing the storeroom at Odysseus' palace – supposedly contemporary with the kingdom of Pylos – tells us that it contained 'plenty of good-smelling oil, and . . . jars of old sweet-tasting wine, with the unmixed divine drink in them, packed in rows against the wall, in case Odysseus might one day come home.'[10]

A food historian might want to modify Renfrew's insistence that Aegean civilization developed locally on the basis of three plant food sources, because human survival, in nearly every society ancient and modern, depends on a wider range of foods than this. The Aegean diet in particular has always necessarily been varied because of the uncertainty of Aegean harvests: farmers are compelled to diversify to make full use of varied terrain. Barley will be a safer choice in southern Greece and the islands than any species of wheat: wheat is good food, but a wheat crop may fail as often as one year in four. In bad years, to guard against shortages of grain, there had better be pulses, which can survive a drought that would ruin a barley crop. But some of these (including the admired *Lathyrus clymenum* of Thera) are seriously bad for human health if overused. They cannot serve alone as a staple. It is good if a forest is not too far away: chestnuts are a useful resource. In a very bad year we may need to let the pigs go hungry and eat their acorns or grind them for flour:

> He gathered some acorns off the ground, shelled them and ate them. As Kosmas looked at him in surprise, he said: 'Those aren't acorns, they're chestnuts. At least we call them chestnuts when evening comes and we've had nothing to eat and can't make things out clearly any longer.'[11]

People in Greece have kept bees since the 17th century BC at the latest, and the thyme-scented honey of Mount Hymettos has been renowned for more than half of that period. Earthenware beehives were once used. Nowadays they are wooden, like these hives among the olive trees on a terraced island hillside.

For such reasons pigs may not survive a bad year. In a drought, grazing animals may find no food and die; then meat for humans will fail in turn. There will very rarely be a year so catastrophic that all food sources fail at once, but the multiple possibilities explain the need for alternative grains, alternative pulses, different vegetable and root crops, and, beyond even this, the need to be aware of what might be found in the wild. All this is bad news, but there is good news to go with it. If you have diversified, and if you remember wild foods, in a good year you will have a tastier, more varied, more nourishing diet. And most years are good.

Already, before the Minoan and Mycenaean collapse, there is plenty to show what varied tastes would have been available to those who organized the great feasts that held these civilizations together. A list of aromas and flavours named on Linear B tablets will include honey, coriander, cumin, celery, fennel, sesame, mint, pennyroyal, safflower and 'Phoenician spice'.[12] Dill, mustard, anise, poppy seed, saffron and mastic can be added, though they are not on the tablets: poppy, dill and mustard seeds are found in Bronze Age archaeological contexts; saffron-gathering is seen in Minoan frescoes; while Fouqué recognized anise seeds and the charcoal of lentisk wood at the two Santorini sites. Several of these deserve a closer look.

A century after Fouqué's discoveries, modern excavations began at the pre-eruption settlement of Akrotiri, which he had barely touched, but which is now famous for its remarkable wall paintings. The new discoveries have brought to light Greece's oldest beehive. Wild honey is a resource known to various predators, but only humans have persuaded bees to live in artificial hives from which their honey can be safely harvested (or stolen, depending on your point of view). The idea may have come to Greece from Egypt, because it is clear from the wall paintings and other finds that Akrotiri had Egyptian contacts.

Coriander is the earliest aromatic in which people in Greece are known to have been interested: a coriander fruit was found in a seventh-millennium BC context at Franchthi cave. At Bronze Age Sitagri coriander was so plentiful that it must have been cultivated. Soon afterwards there was coriander, again in large quantities, at Therasia and Akrotiri (then, not long afterwards, in Tutankhamen's tomb).

Coriander has few uses in modern Greek food, but fennel, which flourishes in the wild, has many: its fronds are used to make fritters; they are cooked together with oily fish, octopus and mussels; they are a flavouring for olives and pickles (*toursia*); and the seeds are sprinkled on loaves and found in sausages from the Cyclades and the south Aegean islands, where the wild plant is a familiar sight.

Celery, again native to the Aegean, is known not just from the tablets but from finds of seed at Iron Age sites. A bag of white mustard seeds turned up in a Bronze Age context at Marmariani in Thessaly. Dill, often mentioned in classical Greek texts, was found as seed at the Bronze Age settlement of Kastanas. Anise would not have been easy for Fouqué to distinguish from fennel and dill, but he may still have been right to identify it at Bronze Age Therasia.[13] It is native to western Anatolia and the eastern Aegean, and is now the aromatic used in the best Greek ouzo: not-so-good ouzo may instead contain Chinese star anise.

Why people at Mycenae wanted *sa-sa-ma* the tablets do not explain. Introduced from the east (it was called *šamaššammu* in ancient Iraq), native to the Indian Ocean shores, it is clearly what we know as sesame: an excellent source of oil, but in Greece it has always been an aromatic used in bread, cakes and sweets. Poppy seeds were being collected at Bronze Age Thermi on Lesbos and at Kastanas; poppies are useful for their medicinal latex as well as their seeds. Three oily and aromatic seeds – sesame, poppy and flax – were all being used to garnish loaves at the beginning of the classical period, when the Spartan poet Alkman happened to list them in a poem from which this small fragment is known:

Seven couches and seven tables
Crowned with poppy-seed bread, linseed bread and sesame bread
And, for the girls, buckets full of honey-and-linseed sweets.[14]

Wild saffron crocus growing boldly between the stones of the path to Zeus's Cave on Naxos. The orange-red stamen, proudly extended, is the world's most expensive spice.

Not far south across the Aegean is Thera (Santorini), where this wall painting of a girl picking saffron was found in the ruins of Akrotiri, destroyed in the volcanic eruption of the 17th century BC.

The saffron crocus is now grown in several Mediterranean and Middle Eastern countries. It is not found anywhere as a wild plant, but seems probably to have been domesticated from *Crocus cartwrightianus*, which grows wild on rough hillsides in southern Greece. If so, domestication would have happened in the Aegean region; how long ago is unknown. The decorative scheme of a remarkable room in a house at Akrotiri obliterated by the eruption of 1629/1627 BC, recently excavated, is devoted entirely to saffron: it shows girls gathering the red stamens in a rocky landscape and ladies carrying them in baskets and finally presenting them to a goddess. The mural clearly shows the importance of saffron in Aegean religion. It doesn't prove that the plant was already domesticated, although the density of saffron crocuses in the painted landscape suggests a plantation rather than a random scattering of wild plants.

Coriander in modern Greece has been supplanted in some ways by cumin, an exotic introduction from Central Asia; its Greek name (*kyminon*,

Linear B *ku-mi-no*) is borrowed, probably from a Semitic language of Syria, where cumin was certainly grown in Mycenaean times. 'Phoenician spice' (as the Mycenaean tablets call it) was something else: surely sumach, a fruity and health-giving spice familiar to Greeks from the earliest classical literature onwards, but hard to find archaeologically. It is 'Phoenician' in two senses: it is dark red, the usual meaning of the classical Greek word *phoinikeos*; it is prepared only in Syria and would have come to Greece in Phoenician ships.

The last in this series of aromatics of prehistoric Greece is, again, a native product. There is a hint of it in the terebinth fruits gathered by the Mesolithic inhabitants of Franchthi cave; another in Neolithic Crete, where, according to pollen samples, terebinth, alongside olive, flourished unexpectedly after about 5000 BC, probably with human help; and yet another at pre-eruption Santorini, if Fouqué was right to recognize the charcoal of lentisk wood. All the species of this genus have useful fruits and aromatic resins: the shrub *Pistacia terebinthus*, the big tree *P. atlantica* (terebinth), the shrub *P. lentiscus* (lentisk, the one that Fouqué identified) and the small tree *P. lentiscus* var. *chia* (mastic). This last, native to southern Chios alone, is the richest in resin. Its resin is the mastic of Chios, valued highly in classical times and today for its aroma and its health benefits. To ancient Greeks the unique taste of mastic was indissolubly linked with the idea of fresh breath and clean teeth: this is why, although various woods could equally be used for making toothpicks, lentisk toothpicks with their residual aroma of mastic were the most fashionable: 'Lentisk is best,' the poet Martial asserts.[15] Mastic was one of the resins used in preparing amphoras for storing wine. Its flavour lingered, but some needed more of it: medicinal mastic wine and oil were

Sumach is best known as a dark red powder: its fruity aroma shows at its best when sprinkled on rice. Its origin, hard to guess at, is the dried, crushed, ground berries of the tree *Rhus coriaria*.

made on Chios for export. Mastic was an ingredient in compound medicines, an occasional cooking spice and very commonly incorporated with the dough when baking bread, as it still is today.

Classical, Not to Say Conservative

As classical Greeks knew, wild food from land and sea came to them by their own efforts. Artemis was a huntress and Poseidon was the all-powerful sea-god, but they did nothing to help human hunters or fishermen. Rather the opposite: both Artemis and Poseidon were dangerous for mortals to know.

Agriculture was different. Greeks knew that they could never have learned to grow field crops, or discovered olives, or understood the proper use of grapes, without divine help. Even the humble acorn, one of the foods gathered by the Paleolithic people of Franchthi cave – the acorn that was still, famously, in use as a food in mountainous Arkadia in the classical Peloponnese – even the acorn, and the grinding of acorns into flour, would not have been known without the help of a mythical hero. 'People used to eat fresh leaves, grasses and roots, inedible and some of them poisonous,' the classical topographer Pausanias tells us in his guide to Arkadia:

> Pelasgos stopped them doing this, and it was he who discovered that acorns were a food – not the fruit of all oaks, only the *phegos*. This diet has survived among some Arkadians, from the time of Pelasgos to the present day. Hence when the Pythian priestess forbade the Spartans to annex that region she spoke these lines:

> Many acorn-eating men live in Arkadia,
> And they will stop you . . .[16]

To most Greeks, most of the time, acorns were for pigs: cereals were the staple food. Cereals were the gifts to humanity of the goddess Demeter. When searching for her lost daughter Persephone, Demeter was given shelter at Eleusis by King Keleus. She learned from Keleus' son Triptolemos how the dark god Pluto had abducted the girl. Her reward to Triptolemos, when Persephone was found, was the gift of wheat and barley and the knowledge of their cultivation, which he then taught to all mankind. But to Eleusis her gift was the Mysteries, the secret rites that the Athenians celebrated there annually ever after:

Rich among earthly men is he who has seen them.
He who does not know or partake in the rites will,
Once dead, in nether darkness, have no such luck.[17]

The Eleusinian Mysteries guaranteed the renewal of the seasons and the flourishing of the earth in spring, the season when, each year, Persephone would return from the Underworld.

Athens was the place where mankind first learned of the olive. Herodotos, father of history, tells it briefly: 'On the Akropolis there is a sacred place of Erechtheus who is called the earth-born, and within it an olive tree and a salt spring. The Athenian story is that the gods Poseidon and Athene, when fighting over this land, placed them there to stake their claims.'[18] Soon to be commemorated in the Parthenon reliefs, this became the standard story, inserted by some into a general myth in which cities became the fiefs of single gods and goddesses. But it was awkward to explain how Athena won the fight:

> Poseidon was the first who came to Attike, and striking the middle of the Akropolis with his trident he made a salt spring appear: they call it Erechtheus. Athena came next: summoning King Kekrops to witness her claim she planted an olive, the one that is now shown in the Pandroseion. Then they fought for the land. Zeus separated them and appointed as arbiters the twelve gods. They determined that the land was Athena's, Kekrops testifying that Athena was first to plant the olive. She named the city after herself.[19]

In the concave mirror of Greek myth, wheat, barley and olives were Greek discoveries but wine was an intruder on the scene, brought to Greece from somewhere beyond its frontiers, the gift of a god who never became one of the twelve Olympians. Dionysos was, famously, the son of Zeus, king of the Greek gods, and Semele. He was fathered in Thebes, one of the most ancient of Greek cities. The grape vine was something he picked up on his travels: in northeastern Anatolia, possibly, where (unknown to the writers of myth) wine had in fact been made thousands of years earlier; or in Thrace, perhaps, whose borders reach to Dikili Tash, where (again unknown to the mythmakers) the earliest evidence of winemaking in Europe would one day be found. The vine with its fruit was Dionysos' consolation gift to Oineus, king of Kalydon in Aitolia, where Dionysos first stayed on his return to Greece – his apology for having seduced Oineus' wife.

This island kitchen garden and orchard displays squashes and several fruit trees, including a fig. The tank is essential to irrigate summer vegetables. The hillside beyond, partly terraced, is planted with olives.

Classical Greece was rich in fruit, even if it is hard to know how and when they arrived there. Enthusiasm for orchard fruit shines out from a lyrical passage of the *Odyssey*, composed, probably, in the early seventh century BC. The wandering Odysseus, shipwrecked and cast ashore on the mythical island of Scherie, makes his way to the town and approaches the king's house:

> Outside the yard is a big orchard on both sides of the gates,
> Of four acres, and a hedge runs along each side of it,
> And there tall trees have grown, lush with leaves,
> Pears and pomegranates and shiny-fruited apples
> And sweet figs and olives lush with leaves,
> Whose fruit never fails or falls short,
> Winter or summer, all the year, but forever
> The West Wind, blowing, engenders some and ripens others.
> Pear upon pear grows old and apple upon apple,
> Grapes upon grapes and fig upon fig.[20]

Lyrical and exactly right. Scherie may be a mythical place but it is generally agreed to be just like Corfu, that fertile island at the northwestern corner of the Greek world. Not all of Greece offers a climate as mild or a terrain as suitable to orchard planting as Corfu does. The hinterland of Athens, for example, ideal for figs and hospitable to vines and olives, is too dry and rocky for temperate fruits. So classical Athens already imported a range of fruits, some of which are handily listed in a scrap of Athenian comic verse of the late fifth century BC. 'Pears and fat apples' grew close at hand,[21] in the fertile plains of central Euboia, from where they could reach Athens by sea in a day or two – fast enough to arrive at a market stall in perfect condition, if carefully handled.

There's no such hurry with nuts, and so the same text lists 'chestnuts and glossy almonds' as coming to Athens from Paphlagonia, a wooded country far beyond the borders of Greece but close to a chain of Greek colonies and to the Greek trade route that followed the southern shore of the Black Sea. From orchard to table might have taken several weeks, and it wouldn't matter. Those well-watered hills of what is now northern Turkey produced more than chestnuts and almonds. Two varieties of hazelnut came from this region to classical Greece, one called 'Heracleotic' after the city whose modern name is Ereğli, the other 'Pontic'. Pontos was the name of the sea itself and also of the further shores of northeastern Turkey, a mountainous region where Greek settlement had begun as early as the seventh century BC and continued without a break until 1922. Although sweet chestnuts, almonds, hazelnuts and walnuts grew in Greece as well, they grew more plentifully in the Pontos.

In the fifth century BC, when Greeks established a colony that they called Kerasous, further along this same route at the harbour now known as Giresun, they found a wealth of cherry trees (*kerasos*). Kerasous was surely founded in full knowledge of the cherries – possibly even because of them – and was named after them. Sweet wild cherries grow plentifully in Europe, but this tastier sour kind, the kind we prize and use in cooking, was well worth finding. Whenever sour cherries were introduced to Greece – probably not long after the foundation of Kerasous – they spread widely. Experiment showed that fine sour cherries could be grafted onto wild cherry stock. Gardeners still commonly do this, as they do with apples, pears and plums. Again, no one knows when the cultivated kinds began to be grown. No one knows, if it comes to that, who invented grafting or where this magical procedure was first employed, but classical Greeks knew all about it. The 'shiny-fruited apples' of the *Odyssey*, the 'fat apples' of the comedy, are no exaggeration: these were real cultivated varieties, though we know little about them. The pears of classical Greece were sweet and succulent (after poaching) and were served at dessert – as seen in this comedy dialogue between two women, one apparently consoling the other for a rival's success:

'Did you ever see pears served in water to men while they were drinking?'

'Lots. Lots of times. Obviously.'

'Doesn't each of the men always look for the ripest of the floating pears for himself and pick that?'

'Of course they do.'[22]

The same poet – Alexis in the early fourth century BC – gives us a picture of the typical plums of the Athenian market: 'Did you ever see a cooked calf's stomach, or a boiled stuffed spleen, or a basket of ripe plums? That's what his face looks like!'[23] The plums in the audience's mind are bulging and purple, and 'he' is evidently apoplectic.

Four more fruits were familiar in classical Greece: pomegranates, quinces, melons and watermelons. Pomegranates are easy to forget: an insignificant bushy tree overladen with heavy, hard-skinned fruits whose juice, mild and sweet in flavour, enclosed in multiple small segments each of which contains a bitter seed, may hardly seem worth the trouble of extracting. Yet prehistoric farmers had spread pomegranates steadily westwards from their point of origin in Iran. They were in the orchard described by Odysseus. They were also important in mythology. Those refreshing segments were the very ones that tempted Persephone during her stay in the Underworld, as a result of which she was compelled to return there for part of each year. Pomegranate syrup, a modern commercial success as refreshing drink and culinary flavouring, has a long history in Greece under the name *petimezi*, which is also applied to grape syrup.[24]

It's clear from written texts that quinces, another Iranian fruit, have been popular in Greece for about the same length of time as pomegranates, at least 2,500 years. Frustratingly for the archaeologists, no one can find early evidence for them. The texts are confusing, too: they distinguish only vaguely, and sometimes not at all, between apples and quinces. Although the three fruits look alike, quinces differ strongly from modern varieties of apple and pear: you can bite into either of those, but wise people don't bite into quinces. It seems that in ancient times apples and pears were less immediately attractive than modern varieties are; in fact, all three fruits were at their best when cooked, and quinces, the firmest and most aromatic of the three, simply wanted more cooking than the others.

The old harbour city of Kydonia (Chania) in western Crete, now the centre of an orange-growing district, was famous throughout ancient times for its quinces. The Latin, French and English names for this fruit (*cotoneum, coing, quince*) are all derived from the ancient Greek *kydonion melon*, 'apple of Kydonia'. Ancient quince orchards have been archaeologically

Quinces Baked in Coke

Less popular than it was in ancient and medieval times, the quince (*Cydonia oblonga*) is beautiful but troublesome. It requires long cooking, eventually to be eaten as a baked fruit or in the classic form of quince marmalade or paste, deep red in colour, sweet and acid, unique in taste and aroma.

6 large quinces, peeled, halved and stoned
400 g sugar
2 cans Coca-Cola
½ bottle red, semi-sweet wine

Put all ingredients in a large pan and simmer the quinces in the syrup till tender. Leave to get cold in the pan: the liquid will gel as it cools. Serve the quinces cold with some of the jelly around them and perhaps some thick, creamy yoghurt.

A novel version of an ancient idea, this recipe makes perfect sense in the modern Greek context: cinnamon, once too expensive to cook with, has become a favourite aromatic in Greek sweets; cassia (cheap cinnamon) is the dominant flavour of Coca-Cola. The recipe comes from Kamares seafood taverna, opposite Aristotle University in Thessaloniki, popular with teachers and students.

Ripe quinces, the fruit first known from Kydonia (Chania) in western Crete.

identified nearby. Greeks and Romans knew this unique flavour by way of quince honey and quince wine, for which we have an ancient recipe:

> *Quince wine.* Remove the seeds from quinces and chop them as if chopping turnips. Tip 12 pounds into 1 *metretes* [6 gallons] grape must; [leave to ferment] for 40 days. Strain and bottle.[25]

In later times most people have used this fruit for what the Byzantine Greeks called *kydonaton*, 'quince paste, marmalade', still popular in Mediterranean lands. The first recipes for this go back to the sixth century AD. At about that date sugar must have become sufficiently cheap, for the first time in Europe, to be used in bulk in such a recipe. There is an older equivalent, however. Quince marmalade is a linear descendant of ancient quince honey, *melomeli*, for which this is the historic recipe:

> *Quince honey.* Remove the seeds from quinces and pack them as tightly as possible into a jar that is then filled with honey. It is ready to use after a year. It tastes like honey wine, and has the same dietary effects.[26]

Most of these fruits had been introduced to Greece from east or south at some prehistoric period. The same is true of melons and watermelons, both of which were native to Africa and apparently reached Greece from Egypt at around the time when the Mycenaean palaces fell.

But the classical period, when Greek literature and art were at the acme of their originality, when great leaps were being made in philosophy and political thought, was a time of consolidation in the Greek kitchen and larder. Just one wholly new food arrived in Greece and became naturalized at the beginning of the classical period. It was the chicken, the barnyard fowl, which had been domesticated in India thousands of years ago. When did the first chicken reach Greece? To the comic poet Krateinos, in the mid-fifth century BC, it was 'the Persian awakener', and to his colleague Aristophanes it was 'the Persian bird'.[27] These names suggest that chicken was at that time very new to Greece and had arrived from the Persian Empire, then just a hundred years old. But that can't be true. Earlier texts speak of a 'return home at dawn, at the first call of the awakeners', and again of 'eggs of geese and of awakeners', with no mention of Persia.[28] There are vase paintings, too, Corinthian, Laconian and Rhodian, as early as the seventh century BC, with unmistakable figures of cocks and hens. An epic

Capers

Kappari, capers (*Capparis spinosa*): the buds are collected together with fruits and leaf tips and all three are salted. In mountain villages caper bushes are commonly found growing from cracks in stone walls, and old ladies are commonly found collecting the buds during the summer. The bushes are spiny and the work is arduous; our advice is to let someone else do it. Caper buds are blended with bread (or mashed potatoes) and olive oil to make a very salty dip similar to *taramasalata*. It is best to soak capers in water, to reduce the saltiness, before using them to top a salad. Natives of Syros are known for their love of capers.

Caper flower and (to the right, not to be overlooked) caper bud, ripe for pickling. Like greens, capers are gathered from the wild: famously, the caper bush refuses to be cultivated, growing wherever it chooses among ruins and in stony places.

migration – which no source even mentions – from India across western Asia had certainly brought chickens to Greece by 600 BC.

They were at first a rare, high-status food, a typical gift from lover to beloved. They gradually came to be seen as a good basis for a nourishing stew or soup, especially suitable for invalids: the very best barley meal or oatmeal, says the dietician Dieuches, could be added 'to chicken soup when it is simmering, not agitating it but letting it dissolve, warming over a fire or in hot water without stirring until it is cooked through, for those with digestive ailments' – adding a roasted poppy head to send them off to sleep. The classic Greek combination, as it may seem now, of chicken with egg-and-lemon sauce was not yet possible: the chickens had arrived but the lemons were yet to come.[29]

One example, then, to demonstrate that innovation never quite ceases. But apart from chickens, there was little new in the larder. Greeks were proud of the Spartan simplicity of their cuisine. They told the story that when the Persian emperor Xerxes fled from Greece after his defeat at Salamis, he left his headquarters behind. When Pausanias, king of Sparta, saw the Persian tents, decorated as they were with gold and silver and embroidery, he ordered the captured bakers and cooks to prepare a Persian dinner:

> They did as they were told. Pausanias, looking at the finely draped gold and silver couches and gold and silver tables and the grandiose layout of the dinner, and amazed by the good things before him, ordered his own servants to prepare a Spartan dinner. There was a big difference between the two. Pausanias, laughing, sent for the other Greek generals. When they came, he said, pointing to the one dinner and then to the other: 'Greeks, I have called you in to show you the foolishness of the Persian who, living in such luxury as *that*, came to rob us of such poverty as *this*.'[30]

New Food Crops, Mainly from the East

It was a good story, like most of those told by Herodotos, and it may have been true. It had a sequel. In the 150 years that followed their victory, Greeks became more and more familiar with the Persian Empire: they travelled in it, they fought for it, and some of them (including Herodotos himself) were born and lived in it. Eventually, led by Alexander, they conquered it. Among Alexander's aims – he was steered in this direction by his teacher Aristotle – was to investigate the natural products of the Persian provinces.

This had immediate practical results. New foods were found. Several of them were soon introduced to Greece and Europe, became major crops, and have long since become so familiar that they seem native.

In the years that followed Alexander's conquest of the Persian Empire, peaches and apricots spread rapidly westwards, to be grown, eventually, in Greece and all around the Mediterranean. Their names in the earliest Greek reports suggest that they were discovered, respectively, in Persia and Armenia, although both originate even further east. Diphilos of Siphnos, physician to Lysimachos, one of Alexander's generals, advised that peaches, 'the so-called "Persian apples", have moderately good juices and are more nourishing than apples'.[31] The Roman encyclopaedist Pliny described 'Armenian plums' as 'the only plums deserving praise for their aroma' as well as their flavour.[32]

A third discovery was made in eastern Persia or Afghanistan, where pistachio trees had long been domesticated and were found growing in great number. As luck would have it, their movement westwards can be traced – mainly through Greek texts – in some detail. Even before Alexander's time the Greeks had heard rumours of nourishing nuts that served as a diet for young Persians learning to survive in the wild; in these stories the nuts were called 'terebinth', the nearest species known to Greeks at that time. Alexander's troops, who encountered pistachio trees on their march through Iran, still had no name to give them. Back in Greece, Theophrastos, who collected the scientific reports from the expedition, described the trees as 'terebinth or something like it' but with fruit as big as almonds.[33] Within a hundred years pistachios had a proper Greek name of their own. They are among the endless remedies for scorpion stings listed by the wordy poet Nikandros, though he still thought of them as belonging somewhere in the distant east – 'all the *pistakia* that grow like almonds on their branches beside the Indian flood of the resounding Choaspes'.[34] Two hundred years later the practical pharmacist Dioskourides, who worked for the Roman army, prescribed pistachios for snakebites. He knew that they were grown as far west as Syria. Their spread had been made easier (and still is) by a simple fact: pistachio can be easily grafted onto terebinth, and terebinths flourish around the Mediterranean.

Another fruit tree encountered by Alexander's expedition in Iran belonged to a different botanical family, one that was eventually to become more important in Greece than any of the *Pistaceae*. This new fruit was the citron. It was a tantalizing vision to the Greeks who first saw it. At any season a tree would be carrying some ripe fruits, some still ripening, and some in flower. This 'Median apple', soon to be called *kitron*, had a beautiful colour, a compelling aroma and an interesting, if irregular, shape, but the heavy oblong, knobbly, bright yellow, pithy fruits seemed to have very limited use. In spite of this, gardeners spread them westwards. Many citron orchards are found in Greece; at least the essence has its uses, and on Naxos there is a citron-flavoured liqueur.

The lemon is a hybrid that arose, far to the east, as a cross between citrons and bitter oranges. Nothing is heard of this new fruit anywhere in the world until the year AD 951, when it was described by an Arab traveller to Sindh in western India: 'In their country grows a fruit of the size of an apple, very bitter and very acid, called *limūn*.'[35] At that date lemons must have already spread across India from the region of Assam, where the hybrid is thought to have originated. From that point they spread westwards in cultivation. A French crusading bishop encountered them in Palestine about 1220: 'acid fruits with a wormwood-like flavour, whose juice is used very liberally in summer with meats and fish, because it is cool, dry to the

Gigantes – *Lima Beans*

Giant beans, now very popular in Greece, belong to the Peruvian species *Phaseolus lunatus*. Like other New World foods – courgettes, squashes, maize, potatoes, tomatoes and chillies – they were added to the Greek culinary repertoire after the Columbus voyages.

500 g dried *gigantes* (giant lima beans)
½ tsp bicarbonate of soda
3 onions, chopped
4 medium tomatoes, grated fresh, or 1 can
large bunch of parsley leaves
handful of dill (optional)
120 ml olive oil
salt
1 tsp tomato purée
1 tsp sugar
4 cloves garlic, finely chopped, to taste (optional)

Soak the beans overnight, drain, then next day boil in water with a little bicarbonate of soda until tender.

palate, and appetising.'[36] It was soon afterwards that the first lemons were grown in Greece, and they are named *lemonia* in a late Byzantine poem that conceals its political satire in a listing of fruits.[37] Lemons flourish in Greece today and have an assured place in Greek cuisine.

Then came the oranges. They too are a cross, this time between tangerine and pomelo; in size they fit comfortably between the two, while in colour they match the tangerine. Tangerines are native to China, pomelos to Southeast Asia, and it was probably in coastal southern China that the hybrid arose. It had a long way to travel, but medieval Arab traders sailed those waters and brought bitter ('Seville') oranges to the Near East soon after lemons arrived there. The first Greek mention comes in the same satirical fruit poem;[38] this time there is the accompanying evidence of a Byzantine scholarly commentary, written, no doubt, by an orange-lover.[39] Sweet

Chop the onions and stew together with the grated or tinned tomatoes and the chopped parsley and dill, if using, in a lot of olive oil. Add salt, tomato purée and ½ teaspoon sugar. When glistening and soft but not coloured, tip the whole lot together with the drained beans into a baking dish. Mix and spread them out so that some of the beans are submerged completely – to a depth of about 3–4 cm – and bake for 30–40 minutes at 170°C. If adding garlic, sprinkle it over after 25–30 minutes and stir it in.

When ready, the top layer should be blistered and dark brown. The juices will be thickened by the collapsed onions.

The parsley can be replaced with chervil or celery, still using the leaves as well as the finely chopped stalks.

Gigantes or 'giant beans', a variety of butter or lima beans, one of Greece's favourite side dishes: the baked beans that England can only dream of.

oranges came later, and orange trees are now a familiar sight all over Greece in gardens and orchards. Those planted along urban streets are mostly bitter oranges, ideal for spoon sweets but not to be eaten as a fresh fruit.

Fruits of a different botanical family, and with very different culinary uses, make up the third group of recent introductions to Greece. Aubergines? Vegetables, surely. Tomatoes? Vegetables. Peppers and chillis? Spices, or, if not spices, vegetables again. Aubergines arrived from the east – the species is native to India – in medieval times: they were known to Byzantine Greece. Their ominous colour earned them such names as 'mad fruit' and 'Devil's fruit', and it was only under the Ottoman Empire that they found their true place in Greek cuisine.

The other two arrived from across the Atlantic as a result of the Columbus voyages and the subsequent Spanish conquest of Mexico. The chilli came quickly: the explorers were looking for spices such as the classic black pepper, and here they had found one that was even more useful than pepper. Not only did it confer heat on food, an important medicinal requirement at that period, but there was no need to import it in bulk because it could be grown in Europe. It made the health benefits of spices available to those who could not afford exotic imported aromas, a good reason, surely, for its rapid spread.[40] The tomato was a more reluctant introduction. Europe accepted it as edible, but no one knew how to classify its dietary properties. The tomato allegedly did not arrive in Greece until around 1815, when it was planted in the garden of the Capuchin monastery in Athens.[41] Doubts, needless to say, are consigned to history, and tomatoes are now beloved of gardeners in Greece and praised for their contribution to a healthy diet. There is a caveat: they have to be watered generously in the hot early summer when the fruit is swelling. Even if this can be managed now, it may not remain possible for ever. For the present, tomatoes have an assured place in Greek food production and in the Greek kitchen. Have they not inspired the fusion chef Christoforos Peskias to create his signature tomato sushi?

Still other exotic fruits have found their place in Greece in recent times, notably kiwis from China, courgettes and prickly pears from Mexico. Then there are the once exotic, now thoroughly familiar New World legumes. Several species crossed the Atlantic as a result of the Columbus voyages, but in Greece the most familiar and distinctive are *gigantes* or 'giant beans', cultivars of the Peruvian species *Phaseolus lunatus*, known elsewhere as lima beans or butter beans.

Alongside the new fruits and legumes, three of the world's great staple foods arrived in Greece after the classical period. All three have added their character to Greek cuisine, although none of them even threatens to replace the true Greek staple – good, fresh wheat bread. The earliest of the three to arrive was rice. Native to China or Southeast Asia, rice was being grown in India four thousand years ago and had reached the heartlands of the Persian Empire by the time of Alexander's conquest. Aristoboulos, who travelled with him and observed the pistachio trees of Afghanistan, also noted that rice in the Indus valley 'is sown in garden beds and grows in water-filled enclosures. The plant is four cubits high,' he continued, exaggerating somewhat, 'with many ears and much grain.'[42] Aristoboulos' younger contemporary, the diplomat Megasthenes, described how rice was part of Indian meals: 'at dinner a table like a pot-stand is placed before each person, and a golden bowl is set on it, in which they first of all put rice, boiled just as one might boil emmer wheat, and then many different relishes prepared according to

Indian recipes.'[43] Rice was too useful to ignore, and under Alexander's successors effective experiments were made with rice-growing in Syria. It has been a Mediterranean crop ever since, but marginal: a basis for puddings recommended to invalids, a popular side dish, but not the daily staple that it is in India. In Greek cuisine it soon found a special place as a main ingredient in the dish once called *thria*, now *dolmades* (see box on page 92).

Maize and potatoes, staple diets of Mexico and Peru respectively, came to Europe after Columbus. Potatoes were late to reach Greece. They do well in eastern Macedonia and Thrace – Nevrokopi near Drama is the potato capital – but they never previously had as much publicity as they achieved in 2012, when the 'potato movement' saw Greek farmers selling potatoes and other basic foods direct to Greek consumers to undercut cheap imports.

Maize is much more important. By the early nineteenth century it had replaced wheat and barley as the basic grain crop in parts of Greece, in the Peloponnese for example, where the English antiquarian W. M. Leake often noticed fields of what he calls 'kalambokki'. He also noted its importance in the household:

> The chief instrument of household furniture is the hand-mill, in which the kalambokki is ground. This is the employment of the women at night, who generally accompany the work with a song in lamentation of some deceased relation who has been killed perhaps by a hostile house ... The *cheiromylon* is a lineal descendant of the ancient hand-mill, as the songs which accompany the grinding are of the *odai epimylioi*.[44]

Elsewhere, Leake writes of the women of Mani: 'At night they turn the handmill, and weep, singing lamentations for the dead while they grind their wheat.'[45] Leake knew that *odai epimylioi*, 'grinding songs', have a history as long as Greek literature. In his time they accompanied the women's milling of maize and wheat; 2,500 years earlier it was barley, when Pittakos ruled Mytilene on Lesbos in the sixth century BC and had never lost his plebeian ways: 'His relaxation was to grind flour, so the philosopher Klearchos said,'[46] and the early scientist Thales confirmed the story. 'I was once at Eresos on Lesbos,' he recalled, 'and heard a slave-woman singing at the millstone':

> 'Grind, mill, grind;
> Even Pittakos grinds,
> King of great Mytilene.'[47]

TWO

Classical Feasts: The First Gastronomy

During the first few centuries of its written history, Greece was like no other region of the world then or now. It was a cluster of cities as fiercely independent, each one from all the rest, as the proudest Swiss canton or the spikiest of nation states. These 'cities' were often tiny – a few thousand or a few hundred inhabitants – and most of them regarded themselves as democracies. In truth they were both more and less democratic than a modern state. Only men, and only free men, and only those who belonged to the city, were part of these democracies, but these free male citizens assembled in person, spoke, voted and legislated. If some cities were ruled by kings or 'tyrants' (Greek *tyrannos*, an absolute ruler) it was because, on some past occasion, the citizens had decided it would be so. In theory they could change their minds. If the cities fought one another, as they continually did, it was because the citizens themselves had voted to fight, and, when the decision was made, the citizens themselves marched to battle.

As prehistory turns into history, as archaeology begins to be supplemented by literature, from about 700 BC onwards, it becomes easier to re-imagine whole meals and individual dishes as Greeks enjoyed them. But there is at first a strange disparity between history and literature. The two Homeric epics, the *Iliad* and the *Odyssey*, composed at about this date, seem to give us a typical meal for a society that the poet imagines, but where are the city-states? In those poems a dinner, in a king's hall or a swineherd's cottage, will always consist of roast meat – pork or mutton, or, if an ox is being sacrificed, beef. There will be bread served in baskets; there will be 'fiery wine'. Men roasted the meat. Women baked the bread. At a wedding at Menelaos' house the male guests 'came to the house of the godlike king, driving sheep and carrying manly wine, while their wives sent in bread for them.'[1]

Breakfast (there is only one breakfast in the *Odyssey*) consists of food left over from yesterday's dinner. But there are other occasions, and tantalizing hints of greater variety. A guest who arrives unexpectedly is offered food, shared by the host: food left over from yesterday's dinner, again, but with 'all sorts of relishes'. The young Nausikaa takes clothes to wash in the river and her mother packs 'all kinds of cooked foods' along with wine for her lunch. Kalypso makes up a similar picnic for Odysseus.

There is cheese in the *Odyssey*. It is not a product of civilized people but of the monstrous Cyclops, whose regular foods are the milk of his sheep and the junket and cheese that he makes from the milk. Odysseus and his sailors found 'wicker trays full of cheeses and pens crowded with lambs and kids; each were in their proper places, the firstlings, the middles and the younglings; and all the vessels were brimming with whey, the neat pails and bowls into which he milked his beasts.'[2] Soon they watched the giant as he 'sat down to milk his sheep and bleating goats, all in turn, and then put a suckling to each. Afterwards he curdled half of the white milk and put it to drain in woven baskets. He stood the other half in jugs as a drink and a dessert for himself.'[3] Cheese made from mixed sheep's and goats' milk was, oddly enough, precisely the kind that Sicily exported to Greece in later times, and Sicily was, oddly enough, precisely where Greeks in later times imagined that the Cyclops had lived. His lifestyle, opportunistic cannibalism aside, is that of a gentle and peaceful shepherd, one of those who would migrate to the mountain pastures in spring and back to the lowlands in autumn.

Woman baking bread: a Tanagra figurine of the early 5th century BC.

A Homeric scene, cer-
tainly. Is it Briseis serving
wine to Phoinix, or is it
Hekamede mixing *kykeon*
for Nestor? In either case
the woman was a noble
captive, which would
justify her formal dress.
Athenian vase painting by
the 'Brygos painter',
c. 480/470 BC.

There were also foods that restored health or took it away. Women, it
seems, had the special skill to prepare them. In the *Odyssey* Menelaos and
his two tired guests need the attentions of Helen, who 'put a drug into the
wine they were to drink, to soothe pain, calm anger and bring forgetfulness
of ills'.[4] She is said to have learned about medicinal plants in Egypt. Other
women, too, though they left the roasting of meat to men, knew the art of
mixing *kykeones*, 'possets, potions', for tired and preoccupied men.[5] In the
Iliad Nestor brings back the wounded Machaon to his tent:

> For them fair-haired Hekamede made a *kykeon* . . . On the table
> she placed a bronze dish with an onion in it as relish to the drink,
> and also yellow honey; and next a heap of holy barley meal . . . She
> made a *kykeon* for them with Pramnian wine, and grated goat's
> cheese into it with a bronze grater, and sprinkled barley meal on
> it, and when she had prepared it she invited them to drink.[6]

No drugs here, yet the context reminds us of Helen, and the procedure
is the same again when the witch Circe entertains: 'She led them in and
sat them on chairs and stools, and stirred (*ekyka*) for them cheese and
barley meal and yellow honey into Pramnian wine, and mixed drugs with
the meal.'[7] That was the mixture that turned Odysseus' sailors into pigs.[8]

A different source, of almost the same date, gives us a farmer's picnic.
The *Works and Days*, Hesiod's poem of advice to a farmer, includes a farming calendar, in which midsummer is the time for eating outdoors:

When the golden thistle blooms, and the noisy cicada,
Sitting in a tree, often pours out its shrill song
From under its wings, in the hard summer season,
Then goats are fattest and wine is best
And women are lustiest and men are weakest,
When Sirius parches the head and the knees,
And skin is dry under the heat: that is the time
For rocky shade and Bibline wine
And creamy barley-mash and the last milk of the goats
And the meat of a cow that feeds in the wood and has not calved
And of firstborn kids; and to drink fiery wine

Sitting in the shade, the innards stuffed with food,
Facing towards the fresh west wind,
And from a perennially flowing and unpolluted spring
To pour three of water and to make the fourth be wine.[9]

This earliest epic poetry tells us of an essentially rural way of life, and there is no doubt that the epic poets drew on oral tradition reaching far into the past. The elegiac and lyric poets, their contemporaries and followers, perhaps lived differently; certainly they saw life differently. They lived in, fought for and wrote for the city-states that were already beginning to flourish. Archilochos, who described a promiscuous Parian woman he knew as 'a fig tree feeding many crows', was one of the citizens of Paros who sailed north to conquer Thasos. They colonized the island, seized the vineyards of the Thracian coast and drank the wine: 'My kneaded loaf is on my spear, a skin of Ismaric wine hangs on my spear, and on my spear I lean to drink.'[10]

At one political extreme was Sparta, and its near neighbours, and the Cretan cities, in all of which the meals of male citizens were strictly equal and communal and took place in the 'men's house', *andreia*. The food was dull, the staple of Sparta being the famous black broth. As was observed on the Athenian comic stage, 'It's no wonder the Spartans fight to the death. They'd sooner die ten thousand times than go home for more black broth.'[11]

At the other extreme were Athens and Corinth, rich trading cities that had their friendships and factions and rivalries, which were very visible around food and wine. Athenians had learned, from the eastern civilizations that they sometimes pretended to despise, to recline on couches to eat and drink. They had learned to eat first and then, as a separate 'meal' and sometimes in different company, to drink. The eating was the *deipnon*; we know what it was like from many comedy fragments, and there is an impression that more eating than talking took place. The drinking party was the *symposion*, familiar from Plato's philosophical dialogues, one of which, the *Symposium*, depicts Sokrates and friends discussing the nature of love. But the best *symposion* menu is in an early elegy by Xenophanes, who explains very clearly just how things came together:

> And now the floor is clean, and our hands, and the cups; one hands out wreaths, another offers a jug of perfumed oil. The *krater* stands full of cheer; a second wine, waiting in jars and promising never to give way, has the mild smell of flowers. Incense gives a holy scent among us; there is water, cold, sweet and clean. Yellow loaves are set out, and a generous table loaded with cheese and rich honey.[12]

It is hard to look at this scene, modelled on a Cypriot vase of about 2000 BC, without thinking of the picnic described by Hesiod in the *Works and Days* about 1,300 years later. But is this a view of the preparations for a sacrifice? Or is it a shepherd and his dog? It amused the potter to include the jug itself in the scene.

Reclining symposiasts holding a drink horn. This bronze statuette, almost contemporary with Xenophanes' poem, was modelled in northern Greece about 525 BC and was intended to decorate the rim of a bronze *krater*, a wine-mixing bowl.

The *krater*, 'mixing bowl', contains wine that has just been mixed with water. The *deipnon* and *symposion* were so different, and felt so different, that scarcely any source links them.

For classical Athens there is a wealth of literary evidence for food, including one short fragment of comedy that offers a whole menu for a festive *deipnon*. The play is just beginning, and a speaker has noticed that something is wrong: the household behind one of the stage doors ought to be toasting a happy event (the *Amphidromia* were celebrated five or ten days after a baby was born) but, for some reason, it isn't:

> Well, then, why is there no wreath in front of the door? Why does no smell of cooking strike the tip of my exploring nose, if it's their *Amphidromia*? – when the custom is to bake a slice of Chersonese cheese, to fry some cabbage gleaming with oil, to stew some fat mutton chops, to pluck wood-pigeons and thrushes along with chaffinches, to nibble little cuttlefish along with squids, to swing and beat many a tentacle, and to drink many a cup of wine not too much diluted.[13]

There, alongside mutton chops from a sacrificed sheep or lamb, we have melted cheese, fried sliced cabbage, wild birds and seafood including octopus (owner of the tentacles that must be beaten to tenderize them).

Fresh meat – meaning specifically the fresh meat of domestic animals – would be on the classical menu only after a sacrifice: this was a firm rule.

Wild game was different – it didn't have to be offered to a god – but there was not much game to be had around classical Athens. The only likely catch was hare, a love-gift that demonstrated the lover's hunting skill or generosity. Which of the two? That would depend on whether it was caught – in accordance with the advice of Xenophon's little manual of hunting, which assumes that hare will be the usual catch – or bought. Hare was no commoner in the classical diet than other fresh meats, but we are lucky enough to have one classical recipe for it, or rather, a choice of recipes from which we are very firmly guided towards one. Archestratos, Greece's first gastronomic poet, writing about 350 BC, pronounces on the subject in his inimitable way:

> There are many ways, many rules for the preparation of hare. This is the best, to bring the roast meat in and serve to each while they are drinking hot, simply sprinkled with salt, taking it from the spit while still a little rare. Don't worry if you see the *ichor* seeping from the meat, but eat greedily. To me the other recipes are altogether out of place, gluey sauces over it, cheese over it, too much oil over it, as if you were cooking a weasel.[14]

Homer and Hesiod never mention seafood at all, but to judge by the written texts fish was far commoner than fresh meat at dinner in classical Athens. Fragments from an astonishing range of Athenian comedies show aspects of the fish business, from market to kitchen to table. Athenians were not fishermen. If they wanted fish, they paid for it, and the price of fish – always higher than it ought to be – was a surprisingly common topic of conversation. There was even a book about it: 'Lynkeus of Samos wrote *Shopping for Fish* for one of his friends who disliked shopping: it told him how much he should offer to the murderous fishmongers to get what he wanted reasonably and painlessly.'[15] From this bible of the fourth-century gastronome one extract survives:

> To quell their steely gaze and unwavering prices it is not ineffective to stand over the fish and criticize it, recalling Archestratos or another such poet, and quoting the line: *The inshore mormyros, a poor fish, never worthy*; and if it's spring: *Bonito? Buy in autumn . . .*; and if it's summer: *Grey mullet's wonderful when winter comes!* There are many possibilities. You will frighten off most of the shoppers and bystanders, and so the man will have to settle at the price you choose.[16]

These little embedded verses are not real quotations but a literary game at which Lynkeus' friend is assumed to be able to beat the fishmonger. It was Hesiod who wrote 'never worthy', not about a bream but about Askra, his home town.[17] Archestratos did advise cooking bonito in autumn, but not in those words.

Once the fish was bought, it had to be cooked, and comedy cooks are full of information on how to treat each species in the astonishingly wide range to be found in the Athenian market. One speaker in a comedy by Sotades, equally proud of his market and kitchen skills, lists a whole marine banquet: shrimps cooked in the frying pan; a *galeos* dogfish – 'I've baked the middle pieces, I'm boiling the rest of it with a mulberry sauce to go with it'; two bluefish steaks – 'into a casserole with them, with a few herbs, cumin, salt, water and a drop of olive oil'; 'a very fine sea bass: to be cooked in stock with oil and herbs, after taking off the steaks to be grilled on spits'; red mullets and wrasses on the grill, dressed with oil and oregano; a boiled stuffed squid; cuttlefish tentacles simply roasted, with 'a side salad of all sorts of greens'; small fry dressed with oil; a conger cooked in 'stock with strong herb flavours'; gobies and rock-fish, dredged in flour and fried; a bonito 'dipped in oil, wrapped in fig leaves, sprinkled with oregano, and hidden like a firebrand under heaped ashes'; 'some little Phaleron anchovies: a cup of water over these is enough; I'll chop herbs and tip them on with a good jug of oil ... That's the art, and you don't learn it from books and notes.'[18] Sometimes the recipes are given as instructions from a cook to a slave. This sharp dialogue is by Antiphanes:

Mid-4th-century BC Apulian (south Italian) fish plate, a very popular pattern in Greek-style ceramics, with a small central well presumably intended for a dipping sauce. The downturned rim (not visible here) served to make the dish more prominent: fish was expensive.

The Arkesilas Cup, Laconian (Spartan) ware of about 560 BC. It shows King Arkesilaos of Kyrene supervising his city's trade. The sacks might hold wool but they are usually thought to contain *silphion*, the spice on which Kyrene's prosperity was built.

'No, no, the stone bass to simmer in brine, as I told you before.'

'And the sea bass?'

'Bake whole.'

'The *galeos*?'

'Boil with fresh chopped herbs.'

'The eel?'

'Salt, oregano, water.'

'The conger?'

'Same.'

'The ray?'

'Greens.'

'There's a slice of tuna.'

'Bake it.'

'The kid?'

'Roast it.'

'The other?'

'The opposite.'

'The spleen?'

'Stuffed.'[19]

What's surprising is that however jokily the topic is inserted into comedy dialogue – 'Do you know how to cook horse-mackerel?' 'I will when you've told me'[20] – the recipes are real. We know this not just because they make good sense, but also because they agree with other recipes on the few occasions when other recipes survive.

Notice the simplicity. No cumin, no coriander, not even onions and garlic, though these were welcome in their proper place. Fish wanted nothing but olive oil, good fresh herbs and occasionally good wild greens. No spices – certainly not pepper, which was still vanishingly rare in Europe. Even the two exotic spices known to have been in use in classical Athens do not show up in fish cookery: fruity sumach, familiar to Mycenaeans, and the legendary *silphion* of ancient Libya.

Silphion was the resin of a sturdy fennel-like plant that was never found naturalized beyond north Africa. It was imported to Greece, sold at a high price and prized by classical cooks and dieticians, who thought it good for the stomach. It was grated, along with cheese, vinegar and oil, on to birds for roasting, and similarly served with cheese and vinegar to flavour fish. It was an ingredient in marinades and sauces. Its role in luxury Greek cuisine can be compared with that of garlic in French cookery. The Romans learned about *silphion* from the Greeks and liked to eat the whole root and stem, sliced and preserved in vinegar. They overexploited it: 'the single stem found within living memory was sent to the emperor Nero,' Pliny reports sadly.[21] Alexander's troops had meanwhile discovered a *silphion* substitute in Central Asia, the resin known to us as asafoetida, but this was never adopted into Greek cuisine.

Central Asian asafoetida, *Ferula assa-foetida*, was adopted in Rome and Byzantine Greece as a *silphion* substitute. This is the asafoetida plant, flourishing in Uzbekistan.

One other important flavour was new to classical Greece. This was *garos*, fish sauce, a Greek or Phoenician invention, first made at Greek colonies in the Crimea and at Greek and Carthaginian colonies on the Mediterranean coast of Spain, where archaeologists have found large-scale facilities. From the producers' point of view it was an excellent way to use the offcuts and innards of fish that were destined for export, dried, smoked or salted. From the ancient cook's point of view *garos* was a fermented sauce, one of those familiar in many parts of the world that add savour and salt-iness. Soy sauce is the best known, but those who want to get closest to the ancient *garos* use Southeast Asian fish sauce, made in exactly the same way. The fashion for *garos* was transmitted to the Romans and preserved (so to speak) in the Byzantine Empire, and the known historic recipes, intended for small-scale production at a farm near the sea, are Byzantine. Two variants follow:

> *Making garos.* The so-called *liquamen* is made thus. Fish entrails are put in a container and salted; and little fish, especially sand-smelt or small red mullet or mendole or anchovy, or any small enough, are all similarly salted; and left to pickle in the sun, stirring frequently. When the heat has pickled them, the *garos* is got from them thus: a deep close-woven basket is inserted into the centre of the vessel containing these fish, and the *garos* flows into the basket . . .

> A rather high-quality *garos*, called *haimation*, is made thus. Take tunny entrails with the gills, fluid and blood, sprinkle with suffi-cient salt, leave in a vessel for two months at the most; then pierce the jar, and the *garos* called *haimation* flows out.[22]

Silphion itself, a tall, sturdy, fennel-like plant whose stem and root produced the aromatic sap,
is shown on the reverse of this coin of ancient Kyrene: the Greek god Apollo is the obverse
type. The plant is now extinct.

Mosaic image, from the house of the businessman Umbricius Scaurus in Pompeii, of his own brand-labelled *garos* (fish sauce). The Latin inscription reads *G(ari) f(los) scom(bri) Scauri ex offi(ci) na Scauri*, 'Scaurus' best mackerel *garum* from the Scaurus factory'.

Well known by the fifth century BC (the tragedian Aischylos, curiously, is the earliest known writer to mention it), *garos* remained an everyday item until the sixteenth century AD, when Pierre Belon, a French naturalist, encountered it in Ottoman Constantinople – but this is its last gasp:

> The *garum*-makers of Constantinople are mostly in Pera. They prepare fresh fish daily, sell it fried, and make use of the entrails and roe, steeping them in brine to turn them into *garum*. It matters a good deal which fish is used. Only the scad, which the Venetians call *suro*, and mackerel, will do.[23]

There were classical Greeks who had no money for buying meat or fish, let alone imported sauces and spices. 'These things the poor cannot buy,' a greedy speaker in a comedy fragment reminds us, 'the belly of a tuna, the head of a bass or a conger, or cuttlefishes, which I think even the blessed gods do not despise.'[24] What proportion of Athenians were 'poor' in this sense is not known, but, since state festivals meant free food, they would certainly have been present in the comedy audience, twice a year, to recognize themselves in speeches like these:

Bulbs

Towards the end of February or the beginning of March the mountains are suddenly covered with flowers. First there are anemones, mauve and purple; then almond blossom, sign of spring on its way; then the invasive Bermuda buttercup carpeting terraces, roads and walls; then crocuses, delicate pink rock roses, sweet peas, orchids and lupins. Lupin seeds make a good and historic addition to the Lenten table, but they need thorough soaking and cooking to rid them of their poisonous bitterness. Then, suddenly, amid the dandelions and knapweed, hundreds of tiny blue hyacinths sprout.

The small bulbs are deeply embedded in the rocky ground, and it takes a long time to collect a kilogram, but in the Peloponnese, Crete and elsewhere these *volvoi*, bulbs of the tassel hyacinth *Leopoldia comosa*, are prized. Their season usually coinciding with Lent, they will be served on fasting days alongside other *mezedes*, slightly bitter yet with a clean taste and crunchy texture to complement the vinegar and olive oil.

The flower of the wild grape hyacinth, *Leopoldia comosa*.

Grape hyacinth bulbs (Greek *volvoi; Italian lampascioni*) have been a popular food in Greece and southern Italy since ancient times. They can be grown in gardens – grape-hyacinths are known elsewhere as garden plants – but are often collected from the wild. Their aphrodisiac reputation faded long ago.

The following method was given to us by Christos Stamatianos. In his native Sparta, he adds, the bulbs are lightly mashed with oil and eaten as a main dish with only bread and a jug of wine to accompany them. People would once follow the mules ploughing the fields to pick the fresh bulbs from the tilled ground. They are now unknown to many younger Greeks. It is unusual to find *volvoi* on restaurant menus except in Crete in spring (and who would pick out the bare word 'bulbs' on a menu anyway?).

Volvoi

Carefully peel each bulb of its dark outer layer, trimming but retaining the root so that the bulb doesn't collapse during cooking. Bring to the boil and simmer in plenty of water for fifteen minutes or so, then drain. Repeat this process three times to wash out the bitterness. Pack into jars with a few whole peppercorns and a bay leaf, and cover with good white wine vinegar. They can be used as soon as wanted, but the flavour matures in storage. Serve dressed with strong extra-virgin olive oil, finely chopped garlic and fresh dill, oregano or Cretan dittany.

My man is a beggar, I am a poor old woman: our daughter, our son a mere child, and this good girl here, that makes five of us, three to dinner and two to share a little barley-cake with them ... The parts and the whole of our life are bean, lupin, potherb, turnip, cowpea, grass pea, acorn, *bolbos*, cicada, chickpea, wild pear, and the sun-baked heritage that I love so dearly, the dried fig.[25]

One of the items in this list of local, traditional, non-meat foods that would have cost practically nothing deserves a second glance. Native to Greece, considered a delicacy by many in ancient as in modern times, *bolboi* (grape hyacinth or tassel hyacinth bulbs) are often gathered from the wild and were seen by ancient Athenians among the vegetables that gardeners from neighbouring Megara would bring to market. They once had an aphrodisiac reputation. 'Bring from Megara the fertilizing seeds of the bulb that arouse men and arm them for intercourse with women,' wrote the Latin agricultural poet Columella.[26] That reputation has long since withered away, but bulbs are still a popular side dish in some parts of Greece, though they need long baking (traditionally under hot ashes) and, as a Greek comedy had already emphasized, sympathetic seasoning: 'Look, if you please, at how highly the bulb is regarded for its extravagance: it insists on cheese, honey, sesame, olive oil, onion, vinegar, *silphion*. All on its own it is mean and sour.'[27] The ancient Roman cookbook *Apicius* suggests some Roman ways with this Greek speciality:

> *Bulbs.* Serve in oil, fish sauce, vinegar, with a little cumin sprinkled over. – Or, mash and boil in water, then fry in oil. Make a sauce thus: thyme, pennyroyal, pepper, oregano, honey, a little vinegar and, if liked, a little fish sauce. Sprinkle pepper over and serve. – Or, boil and press into a pan, adding thyme, oregano, honey, vinegar, concentrated must, dates, fish sauce and a little oil. Sprinkle pepper over and serve.[28]

LOCAL SPECIALITIES

Spices and side dishes are not the main story. In the brief flowering of the classical period – between, say, the first Olympic games, in 776 BC, and the accession of Alexander the Great as king of Macedon in 336 BC – we can see the beginnings of a remarkable, creative interplay between the varied geography of Greece and its astonishingly fragmented political landscape. It was now, for the first time in this region and the first time anywhere in the world, that people began to prize the special products of each island and each city.

This discourse pervades ancient Greek writing. When the goddess Athena recounts Telemachos' visit *Sparten es kalligynaika*, 'to Sparta, city of beautiful women', she is not teasing Odysseus about his son's adventures or filling a verse with a random adjective.[29] This was a real quality attributed to that one city: witness the deadly serious oracle delivered by Apollo's priestess at Delphi to earnest enquirers:

> Thessalian mares, Spartan women,
> The men who drink the water of fair Arethousa,
> But the best fighters live between
> Tiryns and Arkadia rich in sheep:
> The linen-breasted Argives, goads of war.[30]

The same serious tone is adopted by the praise-poet Pindar in a brief list of local specialities: 'From mount Taygetos the Lakonian dog, an eager beast for chasing the prey. Skyrian goats are excellent for the giving of milk.'[31] Somehow food and drink keep recurring: the volcanic spring of Arethousa (which once supplied drinking water to Chalkis in Euboia), Skyrian goats' milk, the mountain sheep of Arkadia. Such listings sound best in hexameter verse, as used in the *Odyssey* and by the Delphic priestess. Even Athenian comedy slips into epic hexameter for its lists of local specialities:

> From Kyrene *silphion* and oxhide;
> From the Hellespont mackerel and every salt fish;
> From Thessaly, emmer meal and ox ribs . . .
> Syracuse supplies pigs and cheese . . .
> Rhodes sends raisins and dreamy figs.
> From Euboia pears and fat apples . . .
> Paphlagonians send us chestnuts
> And glossy almonds, ornaments to the feast.[32]

The listings agree because they are stating real facts. When Polykrates, wealthy king of Samos, looked for the best goats and pigs for his model farm, he selected goats from Skyros (as approved by Pindar) and pigs from Sicily (as in this comedy extract).[33] The lists even supplement one another, tempting the foodie scholar to compile a gastronomic guide to ancient Greece.

Among the mythical followers of Dionysos (Bacchos), Greek god of wine, Silenos took the lead. He is often pictured as a fat, old, tipsy reveller, unsteadily riding a donkey; sometimes carousing with a Mainad, as on this coin of Thasos.

No wonder that Dionysos – a revered god, but also a recurring character on the Athenian stage – is the speaker who recites this comedy listing of the best wines of classical Greece:

> For Mendaean the very gods wet their soft beds.
> Sweet generous Magnesian, and Thasian over which the scent
>   of apples plays,
> This I judge much the best of all the other wines after noble
>   and unhurtful Chian.[34]

That was the late fifth century BC. If someone had asked the wine god for a similar list a few decades later, he would certainly have added Lesbian.

The story of ancient Greek wine is of a very gradual development with a strong focus on local specialities. Several cities were proud of their wine. Their policy, expressed in our terms, was to establish a brand identity. Each wine-producing territory would have its own distinct shape for the big earthenware amphoras in which wine was distributed. Amphoras were stamped or labelled. Grapes, amphoras and other wine-related subjects were chosen as coin types by wine-producing cities: the fifth-century BC coins of Mende illustrate Dionysos, Silenos and vines. The flavour of oak would have been absent, but pine resin – familiar today in retsina – was already present: the first written evidence comes from Dioskourides, a pharmacist who wrote in Greek under the Roman Empire, but archaeological finds

Wine amphoras from an ancient shipwreck in the Dodecanese, displayed in Bodrum Museum as they would have been stacked during transport. The amphoras are Koan, signalling that the wine was probably from Kos and was flavoured with sea salt.

of resinated amphoras show that Greek wines would have had this flavour long before. Resin sealed the porous earthenware and made the wine less likely to spoil, as well as adding a distinctive flavour – not the best flavour that wine can have, but also not the worst.

THE FIRST GASTRONOMERS

If we look beyond wine, searching for the geography of food quality, the first and most important source is the gastronomic poem by the Sicilian Greek Archestratos, written about 350 BC. Well-chosen fragments survive in that venerable gastronomic bible, the *Deipnosophistai* of Athenaios, of which more later.

Archestratos' language is direct, forceful, often argumentative. His lines are very easy to memorize. They were ideal for gourmets to quote to one another over dinner. The reader or listener is told when to buy particular foods at their best:

> When Orion is setting in the sky
> And the mother of the grape-clusters sheds her ringlets,
> Then take a baked sargue sprinkled with cheese,
> Good-sized, hot, slashed with sharp vinegar . . .
> Treat everything in the nature of tough fish similarly.
> When you have good fish, naturally soft, with rich flesh,

Just sprinkle it lightly with salt and moisten it with oil.
By itself, within itself, it has the faculty of pleasure.[35]

Pleasure is the beginning and end of this gastronomic philosophy. Like Hesiod, incidentally, Archestratos looks to the stars ('when Orion is setting') not for any astrological reason but because each ancient city had its own calendar. Since Archestratos is writing 'for all of Greece', month names are no use to him: he has to use the rising and setting of the stars.[36] Archestratos strongly disapproves of his fellow Sicilians' drinking customs: 'Have nothing to do with those Syracusans who simply drink, like frogs, without eating anything.'[37] There is not a word of praise for the cooks of Greek Sicily:

They do not know how to prepare good fish
But wickedly spoil it by cheesing everything
And dousing it with watery vinegar and pickled *silphion*.[38]

Archestratos knows what fish to buy on the seafront at Carthage and in the marketplace of Macedonian Pella. He knows of the industrial bread ovens of independent Athens and of the clay ovens of Persian-dominated Erythrai. He ranges from Hipponion in southern Italy, where people traded with Oscan-lettered coins, to Iasos in southern Asia Minor, ruled by a king who had become a Persian governor. Sixty places are named in the surviving fragments of his poem. He surely visited these places – there would

Fish just caught and ready for sale on the quayside at Ermoupoli (Syros).

have been no other way to do the research. He travelled cheaply enough to take a close personal interest in his food, but not so cheaply that he could not afford to buy and taste the best. Some of his advice – his praise for Athenian bread, Phaleron anchovies and the eels of Lake Kopais – agrees with common gastronomic views. But it is the tip of an iceberg: scores of other opinions take us far beyond what is in any other source, to the smaller Greek harbours and markets and to a great range of foodstuffs (especially fish) unknown in other writings. Quite outside literature there was a local tradition on the sources of good foods in each city, and Archestratos, in spite of his verbal fireworks, writes in accordance with it. We are reading a slice of the knowledge that passed among fishermen, fishmongers and food buyers, among travellers and innkeepers.

Archestratos' favourite topic is fish, but he began his poem with the cereals, the staple foods of Greece, given to mankind (as everyone knew) by the goddess Demeter. His information agrees with archaeological and literary evidence wherever there happens to be any. Looking back to pre-historic times, barley really had been favoured on Lesbos and emmer was the chosen wheat crop in Thessaly. Athens imported wheat and was famous (in Athenian comedy, with support from Plato's dialogues) for its oven-baked wheat bread; clay ovens were widely used.[39]

> First I shall recall the gifts of fair-haired Demeter . . .
> The best one can get, the finest of all,
> Cleanly hulled from good ripe barley-ears,
> Is from the sea-washed breast of famous Eresos in Lesbos,
> Whiter than airborne snow. If the gods eat
> Pearl barley, this is where Hermes goes shopping for it . . .
> Take a Thessalian roll, a circling whirl
> Of dough well kneaded under hand; they call it 'crumble' there,
> Emmer-bread as others say . . .
> Fair is the loaf that famous Athens
> Offers to mortals in her market-place.
> A white loaf from the clay ovens of vinous Erythrai,
> swelling with soft ripeness, gives pleasure at dinner.[40]

Archestratos may have said plenty about wine, but he is quoted only briefly on that subject. He gives advice on relishes: he is against them. 'I say goodbye to saucers of *bolboi* and *silphion* stem and all other side dishes!'[41] There is one fragment on shellfish, interesting for its links with other ancient

The scallops for which Mytilene was famous, smaller than *coquilles St-Jacques* but just as good.

sources and with modern information: 'Mytilene offers scallops: so does Ambrakia, in large numbers, and great big ones too.'[42] The great big scallops of Ambrakia, on the Ionian sea, are surely *coquilles St-Jacques*, much bigger than those known to Archestratos in the straits of Mytilene. The scallops of Mytilene, so much smaller, are probably the *pétoncle*, *Chlamys varia*, as good as *coquilles St-Jacques* in flavour and still known in the waters around Lesbos. In ancient times these were conserved in brine and exported, or eaten fresh, but 'grilled and served with vinegar and *silphium* they tend to loosen the bowels owing to their excessive sweetness; they are juicier and easier to digest if they are baked.'[43] The 'oysters of Abydos'[44] on the Hellespont (Dardanelles) recur several times in later literature: the Roman poet Catullus alludes to 'the Hellespont, more oysterous than other shores'.[45] The real focus of the surviving fragments, and surely of the whole of Archestratos' poem, is on fish as the centrepiece of a meal: what species to choose where, at what season, and how to prepare them. The recipe is always extremely simple. Here is Archestratos on a fish of the tunny kind, 'bonito, in autumn', as good at Istanbul now as it was in medieval Constantinople and in ancient Byzantion:

> Use leaves of the fig tree and oregano (not very much),
> No cheese, no nonsense: just wrap it nicely
> In fig leaves fastened above with string,
> Then hide it under hot ashes, keeping a watch on the time.
> When it will be baked, and don't overcook it.
> Get it from lovely Byzantion, if you want it to be good . . .[46]

Another fragment recommends tuna, the same species whose migration through the newly opened Aegean was interrupted by the Mesolithic fishermen of Franchthi cave:

If you should come to the holy city of famous Byzantion,
For my sake eat another slice of one-year tuna: it is good and tender.[47]

But Archestratos keeps it simple. If, rejecting this simplicity, you want a sauce for your salted tuna, you must wait seven hundred years to look up the ingredients in the Roman cookery book *Apicius*:

Sauce for salted bonito and tunny. Pepper, lovage, cumin, onion, mint, rue, walnut, date, honey, vinegar, mustard, olive oil.[48]

Archestratos was the greatest but not the first ancient food writer. Not one classical Greek cookbook survives, but, thanks again to the *Deipnosophists* of Athenaios, we can read one or two recipes from a whole series of early texts of this kind. The very first author of a Greek cookery book was 'Mithaikos, who wrote the book on Sicilian cookery'.[49] These words come from Plato's dialogue *Gorgias*: evidence already that Mithaikos had a certain notability, or he would never have earned mention in a philosophical text. Plato's Sokrates remarks ironically that Thearion the baker, Mithaikos, and Sarambos the wine-dealer had all three been good at caring for the Athenians in a physical way: they had supplied the city with fine bread, rich cuisine, and foreign wine . . . and the result was not health but decadence. There are a few other references to him, but only Athenaios gives a quotation from Mithaikos' book. It is a whole recipe, but it could hardly be briefer. It is for the fish called *tainia*, a name known in Sicily in the early fifth century BC and to be identified with the none-too-gastronomic ribbon-like fish that the French call *cépole*: '*Tainia*: gut, discard the head, rinse and fillet; add cheese and oil.'[50]

Mithaikos had a neighbour and successor, Glaukos, a native of the Greek city of Lokroi in southern Italy. From his work, too, only a single recipe is known, for a sauce: '*Hyposphagma*: fried blood and *silphion* and grape syrup (or honey) and vinegar and milk and cheese and chopped aromatic herbs.'[51] And then there was Hegesippos from the Greek city of Taras (Taranto), who gave a recipe from which Athenaios quotes only a few words, for a famous ancient dish that was neither Sicilian nor Italian but from Lydia, the pre-Persian kingdom on the eastern edge of the Greek

Octopus in Red Wine

It is still common to see older men and women on the seafront in the mornings, beating their catch on the rocks. Octopus are caught with a long-handled trident, or just by hand, and tenderized by repeated beating with a wooden paddle or by throwing the poor thing on to the rocks. 'The octopus is to be beaten with twice seven blows,' according to the ancient rule. Modern wisdom dictates 42 blows or a brief spell in the freezer.

I whole octopus, cleaned
2 bay leaves
I tsp peppercorns
half an onion, chopped
I clove garlic, sliced
water
I glass red wine, dry or
semi-sweet
²/₃ glass olive oil

An octopus, just caught and killed, soon to
be cooked, waits in the sun.

Put the whole octopus into a neatly fitting saucepan, together with the bay leaves, peppercorns, onion, garlic and enough water almost to submerge it. Cover the pan and boil for one hour. Then pour in the wine and oil and leave to simmer slowly until the sauce thickens to the consistency of single cream and the octopus is tender. Cut it into large pieces and serve warm, together with its sauce, as a fine accompaniment to *revithada*.

A couple of charcoal-grilled octopus tentacles served with a wedge of lemon on a small saucer: this is perhaps the quintessential *meze* to serve with ouzo. In the summer octopus are grilled or boiled and served cold in vinegar, with dried oregano. In the winter they are stewed with wine or made into *chtapodokeftedes*, octopus croquettes. A popular Lenten dish is octopus braised with short macaroni.

Octopus attacking crayfish: detail of a marine life mosaic in the House of the
Dancing Faun, Pompeii, 1st century AD.

world. 'The Lydians', writes Athenaios, 'also spoke of a certain *kandaulos*,
indeed not one but three of them, so versatile in luxury had they become;
made, says Hegesippos of Taras, of fried meat and grated bread and
Phrygian cheese and dill and rich broth.'⁵²

At the same time as the cookery books – which, to judge by this meagre
evidence, were businesslike and laconic in the extreme – a completely different kind of food writing was developing. Around 400 BC appeared the
earliest text, probably in any language, that existed purely to describe a meal.
The *Dinner* of Philoxenos of Kythera is a playful poem, a description of a
lavish banquet by one of the guests, addressed to an intimate friend. Much
of it can still be read, thanks to a series of long quotations by Athenaios, who
clearly found it more interesting than the early cookbooks.

The subject is probably an entertainment given by Philoxenos' patron,
Dionysios the Elder, king of Syracuse. The diners shared many small tables
in a single hall. They washed their hands before eating and again after the
main course. Wreaths and perfumed oils improved the atmosphere. The
number of different dishes was very large: fish and seafood predominated
at the beginning, with early dishes including an octopus stew; there were
thrymmatides, small birds cooked in a pastry or pie; there were many meat
dishes. Barley cakes as well as wheat bread accompanied the main course,
which ended with 'soft-layered rolls' to be eaten with honey, cream or mild

cheese. Wine was served after the main course without any accompanying food (Archestratos would have disapproved). Then came the dessert, which consisted, beside eggs, almonds and walnuts, of 'frumenty ... sesame cakes in honey sauce ... cheese-and-sesame sweetmeats fried in oil and rolled in sesame seeds' and other sweet confections in which safflower, honey and sesame had a prominent role. Then the diners played *kottabos*, classical Greeks' favourite after-dinner game, in which the dregs of wine left in a cup were projected at a target with a deft flick of the wrist.[53]

Contemporary intellectuals hated this *Dinner*. Aristotle, no less, criticized the half-educated who could be observed 'speaking publicly ... while having read nothing except maybe the *Dinner* of Philoxenos, and not all of that': to those people it seemed a piece of serious but approachable literature.[54] A speaker mocked in a comedy fragment by Antiphanes is one of them: 'Far superior to all other poets: Philoxenos! First of all, he put new words of his own everywhere. And then, how well he watered down his lyrics with tones and colours. A god among men, he was, he really knew about literature.'[55] The critics were right – Philoxenos really does put new words everywhere, sometimes a whole recipe for a stew or a cake packed into a single word – but he isn't being serious: the *Dinner* is a *jeu d'esprit*, incongruously applying to a playful topic the dithyrambic language that he was so good at. He surely had no idea that his invented words would be picked apart by food historians two thousand years later.

Archestratos' work followed soon after. It, too, earned satire on the comic stage and criticism from philosophers, who read it as an exemplar of decadence, of literary writing devoted to an unworthy topic.

Whatever may be thought of Philoxenos, we can see now that Archestratos' fault was to be ahead of his time. Aristotle was about to begin his systematic work on animal biology. His successor Theophrastos wrote on botany, alert to geographical variation with the benefit of scientific reports from Alexander's expedition. It's no coincidence that Lynkeus of Samos, a student of Theophrastos, is the single ancient writer on record who referred to Archestratos' work without criticism. He might well have thought it comparable in its light-hearted way to some of his teacher's work. In the Hellenistic period written research was taken up with exactly the kind of detailed explorations and evaluations, in all kinds of scholarly and technical fields, that Archestratos had devoted to his geographical survey of food quality.

Lynkeus, like so many others, is known only from quotations by Athenaios. He had lived in Samos, Rhodes and Athens and has something to say on food customs in all three. His letters, including *Shopping for Food* (already quoted), were apparently all about food, cooking and dining; so were the letters of his correspondents. Lynkeus' *Letter to Diagoras*, of which only a few fragments survive, is evidence of a new stage in Greek gastronomy:

> When you lived in Samos, Diagoras, I know you were often at the drinking-parties at my house, at which a flask beside every man used to be poured out to give each a cupful at pleasure.[56]

Lynkeus sets himself against Athenian practice. In traditional Athenian *symposia*, part of the ritual was deciding the ruling strength of the wine-and-water mixture, after which all participants gradually got drunk together. Lynkeus also has an opinion on what to serve as appetizer and dessert: 'Figs, by the way, I have sometimes served not after dinner, as they do there, when fullness has spoilt the palate, but before dinner when the appetite is virgin.'[57]

When Archestratos advised his readers to prize the special loaves and cakes of one city or another, all they could do in response was to make a special journey. Lynkeus, in the same letter to Diagoras, expects him to do the same if he wantes to taste the Rhodian *echinos* or urchin-cake: 'When you are with me we shall taste them made the Rhodian way and I shall try to explain more fully.'[58] But if you can select dining customs from different cities and construct your own etiquette, you can also select recipes from different cities. Lynkeus' correspondent Hippolochos shows us that things were moving in this way. In a single Macedonian household, in a single menu, Hippolochos enjoyed 'cakes of every kind, Cretan and your own Samian, my dear Lynceus, and Attic, each set out in its individual container'.[59]

To fit these new tastes, a new kind of cookery book would be wanted. Athenaios cites two titles, *Bread-making* and *On Cakes*, by Iatrokles, a writer perhaps of the third century BC. He described cakes from Kos, perhaps Thessaly, probably Syracuse, certainly Athens; he wrote recipes reflecting this new gastronomic freedom and eclecticism. Harpokration of Mendes, the author of *On Cakes*, was Egyptian in origin and gave a recipe for an Alexandrian sweetmeat that came wrapped in papyrus. Chrysippos of Tyana, from whose *Bread-making* Athenaios gives two long quotations, included recipes linked to his native Anatolia, to Crete, to Syria and to Egypt, but in much greater number to Rome and Italy, which is apparently where he wrote in the second or early first century BC.

Paxamos was a second Greek author who probably worked in Rome at that period. He was a man of wide interests, according to a Byzantine

A quiet taverna at Kardamaina on the south coast of Kos.

lexicon: '*Paxamos*, author. *Cookery* in alphabetical order. *Boiotika* in 2 books. *The Twelvefold Art*: this is about sexual positions . . .'.[60] The book on *Cookery* is cited in Athenaios' *Deipnosophists* as if still current. Paxamos is still remembered in a way: the barley biscuit or rusk first named by Galen in the second century AD and well known in Byzantine and modern Greece owes its name *paximadion* to him. Galen gives a recipe not for the ordinary rusk but for a laxative version. It may seem odd, given that special purpose, to prescribe white flour. Wholemeal, however, was regarded as cheap and 'dirty' and would have been unacceptable to the wealthy patients for whom such prescriptions were intended:

> *Laxative paximadia.* Take 2 or 3 drams scammony, 3 drams mastic, 2 drams celery seed, 4 drams polypody, 1 dram cinnamon, 1 pound dough using white flour: mix and add the dry ingredients and knead carefully.[61]

This recipe quoted from Paxamos by way of Galen of Pergamon is a reminder that all through this period, beginning with Mithaikos and continuing into the Roman Empire, another quite different kind of writing about food – books on nutrition and diet – was also flourishing. As far back as the end of the fifth century BC, in the handbook known as *Regimen* or *On Diet* in the Hippocratic collection of medical texts, foodstuffs were catalogued for their effects on health. The seasons of the year and the various human physical types had been matched with appropriate regimens of diet, exercise, hygiene and sexual activity.

From the third century BC onwards, there were many more such texts. Eminent Greek physicians were employed in the royal courts of

Codex Anicia Juliana, the great 6th-century illustrated manuscript of Dioskourides' *Materia Medica*, a classic Greek herbal which had a lasting influence on Arabic and European medicine. To the classical text, in uncial script below, were later added a Byzantine Greek comment above and, still later, the plant's Arabic name. The species illustrated is scurvy-grass, *Cochlearia officinalis*, important as a supplement to sailors' diet.

the Hellenistic kingdoms. One of these was Diokles of Karystos, the first known author of a book of nutritional advice for travellers, from whom Athenaios gives several quotations. A colleague, Diphilos of Siphnos, 'lived under King Lysimachos' and wrote *Diet for the Sick and the Healthy*, another text known through quotations by Athenaios. Another colleague was an Apollodoros who worked for one of the Ptolemies of Egypt and advised on the choice of wine. This was a golden age for dietary writing, and medical authors sometimes went into sufficient detail to provide information that almost amounts to recipes. Also relevant was *On Substances* by Hikesios of Smyrna: a surviving fragment of this work is a reminder that Greek dining engaged all the senses, not just taste. Hikesios considers the perfumes of the *symposion* to be as important to his subject as the foods:

> Some perfumes are ointments, some are waters. Rose fragrance is suitable for a *symposion*, as are myrtle and quince: the latter is stomachic and appropriate to lethargics. Meadowsweet fragrance, a stomachic, also keeps the mind clear. Marjoram and mother-of-thyme fragrances are also suitable for a *symposion*, and saffron when not mixed with much myrrh. Myrrh is also suitable for a *symposion*; spikenard as well. Fenugreek fragrance is sweet and gentle. Gilliflower [stock] is aromatic and very digestive.[62]

For those who want to reconstruct ancient perfume, there are lists of ingredients in Theophrastos' short work *On Odours* (about 300 BC)

In the wilder parts of ancient Greece, especially in the north, there was good hunting. Painted sketch of a wild boar and a wild bull from the rim of a sarcophagus, 4th century BC, Macedonia.

and in an important compilation of the first century AD, Dioskourides of Anazarba's *Materia Medica*. This survives complete, and it set a new standard for comprehensiveness in the study of natural substances, their manmade derivatives and their digestive and pharmacological properties. Relentlessly methodical, it draws on the flora, fauna and food products of the whole central and eastern Mediterranean.

Returning to the food, a medical writer under the early Roman Empire, Athenaios of Attaleia, summarized the seasonal qualities of meat and fish in a fragment reminiscent of Archestratos but far more systematic:

> Pigs are worst from spring until the autumn setting of the Pleiades, and are best from then till spring. Goats are worst in winter, and begin to improve in spring up to the setting of Arcturus. Sheep are worst in winter, but they fatten after the equinox up to the summer solstice; while cows fatten when the grass goes to seed as spring ends and through the whole summer. As for birds, those that appear in winter – the blackbird, thrush and wood-pigeon – are best then, francolins in autumn, and blackcaps, greenfinch and quails are fattest at that season. Hens are not very healthy in winter, especially when the wind is in the south: the turtle dove is finest in autumn. Of fish some are best when carrying eggs, shrimp, langoustine and the soft-bodied squid and cuttlefish, others when they ovate, such as the *kephalos*, grey mullets: these are thin and poor as food when they fill with roe, still more so when they deposit their eggs. The tunny is fattest after Arcturus, worse in summer.[63]

The greatest dietician of the second century AD was Galen of Pergamon, physician to the Roman emperor Commodus and a prolific author. In *On the Properties of Foods* Galen discusses the dietary value of practically all foodstuffs of Greece. There are asides on food and cookery in many of his works. The central role that diet played in ancient medicine shines out from his obsessively careful notes, enlivened with anecdotes, on such subjects as the boiling of eggs and the making of pancakes:

> Let us find time to speak of other cakes, the ones made with club wheat flour. *Tagenitai* as they are called in Attic Greek, *teganitai* to us in Asia, are made simply with oil. The oil is put in a frying pan resting on a smokeless fire, and when it has heated, the wheat flour, mixed with plenty of water, is poured on. Rapidly, as it fries in the

oil, it sets and thickens like fresh cheese setting in the baskets. And at this point the cooks turn it, putting the visible side under, next to the pan, and bringing the sufficiently fried side, which was underneath at first, up on to the top, and when the underneath is set they turn it again another two or maybe three times till they think it is all equally cooked ... Some like to add honey, and others again sea salt.[64]

Galen was an older contemporary of Athenaios. A fictionalized Galen is a character in the dialogue of Athenaios' *Deipnosophists*. This brings us to Athenaios himself, the Greek writer on whom so much in this chapter depends. He lived in the late second and early third centuries. He was a native of Naukratis in Egypt, but he set his fictional dialogue in Rome, the second home of Greek intellectuals, gastronomes and cooks. His great work seems to have been completed soon after AD 223.

The *Deipnosophists* (the 'sophists' or 'professors of dining') takes the form of a series of fictional dinner discussions. In imitation of Plato's *Republic*, these discussions are reported, in a frame conversation, by 'Athenaios' to 'Timokrates'. Several of the speakers have the names of real people, such as Galen, who were Athenaios' contemporaries; others are fictional. They include a couple of doctors, who quote dietetic texts; a cynic philosopher; the pedant Ulpian, who demands the textual authority for strange food names; and the host, the Roman citizen Larensius. The thread running through the discussion from beginning to end is the food and entertainment of the Greeks and some of their neighbours in the last few centuries BC. The speakers talk occasionally about the food and social life of their own time, but nearly always they are appealing to written texts of the classical past: comedies, memoirs, epics, history, science, medicine and lexicography. They are continually quoting, and frequently interrupt and dispute the quotations of others.

Athenaios loved the Athenian comedy of the fifth to third centuries BC – hence the quotations of cooks' speeches earlier in this chapter. He was bored by recipe books, but interested in medical texts on diet, and he liked the anecdotal history books of Hellenistic times, full of information on food and festivity. On the rare occasions when his quotations can be checked against the originals, he is relatively accurate. But there are thousands of occasions on which he can't be checked, because, but for his quotations, the texts he cites would be entirely lost. This is the real value of the *Deipnosophists*, an astonishingly generous resource without which our knowledge of the history of Greek food and food writing would be immeasurably poorer.

THREE

Roman and Byzantine Tastes

Athenaios lived and wrote in Rome, under the Roman Empire of which Greece was part, but in the whole vast *Deipnosophists* there is little to be found about life as a Roman subject in the early third century AD. He focused on the Greece of the past.

The food and cookery of Greece as part of the Roman Empire, a topic that did not matter to Athenaios, matters to us. It is the historical link between classical Greece and the Byzantine Empire, and it explains how the one developed from the other. Under the pressure of internal political crises, frequent rebellions and continual frontier warfare, the Roman Empire split. The split was a deliberate decision, initially by the emperor Diocletian, who planned a hierarchy of four emperors, a tetrarchy, one of whom (Diocletian himself at first) would hold supreme power. It did not work out like that. Successive struggles reduced the number of power-holders to two and created a balance between them. From the beginning of the fifth century there were effectively two empires, and the western, in less than a hundred years, collapsed.

The eastern was what we call the Byzantine Empire. It was bilingual: both Greek and Latin were used in official documents. The lands long inhabited by Greeks, Greece, Macedonia, Thrace and Asia Minor were all part of it. The capital, Constantinople, was Greek-speaking. Greek food habits were ingrained in the central lands of the Empire, but for about four hundred years they had mixed, through travel, migration, intermarriage and empire-wide trade, with the foods and ways of life of Romans and others. With what result?

There is no shortage of information. Luxury dishes are named in the *Historia Augusta*, a series of fictionalized imperial biographies written about AD 380. Foods are listed, alongside other supplies, in the emperor

Diocletian's Price Edict, a failed attempt in AD 301 to fix the maximum prices that the army would pay for its supplies. The Edict was promulgated in Latin and Greek, the two official languages of the Empire. But the single greatest source on Imperial cookery and cuisine is a collection of Latin recipes, probably of the late fourth century, known under the name of the legendary gourmet Apicius.

Some recipe books are intended for armchair reading, not for practical use by cooks. People have said this about *Apicius*, but wrongly. It is not a book that anyone would have read for pleasure. This is obvious from its style and its language. It is a bare sequence of recipes that are mostly no more than lists of ingredients, and it is written in vulgar Latin, the colloquial language of the Roman Empire. People of culture read and wrote literary classical Latin; *Apicius* displays the everyday speech and technical jargon used by cooks and servants in Roman households. As one of the major sources for vulgar Latin, this book gives an unrivalled picture of the linguistic and cultural interchange that was happening under the surface.

Apicius has many recipes for dishes with Greek names. Inside the recipes are food names and cooking terms borrowed from Greek. This was nothing new. The same Greek words crop up in other texts too: in Petronius' Latin novel *Satyricon* of the first century AD and in *Daily Conversation*, a bilingual Greek-Roman phrase book of the later Roman Empire. It was in fact a two-way exchange. In modern Greek there are Latin loanwords in the names of foods and dishes; there are Greek elements in the modern Romance languages that grew out of Latin. Greek terms in *Apicius* were real linguistic borrowings into Latin some of which survive today in Spanish, Portuguese, Catalan, French, Italian and Romanian.

It was natural for new foods and dishes in Roman imperial cuisine to end up with a single name used in more than one language. Examples are sausages. There was the one called *isikion*, discussed in the *Deipnosophists*, with a variant version (perhaps salted) called *salsikion*. It goes back to the second century BC, but was it Latin or Greek? The Latin form *salsicia* survives today in modern Italian *salsiccia* and French *saucisse*; meanwhile, in mid-Byzantine Greek, in the *Miracles of Saints Cosmas and Damian*, we find the useful phrase *seira salsikion*, 'a string of sausages'.

There is no early recipe for *salsikion*, but in the case of the popular smoked sausage *loukanikon* we know that not only the word but some details of the recipe were shared between cultures. It was originally brought to Rome, the Latin author Varro tells us, by soldiers of the second century

BC who had served in the southern Italian region of Lucania, after which the sausage was named. *Apicius*, some centuries later, gives a Roman method (*liquamen* in this Latin recipe is a form of *garos*):

> *Making of lucanicae.* Pound pepper, cumin, savory, rue, parsley, bay berry spice and *liquamen*. Add meat which has been thoroughly pounded so that it can then be blended well with the spice mix. Stir in *liquamen*, whole peppercorns, plenty of fat and pine nuts. Put the meat in the skins, draw them quite thinly and hang them in the smoke.[1]

At about the same period at which this recipe was written, the word is first recorded in Greek. *Loukanika* are familiar today from end to end of the Mediterranean and far beyond: in southern Italy, Greece and Cyprus; in Bulgaria; in Portugal and Brazil as *linguiça*; in Spain as *longaniza*; in the Arabic-speaking Levant and among Levantine Jews. Modern *loukanika*, under these various names, are usually spicy, usually smoked, usually lamb rather than pork, usually formed of a single long casing, not twisted into segments.

Moving from sausages to sweets brings us to another exchange between the two great languages of the Roman Empire. The Latin suffix that appears in Greek as *-aton* is applied to concoctions based on a single main ingredient. In the case of a typical Mediterranean conserve, quince paste, made by long, slow cooking of sliced quinces in sugar syrup, the usual medieval name was based on the Greek *kydonion melon* ('apple of Kydonia or Chania', that is, quince) with this Latin suffix, giving *kydonaton*. There was another name, Greek *melimelon*, 'honey apple', stemming from an earlier period when – sugar being still too costly – similar conserves were made with honey. This alternative name passed by way of Latin *melimelum* into Portuguese, where quince paste is *marmelada*. As Portuguese quince paste became popular in Elizabethan England, the word travelled on into English in the form marmalade, now used for citrus fruit conserves rather than for quince.

At this period of empire-wide cultural exchange in farming, some food species already familiar in Greece were given new Latin names, and the Latin names have stuck. Thus the modern Greek term *kitron*, 'citron', is totally different from the older Greek *melon medikon*, which meant 'Median apple' because this was a fruit that the Greeks first encountered in Central Asia, in Media to be precise, in the orchards of the Persian emperor. Instead, the modern term is borrowed from the Latin *citrus*, which has another origin.

Roman gardeners and farmers put great effort into plant-breeding, and new varieties sometimes became so widely popular that the new variety name, which might well be Latin, replaced the older species name. The modern Greek word *marouli*, 'lettuce', has nothing to do with the ancient Greek *thridakine*; instead, it seems to come from a Latin variety name, now forgotten, which would have been something like *amarula*, 'bitterish'. Rome had a special liking for the Damascus variety of plum, Latin *damascenum*; this is still a variety name in most of Europe – English damson, for example – but in modern Greek it has become a general name for prunes and plums, *damaskino*. The apricot, which flowers and fruits early, was called *praecocium*, 'precocious', in Rome in the first century AD; from this came a medieval Greek term *brekokion*, the modern Greek *verikoko*, and by way of medieval Arabic a whole series of modern West European names including the English apricot. At about the same period a kind of peach was given the Latin epithet *duracinus*, 'hard-kernel'. This, too, passed into Greek as *dorakinon*, but the Greek name seemed to make better sense with the consonants transposed, hence the modern Greek *rodakinon* (which appears to mean 'rosy-skinned'). Names of this kind, too, could be transferred in the other direction, from Greek to Latin. A cultivated fleshy variety of carrot emerged in Hellenistic times and was named *karoton* (perhaps meaning 'heavy-headed') in the Greek of the Roman Empire. This later Greek term not only replaced the ancient name for the wild species, which was *daukos*; it also passed into vulgar Latin and the languages of Western Europe, whence English carrot.

Out of all the interactions between Greek and Roman culture in a gastronomic context, the story of the names for 'liver' is the strangest. The medieval Greek word is *sykoton* (modern *sykoti*) and the vulgar Latin word is *ficatum* (the ancestor of French *foie*, Spanish *higado* and other West European names for 'liver'). The Greek and Latin terms both transparently mean 'figged' or, to say it more explicitly, 'stuffed with figs': they derive from classical Greek *sykon* and from classical Latin *ficus*, 'fig'. Why did words with the literal meaning 'stuffed with figs' develop the sense 'liver' in both these early languages? The clue is in Greek. It was in ancient Greece that gastronomes first took a special interest in force-fed geese: we know this because Penelope, the wife of the wandering Odysseus in the *Odyssey*, narrates a dream in which she is fattening twenty geese in her farmyard (they represent, as Homer and Freud would agree, her avid suitors). It was also in ancient Greece that gourmets first noticed something special about the livers of such geese; and it was in Greece, where dried figs are two a penny, that geese were fattened by being fed with figs. In Greece, therefore, and nowhere else, it made perfect sense to use a term meaning 'stuffed with figs', *sykoton*, for *foie gras*. The second step, since this was the nicest kind of liver, was to use the same word optimistically for all liver (just as *koniak* is used optimistically in modern Greek for all brandy). The third step was for Latin speakers to create a Latin word to match: so Latin *ficatum*, from its very first use in a recipe in *Apicius*, means simply 'liver', only ideally and not in everyday reality 'the liver of an animal fattened with figs'.

Cultures were truly mingling. A technical term from one of the two languages would be seen as the best way to denote a newly developed food idea. In the case of some of the new technical terms of Latin and Greek that were first recorded during the Roman Empire, it is strangely difficult to say which language they started in. Is *isikion* Greek or Latin? No one knows. Is *kydonaton* Greek or Latin? Half and half. A kind of coalescence was under way, but was never completed, as the administrative division made by the later emperors between eastern and western provinces eventually hardened into a cultural and linguistic frontier. The eastern Empire, Greek-speaking, Roman in government, proud of its Greek and Roman cultural heritage, became what we know as the Byzantine Empire: it lived and flourished, though gradually shrinking, for a thousand years. Food was a major part of that Greek and Roman heritage, and many of the terms used by the Greeks of Constantinople, in speaking and writing about their food, survive in everyday Greek today.

THE UNIQUENESS OF ROMAN GREECE

'We are in our prime,' the Latin poet Horace asserts with less than total conviction, 'we paint and sing and fight better than the greasy Greeks.'[2] In spite of their ambiguous feelings about this conquered province, the Romans had plenty to say about its local food specialities. Athens was the usual destination of Roman voyages eastwards, but the once-rich city was now relatively poor and its history was for sale; or so the poet Automedon implies:

> Bring ten measures of charcoal and they'll make you a citizen
> ... To your local contact you must give cabbage-stalks, lentils or snails. Be sure to have these and you may call yourself Erechtheus, Kekrops, Kodros, whatever you want; nobody cares at all.[3]

Snails Stifado

Snails are appreciated almost everywhere in Greece. Various villages are famous locally for their snails. For example, Lefkes is known on Paros as the village of snail-eaters, *karavolades*, and a snail festival is held there every July (which is, oddly enough, the time of year when snails are least likely to be found). On Crete they are popular stewed with tomatoes and onions in a stifado or simply cooked with plenty of garlic. This recipe is from Diana Farr Louis's *Feasting and Fasting in Crete*.

Stifado implies 'stewed with onions and spices'. Take each baby snail and suck it out of its shell.

½ kg snails
1 large onion, finely chopped
120 ml olive oil
500 g tomatoes, chopped
salt and pepper, to taste
400 g bulgur or trachanas

Put the snails in a saucepan with water barely to cover, bring to the boil and cook for 5–8 minutes, skimming all the while. Drain and rinse well.

Athens, by this time, obviously had not much to offer gastronomically, but there was the thyme that grew freely on the slopes of Mount Hymettos, just outside the city. Along with wild greens such as rocket, thyme served as a relish to set beside the bread of the poorer students of Athens. Far beyond Athens, its thyme was known indirectly. 'The best honey is Attic, and the best of Attic the Hymettian': the honey from those sunny slopes was a cliché of ancient gastronomy, and, then as now, it was the thyme that made it special.[4] Hymettian honey was required for *mulsum*, the sweet aperitif that preceded a Roman meal, a truly Graeco-Italian blend, 'mixed from new Hymettian honey and well-aged Falernian wine' from the hills that divided Lazio from Campagna.[5]

The epigram by Automedon quoted above is a rarity. Roman literature generally says as little as possible of the real state of Greece, the

Sauté the onion with the snails in the olive oil until the onion is translucent and starting to brown. Add the seasoning and tomatoes, stirring. Cover and cook over moderate heat until the tomatoes release their juices. Uncover and simmer until most of the liquid has evaporated.

Test the snails to see if they are done by spearing one and cutting the meat. If tender, remove them from the saucepan and add the bulgur or trachanas along with 360 ml of water. Cover and simmer until most of the water is absorbed (10–15 minutes). Put the snails back in the pan and simmer for another 5–10 minutes.

Serves 4–6

Snails on sale in Athens, some of them not yet resigned to their fate.

cities shrunken or abandoned, the wealth (if there had been any) spent or stolen, the politics parochial and dependent on Rome. Instead, it builds a picture of Golden Age Greece, when grapes were trodden by Dionysos' own feet 'and honey dripped from sticky leaves, and oil from the fat olive tree', and the sounds of hunting were heard across the mountains.[6] The mountains, though, were of real economic importance. Crete was the best source of medicinal herbs in the Mediterranean; second best were the slopes of Mount Pelion in southeastern Thessaly. The centaur Chiron, native of Pelion, was a skilled herbalist according to the myths, gathering his herbs on the slopes near Pagasai. There was more too. 'I hunt about through Thessaly, Aitolia, Boiotia, for honey and cheese and all that line of grocery,' announces a character in the *Metamorphoses* of Apuleius.[7] The mountain cheeses of northern Greece were in great demand, and Greek

A feast shared by the dead person and the surviving family is a typical scene on gravestones from ancient Greece. On this example, broken across the top but otherwise well preserved, traces of the original colouring survive. The food is served on a small three-legged table.

mountain honey, even if not from Hymettos, was reputed to be the finest in the Empire.

From the viewpoint of classical Greece, a characteristic shared by the northern regions of Macedonia and Thrace was their lush fertility, seen in literature in occasional rumours of twice-bearing fruit trees or ridiculously high-yielding crops, and in Pindar's poetic celebration of Thrace, 'of abundant grapes and of fine fruit'. This commonplace emerges once more in Roman literature. Odysseus in the *Odyssey*, telling the story of his ten-year wanderings, had spoken of a wine given him by the Thracian Maron, which was so strong that it needed to be diluted with twenty parts of water. The Roman encyclopaedist Pliny was ready to believe it, because his trusted informant 'Mucianus, three times consul', while touring in the Maronea district of Roman Thrace, had tasted a wine that was very nearly as strong: 'each pint was mixed with eight of water; it was black in colour, fragrant, and became fuller with age.'[8] It is no coincidence that Thracians were said to drink themselves to madness. In classical Greece it was accepted as a matter of simple fact that drinking neat wine (which Thracians and Macedonians were well known to do) would lead to insanity, and insanity in turn led to fighting: 'It is a Thracian habit to fight with the cups that are meant for pleasure', said Horace.[9]

As for Crete, the island was already well known for the quality and efficacy of its herbs when Theophrastos was compiling the *Study of Plants* in 310 BC. Even in his time there were people who said that in leaves and stems and all parts above the roots Cretan herbs were the best in the world. Some of them, such as the two gynaecological drugs *diktamnon* (Cretan dittany, *Origanum dictamnus*) and *tragion* (perhaps *Hypericum hircinum*), could be found nowhere else. Dittany leaves, pounded in water, would bring on labour; *tragion* was used to promote lactation and to cure breast ailments.

Mark Antony acquired large estates in Crete and gave them to his beloved Cleopatra. On her defeat and death these estates fell to the victor, Octavian – soon to be the emperor Augustus – and they formed the basis of a Roman imperial monopoly in the medicinal herbs of Crete. The full development of the trade in Cretan herbs is tentatively dated to the time of Nero, the fifth emperor, whose personal doctor Andromachos was a native of the island. Galen describes the business in full vigour in his own time, a century later: 'Many herbs are imported every summer from Crete: the plantsmen whom the Emperor maintains there send great trays full of them not only to the Emperor himself but to the city at large.' They went to some provincial markets too. They were gathered whole 'so that everything is present, plant, fruits, seeds, roots, juice', and loosely enveloped in rolls of papyrus. The rolls were packed into baskets woven from withies of agnus castus, and the herbalists of Rome bought Cretan herbs by the basketful. The rolls were labelled on the outside, sometimes just with the name of the particular species, sometimes also with the district of origin – and if this was Pedias, said Galen, the quality was likely to be best of all. Pedias is modern

Spices and herbs on sale near Athens Central Market. Visible here are cassia and the finer cinnamon, beeswax, lavender, thyme (*enchorio*, 'local'), star anise and Indian turmeric.

Peza, a wine appellation, the green, well-watered district of hills and valleys southeast of Knossos.

Galen adds that the imperial pharmacists always preferred the Cretan dried supplies of such plants as *polion* (ja'adah or hulwort, *Teucrium polium*), *hyssopon* (hyssop, *Hyssopus officinalis*), *thlaspi* (perhaps shepherd's purse, *Capsella bursa-pastoris*), *helleboros melas* (black hellebore, *Helleborus niger*), *chamaidrys* (germander, *Teucrium chamaedrys*) and *chamaipitys* (perhaps herb ivy, *Ajuga iva*): if presented with the fresh plants those timeservers would not have recognized them. But he himself had found fresh specimens of all these plants growing wild in the country round Rome. Even so, if Rome happened to have had a wet spring, the dried Cretan herbs would be better than the fresh Italian.[10]

Being easier to store and transport than almost any food, wine was one of the Greek products that reached a new market after the Roman conquest, but this led to changes in the product and, as we shall see, to adulteration with seawater. Dionysos' list of fine wines, if it had been given in Roman times, would have omitted Mendaean and Thasian and included sweet Cretan instead. Suddenly there were good wines, even great vintages, from the mainland vineyards of Asia Minor, where there were apparently none before. There would be three high-quality Lesbian appellations and a *premier cru* Chian: unmentioned in earlier Greek texts, the Chian sub-appellation Ariousion was 'a rugged and harbourless district that produced the best wine of Greece', the geographer Strabo asserted.[11]

Two centuries later there is a list of good Greek wines in the writings of Galen, who had impressive qualifications for the task: he was a Greek-speaking native of the best wine-producing region of Asia Minor, and also a careful wine-taster. He writes for colleagues who will be prescribing a regime for wealthy patients:

> In Asia Minor and Greece and neighbouring provinces Italian wines are not to be found. Often the best wine to prescribe, of what is available in those parts, will be Ariusian (grown in certain districts of Chios) or Lesbian. There are three cities of Lesbos. The least aromatic and least sweet comes from Mytilene, more aromatic and sweeter from Eresos, then Methymna. Prescribe the 'unmixed', so called because there is no seawater mixed in. But they have not usually included seawater in the *best* wines of Lesbos or of Chian Ariousion, and, after all, it is the best wines that I am talking of.[12]

Most Roman sources rank Chian first on the list of fine wines. It had been a rare luxury in early Rome, taken only on doctor's orders, until as dining became more lavish and expensive it was eventually adopted as the acme of luxury. In a Latin satire by Horace the ambitious host Nasidienus, anxious to follow every fashionable gastronomic rule, boasts that he is serving Chian wine and that his cooking vinegar comes from Lesbian Methymna.[13]

Other Greek vintages were among the worst in the Roman Empire, and this surely applies to those that were salted with seawater. The typical salty wine was Coan: 'The invention was owed to the dishonesty of a slave: it was his way of fulfilling his target,' Pliny tells us, and it was one of the most successful examples of adulteration in the whole history of food.[14] In addition to its obvious attraction to the merchant – salt gave it stability – Coan wine turned out to be a laxative. The typical shapely amphoras of Cos were eventually manufactured at many sites across the Mediterranean, demonstrating that so-called Coan wine was being made all over the place. Since salt would tend to conceal any native delicacy of flavour, this was easy to do. We even have two recipes for it. One is in the early Latin farming handbook by Cato the Elder, the other, quoted here, in the Byzantine collection *Geoponika*:

> *Making Coan Wine.* Some people boil 3 parts grape must and one part seawater down to two-thirds. Others mix 1 cup salt, 3 cups grape syrup, about 1 cup grape must, 1 cup vetch flour, 100 drams melilot, 16 drams apple, 16 drams Celtic nard, into 2 *metretai* [12 gallons] white wine.[15]

THE EXOTICS

Roman cookery at its most elaborate surpassed, in complexity and in sheer number of ingredients, anything that we know of the cuisine of early Greece. Rome's most important contribution to the Byzantine gastronomic mix was its use of spices. Apart from *silphion*, imported spices had been used in earlier Greece to make perfumes, perfumed oils, medicines and spiced wines, but hardly ever to flavour food. Like some twentieth-century Martini-drinkers, there were ancient Greeks who loved the taste of spiced wine but hated spices in their food. Theophrastos, the botanist successor to Aristotle, was one of them: 'One might wonder,' he wrote, 'why exotic and other fragrances improve the

Cupids picking grapes
from trellised vines in
a detail from a carved
sarcophagus, Roman
period.

Tipping fruit into
the vat.

Treading the grapes.

taste of wines when, so far from having that effect on foods (whether cooked or uncooked), they invariably ruin them.'[16] Later, however, when dining fashions among the wealthy of the Mediterranean world had coalesced, those who dined from *Apicius* must be imagined experiencing complex mixtures of herbs and spices from all over the Empire and beyond its frontiers, mixtures that would have disgusted Theophrastos. Let's consider a few of those exotics, and first of all one that Theophrastos himself briefly describes in an appendix to his *Study of Plants*:

> Pepper is a fruit, and is of two kinds: one round like bitter vetch, with a shell and flesh like bay berries, reddish; the long kind with poppy-like seeds, and this is much stronger than the other. Both are heating; thus, like frankincense, they are antidotes to hemlock.[17]

The classical Greek word *peperi* is of Indian origin, borrowed from Prakrit *pippali*, but in Indian languages the word always denotes the pungent long pepper of northeastern India, *Piper longum*: this, the species that is listed second by Theophrastos above and is far less familiar nowadays, is the one that Greeks got to know first. From the second century BC, when the Ptolemies, the Macedonian rulers of Egypt, developed the monsoon sailings directly across the Indian Ocean, they began to buy the round black pepper of southern India, *P. nigrum*, in ever larger quantities. It came to the Roman Empire from the port of Muziris, near Cochin, on the Indian Ocean trading ships: 'They arrive with gold and depart with pepper', wrote the Tamil poet Tāyan-Kannanār, speaking of the Graeco-Roman traders.[18] This, more than any other spice, was what they wanted from India. 'Ships at these trading ports carry full loads because of the volume and quantity of pepper', the Greek Indian Ocean sailing guide confirms.[19]

Pepper was used for centuries in sacrifices and as a medicine before anyone in Greece admitted to liking the taste of it. It is a recipe ingredient in a fragment of Diphilos of Siphnos (about 300 BC), but he is speaking as a dietician: 'Scallops in general are good to eat, good to digest, and good for the bowels if taken with cumin and pepper.'[20] Medicinally again, pepper is wanted in Petronius' Latin novel *Satyricon* in a cure for impotence. As far as taste is concerned, one of the speakers in Plutarch's *Symposion Questions* makes a telling comment: 'Many older people still cannot enjoy melon, lemon or pepper.'[21] By the time of *Apicius* this was no longer the case: pepper is called for in nearly every recipe in that collection. In Byzantine cuisine and diet, it remained a notable ingredient in foods and medicines.

Mushrooms

In Greek supermarkets and groceries it is difficult to find anything other than button, field or oyster (*Pleurotus*) mushrooms, yet around 150 edible species grow in Greece and many of these are collected to eat at home. Don't collect from olive groves, people say, but for no very good reason. On Paros, one of the drier islands, blewitts are common: they are dredged in flour, fried in olive oil, and lemon juice is added before they are eaten piping hot. Elsewhere wild mushrooms are cooked in a casserole with pork or made into a fricassée scented with dill and served with avgolemono.

Grevena, southwest of Koritsa and Siatista, calls itself 'the home of the mushroom' and holds a mushroom festival each November. In Grevena wild mushrooms are served fresh in mushroom pies (*manitaropites*), dried for rehydrating in pilafs and risottos (a none-too-Greek recipe), candied in loukoum or used in an unexpected mushroom spoon sweet, which can be eaten on its own as an accompaniment to coffee, or with thick yoghurt as a dessert to cleanse the palate.

Cantharellus cibarius, the chanterelle or girolle.

Ginger, classical Greek *zingiberi*, arrived later. It, too, was a medicine. We first hear of it in a Greek-speaking context when the Roman medical writer Celsus lists it as one of the ingredients in the famous *mithridateion*, the poison antidote of King Mithridates of Pontos. Soon afterwards the Greek pharmacist Dioskourides of Anazarba admits that it is worth eating:

> Ginger is . . . grown mostly in Eritrea and Arabia, where they make much use of it fresh, as we use leeks, boiling it for soup and cooking it in stews . . . Some producers pickle it (otherwise it dries out) and export it in jars to Italy: it is very nice to eat; it is eaten pickle and all.[22]

A Far Eastern tropical plant, ginger was surely brought to the shores of the Red Sea by the monsoon sailings in the second century BC – and was traded northwards just in time for it to be included in the *mithridateion* if Celsus' recipe for that mysterious drug happens to be correct. Ginger is much less prominent in *Apicius* and in Byzantine food texts than pepper. This is evidently because it was used not so much in cooking main dishes as in confectionery, for which hardly any recipes survive.

Pliny, the first classical author to mention cloves, says that they were imported 'for their aroma'. Their actual source, far beyond Greek and Roman knowledge, was the Banda islands in Indonesia. By the end of the Roman Empire Greek medical authors knew of various uses for cloves, whose name was *gariofilum* in Latin, modern Greek *garifalo*.

And so the use of spices in Western cuisine, which began with one or two strange flavours in Mycenaean texts, and increased fairly slowly to three or four in classical Greece, grew towards its medieval climax. Some flavours, experienced under the Roman Empire only by those with delicate health and well-paid physicians, would become sources of gastronomic pleasure in medieval Constantinople.

Nutmeg, produced only in the distant islands of Ternate and Tidore, was little known to the Romans. It was certainly familiar to the Byzantines: they called it *moschokarydion* and sprinkled it on pease pudding served on fast days.

The case of cane sugar is similar. Greeks first heard of this wonderful sweet spice in India, in Alexander the Great's time, as recorded by the scientist Eratosthenes (he writes of 'large reeds, sweet both by nature and by the sun's heat').[23] Pliny lists it among Indian spices, but had heard that it was grown in Arabia too: it was 'brittle to the teeth', he adds, but was 'used only in medicine'. Greek medical authors, Dioskourides and Galen, agree. Honey, familiar and cheap, was the natural sweetener; sugar, rare and costly, had to be prescribed by physicians. The first evidence of its use in European food comes in mid-Byzantine times, and the sweet conserves and sweet drinks that were so much loved in Constantinople seemed all the healthier because they incorporated this exotic, medicinal spice.

Next in the list of the spices that Rome knew and that Constantinople loved are cinnamon and cassia. Tall stories were told of their distant origin, rendering them so fearfully expensive that no Roman dreamed of adding them to food: they were medicines and offerings to the gods. Galen tells of making up an antidote for the emperor Marcus Aurelius using cinnamon that had come in a 'box shipped from the land of the barbarians, four and a half cubits long, in which was a whole cinnamon tree of the first quality'.[24] Cinnamon was likewise wanted in the medical chest that the Byzantine emperors took with them on campaign in the tenth century, but by mid-Byzantine times it had culinary uses too. As did saffron, whose only known place in the earlier Greek diet was as an ingredient in spiced wine. As regards cinnamon and saffron, the change is clearly visible from the *Prodromic Poems* of the twelfth century: there in two and a half lines of verse we have one of the tastiest of Byzantine recipes, 'a sweet-and-sour saffron dish with spikenard, valerian, cloves, cinnamon and little mushrooms, and vinegar and unsmoked honey'.[25] The anonymous poet, satirist of greedy abbots and self-important officials, was also a true food-lover: note the insistence on unsmoked honey. Other sources of the same period add that the unprepossessing bulb of squill, *skilla*, poisonous according to modern information but used in Roman medicine, came into its own in Byzantine flavoured wines and vinegars.

BYZANTINE FOOD AND WINE DEVELOPMENTS

Greek medical authors who wrote about diet have often been quoted earlier in this book, not least in the last few paragraphs. This tradition had reached a kind of apogee in the writings of Galen, which held the field almost unchallenged for nearly two hundred years.

From that point onwards the aim of Greek medical writers was not to contradict Galen – he rapidly became a classic, universally revered – but to set out the state of medical knowledge more briefly, more accessibly, with adjustments that would take account of new information, new foods and new habits. This was the aim, for example, of Oreibasios, in the mid-fourth century AD, whose large-scale, well-organized sixteen-book *Medicine* begins with a long section on diet consisting mainly of well-chosen extracts from Galen and others. He was followed in turn by Aetios of Amida in the fifth century, Alexander of Tralles in the sixth and Paul of Aigina in the seventh. All three, especially Paul, made important progress in other areas of medicine, but as regards diet they held true to tradition, adding brief information on such things as newly available spices. Their works were, in a sense, successive incarnations of the ideal practical textbook of current medicine that every medical student needs to know from beginning to end.

Paul of Aigina, like Galen long before, wrote a standard work whose popularity endured. But his textbook, like its predecessors, was too big, specialized and difficult to be of use to the general reader. Two observant, imaginative mid-Byzantine humanists became aware of this and, between them, did something about it. Michael Psellos, politician, historian and writer on many subjects, wrote a brief guide to the dietary qualities of foods and addressed it to his imperial patron, the emperor Constantine IX Monomachos. Being Psellos, he wrote it in bland but classical iambic verse:

All cheese is indigestible, producing stones,
But *prosphatos* when not too full of salt
Is mild and nourishing and nice to eat . . . [26]

The main credit goes not to Psellos but to his modest friend Simeon Seth, whose patron was Constantine's successor, Michael VII Doukas. A trained physician with knowledge of Arabic and Jewish as well as Greek traditions, Simeon was able to produce a handbook that was better informed and more innovative than Psellos could have managed. For the first time, in Simeon's *Alphabetical Handbook of the Properties of Foods*, we have a handy survey that reflects a truly Byzantine range of knowledge.

Meanwhile, where earlier dieticians, from the Hippocratic *Regimen* to Oreibasios, had said very little of the effect of spices in food, the Byzantine dietary manuals from Aetios of Amida and Paul of Aigina onwards insist on this issue over and over again, urging different strengths and combinations of aromatics depending on the eater's physical condition, the season of the year and even the time of day. Spices and seasonings were, more than ever before, an integral part of the diet, used both during the cooking process and at table to adjust the flavour and the dietary qualities of each dish.

So the new medical writing about diet is the background for fundamental changes in the food itself. The cuisine of the Byzantine Empire was,

Tylichtaria (*Dolmades with Mallow Leaves*)

Once a food ingredient, used as wrapping in the ancient *thria*, fig leaves have now been supplanted by vine leaves in a similar dish, *dolmades* — which is often seen in restaurants but is hardly ever prepared at home except for Clean Monday, the first day of Lent. Figs are generally dried and eaten as a sweet snack. A second alternative wrapping, more easily available in northern Europe, is mallow leaves. This recipe comes from Myrsini Lambraki's book on Cretan wild herbs, Τα χορτά.

60 fleshy mallow leaves
2 chopped carrots
1 large sundried tomato
2 cloves of garlic
1 finely chopped onion
2 fresh spring onions
1½ cups (300 g) sticky rice
2 large potatoes
240 ml olive oil
1 tsp chopped green coriander
juice of 2 lemons
salt and pepper

Take these fresh young leaves . . .

Rinse the mallow leaves and remove their stalks. Blanch them for 6 minutes in boiling water. Drain them and spread them flat in a large dish. Prepare the filling: thoroughly mix the carrots, onions, garlic, tomato, coriander, pepper and rice with half of the lemon juice and half of the oil. Take each mallow leaf, put a teaspoonful of filling on it, and fold the sides over to wrap firmly.

Place the potatoes, chopped in quarters, at the base of a casserole and on top of them in layers the filled mallow leaves, top downwards. Add 5 tbsp olive oil, a little salt and the remaining lemon juice, and cover with a shallow plate. Pour in 450 ml of water, put the lid on the casserole and cook slowly for about 40 minutes. Serve warm or cold.

. . . or, if you prefer, wait for the ripe fruit.

naturally, a synthesis of what had gone before. It inherited the culinary knowledge of the Roman Empire and set beside it an emphasis on local produce, notably seafood, typical of classical Greek gastronomy. But there is room for many novelties.

Alongside the meat foods known in earlier times, the Byzantines experimented with dried meat, one of the forerunners of the *pastirma* of modern Turkey. The attention they paid to inland Anatolia and Syria is reflected in the high reputation as game of the gazelles of the Near East, 'the deer that are commonly called *gazelia*', overlooked by earlier authors but recommended above all other game by Simeon Seth.[27] The emperors had their hunting parks, and in particular maintained a herd of wild asses of which they were very proud (though one wonders whether the cynical bishop Liutprand of Cremona was right and the wild asses of tenth-century Constantinople, so prized by gourmets, were merely a semi-feral herd of the domesticated species after all). Closer to home, sparrows, *pyrgites* in Byzantine Greek, were added to the list of small birds that were caught for food.

Constantinople, classical Byzantion, modern Istanbul, has always been famous for its seafood. The medieval handbooks specify a great many kinds, singling out this or that quality in each, and again there was plenty of room for gastronomic adventure. The Byzantines definitely appreciated salted grey mullet roe, botargo, in spite of the dieticians' disapproval: according to Simeon, 'botargo is indigestible, produces bad humours, and is heavy on the stomach; therefore its use must be avoided totally.'[28] He was not obeyed. Kippered herrings, Byzantine Greek *rengai*, were imported from distant Britain. From the twelfth century onwards Constantinople knew the taste of caviar, the fish delicacy of the northern Black Sea coasts.

Herbalists, gardeners and food-collectors could still draw on all the native plant species whose properties had been set out in the *Materia Medica* of Dioskourides, a work that was never superseded. Dieticians might even recommend vegetarian meals, perhaps dressed with vinegar (as a spoonful of vinegar may nowadays be added to lentil soup). We have already noted the new species introduced to Greek gardens and orchards at this period: the aubergine, Byzantine Greek *melitzana*, and the orange, *nerantzion*. New flavours and combinations continued to be tried. Where classical cooks had wrapped food in pickled fig leaves and called them *thria*, it was in Byzantine times that stuffed vine leaves were used in similar recipes. This historic recipe is supplied by a scholar of the Roman period:

> *Thria were made thus:* Take fried pork fat with milk and mix with boiled barley grains; combine with soft cheese and yolks of egg; then roll in a fragrant fig leaf and fry in chicken or pork fat. Place in a jar of boiling honey-water . . . The ingredients are taken in equal quantities but with plenty of egg yolk because that binds and solidifies.[29]

The direct descendants of this recipe are modern *dolmades*, 'vine-leaves stuffed with minced meat, rice and herbs', familiar under this newfangled Turkish name from ten thousand restaurant menus.[30]

The bakers of Constantinople were in the most favoured of trades, with a range of privileges specified in the *Book of the Eparch*, rules laid down for the city's trade guilds around the year 895: 'Bakers are never liable to be called for any public service, neither themselves nor their animals, to prevent any interruption of the baking of bread.'[31] Bread was classically *artos* but in everyday speech *psomi*, literally meaning 'crumb', a word adopted from familiar New Testament stories. Bread came in varieties already known from classical texts: white and brown were distinguished as *katharos* 'clean' and *ryparos* 'dirty', and there was a middle-grade *kibaros*, 'everyday bread'. 'I love bread, both crust and crumb', and 'I am not to eat the white bread they call foamy but the halfway kind they call *kibarites*', said the Prodromic poet.[32] *Silignites*, raised bread made from what is now called bread wheat, becomes more common in Byzantine sources.

Army bread took a special form. 'The bread that soldiers are to eat in camp', the historian Prokopios explains, 'has to go into the oven twice and be so thoroughly baked that it will last as long as possible and not quickly spoil. Bread so baked is much lighter in weight.'[33] There was a hard ring-shaped loaf of this type, *boukellaton*, and an equally hard barley rusk named after the ancient cookery author Paxamos. This *paximadion* reached its greatest fame, as narrated again by Prokopios, when Leo I was emperor:

> Three young farmers of Illyrian origin, Zimarchos, Dityvistos, and Justin . . . determined to join the army. They covered the whole distance to Constantinople on foot, carrying on their shoulders knapsacks in which on their arrival there was nothing but what remained of the rusks that they had packed at home.[34]

One of those three, Justin, was destined to become emperor himself and father of the famous Justinian.

Cheese begins in Byzantine texts to resemble more closely the types we know from the modern Aegean. The whey cheese *myzethra* is mentioned. The *prosphatos* singled out in the poem by Psellos quoted above seems not unlike feta. For the first time in Greek literature since the Homeric description of the Cyclops' cave, a Byzantine text offers a few practical notes:

> *Making cheese.* Most people curdle cheese using what some call *opos* and others rennet; the best is from kids. Roast salt also curdles milk, and the sap of the fig tree and its green shoots and leaves,

and the hairy inedible parts of globe artichokes, and pepper, and the rough lining of the stomach of the domestic hen which is found in its droppings and looks like skin . . . Green cheese keeps longer if safflower seed made up in a little warm water, or also with warm honey, is added to it.

Cheese keeps if washed in drinking water, dried in the sun and put up in earthenware jars with savory or thyme, the cheeses kept apart from one another so far as possible, then sweet vinegar or

---

The Hall of the Nineteen Couches

Christian and Muslim visitors to 10th-century Constantinople admired the Great Palace dining room, 'wonderfully lofty and beautiful, called Decaenneaccoubita, the House of the Nineteen Couches,'[37] 'a room two hundred paces long and fifty wide, in which are a wooden table, an ivory table, and a gold table. After the Christmas festivities, when the Emperor leaves the church, he enters this room and sits at the gold table . . . They bring him four gold dishes, each of which arrives on its own little chariot. One of these dishes, encrusted with pearls and rubies, they say belonged to Solomon son of David (peace be upon him); the second, similarly encrusted, to David (peace be upon him); the third to Alexander; and the fourth to Constantine.'[38] 'After the meal fruit is brought on in three golden bowls, which are too heavy for men to lift . . . Through openings in the ceiling hang three ropes covered with gilded leather and furnished with golden rings. These rings are attached to the handles projecting from the bowls, and with four or five men helping from below, they are swung on to the table by means of a movable device in the ceiling.'[39] These travellers were luckier than they knew. Just twenty years later the hall was demolished, when Nikephoros Phokas, with that passion for reducing the cost of government that many unlucky rulers have shared, cut the Great Palace in half. He did not, however, destroy the nineteen semicircular marble tables. Parsimonious but pious, he gave them to his

honey vinegar poured over until the liquid fills the gaps and covers them . . . Cheese keeps white if stored in brine. Firmer and sharper-tasting if smoked.[35]

The distinctive flavour of Byzantine cookery emanates from sweets and sweet drinks above all. There are dishes that we would recognize as puddings, such as *grouta*, a sort of frumenty, sweetened with honey and studded with carob seeds or raisins. Simeon recommends rice pudding, 'rice cooked with milk and served with honey'.[36] William of Rubruck, a

new religious foundation, the Great Lavra, which is now the most venerable of the monasteries of Mount Athos. In the vast refectory at the Great Lavra there are still, today, nineteen marble dining tables. Needless to say, the monks do not recline to eat: they sit at benches, but the tables they use are the same at which emperors and their guests, a thousand years ago, used to dine to celebrate the great festivals of the Byzantine year.[40]

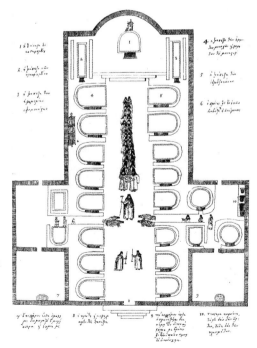

This drawing of the nineteen tables, with the monks of the Great Lavra about to take their places, is by the Russian traveller Vasilii Barskii, who made sketches of the monasteries of Mount Athos during his visits there in 1725.

thirteenth-century diplomatic traveller, looking for worthwhile gifts to take on from Constantinople to Khazaria in the southern Russian steppes, made up his mind 'on the advice of merchants' to select 'fruit, muscat wine and fine biscuits to . . . make my passage easier, since they regard no one with favour who arrives empty-handed'.[41] The fruit would have been dried, candied or preserved in grape syrup or sugar syrup. William obtained his biscuits, we may guess, just where travellers of the seventeenth century would have done: at that period, according to the Turkish traveller Evliya Çelebi, along the sea-front on the European shore of the Bosporos at Yeniköy were 'some hundred biscuit-factories; the ships sailing for the Black Sea all take in biscuit either at this place or at Galata' [Pera].[42] Byzantine quince marmalade must have been very much as we know it today, since sugar by this time had supplanted honey as the preserving medium. There were other jams or conserves too, including pear and citron.

The drinking of wine under the Byzantine Empire was as enthusiastic as before, and the wine was tastier. No longer, as in classical Greece, was wine almost compulsorily mixed at least half-and-half with water. The change was favoured by religion – wine of the Eucharist, like wine once offered in libations to the Greek gods, was unmixed – and was encouraged by the medical writers, who found desirable dietary effects in wine and noted (rightly, of course) that these effects would be stronger if the wine were mixed with less water. They allowed their readers to take a dose of neat wine on a winter morning, and recommended stronger than half-and-half mixtures.

There was a problem, though, with Greek wine. The Italian bishop and diplomat Liutprand, who visited the Constantinopolitan court twice in the mid-tenth century, put it in a nutshell: 'Greek wine, owing to its mixing with pitch, resin and gypsum, is undrinkable by us.'[43] Dioskourides, nine hundred years before, had already mentioned the use of resin in wine. Liutprand may have been right about the pitch – used, like resin, in the preparation of earthenware vats and amphoras – and about the gypsum, used in fining: they linger. In his Italy wooden barrels had long ago taken the place of earthenware, like a Californian, and he hankered for the taste of oak. But even a Byzantine author, Michael Choniates, archbishop of Athens in the twelfth century, disliked Athenian retsina, and his older contemporary Nikephoros Basilakes disapproved of the resinous wine of Philippopolis (Plovdiv) in Thrace. It took until the early nineteenth century for a traveller from Western Europe to like retsina – if W. M. Leake, with his judicious comparison to hopped beer, truly liked it:

The plain [of Levidi in Arkadia] is chiefly occupied by vineyards, from which a wine is made resembling small beer in colour, strength, and even taste, as far as the aromatic bitter of the hop flower can be imitated by the resin of the pine tree.[44]

Around the year 1340 the Florentine merchant Francesco Pegolotti enumerates the wines that people in late Byzantine Constantinople wanted to buy and the Greek wines that would sell elsewhere. The first list shows that Italian vintages were competing with Greek (but there were, of course, Italians living in Constantinople, and they may have preferred the wines they knew): *vino Greco* from Naples, wines from the March [Abruzzi], Apulia, Sicily and the wines of Turpia and Crotone in Calabria, wine of Crete, *vino di Romania* (see below) and *vino del paese*, that is, the local wine of Thrace or Bithynia.[45] This list can be extended from Greek authors: Ioannes Choumnos, an almost exact contemporary of Pegolotti, writes that 'others sacrifice to Dionysos . . . by pouring out the wine of Triglia and the Doric wine of Monemvasia in the Peloponnese.'[46] These two names both occur in Pegolotti's second list, of Greek wines worth exporting: Triglia (on the southern shore of the Propontis, within easy reach of Constantinople), *vino di Rimbola* (the *robola* variety, from the Ionian islands and northwestern Greece, close to southern Italy), and then four names representing the classic wines that were the staples of medieval trade to Western Europe. *Vino di Malvagia* and *di Candia* were worth exporting to Tana in the Crimea, the same route that William of Rubruck followed; *vino di Creti* and *vino di Romania* found a market in Venice. *Vino di Creti* and *di Candia* are the two sweet Cretan wines from muscat and malmsey grapes, *Malvagia* is malmsey exported from Monemvasia and *vino di Romania* is the wine of the western Peloponnese exported from Modon (Methoni).

These were sweet, fortified wines, but fortified in a special sense. Distilling was not yet applied to alcoholic drinks, which were, instead, encouraged towards sweetness, maximum strength and stability by late harvesting and the careful addition of honey or grape syrup. Such export wines already went from Greece to classical Rome, but their heyday was in the medieval trade to Western Europe.

The muscat grape, yielding the *vinum muscatos* that William of Rubruck took to Khazaria, is now widely grown in southern Europe. Its name derives from early medieval Greek, in which *moskhatos* meant 'musk-flavoured' (reminiscent, that is, of the aromatic musk that came in the spice trade from

Black-eyed Peas

The young whole pods of black-eyed peas, *ambelofasoula* (literally 'vineyard beans'), are a summer delicacy, readily available at markets and, if not listed on a taverna menu, worth asking for: they are topped and tailed, boiled until quite soft and served warm or at room temperature with oil and vinegar or with the dip *skordalia*. *Ambelofasoula* are the only legume eaten in this fashion; string beans or immature broad beans are usually stewed in oil or in a tomato sauce (*kokkinisto*) rather than simply boiled. But young black-eyed pea pods are also eaten in mixed salad dishes with green leaves and raw vegetables, and as part of a boiled vegetable salad with beetroot, *horta*, courgettes and potatoes.

They are served as a popular *meze* for the Clean Monday Lenten feast. For a modern Lenten banquet, serve them alongside *taramasalata*, fresh clams or sea urchins sucked (or, more delicately, scooped with a piece of bread) raw from the shell, and *lagana*, the unleavened loaves made especially for Clean Monday. For a more Byzantine feast, serve black-eyed peas in the early spring to accompany a dish of grey mullet or bass and perhaps some of the new season's asparagus (better still with wild asparagus). Moderate sex afterwards, as the Byzantine diet handbooks advise.

Mature black-eyed peas were recommended by Byzantine dieticians. As noted by Ilias Anagnostakis, they were combined

Tibet). The vineyards of Samos and Lemnos today produce muscat wine very much of the style that William might have selected.

The other grape, whose wines were better known than muscat in medieval Western Europe, was *monembasios*. This is the name not only of a grape variety but, and initially, of the style of full, amber-coloured, sweet wine that was identified in the twelfth and thirteenth centuries with the Peloponnesian coastal fortress of Monemvasia. It was known in French as *malvoisie* and in English as malmsey, names that have continued to resonate long after the export trade of Monemvasia died away. In the fourteenth and fifteenth centuries it was commonly said in France and England that the best malmsey came from Crete; and it was in the

with chickpeas, lentils and pomegranate in a bean salad, a New Year dish, called *pallikaria*, 'brave boys'.[47] Claudia Roden, in *The Book of Jewish Food*, writes of a very similar preparation for a cumin-spiced Egyptian black-eyed pea salad, *loubia*. In Armenia boiled beans are served warm or cold as a salad and dressed in this fashion, often with the addition of tomatoes, hard-boiled eggs and aromatics.

Ambelofasoula, whole young black-eyed pea pods, served as a side dish. Beside them, when first served, is *skordalia*, the fiery garlic dip: as shown, the two go well together.

late fifteenth century (on 18 February 1478, to be precise) that malmsey reached the peak of its fame in England, when the rigorous sentence for high treason passed on George, Duke of Clarence, was commuted to a quick and sticky drowning in a butt of malmsey. Later still, as fashions and trade routes changed, the malmsey grape and the malmsey style were found to be ideally suited to the volcanic slopes of Madeira. They are now hardly known in Greece.

In Constantinople itself flavoured wines were at least as popular as malmsey and muscat. They already had a long history, but it is in the last years of the Roman Empire, and after, that they gained in importance. Three were listed in Diocletian's *Price Edict*. The price of the complex, multi-spiced *conditum* was fixed at three times the price of ordinary table wine, 24 *denarii* per pint, and absinthe wine and rose wine were valued almost as highly. There were far more varieties than these three. Those flavoured with mastic and aniseed may be set beside the rose and absinthe wines of the *Price Edict* as already in fairly wide use. They are ancestors of modern vermouth; they are more distant ancestors (no distilling is yet involved) of the masticha, absinthe, ouzo and pastis of the modern Mediterranean.

A typical, though over-generous, menu for a Byzantine meal can be extracted from one of the *Prodromic Poems*. The translation is interlarded here with addenda suggested by Anagnostakis on the basis of meagre clues in many other sources.[48] Bread, wine, various sauces, olives and pickles might always be on the table, and first to be served might be salads or boiled greens and pulses, perhaps with oil and vinegar or *garos*, and soups. Then 'first comes the baked dish, the little plaice in their stew. Second the saucy one, a hake weighed down with gravy. Third, the saffron dish' already quoted above, 'and in the midst a big golden gurnard and a grey mullet and dentex from Rygin harbour . . . Fourth the grill and fifth the fry-up: chopped morsels from the middle; red mullets with their moustaches; a double-sized deep pan of big sand-smelts; a flounder, nicely grilled on its own, with *garos*, sprinkled from top to tail with caraway; and a steak from a big sea bass.'[49] There seems no room for meat, but, as in a classical Greek menu, it would arrive sparingly alongside the later fish dishes. Desserts would consist of fruit and cheese. Dried fruit, nuts and sweets would be snacks to take alongside wine, not part of the meal.

Constantinople ruled a Christian Empire, and the feasts and fasts of the Church were built into the calendar. To put it the other way round, the religious calendar structured the Greek diet, as it still does (see pages 254–6). In explaining why shellfish were so often seen in the markets of Constantinople, the fifteenth-century traveller Pero Tafur appeals correctly to these religious observances: 'At certain times of fasting during the year they do not merely confine themselves to fish, but to fish without blood, that is, shellfish.'[50] For those in monasteries, food and drink was regulated as never before. Weekly fast days were observed even more strictly than in the world outside, and fasting was the rule during certain longer period: Lent, the fast of the Apostles, the fast of St Philip. Monks ate only once on each fast day, and without oil or seasoning: the rule was *xerophagia*, 'dry eating', and *hydroposia*, 'water drinking', though the water might be flavoured with pepper, cumin and anise.

Black-eyed Pea Salad

Diane Kochilas, in *The Glorious Foods of Greece*, gives a recipe from the island of Nisyros for plainly boiled black-eyed peas topped with caramelized onions, a trademark of Dodecanese legume dishes, commonly used now for topping pea or bean purées (including the so-called fava of Santorini).

200g dried black-eyed peas
black pepper
1 medium sweet red onion
flat-leaf parsley
good fruity green olive oil such as Cretan oil
from Kolymbari
white wine vinegar
caraway seeds (optional)

Put the peas in a deep pot with plenty of water and pepper and boil vigorously for about 40 minutes until tender. Drain and leave to cool completely.

Pile on to a serving plate. Chop the onion into small dice, roughly chop the parsley and mix them into the peas on serving: the ratio should be twice as many peas as onion, and enough parsley that it virtually covers the surface before you stir it in. The mealy, nutty taste of the beans rounds out the spiky greenness of the herb like a tabbouleh. Dress with a sprinkling of vinegar and plenty of olive oil (and caraway seeds if feeling Byzantine). This salad is as served in the seafood restaurant To Thalami, 'The Octopus's Lair', on Paros.

Even outside the fasts, the average monk's diet was fairly exiguous. The *Life of St Sabas* (set in Palestine in the early sixth century) nicely demonstrates the asceticism that characterized early monastery catering:

It happened that this Jacob was put in charge of the refectory at the Great Lavra and had to cook food for the hermits when they gathered there for a meeting. He boiled up a large quantity of dried peas. They served for one day, they served for the next, and after that he threw the remainder out of the back door into the ditch. Old Sabas saw this as he looked out of his own hermit tower, and he went down quietly and gathered up the peas, very carefully and cleanly, and dried them out again. In due course he invited Jacob, on his own, to share a meal with him. For the occasion Sabas boiled these same peas, cooking them and seasoning them with all his skill.

'Forgive me, Brother. I'm afraid I have no skill at cooking,' he said to Jacob. 'You aren't enjoying your meal.'

'On the contrary, Father,' said Jacob, 'it's very good. It's a long time since I enjoyed a meal so much.'

'Believe me, Brother,' said Sabas, 'these are the very peas that you threw out of the kitchen into the ditch. One who cannot manage a jar of pulses, the food of his own people, without waste, will certainly not manage a synod.'[51]

In later Byzantine monasticism the most prominent constituents of a monastic meal would be cereals, pulses and meatless soups, with the occasional addition of shellfish and salt fish. Ex-emperors, if they retired to a monastery, were subject to the same discipline as the rest. Romanos Lakapenos, on being deposed by his sons in the year 944, was forced to take the tonsure. A few weeks later exactly the same fate befell those unfilial sons, Stephen and Constantine: on the orders of their sister (to the benefit of her husband, Constantine VII) they were exiled to the same monastery. They were greeted by their amused father, so the story went, and congratulated on the gourmet food they were soon to enjoy. 'Here is boiled water for you, colder than Gothic snows; here are sweet broad beans, greens and leeks. It is not luxury seafood that will make you ill, but our regime of frequent fasts!'[52] In 1081 the emperor Nikephoros Botaneiates was also forced to become a monk, and it was afterwards said in the royal family that, when asked by one of his fellow monks if he found the change easy to bear, he replied: 'I hate not eating meat. Nothing else troubles me much.'[53] The story is told by his successor's daughter, the historian Anna Komnene.

How was it, then, that bishops had their choice of rich food? So it appears according to the pained meditations of John the Almsgiver, bishop of Alexandria: 'How many would pine to be filled with the outer leaves of the vegetables which are discarded from my kitchen?' he reflected anxiously. 'How many would like to dip their bread into the cooking liquor which my cooks throw away? How many would long even to have a sniff at the wine which is poured out in my wine-cellar?'[54] The answer comes in the satirical *Prodromic Poems*, in which the abbots' abstinence every Wednesday and Friday from meat and fish allows the impressive ingenuity of Byzantine cooks to be expended on making shellfish and vegetable foods as attractive as the flesh on which they could gorge themselves on the other five days of the week. In the fourth poem of the series, the contrast is pointedly drawn ('they' are the abbots, 'we' the ordinary monks):

> They munch angler-fish, we have our Lent Soup. They drink their Chian wine till they can take no more, we have Varna wine mixed with water. They have their sweet wine after the table wine, we have some nice water after our one-course meal. They have white bread, we have bran bread. They have a mousse after their sesame sweet; we have wheat gruel with the wheat filtered out. They have second helpings of fritters with honey . . . we have our smoky-smelling Lent Soup.[55]

Under these influences, medical and religious, spices and seasonings became ubiquitous. From the twelfth century onwards, as a new popular and colloquial literature emerges (the *Prodromic Poems* are a part of it), there is evidence of complex recipes, with a new adjective, *oxinoglykos*, 'sweet and sour'; there are compound names for cooked dishes with a main ingredient, tuna, *thynnomageireia*, salt meat or fish, *pastomageireia*, pork, *choirinomageireia*, and the famous one-pot stew *monokythron*.[56]

The fearsome-looking anglerfish, called *batrachos*, or 'frog', in Greek and *Teufelsfisch*, 'devil-fish', in German, for sale in Catalonia, Spain.

FOUR

An Empire Reborn

We have seen classical Greek food through Greek eyes. It was the only way. With the Byzantine Empire it is different: we can compare native and foreign views of this long-lost cuisine. Byzantine cookery pleased natives, even those who did not taste the best very often, as it seems from the lingering, mouthwatering descriptions in amusing texts such as the *Prodromic Poems*. On the other hand, there was much to startle visitors to Constantinople, and foreign ambassadors were on the whole uncomplimentary. It seemed odd to provide knives and forks on the table in numbers almost sufficient for each diner to have a pair in his hands. It seemed luxurious indeed to have heated dishes for sauces and to offer individual table napkins. *Garos*, the venerable fish sauce, was an acquired taste. Most foreigners disliked retsina and some refused to drink it.

Strong views on Byzantine culture were expressed by Bishop Liutprand of Cremona, ambassador to Constantinople in 949–50 and again in 968: his lively and querulous *Embassy to Constantinople* and *Antapodosis* are rich sources for the foods that he swallowed or spat out in the course of his mission. At the first formal dinner he attended in 968, when Nikephoros Phokas was emperor, 'as he did not think me worthy to be placed above any of his nobles I sat fifteenth from him and without a tablecloth … The dinner was quite nasty and unspeakable, drunkenly awash with oil and seasoned with another very unpleasant liquid made from fish.'[1] Graeco-Roman tradition, physically manifest in the aroma of *garos* (which is surely Liutprand's 'unpleasant liquid made from fish'), clung tenaciously. A generous use of olive oil is one of the often-criticized features of modern Greek cookery among those who wouldn't like it anyway. Liutprand remarks ironically on food afterwards sent to him at his lodgings: 'The holy emperor alleviated my sorrow with a big gift, sending me one of his most delicate dishes, a fat kid of which he had himself partaken – proudly stuffed with garlic, onion, leeks, dressed with *garum*.'[2]

Liutprand's dry wit gives us only a hint of the range of foods that he would have sampled. His experience of being placed in one of the imperial residences, to which the imperial kitchens delivered ready-cooked dishes, was not unusual. Three centuries later a party of Muslim ambassadors, who had travelled with the Byzantine princess Maria (illegitimate daughter of the emperor Andronikos II) on her return to Constantinople, were assigned 'a house near the residence of the princess . . . We remained indoors for three nights, during which hospitality-gifts were sent to us of flour, bread, sheep, fowls, ghee, fruit, fish, money and rugs.'[3] A third similar story is told from the Byzantine perspective by Anna Komnene. Bohemond of Taranto, later prince of Antioch, visited Constantinople on his journey east during the First Crusade. His host is Alexios Komnenos, Anna's father. The residence in which Bohemond was placed was at the Kosmidion, just outside the land walls:

> There a rich table was laid full of food, including fish dishes of all kinds. Then the cooks brought in meat of animals and birds, uncooked. 'This fish, as you see, has been prepared in our custom-ary way,' they said, 'but in case that does not suit you we have here raw meat which can be cooked in whatever way you like.'

Suspecting poison, Bohemond shared the fish out generously among his followers and told his cooks to cook the raw meat for himself. No one was ill.[4]

Travel to and from Constantinople was less comfortable. Inns were few and far between. Life without festivity is a long road without an inn, said the ancient philosopher Demokritos: he knew some roads of that kind. In the whole Byzantine Empire, only one country inn can claim a gastronomic reputation. According to the *Life of St Theodore of Sykeon*, Theodore himself was born at the inn in Sykeon, in Bithynia, in the sixth century. His mother, his grandmother and his aunt, all three of whom had begun their careers as prostitutes, came to rely instead on the quality of their food to attract customers. Their cook, 'a God-fearing man called Stephanos', is the first restaurant chef anywhere in the world whose name is known.[5]

Those who were lucky enough to be invited to stay with friends while travelling found that this was much the most comfortable way to get a dinner. 'There was always someone to meet us,' said Timarion, speaking of the nightly stages of his imaginary journey to Hell via Thessaloniki.[6]

Luckily, perhaps, the pattern of Byzantine eating meant that one looked for little food during the day, awaiting, instead, that single big meal in the evening. Travellers would carry a midday snack with them or buy what little was necessary. A party of Anglo-Saxon backpackers – the future saint Willibald and his brother, sister and father – visiting the holy sites of Asia Minor around the year 725 and reaching the small seaside town of Phygela under the midday sun, 'got some bread and went to a spring in the middle of the town and sat on the bank and dipped their bread in the water and ate it'.[7] Even an imperial party, when out for a day's hunting, would picnic no more elaborately than on black bread with cheese and cress. Hoping possibly for some meat or fish, Bishop Michael Choniates, on disembarking at the island of Keos, asked those at the harbourside: '"Do you have any *prosphagion* [relish], children?" They at once offered me cheese, because these islanders use the general word *prosphagion* in the special sense of "cheese".'[8]

For those arriving in Constantinople without imperial or other patronage, monasteries were the best choice. Of a monastery at Pera, a Russian pilgrim reported that, in accordance with the founder's will, 'they offer to all bread, soup and a cup of wine. Every Christian on his way to and from Jerusalem is fed there for several days; the Greeks, also, are fed there, and thanks to the prayers of the Mother of God this monastery never becomes impoverished.'[9] Having found a place to stay, the traveller would necessarily explore other food resources of the imperial capital.

Byzantion itself, refounded by Constantine the Great as Constantinople and often described as the 'New Rome', had continued to flourish as the eastern, and soon the only, capital of what was still called the Roman Empire. After a hundred years of this new status, its people were as insouciant as ever, according to a contemporary poet:

> Youngsters avid for sex and old reprobates whose great glory is gluttony and whose pride is to have achieved variety in their corrupt banquets: their hunger is only aroused by costly meats, and they tickle their palates with foods imported from overseas, the flesh of the starry fowl of Juno, or (if they can get it) the green bird that can speak, supplied by the dark Indians. Not the Aegean, not the deep Propontis, not the marsh of Azov can sate their appetite for foreign fish![10]

Foreign visitors were as impressed as any native by the wealth and resources of Constantinople. The Jewish adventurer Benjamin of Tudela remarked in the twelfth century that 'the land is very rich in all fabrics and in bread, meat, and wine: wealth like that of Constantinople is not to be found in the whole world. Here also are men learned in all the books of the Greeks, and they eat and drink every man under his vine and his fig-tree.'[11] And here is the Muslim traveller Ibn Battuta, who visited in the 1320s or 1330s:

> Its markets and streets are spacious and paved with flagstones, and the members of each craft have a separate place, no others sharing it with them. Each market has gates which are closed upon it at night. The majority of the artisans and salespeople in them are women.[12]

The *Book of the Eparch* tells us what was sold and how it was sold in the shops and market stalls of Constantinople at the end of the ninth century. Among spices the perfumers were to sell pepper, spikenard, cinnamon, aloeswood, ambergris, musk, frankincense, myrrh, balsam of Mecca and styrax; much of their stock arrived either via Trebizond, at the western end of the overland Silk Road, or through Chaldaea (Iraq), to which the Indian Ocean spice route led by way of the Persian Gulf. Their shops were to be

Date palms flourish in southern Greece but do not produce ripe fruit. Good to eat, a culinary ingredient and a source of sugar, dates have been imported to Greece for at least 3,000 years. This date palm grows in what used to be the garden of a Jesuit seminary in a hidden valley on Naxos.

Tavern in the Byzantine city of Sergilla.

placed near the Chalke, the entrance to the Great Palace, where they would 'improve its atmosphere with their aroma'. Grocers could set up shop anywhere in the city, and were to sell beef, salt fish, pulses, cheese, honey and butter. Butchers, who were to deal in mutton and not pork, were to go to the River Sangarios, in Bithynia, to await the drovers; they must sell their animals at the covered market called *Strategion*, 'the Commandery', except that spring lambs were sold between Easter and Pentecost at the *Tauros*, 'the Bull'. Pork butchers were to buy at the *Tauros*. Fishmongers were not to go out to the fisheries; they must buy at the harbours, they must sell at the designated markets in Constantinople, they must not salt any fish, and they were discouraged from selling their fish on for resale. Their profit margin was closely watched.

A long list of the foods and spices that came to Constantinople by sea can be extracted from the trading handbook of Francesco Pegolotti. He lists comfits, salt, raisins (including those from Syria), dates, hazelnuts (including those from Naples), walnuts, almonds, chestnuts, pistachios, rice, cumin, safflower, sugar candy, granulated sugar, ginger, zedoary, cloves, nutmeg, mace, camphor, cardamom, long pepper, rhubarb, mastic, saffron, scammony, manna, dragon's blood, squinanth and smoked sturgeon; among olive oils he distinguishes the clear and yellow oils of Venice and of the March, oil of Apulia, of Caieta and of all other parts, in Naples jars, Apulian jars and Seville jars.[13]

Among those wide streets and enclosed markets of Constantinople were taverns supplying food and drink and somewhere to sit and enjoy them. There is an epigram of the sixth century in which a tavern speaks for itself:

> On the one side I have close by me the Zeuxippos, a pleasant public bath, and on the other the Hippodrome. After seeing the races at the latter and taking a bath in the former, come and rest at my hospitable table. Then in the afternoon you will be in plenty of time for the other races, reaching the course from your room quite near at hand.[14]

It is not by chance that this tavern advertises itself at midday, at siesta time. In the late evening, if the rule as stated in the *Book of the Eparch* applied at this earlier period, it would have been closed:

> Innkeepers must not open their taverns or sell wine or cooked dishes before 8 a.m. on the mornings of great feasts or Sundays. They must close by 8 p.m. and put out their lights, because, if the customers of these inns had the right of access to them at night as well as through the day, the result might be that under the influence of drink they would be able to indulge in violence and rioting with impunity.[15]

According to the same rulebook, the price of wine at taverns was fixed centrally by reference to the current market price. It was served in standard measures, of which each tavern-keeper must have a set, officially stamped. But the *phouskaria*, where beer was sold, were separate businesses, as they still would be in Ottoman times, and the *Book of the Eparch* has no rules for them.

Finally, there were stalls where street food was sold ready-cooked. We know this, and we even know exactly where they were, thanks to the Spanish adventurer Pero Tafur:

> Outside St Sophia are great squares with porticoes where they are accustomed to sell wine and bread and fish, and more shellfish than anything else, since the Greeks are in the habit of eating these ... Here they have great tables of stone where they eat, both rulers and common people, together.[16]

So, thanks to Tafur, we know where to place this anecdote from the historian Niketas Choniates. He wrote at the exiled court at Nikaia, after

Constantinople itself was lost to the Crusaders in 1204, and recalled the city he had known so well, the imperial family he loved to hate, and its ministers who had been his colleagues:

> John Hagiotheodorites had spent the day at the palace at Blachernai. Returning from there late in the evening he passed the saleswomen who had street food – 'snacks', in everyday speech – out on display. He suddenly felt like a drink of hot soup with chopped cabbage on the side. One of his servants, called Anzas, said that they had better wait and control their hunger: there would be plenty of the right kind of food when they got home. Giving him a fierce glance John said sharply that he would do exactly as he pleased. He went straight up to the bowl that the market woman was holding, full of the soup that he fancied, leaned over, drank it down greedily and had several good mouthfuls of the cabbage. Then he took out a copper penny and handed it to one of his people. 'Change this for me,' he said. 'Give the lady her two farthings, and be quick about giving me back the other two!'[17]

An End and a Beginning

To say that the Byzantine Empire was a static civilization, obsessed with its own distant past, is to tell much less than half of the story. To say that the Byzantine Empire shrank is to say that on what used to be Byzantine soil other peoples and their cultures mingled with Greek, while Turkish power grew and became established.

In the early Islamic conquests of the seventh century the Arabs ('Saracens' in Greek sources) took Egypt, north Africa and Syria from the Empire. They took Crete and lost it again; they besieged Constantinople but failed to take it. This warfare was soon followed by a remarkable flowering of scholarship in newly Islamic lands. Greek practical handbooks, including the farming manual *Geoponika* and the dietary textbooks of Galen and his successors, were translated into Syriac and then Arabic. This work catalysed original research and new writing in Arabic. The once-Greek medical schools of the east now taught in Arabic, and some of the physicians who emerged from them, like Simeon Seth, were ready to transfer their new knowledge back into Greek. Contact between the religions sometimes led to friendly compromise: Harun ibn Yahya, one of the Muslim hostages invited to Christmas dinner at the Imperial palace in the late ninth century, understood the herald to have announced: 'I swear on the Emperor's head that there is no pork at all in these dishes!'[18]

After the Arab conquests Constantinople still had its supplies of eastern spices, though now they crossed Islamic territory on their way west: 'The best cinnamon comes from Mosul,' writes Simeon Seth in the eleventh century, telling us that this aromatic now arrived from India by way of the Persian Gulf, Iraq and Syria.[19] Thanks to new patterns of trade, unfamiliar aromatics such as ambergris and red sanders reached Constantinople for the first time. New crops appeared, transmitted from the east to farmers in Islamic lands and from them westwards to the Byzantine Empire; they included aubergines, lemons and oranges. Fine varieties of other species owe their existence to plant-breeding in Islamic territory, such as 'the so-called Saracen melon'.[20] Among new culinary herbs came tarragon, very important in Arabic cookery. Still other products, notably sugar, were becoming gradually commoner and cheaper in the Mediterranean world, although rarely grown in Byzantine territory.

As for the Crusaders and other Western intruders, it may seem that they and the Greeks had nothing to learn from one another. So thought the Byzantine emperor Nikephoros Phokas, if Liutprand, the German emperor's ambassador, quotes him fairly. 'Your master's troops', Nikephoros is said to have asserted, 'are rendered useless by their gluttony, their greedy guts: their stomach is their god, their boldness is a hangover, their bravery is drunkenness, their abstinence is nausea, their fear is sobriety!'[21] When the Crusaders eventually passed through imperial lands, they naturally tasted Byzantine food, like those accompanying Bohemond on the first Crusade in 1097, who 'came to Constantinople, set up their tents, and restored themselves for fifteen days, buying food and whatever they needed from what the citizens copiously supplied'.

What they did with these supplies did not impress their hosts, though. The Norman invaders who captured Thessaloniki in 1185 'took no account of our well aged wine because of its lack of sweetness, treating it as if it were an evil-tasting medicine', archbishop Eustathios lamented; 'the fair liquid was poured out as if in rivers.' Spices and aromatics, too, were criminally wasted. New wine, on the other hand, was consumed in vast quantity, as were pork, beef and garlic.[22] The crusader captors of Constantinople in 1204, according to Niketas Choniates, 'revelled and drank strong wine all day long. Some favoured luxury foods; others recreated their own native dishes, such as an ox rib apiece, or slices of ham cooked with beans, and sauces made with garlic or with a combination of other bitter flavours.'[23]

Wall painting from the Mycenaean palace of Tiryns, shortly before its destruction around 1200 BC. Reconstructed from fragments, this is one of the oldest Greek depictions of a boar hunt, notable for what it tells us of 2nd-millennium BC dog-breeding as well as hunting.

To this meticulous Byzantine author, filled with bitter hatred for the destroyers of the world he had known, we owe the very first record of that favourite dish of the savage warriors of southern France, cassoulet; but it never entered the Greek culinary repertoire. Yet rosemary (*dendrolibanon*) certainly did. Though well known under the Roman Empire, it was never used as a food flavouring. Was it the Crusaders who taught Constantinople the use of it? It is recommended for roast lamb, quite in the western fashion, by the Cretan monk Agapios Landos, who published his Greek handbook of farming, *Geoponikon*, at Venice in 1634.

Eventually the westerners came to stay. Italian traders from Venice, Genoa, Pisa and Amalfi had their independent enclaves around Constantinople. From 1204 onwards, French and Italian noblemen and adventurers established little principalities in the once-Byzantine mainland and islands. Although they were Christians, like their Greek neighbours, the westerners had their own interpretation of the rules that Christianity imposed on food.

It was in the rural principalities that Cyriac of Ancona, pioneer of the study of Greek antiquities, found light relief, as in a hunting expedition mounted by the court of Carlo II Tocco, despot of Epiros, in the summer of 1448 near Ambrakia, at which 'several boars' were taken and the first catch, 'a quivering young sow', adjudged to Carlo's son Leonardo. Meanwhile the squires and servants fished in the Gulf of Ambrakia. Ingeniously, it being a Friday, the fish was eaten first as a proper fast-day entrée, which, as the sun set, gave way to a huntsmen's feast of wild boar.[24]

Cyriac had previously visited Constantinople itself and the Italian enclaves on 15 August 1446, the feast of the Assumption. He saw the ceremonies at Agia Sophia, presided over by the patriarch Gregory, then took the ferry to Genoese Pera, where the ceremonies at the church of St Francis were followed by a 'respectable *symposion*' or 'decent drinking party' at which women (there was one young woman in whom he was particularly interested) took equal part and spoke on equal terms with men – which on the other side of the Golden Horn they would surely not have done.[25]

It might well have been the Italian traders who first brought caviar to Constantinople.[26] This delicacy was normally called *kabiari*, but at least one author rejected the new, foreign-sounding word and devised a classical name for it. Indeed, there was never an author more classical than Michael Apostolios, prickly fifteenth-century Cretan humanist, who wrote to thank a friend from Ierapetra for the most traditional gift of a 'large and plump hare, equal to the best you ever sent me', and sent in return, 'as a token, though unworthy, of my friendship, a box of black egg-pickle' (*melan oon tetaricheumenon*).[27] Caviar is more fully described by an early seventeenth-century writer on the history of seafood, Ludovicus Nonnius, who links it with the Italians in the Black Sea and also makes a comparison with the native Greek delicacy botargo. Nonnius begins by explaining that the strong-tasting fish sauces of the ancient world have disappeared from use. In their place 'we have botargo and what the Italians call *caviaro*, which is prepared beside the Black Sea from sturgeons' eggs. They are compressed into masses, packed in pots and exported mostly to Italy where they are prized and fetch a high price: they are very good at restoring a feeble appetite and reviving the sluggishness of a nauseous stomach.'[28]

Caviar, then, was probably introduced from the Black Sea ports by the Italians. Because it comes from sturgeons, caviar is ruled out, for observant Jews, by the general prohibition of fish without scales. For this reason, strangely, a flavour that is much more ubiquitous in modern Greece than caviar may have been invented at the impulse of the Jewish community of Byzantine and Ottoman Greece. The French sixteenth-century natural historian Pierre Belon explains how it happened. Tana is the medieval trading port in the Crimea:

> There is a product made of sturgeons' eggs, universally called *caviar*, which is so common at Greek and Turkish meals throughout the Levant that there is no one who does not eat it except

Fasolada

Fasolada, bean or black-eyed pea soup, is a comforting winter dish. Between soup and stew in consistency, it is eaten all over Greece and far beyond (it is *bob chorba* in Bulgaria, *ciorba de fasole* in Romania, *tavce gravce* in Macedonia). Every family has its favourite recipe, which is, naturally, the best version possible. In Greece *fasolada* is most commonly made with dried white haricot beans, cooked with onion, celery or chervil and carrots in a tomato-enriched broth and eaten with an accompanying saucer of black olives and slices of raw red onion. Butter beans or borlotti beans can be substituted; spinach or wild greens can be included.

Chrisoula's springtime *fasolada*.

the Jews, since they know that the sturgeon has no scales. But the people of Tana, who take a large quantity of carp, will set the eggs aside and salt them so that they taste better than one could well imagine. They make red caviar with them for the Jews, and this also is sold at Constantinople.[29]

This 'red caviar' is the true Turkish and Greek *tarama*, the traditional and best ingredient for *taramasalata*, though modern *taramasalata* is

In northern Macedonia, Thrace and among the Pontic Greeks *fasolada* is made with *tsouknida* ('nettles') or *mavrolachano* (literally 'black cabbage', a kind of kale) and flavoured with red chilli flakes and dill.

What follows is an early spring *fasolada* to make when semi-wild or cultivated chard is just pushing up in the fields and demanding to be used. The quantity given will feed eight – but then it tastes better reheated the next day or the day after that.

Fasolada – *Black-eyed Pea and Chard Soup*

500 g black-eyed peas
1 large onion, sliced
2 or 3 carrots, peeled and sliced into 1-cm rounds
125 ml olive oil
salt and pepper
1 generous tsp tomato purée
chard – two handfuls, three, however much you want –
washed and roughly chopped

Many other dried beans would need to be left in water overnight to soften before cooking, but black-eyed peas need no soaking. Put all the ingredients into a *pilino gastra*, a casserole with a tight-fitting lid. Add enough water to cover to a depth of two fingers. Leave to cook in the oven at 150°C for three hours.

This *fasolada* is good on its own with bread, or with fatty pork sausages plainly grilled, and better still alongside *taramasalata*.

usually based on other fish roes, and the colour of the mass-produced product artificially adjusted to a traditional gourmet pink.

Travellers in the Ottoman Empire were also familiar with Pera, which, though still a Christian enclave, was by the seventeenth century inhabited largely by Greeks and was known as Galata. George Wheler, one of those travellers, notes that in the city of Constantinople all sorts of provisions, corn, flesh and fish are plentiful: 'Only wine is scarce, by reason that it is prohibited. But though there be none permitted to be sold in the City,

Chrisoula's Taramasalata

A lump of cod roe no more than the size of two walnuts
½ onion, finely chopped
2 tbsp finely chopped dill (optional)
olive oil and water

Place the roe, onion and dill in a blender or food processor. Add a drop of oil and blend, then a drop of water and blend again. Repeat this process, blending well after each addition; the mix will emulsify like a mayonnaise and the amount of oil and water used is flexible — a matter of taste. Most people mix the oil and onion with potato or breadcrumbs to stretch the fish roe, but for a small amount there is no need, and the result will be a lighter and tastier dip.

The monks of Athos use dill in their recipe for *taramasalata*. This gives a slightly greenish hue and a fresh flavour, and works well with *fasolada*.

Taramasalata served alongside *fasolada* (black-eyed pea soup).

at Gallata there are some Christian cabarets, but the wine is dear . . . The best wine is made by the Jews, who by their law must not make mixtures.'[30] Others do not say that wine made by Jews was the best, although Antoine Galland, Orientalist and translator of the *Thousand and One Nights*, confirms that at Ottoman Smyrna the Jews (no doubt for the same reason) 'do not drink wine made by Christians but only what they make themselves.'[31]

A Muslim traveller at the same period comments severely on the drinking that went on at Galata (on the southern side of the Golden Horn, such behaviour was no longer seen). This Muslim author, to be quoted again from time to time, is Evliya Çelebi.

> In Galata there are two hundred taverns and wine-booths where the infidels divert themselves with music and drinking. Fish, fruit and milk are excellent as is also the *mubtejil*, a kind of syrup prepared here for the Sufis . . . The Greeks keep the taverns . . . Of the exquisite eatables and beverages of Galata, the first and best is the white bread called *franzola*. The sweetmeats, liqueurs and preserves sold here in the sugar market are nowhere else to be found in such perfection unless it be at Damascus. *Halva* is sold wrapped in coloured paper. The white bread called *simit* is seasoned with spices . . .
>
> The taverns are celebrated for the wines of . . . Mudania, Smyrna and Tenedos. When I passed through this district I saw many hundred, bareheaded and barefoot, lying drunk in the street; some broadcast the state they were in by singing such couplets as these . . .
>
> > My feet go to the tavern, nowhere else;
> > My hand grasps tight the cup and nothing else;
> > Cut short your sermon, for no ears have I;
> > But for the bottle's murmur, nothing else.
>
> But I drank only *mubtejil*, the syrup made with Athenian honey.[32]

The wine of Mudania is what was called wine of Triglia in earlier sources: it came from vineyards south of the Propontis at no great distance from Constantinople. The bread called in Turkish *simit*, ring-shaped and seasoned with spices, has a quite different name in Greek. *Koulouria*, as Patrick Leigh Fermor puts it in *Roumeli*, are hard circular rolls 'with a hole in the middle, crusted with sesame seeds'; he might have added that poppy seeds are an alternative, but instead he goes on to provide the reason why under the Ottoman Empire these

Wherever Greeks are on their way to work, *koulouria*, studded with sesame or poppy seeds, will be seen on sale.

ring-shaped loaves would have been sold by Greeks in Galata. In the 1930s the people of Ioannina and Epirotes in general were nicknamed *plakokephaloi*, 'tile-heads':

> Their mothers are said to smack their babies on the crown to make it more convenient, later on, for balancing a *koulouri*-tray. Traditionally this smack is accompanied by the words 'May you become a *koulouri*-seller in the city!' The city – Constantinople – drew young Ioanniniots like a magnet for centuries.[33]

Other migrant and trading peoples were naturally noted for dealing in, and eating, strange foods. Galland was possibly mistaken on his visit to Smyrna in 1678 to identify as Arabs the street-sellers of '*kiureks* or cakes' and '*alva*, which is a kind of conserve made with almonds' (*çörek* and halva),[34] but he was right about the devoutly Christian Armenians: their fasts, he observed, were more rigorous than those of the Greeks. 'They abstain from wine, from the use of oil, and from eating shellfish and other bloodless seafood that is not forbidden to the Greeks.' It was true, he went on, that they drank wine rather freely when their religious rule permitted it, but 'one never hears it said that their drinking leads to great disorder.'[35]

The same author, a young scholar on his second journey eastwards, had some sharp comments to make about other Europeans. The Dutch at Smyrna, dissatisfied with the varied and much-praised wines of Asia Minor, were choosy enough to import white wines from Western Europe, Rhenish hock and Italian *verdea*, or so Galland reported. The English he admired even less: 'They drink as much wine as all the other nations combined. The damage to their health caused by this lack of moderation hardly worries them.' He found especially tiresome the hospitable English custom of 'forcing drink on those who visit them and taking offence at any refusal', but admitted drily that at least in the matter of drinking in company, 'we French can meet them on their own terms and beat them.'[36] Galland observed that the English – already in 1678 – were accustomed to have beer shipped in from England 'and even have

Wall painting at Vatopedi monastery, Mount Athos, 1312. A dinner of Byzantines, Mongols and others, of which the painter – an anonymous monk – evidently disapproves. The host, with the bulbous white hat, may be Theodoros Metochites, minister of Andronikos II; the topic may be the diplomatic marriages of Andronikos' daughter Maria.
In 1312, on the death of her first husband, an animist, she became one of the wives of his successor, Özbeg, a convert to Islam.

it brewed in Smyrna, although it is not as good as what they have at home'.[37] This same north European product, strangely enough, was to become popular once again in newly independent Athens.

FELLOW TRAVELLERS

Never mind the unshakeable pride in their empire that they displayed at home; Byzantine Greeks were rather impressed by the entertainment they had when they travelled abroad. It is no coincidence that the narrator of the Greek medieval satire *Timarion* applies to a fine meal the adjective *tyrannikos*, 'fit for a [foreign] king'.[38]

Princes and diplomats who travelled to Central Asia disliked the flavours but enjoyed the hospitality. The ambassadors from Justinian I and Justin II in the mid-sixth century, the first European envoys to make contact with the Turks, reported respectfully on their whole day of feasting in a tent decorated with silk hangings, but were taken aback by the 'wine', which was 'not a wine pressed from the grape as ours is, because the grape vine is not native to that country and will not grow there: some different, barbarous liquor was served instead.'[39] The beverage was surely kumiss, fermented mare's milk. We meet it again in the story of the Byzantine princess Maria, illegitimate daughter of Andronikos II, who in the early fourteenth century was married to two successive Mongol rulers of the Golden Horde: the first Toqta, a shamanist; the second Özbeg, a Muslim. Ibn Battuta visited her soon afterwards with a party of Muslim diplomats:

> Özbeg's third wife . . . is the daughter of the emperor of Constantinople the Great. She was sitting on an inlaid couch with silver legs; before her were about a hundred slavegirls, Greek, Turkish and Nubian, some standing and some sitting, and pages were behind her and chamberlains in front of her, men of the Greeks . . . She called for food, which was brought, and we ate before her, while she looked on at us . . . She showed herself to be of a generous nature, and sent more supplies after us.[40]

Thus all four wives welcomed the party in turn, but Maria, the Byzantine far from home in the Central Asian steppes, was the only one thoughtful enough not to force them to drink kumiss while she watched.

The next two Byzantines abroad whom we are able to observe are emperors, though by now they ruled a tiny empire. In December 1391 the young Manuel II Palaiologos had just succeeded to the throne, but immediately, as a vassal of the Ottoman sultan Bayezid, he was summoned to the front. The Ottoman army was at war, and his duty was to join the campaign in person and supply a hundred Greek fighters. He writes to a scholar friend from somewhere south of Sinope in Asia Minor, a region that belonged to his ancestors: 'I see the messengers coming to invite us to the emir's tent. I suppose he again wants to drink a few toasts before dinner and to force us to fill ourselves with wine from his varied collection of golden bowls and cups.'[41] Not long ago it was the Byzantine emperor whose sideboard was loaded with golden bowls and cups and whose feasts were enlivened by mimes, dancers and musicians. Now, a mere parasite at the sultan's table, Manuel reports on how it feels to lead a small Christian contingent to fight for the future Islamic world empire:

> Added to this is the scarcity of provisions. The terribly high price one must pay for them overwhelms the mind, since we have already spent so much in warfare away from home. The men with me are strangers here in customs, language, and faith, and . . . they are barely able to buy the leftovers of what is being sold in the marketplace . . . Beyond all this, should we not mention the daily hunting, the dissipation at meals and afterwards, the throngs of mimes, the flocks of flute players, the choruses of singers, the tribes of dancers, the clang of cymbals, and the senseless laughter after the strong wine?[42]

Manuel's son was the last-but-one Byzantine emperor, and the very last whose personal involvement with food is recorded. John VIII Palaiologos bravely travelled in person to the Council of Florence in a vain attempt to save Constantinople from Turkish conquest by forging a reunion of the Catholic and Orthodox churches. Unable to walk, and probably suffering more than ever from gout after a year of immoderate dining among Christian prelates, he rode into the countryside one day in early 1439, and at Peretola was invited by a householder to pause and rest in his courtyard. The emperor slept under the trees until his people had got together something for him to eat. He had a small table placed before him:

> I found him some white tablecloths, and he ate alone; the others, his companions, ate under the arbor, outside and inside, like a

Strapatsada – *Scrambled Eggs*

3 large eggs, beaten
1 medium tomato
1 tbsp olive oil
a chunk of feta cheese – about 30 g
2 thick slices of sourdough bread, toasted
salt and pepper
dried oregano and a few cherry tomatoes, to garnish

Lightly beat the eggs and season with pepper and just a little salt (the cheese will be salty). Dice the tomato and squeeze out most of the watery juice. Heat the oil in a frying pan and pour in the eggs. When they start to solidify, add the tomato and mix together to scramble the eggs. Remove from the heat when only just set and crumble in the feta.

Place the hot toasted sourdough on a plate and pour over the eggs. Sprinkle with oregano and garnish with the cherry tomatoes, left whole or in half as you like.

The emperor's dish (see text below), which he would probably have called *sphoungaton*, was something very close to the modern *strapatsada* (an Italian loanword). *Strapatsada* should be a midday meal with bread or else one among several *mezedes*, but globalism confuses this peasant dish with the scrambled eggs of world breakfast menus so that it becomes a falsely typical Greek breakfast to rival that truly typical Greek breakfast – a cup of coffee and two cigarettes.

soldiers' mess. The first food the Emperor ate was a salad of purslane and parsley, with some onions, which he himself wished to clean. After that there were chickens and pigeons, boiled, and then chickens and pigeons quartered and fried in the frying pan with lard. As the dishes came, they were all placed before him, and he took what he wanted and sent the dishes along to the others. His last dish was eggs thrown on hot bricks where the other things were cooked, and then set before him in a plate with many spices.[43]

Why purslane and parsley? It has been suggested that they were part of a regime intended to treat gout; in any case they were, no doubt, flourishing on that day close at hand in John VIII's host's garden. And the eggs? Giovanni de' Pigli had no name for this favourite Byzantine dish, but in Greek it is *sphoungaton*, mentioned in many sources; we may call it scrambled egg or omelette. This simple meal, chosen by the last-but-one emperor himself and partly prepared by his own hands, shows him at ease with his food and at ease, at last, with the non-Byzantine world around him.

FOOD OF THE OTTOMAN EMPIRE

After the incessant warfare and inexorable decline of the last Byzantine centuries, the years that followed the Ottoman capture of Constantinople in 1453 appear, through the eyes of contemporary travellers, as something

Purslane Salad

The fleshy leaves and tender stems of purslane, *glistrida* or *andrakla*, are gathered from late spring to early autumn. Prized for their clean and slightly bitter taste, they may be cooked *yiachni* (stewed in tomato sauce) and served with rice, or else eaten raw in salads. They are among the best green vegetable sources of omega-3 fatty acids.

2 handfuls fresh purslane
½ peeled cucumber, sliced into thin rounds
2 baby courgettes, cut into batons
a pinch of oregano, more salt, some pepper
dressing made with six parts olive oil to one of vinegar
and 1 tsp of mustard

Wash and only very roughly chop the purslane. Place it in a bowl and top with the cucumber. Arrange the courgette batons around the edge of the dish and scatter over the oregano, salt and pepper and the dressing. Toss and eat.

Serves 2 as part of a light meal with one or two other dishes.

of a new golden age. Pierre Belon, for example, considered the Greeks who lived in Crete under Venetian domination (a remnant of the medieval political fragmentation of the Aegean) no better off than those who were Ottoman subjects. Belon gives a general overview of the dining customs of 'Turkey', which includes lands largely populated by Greeks:

> They have no tables to eat at, so they sit directly on the ground and put before them a round piece of leather which they keep laced like a purse. There is no one in Turkey, however great a lord he may be, who would choose not to carry his own knife at his belt. Everyone brings his spoon: this is their way to avoid getting their fingers greasy, because they make no use of table napkins. It is true, though, that they generally carry large handkerchiefs which they use to wipe their fingers.[44]

Ottoman food and cuisine, while to some extent a continuation of the Byzantine, included novelties. Some cultivated vegetables and fruits that now became familiar would have been previously unknown in the region, including the currant or 'Corinthian' vine, which is not mentioned in earlier texts. The artichoke, a cultivated variety of the cardoon with a remarkably developed flower head, reached its modern form in fifteenth-century Italy,

Baklava, as it is now known in Greece under its Turkish name, is a direct descendant of the ancient Greek *gastris.*

Grape syrup, now known as *petimezi* (the Greek variant of its Turkish name, *pekmez*), was already used in classical times as a culinary ingredient. Its Greek name then was *hepsema*.

according to historians of horticulture. It soon spread to Greece and is described in the mid-seventeenth-century *Geoponikon* of Agapios Landos. New food plants had arrived from India, Indochina and the New World, including the chilli pepper, again known to Landos, whose name for it is *spetsiai*, literally 'spices'. He gives rather full advice on the food use of haricot beans, which arrived from South America soon after chilli: he recommends cooking them with vinegar, oil, mustard and pepper. Three more species – potatoes, tomatoes and (from the Middle East) spinach – were now for the first time introduced to the Greek diet.

In spite of this, travellers to the Aegean lands from Western Europe tend to notice the foodstuffs that have been there for a long time – grapes, figs, pomegranates, cheese and wine. Rather than by the range and choice of foodstuffs, they are struck by aspects of cuisine. After the observations quoted above, Belon adds a note from the kitchen: 'Their method of cooking differs much from ours. When the meat is cooked they take it out of the pot and then put in whatever it is that they will use to thicken the soup, stirring it, since they are making a large quantity, with a long wooden stick.'[45]

The interaction between Greek and Turkish food customs has been very deep, not surprisingly, for these two cultures have lived side by side for a thousand years and had been in contact for four hundred years before that. Exactly as earlier with Greek and Latin, language interchange shows the scale of mutual influence. One one side, Greek names for the raw materials of food were borrowed by speakers of Turkish: names for wild greens and some vegetables, for chestnuts, hazelnuts and other nuts and fruits, and for almost all the fish of Aegean waters. This is natural, since the Turks came as a result of a long migration whose ultimate source was

Tzatziki

3 small cucumbers (or half a regular cucumber), roughly 250 g
at least ½ tsp salt
250 g thick Greek yoghurt – Total is the best brand; 'Greek style'
yoghurt is not suitable unless it is left to strain through
muslin overnight
3 cloves garlic, crushed
a glug of white wine vinegar
at least 3–4 tbsp really good extra-virgin olive oil

Peel the cucumbers, not so precisely that there is no dark skin left, just removing most of it. Grate them coarsely. Put the grated cucumbers in a colander with a good amount of salt sprinkled over. Suspend the colander over a bowl, with a saucer pressed on top and weighted down to squeeze out the water. Leave for at least four hours – overnight in the fridge is even better – until as much liquid has drained out of the cucumbers as possible. Squash the saucer onto them to make sure.

Scrape out the poor limp cucumbers into a clean bowl and mix with the yoghurt, some more salt and the crushed garlic. Add a good squirt of vinegar and a generous slosh of olive oil and mix again.

Now taste the *tzatziki* and add more salt or vinegar as you think. Continue to stir and taste, pouring in more oil, bit by bit. The yoghurt will 'drink' or absorb more oil than you think, and it is essential that plenty is used, since it gives the dip a lovely creaminess. So often bad *tzatziki* is the result of nothing more than a lack of oil. The thicker the yoghurt, the

the mountainous country of northeastern Asia, where the sea and its fish were unknown and the wild greens would have been utterly different. On the other side, once Greek rule had given way to Turkish, cooked dishes would need to be named and described in words that the rulers could understand, which explains how Turkish tended to replace Greek in this area too, just as (in a different context) Norman French replaced Anglo-Saxon English. Hence for savoury *dolmades* (compare older *thria*)

more oil it can take, so these measurements are simply guide-
lines. Don't worry if small bubbles appear in the yoghurt when
you add the vinegar – just beat the mixture firmly. Similarly,
it is no big deal if the consistency is a little soupy, so long as
the flavour is salty, garlicky and cooling all at once.

Serve as a dip or as part of a choice of *mezedes*. Garnish,
maybe, with an olive, a couple of cucumber slices decorating
the edge of the plate, a slick of extra oil poured over.

With so much oil this is not a low-fat dip, but it is a delicious one and probably the most popular item on the menu
in any Greek taverna in the world.

Some recipes include fresh dill, others finely grated carrot
– in this case add a little ground cumin for a more Smyrneika
taste. Other variations include beetroot, purslane (in a recipe
by Diane Kochilas) and fresh fennel (in a recipe by Aglaia
Kremezi).

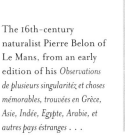

The 16th-century
naturalist Pierre Belon of
Le Mans, from an early
edition of his *Observations
de plusieurs singularitéz et choses
mémorables, trouvées en Grèce,
Asie, Indée, Egypte, Arabie, et
autres pays éstranges* . . .

and sweet *baklava* (compare older *gastris*) the Turkish name survives; the
Greek does not. For grape syrup, which has been a culinary staple for at
least two millennia, there was a classical Greek name, *hepsema*, but this,
too, is forgotten, replaced by the modern *petimezi* (Turkish *pekmez*). The
seventeenth-century writer Bernard Randolph attributes the use of *pekmez*
to the Islamic prohibition of wine, unaware that it has a much longer history: 'Though the Turks drink no wine, yet they take new wine and boil

Tzatziki in Greek, *cacık* in Turkish, a yoghurt and cucumber dip with garlic, olive oil and salt.
The 16th-century traveller Pierre Belon approved of the yoghurt and garlic mixture.

it up to a syrup (which they call *becmez*, and we call *cute*): putting it into small jars they drink it mingled with water.'⁴⁶

One food plant that had been known in Greece ever since the Mycenaean age, and was highly popular in classical times as an ingredient in sweets, gained additional uses under the Turks. It was really at this period and not before that sesame seeds came into common use in Greece for their oil, as Belon explains:

> The Turks make as much use of sesame oil as they do in France of walnut oil and in Languedoc of olive oil. The making of it is laborious and is generally work for slaves. It is only made in winter. They soak sesame seed in brine for twenty-four hours, then take it and beat it until it is husked, then soak it in brine again: this brings the husk to the surface to be discarded. From the bottom they take the seed, dry it in the oven and grind it, and at this point the oil flows as soft as mustard, because there is little sediment. Then they boil it gently and separate the lees. It is a very pleasant and tasty oil, and cheap.⁴⁷

Alongside this the Turks brought with them a few other products unfamiliar to the Greeks and worth adopting. *Yaourti*, 'yoghurt', was one. This is really a group of foods with which earlier Greeks had already experimented. Galen, long ago, had discussed a soured cream product that he called *oxygala*, 'acid milk', and this was no chance observation: the product

must have remained familiar in some form because the same name reap-
pears in modern Greek in the form *xinogalo*, now regarded as a synonym
of *aïrani* or Turkish *ayran*. These are the modern names of a refreshing
yoghurt drink, diluted and slightly salty. There is another yoghurt preparation, thicker, mixed with cucumber, garlic and olive oil, often flavoured
with herbs, served among *meze* as a dip and called *tzatziki* or in Turkish
cacık. Although Belon uses the rediscovered name *oxygala* (he liked redis-
coveries), he appears to be describing something more like modern *tzatziki*
than Galen's *oxygala*:

> All the carmen and muleteers of the caravan had a kind of sour
> milk, called *oxygala*, which they carry in cloth bags hanging at
> their beasts' flanks. Although quite liquid, it stays in the bag
> without seeping through. The Greeks and Turks customarily take
> cloves of garlic and beat them in a wooden mortar and mix them
> with this sour milk. It makes a lordly dish.[48]

Or, since this 'lordly dish' is described as 'quite liquid', is it the thinner version
of *tzatziki* now known among the Greeks of Cyprus as *talatouri* and in Turkish
as *tarator*? But, after all, in the Balkans, *tarator* can be as thick as *tzatziki*.

All these, in any case, derive from the basic ingredient yoghurt, which,
though in some form it must have been known to earlier Greeks, was certainly
developed and popularized by the Turks. In the early nineteenth century W. M.
Leake, who had observed its production at home, gives full instructions:

> Yaourt, which seems to be a Tartar invention introduced into
> Greece by the Turks, is made from the best milk of sheep or goats.
> To make the *pityá* or coagulum: — Take some leaven of bread, that
> is to say, flour and water turned sour, and squeeze a lemon upon
> it, dissolve it in boiling milk, and keep it twenty-four hours. To
> make the yaourt: — Boil some new milk till it foams, stirring it
> frequently, leave it till it is cool enough for the finger to bear the
> heat; then throw in the *pityá*, of which a Turkish coffee-cup full is
> sufficient to make several quarts of yaourt. Then cover it that it may
> not cool too fast, and in three hours it is fit for use. On all future
> occasions a cup of the old yaourt is the best *pityá* for the new.[49]

As Belon's description showed, yoghurt was a natural product
for horse-mounted travellers to adopt, though easy afterwards for

Dakos

The basis of *dakos* the salad is *dakos* the twice-baked barley rusks. They are too hard to eat dry: first sprinkle with water, then dress with oil, vinegar and grated tomatoes, which help to moisten them while retaining their own flavour.

These rusks are found in various shapes and with different names: *paximadia*, barley rusks; *kritharokouloura*, ring-shaped barley rusks; and in parts of eastern Crete *koukouvaia*, 'owls', so called because the shape of the rusk is like the large eye of an owl. Stale bread is given a new lease of life throughout the Mediterranean in salad dishes such as the Middle Eastern *fattoush*, with pita bread, and the Italian *panzanella*. *Paximadia* or *dakos* were the staple in the 'very indifferent diet' enjoyed by the Dutch travellers Egmont and Heyman when they were on Kythera (Cerigo): 'only eggs, and a kind of biscuit softened in water. Our liquor was Cerigo wine, as strong as brandy.'[50]

The recipe is for 4–6 people as one dish among others.

Dakos *Salad*

10-12 slices *paximadia* (see recipe below) or 6 Cretan *dakos*,
sprinkled with water to soften them slightly
4 medium tomatoes, as ripe as possible
½ red onion, diced
2 tsp red-wine vinegar
100 g feta cheese (*xinomyzithra* would be used on Crete, but
feta is a fine substitute)
¼ red pepper, finely diced
1 heaped tbsp capers, drained — and rinsed if they are very salty
salt
oregano and olive oil, to serve

Arrange the rusks on a large serving plate, breaking them a little if you like, and set to one side.

Grate one of the tomatoes into a small bowl, leaving the skin behind. Dice the other three and add them to the tomato pulp together with the onion, some salt and the vinegar.

Dakos the bread and *dakos* the salad. Its basis is formed by the twice-baked barley bread or rusks that Cretans may call *dakos* but other Greeks *paximadia*. It is too hard to eat dry, but the oil, vinegar and juices from the tomatoes are the ideal way to soften it.

When you are ready to serve, spoon the tomatoes over the *dakos*, heaping them in the middle. Crumble the cheese over the top, then add the pepper and the capers on top of the cheese. Sprinkle with some dried oregano and drizzle a little oil over — not much is needed.

Purslane, olives and chopped parsley are common additions to a *dakos* salad, depending on what is available.

Paximadia

Cut slices of stale sourdough or baguette 2 cm thick. Lay them out on a rack and bake at the lowest oven temperature for $1\frac{1}{2} - 2$ hours until completely dehydrated and crisp. Unused *paximadia* will keep for up to six months.

non-nomadic people to make. It is no surprise that the Turks, pastoral nomads turned conquerors, introduced some foods especially suitable to travellers. If this is true of yoghurt and its children, it is also true of *pastourmas*, Turkish *pastırma*, wind-cured dried beef. Although earlier Greeks liked salted and cured meats, and although it can be suggested that *pastırma* is a Turkish word built on a Greek stem (Byzantine *pastos*, 'salted'), Byzantine Greeks rarely ate beef and knew nothing of *pastourmas*. According to Michel Baudier, who wrote of the Great Palace in the mid-seventeenth century, by his time it had become a prized delicacy:

> At the end of autumn the Grand Vizier spends some days over-seeing the manufacture of *pastırma* for the Sultan and Sultanas' consumption. Made of the meat of pregnant cows, so that it will be more tender, it is salted just as in Christendom venison and pork are salted ... At the Palace this product is counted among the luxuries of banquets, while Turkish private households, even those of very modest means, also use it.[51]

Pastırma is now said to be an invention of the Anatolian Turks. So it may be, but the Turks of Constantinople got their beef from the country now called Romania: in the seventeenth century the cattle farmers, 'infidels of Moldavia and Wallachia', brought their beasts to Constantinople and sold them for slaughter at an annual fair lasting forty days, beginning on the feast of St Demetrios.[52] *Pastourmas* in Greece now is a speciality of the north, and particularly of the Vlachs, cousins of those same 'infidel' cattle-farmers, who, incidentally, season it with paprika.

Writing a century earlier, Belon attempts a general description of Turkish food choices and customs. In his day it still seemed natural to assume that the Turks were always on the move: 'Since they do not stop for a midday meal but travel all day they need to prepare today what they are to eat tomorrow.' They were far from delicate about their food, he continues, being satisfied with onions, bread, raisins and other dried fruit. 'It is usual with all Turks, ordinary people and great lords, to eat onions raw ... they eat them at every meal.' Onions and garlic kept the Turks healthy, he argues scientifically, 'saving them from all the dangers of water but also making them salivate, thus giving them the appetite to eat plenty of dry bread'.[53] But Greeks were as devoted to garlic as any Turk.

This mobile lifestyle helps to explain why the philanthropic Mehmet II, Constantinople's Turkish conqueror, gave special attention to the restoration of inns and hostelries on the roads that led to the City. 'No Turk is ashamed to stay in a hostel of this kind or to accept its free food charity because this is the custom of the country. The stranger will be offered no less than the grandest personage,' Belon writes.[54]

Travellers need a portable, durable staple food, whether in bread-like or porridge-like form. From the early Ottoman empire both are reported. On the one hand barley rusks, *paximadia* – already of great importance – survived and flourished. A German pilgrim who sailed through Greek waters in 1483 on his way to the Holy Land called at Modon (Methoni) in Messenia and noted the food as well as the wine: 'We went to the house of the bakers, where *paximates* or *paximacii* are baked for seafarers. An old German keeps the house. There we got our dinner, cooked it, and ate it.'[55] On the other hand a porridge-like staple made from emmer wheat, already known under the Byzantine Empire and even before, became more commonly used in Ottoman times. Its Greek name was *tragos*:

> *Making tragos.* Soak and pound Alexandrian wheat and dry it in hot sun. Then repeat the process until the glumes and fibrous parts of the wheat are all removed. *Tragos* from other good-quality emmer can be dried and stored in the same way.[56]

By the sixteenth century its common name was *trachanas*, as it is today, and a second method was in use: soaking the pounded grain in sour milk before drying into balls, the result of which is a more complete, more nourishing food when the balls are eventually turned into soup. Belon found that this was one of the regular foods available free to travellers at the officially maintained inns of the Empire. 'When the soup at the hostel is ready, anyone who wants some must bring his bowl. They also give meat and bread ... No one is refused who comes there, Jew, Christian, Idolater or Turk.' He catalogues rice and black-eyed peas as alternative mainstays, but focuses on *trachanas*: 'The people of Lesbos have a method of preparing grain and binding it with sour milk. First they boil the grain, then they dry it in the sun and make a compound which ... is exported from Lesbos to all parts of Turkey and is much used in soups.'[57] There is another name, *xynochondros*, borrowed from and perhaps redolent of an ancient emmer porridge or soup, *chondros*. As in the early sources, modern *trachanas* is usually made from emmer or other wheats, but sometimes not: the food writer Aglaia Kremezi reports a *krithinos trachanas*, 'barley *trachanas*', from Kythera.[58]

FIVE

A Culinary Geography, Part 1: Beyond Greece

Before and after the milestone year 1453 the Ottoman expansion engulfed a great number of communities of Greeks and Greek-speakers, most of which, long established, widely scattered geographically, had lost any link they may once have had with the Byzantine Empire.

Greeks have traded by sea around the coasts of the Mediterranean ever since Mycenaean times, when their presence in southern Italy is already demonstrated archaeologically. As they began to write history, a few centuries later, their own trade routes and their early achievements in colonization are among the subjects on which they naturally went to town: they recount the origins, founders, traditional dates of foundation and early municipal histories of a whole series of Greek colonies, many of which have prospered ever since, their Greek origins in some cases almost forgotten.

Beyond what we now call Greece, Greek food and wine customs were flourishing by the fifth and fourth centuries BC in most of Sicily and along the southern coasts of Italy. Sicily, as we have already seen, was a byword for convivial luxury. It was the home of famous cooks (such as Mithaikos) and gastronomes (not least Archestratos). To the south the great city of Kyrene on the coast of what is now eastern Libya exported its legendary spice, *silphion*, prized by all Greeks who cared about healthy eating, and eventually to Rome as well, until the Romans ate it all.

Greek cities studded the Adriatic shores northwards from Epiros and modern Albania. Much further away to the northwest was the prosperous colony of Massalia, modern Marseille, with a string of outlying coastal towns from Monaco and Nice in the east to Ampurias in the west. If they did not introduce viticulture to this region, the Greeks of Marseille certainly helped to spread wine and the desire for wine: Romans reported that around the first century BC a Gaulish slave could be exchanged for an amphora of wine.

The Black Sea (Pontos), unlike the Mediterranean, was practically a Greek sea during the last few centuries BC: the only seaborne access to it was by way of the Hellespont and Bosporos, controlled by some of the earliest Greek colonies. Eventually Greek cities almost surrounded the Black Sea. Many exported wheat to the homeland, where the demand for wheat bread always exceeded the local wheat supply. Cities at the mouths of the great rivers engaged in river trade. Those on the Crimea (Chersonesos Taurike) produced wine and *garos*. Those along the northern coast of what is now Turkey preyed on the shoals of tunny on their annual migration and also exported hazelnuts and walnuts. The hinterland of this coast came to be called Pontos in Greek, after the sea that gave access to it.

All of this was before Alexander the Great. By conquering the Persian Empire he began a cultural merger that swept the whole Near East in the last three centuries BC, a merger in which Greek language and the Greek way of life – as interpreted by Macedonians – ruled. In the successor kingdoms, Greek culture eventually spread far and wide. Three centuries after Alexander, the Roman Empire gradually engulfed nearly all the territories still ruled by his successors. By that time Greek was so firmly embedded that it became Rome's second language, the language normally used for communication in the whole eastern half of the Empire, and a lingua franca in great Roman households and kitchens where easterners ('Greeks' in the wide Roman sense) worked as slaves or former slaves. Thus a second cultural merger was under way. And thus as the eastern Roman Empire became the Byzantine Empire its majority mother tongue was already Greek; to call oneself 'Roman', in this whole vast region around the eastern Mediterranean, meant that one spoke Greek and lived and ate in a Greek way.

At that period the number of Greek-speakers who lived beyond the reach of the government in Constantinople would have been relatively small – most of them in the coastal cities of Sicily, southern Italy and the Adriatic shores. This was to change as the Byzantine Empire steadily shrank. The biggest change, ironically, came in the mid-seventh-century reign of Heraklios, the same emperor who ended the official status of Latin, leaving Greek as sole ruling language of the empire. A few years later he lost the southeastern provinces at a stroke to the Islamic advance, and with them the large and prosperous communities of Greek-speakers in Egypt and Syria. In the eleventh and twelfth centuries most of Anatolia was lost, in the twelfth century most of the Balkans, while the thirteenth century, beginning with the Crusaders' capture of Constantinople, saw the Empire's remaining heartlands, even Greece itself, partly under the non-Greek rule of French- and Italian-speaking lordships. The Greek islands, too, fell to several different rulers. Chios was acquired by the Genoese in 1304. Crete (which, in a unique episode, had been an Arab possession and a nest of pirates back in the ninth and tenth centuries) belonged to Venice by 1212. Rhodes was the stronghold of the Knights Hospitaller from 1309 onwards.

Four important regions of age-old Greek culture had a special destiny, and the following sections focus on the food culture of those four regions. With the unwilling help of a Byzantine rebel and by the final decision of Richard the Lionheart, Cyprus passed from the Byzantine Empire to the Crusader dynasty of Jerusalem at the end of the twelfth century. French was thenceforth its official language, but Greek remained its everyday speech. Not long afterwards the northeastern region of Pontos, which unlike the rest of Anatolia had remained solidly Byzantine until 1204 and was never threatened by the Crusaders, became the breakaway empire of Trebizond under a dynasty of Greek rulers related to the later Byzantines. Pontos continued to have a large Greek-speaking population, alongside Armenians and Turks, even under Ottoman rule. The busy port of Smyrna (modern İzmir) on the Aegean coast of Anatolia, long disputed among Turks, Greeks and Crusaders, finally became Ottoman in 1426, but it and its hinterland also remained largely Greek-speaking for several centuries. The fourth of these regions is the ancient capital itself, Constantinople (modern İstanbul), familiarly and simply known to Greeks as *i Poli*, 'the city'. It was to be the capital of the Ottoman Empire for just over 450 years, and never lost its status as the greatest Greek city in the world.

THE CITY

In 1453, when Ottoman forces were massed around its walls for their final and successful assault, Constantinople was a shadow of its former self: its money uselessly spent, its trade decayed, and much of its population having long since emigrated. The last emperor, Constantine XI, fell heroically as he led its defence.

Under Mehmet II 'the conqueror', thus named in commemoration of his victory that year, the city's rebirth began. He immediately moved his court from Adrianople to Constantinople, and fully atoned for the damage done in the city's siege and capture with a programme of restoration. A notable patron of architects and landscape gardeners, he re-created the old Imperial palace at the eastern end of the peninsula. His new gardens were laid out on the foundations of the gardens that had given pleasure to the emperors of Constantinople, and they were useful as well as beautiful:

> Around the palace he laid out a circle of large and beautiful gardens, burgeoning with various fine plants, bringing forth fruits in season, flowing with abundant streams, cold, clear, and good to drink, studded with beautiful groves and meadows, resounding and chattering with flocks of singing birds that were also good to eat, pasturing herds of animals both domesticated and wild.[1]

It was one of Mehmet's successors, sultan Ibrahim in the early seventeenth century, who laid out the garden along the northern shore of the Golden Horn at Hasköy, 'a garden that reminds one of Paradise . . . The peaches and apricots have the most exquisite flavour . . . Here they catch oysters which are eaten with lemon and washed down with wine.' People who eat oysters without wine, Evliya Çelebi warns, will find them a powerful aphrodisiac. He notes that the fishermen paid an annual rent for permission to sell their seafood.[2] In the district of Kasımpaşa he enjoyed 'peaches of exquisite flavour, apricots, grapes' from a nearby garden whose roses were the finest in the Empire.[3]

Visitors in the sixteenth and seventeenth centuries were as impressed as any of their predecessors by the wealth of the city, and the years of poverty and decline were already forgotten. George Wheler in 1682 especially noted the seafood:

> They have great plenty of many sorts of good fish. Oysters here are better than I tasted them anywhere except in England. The swordfish is another I took notice of for its goodness and firm fleshy substance. Their fruits are excellent, figs, peaches and apples, very fair and good. The Turks are very sweet-toothed and love all kinds of sweet meats.[4]

The single most informative source of information on the foods and luxuries of Constantinople in the early Ottoman centuries is the seventeenth-century work of Çelebi, which includes a description of the annual procession of the trade guilds as they paraded before Sultan Murad IV. Ottoman Constantinople was not unique in its guilds – retail

İmam bayıldı – *Baked Aubergines*

Imam bayıldı 'the imam fainted' is the most famous of Turkish stewed vegetable dishes, popular too in Bulgaria and Greece. The imam, they say, fainted with pleasure on tasting it. Recipes vary; this is the version of Vangelis Chaniotis.

Imam is often made without cheese, although Chaniotis's customers (who are mainly Greeks) prefer the dish with feta. Other cooks use a greater proportion of onions in the sauce, making the final flavour substantially sweeter, like a *stifado*. Bay leaves can be added, together with allspice and whole cloves. The aubergines can be left whole, or halved, and stewed in oil without being fried first, which results in a more slippery, soft-textured dish.

4 medium aubergines, quartered
vegetable oil, for frying
2 tbsp olive oil
1 onion, finely diced
2 cloves garlic, chopped
1 small red pepper, finely diced
6 tomatoes, grated (or a 425 g tin chopped tomatoes)
1 tsp dried spearmint
a little water
1 large handful grated yellow cheese, such as *kefalotyri*
or emmental
150 g feta cheese

trades have enjoyed similar regulation and protection elsewhere – but it was remarkable for their vigour, inherited from Byzantine times and flourishing anew. Çelebi lists no fewer than 735 guilds. They included the apothecaries who distilled cordials from Indian spices and fruits, the perfumiers who sold rose water and other scents redolent of frankincense, ambergris and jasmine, the herbalists and the greengrocers. Incidentally, the stock typically held by the merchants of these guilds was already listed in two earlier sources, Francesco Pegolotti in the late Byzantine period

Wash, top and tail the aubergines and cut them into quarters along their length. Deep-fry them in plenty of vegetable oil for ten minutes or so until soft and golden but not completely cooked through. Leave them to one side to drain well.

Now make the tomato sauce: heat the olive oil in a pan and soften the onion, garlic and pepper. Before they colour, add the tomatoes, the spearmint and a little water if the tomatoes are not very juicy. Allow to simmer over a medium heat for twenty minutes until the sauce is reduced and thickened slightly.

To assemble the dish, place the aubergine wedges, skin side down, in neat rows in a baking dish. Scatter the aubergines with the grated yellow cheese and carefully pour the sauce on top. Roughly crumble over the feta so that most of the surface is covered, but with some gaps. Bake for 35 – 40 minutes in a medium-hot oven.

Serves 4

Vangelis Chaniotis preparing aubergines in his restaurant as he has for the past 30 years.

and Pierre Belon in the mid-sixteenth century. We can also glance at the *Geoponika*, the tenth-century Byzantine farming manual, which includes a list of the garden vegetables planted in the latitude of Constantinople month by month: 'In January seakale is sown, along with orach and fenugreek. In February parsley is sown along with leek, onion, chard, carrot, beetroot, savory, salad mixture . . . sprouting broccoli, coriander, dill and rue. Lettuce and chicory are planted out,' and so on through the year.[5] The mention of rue is worth noting; this aromatic herb was popular in

Early photograph of a cooked food street stall in mid-19th-century Constantinople.

ancient and medieval cuisine and easily grown in Greece, where it may well have originated, but is scarcely used in modern Greek food.

As for Belon, immediately on his arrival at Constantinople in 1547 he made for the markets along the shore of the Golden Horn, guided, probably, by the topographer Pierre Gilles, who was there before him.[6] Belon noted the names in several languages of the fish, fruits and spices he found. With his special interest in edible plants, he is the earliest author to mention *vrouves*, mustard greens, eaten raw in spring 'when they have shot and begun to flower . . . they have a flavour of radish, but if boiled they become bitter.'[7]

Continuing with the food trade of Ottoman Constantinople, the bakers of bread, the pastry-cooks and the bakers of *paximadia* all belonged to separate guilds. Then there were the makers of 'musk-sherbets': Çelebi, an expert on sherbets, knew not only of ambergris and musk but of rhubarb, roses, lotus, grapes and tamarinds as flavourings. And then there were the coffee-sellers. Coffee was still something of a novelty in his time – 'an innovation which curtails sleep and the generating power in man. Coffee-houses are houses of confusion', or so the butchers' guild claimed in a celebrated debate on precedence.[8]

Also prominent in the procession of the trade guilds were butchers, drovers and shepherds, milkmen, cheese merchants and many kinds of cooked food sellers, not least the tripe merchants, who were in great favour with Muslims because Muhammad himself, according to Çelebi, called tripe 'the prince of dishes'. In spite of this, according to Çelebi again, the seven hundred tripe-cooks of the City were all Greek. They were exempt from taxes, but every day they had to deliver to the imperial kennels 'sixty donkey-loads of intestines as food for the greyhounds and sheepdogs. At night their shops are full of drinkers who eat tripe soup all night to get rid of their wine', owing to its reputation as an antidote to drunkenness. In the procession the tripe-cooks would theatrically fish offal out of their cauldrons and serve it up in bowls, seasoned with pepper and cloves, while singing Greek songs.[9] Their legacy is to be found in the tripe restaurants of modern Thessaloniki, *patsatsidika*, and of Thessaly, *skebetzidika*.

Among the makers of sweet and hot drinks were the sellers of *salep*, that traditional, fortifying beverage made from ground orchid roots. They, too, have a modern legacy. Then came the sellers of snow from the mountains of Bithynia; then the confectioners, five hundred of them, the best of whom (according to Çelebi) were the Greeks of Chios, great masters of their art and deeply versed in pharmacy: 'They display all kinds of crystallized fruits such as almonds, filberts, pistachios, ginger, orange-peel, coffee … covered with sugar icing of various colours and preserved in fine crystal jars. Their shops are hung with silk hangings of satin and brocade.' At public shows they displayed sugar-trees decorated with crystallized fruits.[10]

Living crabs and lobsters, hardly soothed by their journey to Thessaloniki market, must be handled with care.

Incongruously, among the local fresh fish on sale – bass, red mullet, bream and so on – can be seen fillets of an exotic species (back right), hopefully labelled 'perch' in Greek. The scientific name *Pangasius* and the origin 'Vietnam' suggest a Mekong catfish: let's hope it isn't the critically threatened *Pangasionodon gigas*.

Fried *marides* (smelts) are served whole (with a green salad alongside) and will be eaten whole, just discarding the tail.

The fishermen of seventeenth-century Constantinople were mostly Greeks. In the few days before the procession they did their best to catch a few rarities and 'sea-monsters' to display to the crowds on their floats (which were pulled by buffaloes). The fish-cooks, too, were 'infidel Greeks' who cooked their fish in olive oil or in the linseed oil that came from Raidestos (Tekirda) in Thrace, no surprise if we remember that flax had been the usual oil plant five thousand years earlier in Neolithic Thrace and Macedonia. 'These Greeks', Çelebi adds, 'have certain fast-days including Saints Nicholas, Mary ... Demetrios, George, Elias, Symeon and Kalikanzaros. On those days they prepare their dishes without butter.'[11]

Grocers, butter-merchants, oil-merchants, fruit-merchants and poultrymen followed in turn. Last of all were the dealers in strong drink, *buza* or 'millet beer' (this alone was explicitly permitted to Çelebi and other Muslims), rice wine, mead, arrack and *petimezi*, 'grape syrup'. Then, last of all, the tavern-keepers:

> There are in the four jurisdictions of Constantinople one thousand such places of misrule, kept by Greeks, Armenians and Jews ... Besides the open wine-, brandy- and beer-houses there are many secret spots known to amateurs by their particular names, of which, naturally, I am ignorant.[12]

One of the classic modern Greek cookbooks came out of the nineteenth-century Greek community of Constantinople: Nikolaos Sarantis's *Syngramma magirikis* was published there in 1863. The Greeks of the city, unlike those of the rest of Turkey, were not forced into exile in 1923, but many emigrated in those years and the community has dwindled since then, with an especially sharp decline in the 1960s.

The food traditions of Greek Constantinople – of those people who were, long ago, the ruling caste in a metropolis that was far richer and more powerful than any other in southeastern Europe – survive today in the families of those who once lived there. Such traditions, threatened in each generation by change, dispersal and forgetfulness, need recording and celebrating. Currently the pre-eminent recorder is Soula Bozi. Her *Politiki kuzina*, 'the Cuisine of the City', appeared in book form in 1994 and afterwards lent its title and theme to a film. She showed how food traditions from all over the Ottoman Empire had influenced the Greeks of Constantinople, and how, migrating to 1960s Greece, they transformed the relatively Spartan culinary repertoire of Greece of that period.

SMYRNA AND BEYOND

Bozi has written more recently on the culinary traditions of the Greeks of Ionia, Cappadocia and Pontos, all very different from those of Constantinople and each different from the others. Ionia is a name applied by modern Greeks to the region that stretches inland from the Ionia of ancient geography (the twelve luxury-loving early Greek cities

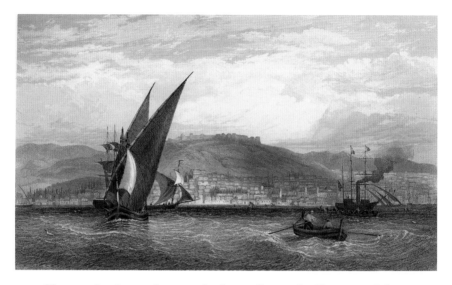

The approach to Smyrna, the greatest Greek city in Ottoman Asia Minor, around 1850,
engraving by A. Willmore after a sketch by E. Duncan (London, 1854?).

on the eastern shore of the Aegean). The Ionia of recent history, whose Greek minority fled in 1923, centred on the coastal metropolis of Smyrna with its large Greek population.

By the late seventeenth century, Ottoman Smyrna had become a considerable port of trade that channelled the produce of Asia Minor for export westwards. The city is described in memoirs, many of whose authors were interested in its grapes and wine – which would not have surprised the ancient physician Galen, a native of this region and a connoisseur of the wines that it produced fifteen centuries earlier. Smyrna exported 'a great quantity of raisins to England', Richard Pococke reported in 1743, and also 'a small quantity of muscadine wine, for which this place is famous, as well as for the drier virgin white wine'.[13]

The best and sharpest description of Ottoman Smyrna is by the young Antoine Galland, who spent a mere five months in the city in 1678. His survey, intended for publication under the title *Smyrne ancienne et moderne*, lay forgotten until the year 2000. There were thirteen bakeries for the Turks and Greeks, he reported, and recently one for the English and one for the French, who had not been allowed to build them before the Turkish conquest of Crete, for fear that they might be used to supply 'biscuit' (that is, *paximadia*) to the Cretans and Venetians under siege. He counted 26 sheep butchers and 15 for cattle: 50 cows and 150 sheep were slaughtered daily, not counting lambs and kids, which were much in demand at Easter. There was cheap chicken (and expensive fat capons for the English), and partridges, francolins and woodcocks almost as cheap. Galland gives especial attention to the wine, which, he says, 'the Turks do not drink, or, if they do (and some admittedly do), they keep no stock of it but buy it from the Christians'. What did the Turks drink instead? The answer is water, coffee and sherbet, a refreshing beverage made of lemon juice, sugar and water. The rich might enjoy their sherbet flavoured with ambergris or with cooling camphor:

> They chill water in summer by adding snow which is carefully gathered from the mountains in winter and carefully stored. For drinking water there are public fountains in each district and some in private houses. Then they have *cahvé*, which comes to them from Cairo, and *cherbet* from the same country (but only for the rich) and what is made locally with roses, violets and other flowers. The common people, however, make it only with raisins, dried figs or prunes, soaked in water.[14]

All the other 'nations' at Smyrna drank wine and brandy. The wine was made locally from the grapes of neighbouring districts; it was very good and unusually strong, said Galland. 'It sometimes has a certain sweetness . . . not unpleasant when one is used to it . . . but it nearly always spoils before the next season. As a result, those few who have good wine make a great profit by selling it to the English, who must have it at any price.' A little wine was brought in from the islands, notably the excellent muscat of Tenedos (which in the twentieth century was supplanted by the equally excellent muscat of Lemnos). Local brandy was 'better when drawn from raisins than from the marc', and was sold in great quantity. The Greeks took one another to taverns for a brandy and rarely stopped at a single glass: 'it often happens that a party that begins in the morning is only driven home by the fall of night.' But the English, Galland repeats, were the heaviest drinkers. He goes on:

> The Greeks drink their full share, particularly at their festivals which they think they have properly celebrated only when full of wine. They drink very little during their fasts, when they only eat fish, saying that wine should be reserved for *pascalino*, in other words, the meat permitted during Easter, and that only water should accompany fish.[15]

Dolmadakia (miniature *dolmades*), a speciality of the cuisine of Smyrna.

Smyrna flourished as a relatively Greek city in a relatively Turkish countryside until the early years of the twentieth century. Successive adjustments of boundaries between Greece and Turkey made community relations in Smyrna no easier, but had no direct local effect, until Greece occupied Smyrna and began to expand inland into Asia Minor in 1921. The Greek advance was eventually halted, and retreat turned into rout. In this catastrophe Smyrna was largely destroyed. The surviving Greek population not only of the city but of almost the whole of Asia Minor was driven into exile. Many from Smyrna and its neighbourhood fled to Thessaloniki and helped to turn its Greek minority into a majority, most of the Turkish inhabitants of Thessaloniki, Greek Macedonia and Thrace having been forced to migrate in the opposite direction.

For the wealthy Greek merchant families of Smyrna, the latest fashion in food had been French. This had blended with the Ottoman Turkish influence of Constantinople, the imperial capital, traceable partly to the Byzantine Empire and partly to medieval Turkish nomads and conquerors. Also in the mix were the local food traditions of western Asia Minor, partly Greek, partly Turkish, and the ethnic cuisines and customs of Smyrna itself. All of this enriched the cookery of the Greek cities where the refugees settled. Without the catastrophe and the resulting migrations, a whole constituent of modern Greek food would be absent, a cosmopolitan 'Smyrniot' element opposite to the country food of the Greek regions. Visitors to Greece may never notice these nuances, but they are easily distinguishable by Greeks. Smyrniot are the stuffed vine leaves (*dolmadakia*) and their relatives, the lamb with rice (*atzem pilaf*) and many other rice dishes, and the carefully kneaded meatballs (*keftedes*, Turkish *köfte*). And then there are the cumin-flavoured meatballs with tomato sauce called *soutzoukakia* in Greek, but in Turkish simply *İzmir köfte*, 'meatballs from Smyrna'.

GREEKS OF CAPPADOCIA AND THE PONTOS

Nearly all the surviving Greeks of the Pontos in northeastern Turkey and of Cappadocia in the inland mountains were compelled to change places with the Muslim population of Greece in the population exchanges of 1923. Memories are not so easily effaced, however, and their children and grandchildren still re-create the foods of homelands that some have never seen and that were in many ways very unlike the Greece in which they now live.

The Greeks of Cappadocia, rural and traditional where those of Smyrna were urban cosmopolites, have contributed in modest but distinct ways to the general food culture of modern Greece, reinforcing and adding their own nuances to the special foods of the major Christian festivals. They also claim *pastirma* as one of their specialities. In spite of such Byzantine precursors as *apokti*, it is true that the *pastirma* tradition has deep roots in the nomadic culture of the medieval Turks. It is highly probable that they transmitted the idea to the Cappadocians a long time before Constantinople was conquered, and, although Constantinople knew all about *pastirma* from the seventeenth century onwards, it is certain that after the population exchanges of 1923 modern Greece acquired its knowledge of *pastirma* from the Cappadocians. *Apokti* might be the salted dried meat of several animals, but *pastirma* is beef (or camel, the food historian Mariana Kavroulaki is careful to add): the meat pressed, salted, sun-dried and often generously coated in garlic and spices.[16] For eighty years Athenians have relied for their *pastirma* and other Cappadocian meats and cheeses on producers in Thrace and on Arapian, the famous shop whose founder, Sarkis Arapian, was not a Cappadocian Greek but a Cappadocian Armenian.

Today there are communities of Pontian Greeks sprinkled across Greece, from Corfu to Lakonia in the Peloponnese, from Chania in Crete to Mount Pelion in Thessaly, but it is in Macedonia and Thrace that the majority settled. There is a second Pontian culinary tradition too,

Soutzoukakia Smyrneika

Sucuk is 'sausage' in Turkish; *-aki* is a Greek diminutive suffix: thus, in a single-word compound of Turkish and Greek, *soutzoukakia Smyrneika* are 'little sausages from Smyrna'.

For the *soutzoukakia*:
600 g minced meat, ideally a mix of beef and lamb, or beef and pork; just beef is not a disaster
3 cloves garlic, finely chopped
1 tsp ground cumin
2 eggs
small handful of finely chopped parsley

For the tomato sauce:
4 tbsp olive oil
1 finely chopped onion
a 400 g tin of chopped tomatoes or tomato passata
a little sugar
a bay leaf and a cinnamon stick
a small wine glass of dry red wine
salt and pepper

First make the *soutzoukakia*: mix all the ingredients in a large bowl, adding lots of salt, kneading by hand to ensure a good homogeneous mix. Taking roughly 50 g of mixture at a time (wetting your hands if it sticks too much), form into small sausages. Cover the torpedos with cling film and put in the fridge for half an hour or so to firm up.

In the meantime, heat 2 tbsp of the oil in a large frying pan and fry the onion for a few minutes till soft but not yet colouring. Add the tomatoes, half a spoon of sugar, the bay leaf and cinnamon stick and pour in the wine. Season, bring to a boil then lower the heat and simmer for 20 minutes, till the sauce has thickened and reduced slightly. Put the sauce to one side, clean the pan and put it back on the heat with the remaining oil.

Fry the *soutzoukakia* over a medium heat, five minutes a side so they are nicely coloured, then pour in the tomato sauce. Cover and simmer for 20 minutes over a low heat till they are cooked through and the cinnamon is fragrant.

Serve three *soutzoukakia* per person with some of the sauce spooned over, and a plain rice pilaf or potatoes fried in olive oil. Perhaps add grated cheese over the rice and a salad of shredded cabbage and carrot dressed with olive oil and lemon juice (never vinegar on this salad). This recipe is by Vangelis Chaniotis.

Traditionally *soutzoukakia* should have a dense, almost salami-like, toothsome quality very different from the softer *keftedes* (meatballs) so popular all over Greece. However, this can make them weigh heavily on the stomach, so add two good handfuls of breadcrumbs to the meat mixture if you prefer a lighter dish. *Soutzoukakia* also differ from meatballs in their inclusion of cumin and garlic, two popular Constantinopolitan flavourings. Cinnamon is commonly used in tomato sauces throughout Greece.

Soutzoukakia Smyrneika, another speciality of Smyrna's cuisine.

Pontos

Theofilos Giorgiadis has spent the past thirty years travelling back and forth from his home, the destination of his grand-parents' compulsory migration near Kilkis, to the Pontos, their original homeland, and the ancestral village of Ragias. In Greece in the late 1960s he was discouraged at school from speaking the Pontian dialect, but chose to learn it himself from his grandparents. His wife, Eleni, has roots in Constantinople, her father was a Smyrniot refugee, and now she is Pontian because of her husband.

They have a cheese-producing farm in Kilkis, run by Theofilos, and a Pontic shop in Thessaloniki, run by Eleni,

Ragian, home from home for all who want to taste the delicacies of the Pontos. Cheeses steal the show . . .

stemming from a community that has migrated twice, in the nineteenth century northwards across the Black Sea to Mariupol and eastern Ukraine, then, as the Soviet Union broke up, to Greece. *These* Pontians cook dumplings and complicated dough-based dishes in heavy sauces.

So Pontian traditions are again very different from those of familiar Smyrna, which faced Greece and communicated with it continually across the busy Aegean. Pontian is peasant farmers' cuisine – like much of Greek food – but from a different and distant landscape, and based on grains, whole wheat and cracked corn, maize, dairy products and fish. The fish once came from the Black Sea coast and the wide rivers that fed it from

. . . especially *gaïs* pulled cheese, from young to old, from white to black.

named Ragian. This is their passion, and it shows as soon as
a customer walks in: Eleni knows inside out the products that
Theofilos makes in the ancestral way. Hidden in the maze-like
streets around Aristotelous Square, Ragian is an encyclopaedia
of Pontian food: the *perek*, a flatbread 30 cm in diameter,
often used as the crust for a simple pita or pie; a cornucopia
of cheeses farm-made by Theofilos; cured meats, dried herbs,
biscuits and sweetmeats from Pontian culinary tradition. Some
of their products can be found elsewhere in Greece wherever
Pontians have settled.

the Turkish mountains, but now from the northern Aegean and the rivers
of Thrace that flow south out of the Balkans.

Being cattle-farmers rather than goat-herders, Pontians' preferred cooking fat is butter. Olive trees did not thrive in the Pontos and do not thrive in
the colder climate of the Rhodopi mountain range in the north of Greece
– we have seen that even in Neolithic times other oil plants were grown
there – so, for Pontians who now live in Macedonia and Thrace, olive oil is
a luxury just as butter would be further south.

Fresh yoghurt (*douvana*) is churned in a similar manner to butter and
so makes *tan*, which, as far as Greece is concerned, is unique to the Pontian

kitchen. *Tan* is used fresh and the excess left for two months to mature into *paskitan* (rather like the Greek *myzithra*). If this is then left to air-dry thoroughly it becomes *chortan*, a hard, caramel-coloured, brittle-toffee-textured cheese-tasting *meze*, to be chopped up into small pieces alongside *tsipouro*. This alone demonstrates the amazing ingenuity of the Pontian farmers – absolutely nothing was wasted. Soups and stews are thickened with *paskitan*. One of the best examples of this technique is *tanomenos sorbas*, originating in Armenia but named in Pontic Greek, which was eaten as a good breakfast before starting work in the fields. The name translates literally as 'soup with *tan*' (*çorba* is the word for soup in Turkey and the Balkans, whereas the ordinary Greek word, borrowed from Italian, is *soupa*). *Korkoto* (cracked and dried maize kernels, alternatively bulgur wheat or barley) is boiled until tender and then simmered gently with *tan* or *paskitan* to thicken it gently and add a slightly sour and creamy flavour, before butter-fried green onions and spearmint are stirred in. This is a completely different style of soup from those of southern Greece and the islands.

Whey – at Ragian, for example – is made into pulled cheese or *gais*, a product known in many countries under different names and forms, not least in Italy, where it is known as *mozzarella*. In Kilkis in central Macedonia this cheese is stretched into long ropes (perish the thought that it should be compared with the commercial and processed string cheese, but there is a similarity in texture) and rolled into spirals, ultimately to dry out for as many years as it may take before it is used.

A strong feature of Pontian cuisine is the many dough-based dumpling and pasta-style recipes. Milk is used to enrich the cornbreads, pie crusts and dough for Russian-influenced dumplings, *piroski*, and the dumplings are served with butter and *paskitan*. The *piroski* of the Pontians are generally fried, rather than boiled or poached, but for the most part the fillings are remarkably similar: potato, meat or cheese-based; fruit is not as popular as in other countries. Turkish influence is seen in pasta-making: the meat-stuffed *giannoutsia* (*giohadas* in Turkish) and the *manti* style of ravioli or dumpling that is found in various forms from Turkey all across Asia as far as the *man tou* of China, but also in many other everyday dishes.

Beans and vegetables are prominent, as they are in the culinary traditions of the rest of Greece. The preferred Pontian *horta* – or greens – are nettles, which thrived along the Black Sea coast as they do in northern Greece. They are boiled in salads as elsewhere, made into a purée or soup and stewed together with the local red or white beans. Also common (and often used

Cypriot halloumi cheese, sometimes aged in brine, has a firm texture and a high melting point, making it ideal for frying or grilling. It is traditionally made with sheep's or goats' milk, now often with cows' milk.

interchangeably with the nettles) are dark green cabbages, sorrel and other leaves of the dock family, and beetroot – especially the beetroot greens. The *mavrolahano*, 'black cabbage', is sometimes cultivated and also grows wild. As in many Balkan cuisines, pickled vegetables are a staple in kitchens.

Homemade pasta (*makarina*) is shaped into thick tagliatelle-like ribbons and eaten with yoghurt or butter and fresh *gais* cheese. Fruits such as plums, raspberries and wild pears grow well in the extreme north of Greece, as they did in the Pontos, and are eaten fresh or made into *kompostes* (compotes), or else into *petimezia* (concentrated fruit syrups) and dried in the sun.

Even today, when the cooking of other minorities has been all but absorbed into a 'national cuisine', the food of the Pontian Greeks retains identity and continuity.

Cyprus

Cyprus, the great possession of the Crusader kingdom of Jerusalem, and retained long after Jerusalem itself was lost, fell to the Ottoman Empire in 1571, and by the nineteenth century the island had a significant Turkish minority. It fell into British hands in 1878. From British possession Cyprus became independent in 1960 and is so still, though with its British military bases in the south and its breakaway Turkish enclave in the north.

Historically Cyprus is entirely comparable to Constantinople, Smyrna and the Pontos, regions with historic Greek populations lying beyond the borders of modern Greece. Cypriot food is important to this story because

Seftalia

For *souvla* (spitted dishes) pork mince is combined with spices and herbs, formed into fat sausages, wrapped in lamb or pig caul, skewered and grilled. This is good as a *meze*, or else stuffed into a Cypriot pita with the usual *gyros* additions of *tzatziki*, onion, tomato and lukewarm chips.

Cypriot pita bread is roughly oval in shape and can be easily split down the middle and stuffed, whereas Greek pitas are thicker and round, cannot be split in the same way and have to be wrapped around the desired filling.

Seftalia are so popular in Cyprus that pigs' caul is imported especially for making it.

Cypriot seftalia

500 g fairly fatty pork mince
100 g dry bread, soaked in water and squeezed out
a handful of finely chopped parsley
a little less of spearmint
½ tsp ground coriander
½ tsp cinnamon
salt and pepper
6 pieces of pigs' caul, washed thoroughly and patted dry
with kitchen paper

Mix all the ingredients, except the caul, by hand to achieve a smoothish sausage-meat consistency. Divide the filling into six and shape each into a rough elongated ball. Laying out one piece of caul at a time, wrap up each meatball tightly as you would a spring roll or *dolma*. Thread individually onto long wooden skewers. Serve hot.

(in contrast with those other regions) the island's majority population is Greek today – and also because, across the world, the modern Cypriot and Greek diasporas interact and merge.

Cumin (known locally as *artisha*), coriander (both the fresh herb and the ground seed) and mint are typical Cypriot flavours. Coriander

---

Greek Gyros

Souvlaki merida is on every grill-house and fast-food menu: lit-erally a *'souvlaki* plate' of meat sliced from the large rotating kebab, finely sliced onion, *tzatziki*, tomato, triangles of toasted pita bread and nicely fried chips. A thousand photos in a thousand *souvlaki* shops show this dish, and it is a better combination than it sounds. As with a *gyros*-pita (meat etc. wrapped in the pita and eaten on the hop), specify if you want *apo ola*.

This recipe is inspired by *gyros* served on Paros one evening in May, before the local tomato season had started and avoiding the tasteless excuse for a fruit that is an imported tomato.

For two people, allow 3 skewers of pork marinated in oil,
lemon and oregano, and grilled
2 round pitas, or Cypriot pitas, toasted and quartered
a nice mound of *tzatziki*
½ small red onion, finely sliced
a couple of handfuls of rocket, roughly chopped

Arrange the pitas on a large plate and place the kebabs on top. To one side dollop the tzatziki, next to that pile the onion, next to that the rocket leaves. With a beer or two, it is a perfect meal on one plate.

---

seeds, scarcely used in much of Greece, are the dominant spice in Cypriot dishes such as *afelia* (pork sautéed with red wine and coriander seeds). Fresh coriander is used in salads, olive bread and *spanakopita* and may give its unmistakeable aroma to cooked dishes such as *giachnista*. Mint is particularly popular with meat: in *pastitsio*, for example, and in *keftedes* or meatballs. *Pastitsio* is locally called *makaronia tou fournou*, a name much more Greek than Italian.

Şeftali kebabı or *seftalia*, typically Cypriot grilled sausages wrapped in caul instead of intestines, are Turkish to judge by their name: *şeftali* means 'peach', but why this term should apply to sausages is mysterious. *Souvla*, historically a dish for special occasions, is meat marinaded, spitted and grilled over charcoal; its name is Latin (*subula* = 'spit'). Also skewered are

Lountsa

The most famous cured meat of the whole region, *lountsa* was probably introduced to Cyprus by the Venetians and was originally a useful cash product for impoverished Cypriots, made each November with the slaughtering of the family pig and sold to passing ships. The tenderloin of the pig is salted, soaked in red wine and aromatics for at least a week, stuffed inside the intestine of the animal, smoked and hung to dry out for a few months. The astonishingly aromatic meat is then served sliced as a *meze* or used in omelettes, pies or other dishes – as in this sandwich, served in Marina Cafe on Paros every day for an entire summer to two homesick Cypriots.

Cypriot Sandwich

4 thickish slices of good and sturdy white sandwich bread,
or 2 small ciabatta rolls
a little mayonnaise, enough for a slick, but not too much
1 vacuum pack Cypriot *lountsa* – or 4 thick slices of smoked
pork
a vacuum pack of *halloumi*
a ripe but firm tomato cut into rounds
piccalilli

Slice the bread and spread each slice with mayonnaise. Arrange the *lountsa* or pork slices on two of the pieces of bread, creating a nice mosaic with as few gaps as possible.

Cut the halloumi into ½-cm oblongs or a little thicker. Heat a dry, non-stick frying pan over a medium-high heat and

souvlakia – but this diminutive name is used in Greece too – whether pork, chicken, *seftalia*, *loukaniko* sausage, mushrooms or halloumi cheese – and then stuffed into or wrapped in pita.

Cyprus is great, some say, for its preserved meat: lamb and kid as *tsamarella*, perforce very salty; beef, salted and powerfully spiced, under the Turkish name *pastourma*, or sometimes turned into *loukaniko* sausages; but most notably salt pork, whose special Cypriot flavour comes from the

Lountsa and local sausages hanging outside a butcher's shop.

toast the cheese in batches, turning each piece once so that it is nicely coloured on both sides. Cover the *lountsa* with the halloumi slices and eat the leftover cheese before it gets cold and rubbery: this is the chef's portion. Top the sandwiches with the remaining bread slices, mayonnaise down.

Toast the sandwiches in a panini press, or otherwise pressed. When browned, open up, cover the bottom half with thick slices of tomato and spread the other generously with piccalilli. Gently squash back together, cut into triangular quarters and eat to the accompaniment of a cold beer. An imperial relish of Indian origin, piccalilli retains the popularity in Cyprus that it gained when Cyprus lay astride the sea routes that linked Britain with its Eastern possessions.
Serves 2

red wine in which it is marinated. *Lountsa* is made from pork tenderloin, brined, marinated in red wine, smoked and (for those who like it even stronger in flavour) aged.

Cyprus has its bulgur wheat (*pourgouri*), steamed with tomato and onion, and its *trahanas*, to which, when it is turned into soup, squares of old halloumi cheese may be added. Mediterranean trade brought salted herrings and salt cod, which was baked in outdoor ovens with potatoes

The grape harvest in 1860s Cyprus: bringing the grapes to the treading vats.

and tomatoes. Among the newer vegetables of the island, good use is made of aubergines and of the waxy Cyprus potatoes, baked, and accompanied by cumin, oregano, and sliced onion.

Of its cheeses, the best known is halloumi, a brined cheese from mixed goat and sheep milk, often sliced and grilled or fried. Aged halloumi can be grated. *Anari* is a whey cheese, either fresh and crumbly like ricotta and eaten with honey, or dry, hard and salty, grated with pasta dishes, notably *giouvetsi*, a spicy meat stew served with pasta. The island's fruit sweets and syrups are as distinctive as its *soumada*, almond spread, recorded as a gift from King Peter II of Cyprus to King Casimir of Poland in 1364, and its white pudding, *mahalepi*, flavoured with St Lucy cherry or with rosewater. Yet none of these is as proud of itself as is Commandaria fortified wine, inheritor of a medieval style and flavour that, it seems, triumphantly survived to our time while the malmsey of sixteenth-century Greece is almost forgotten. Just such a Cypriot vintage was the only wine from beyond the borders of France to achieve star billing in the early thirteenth-century French poem by Henri d'Andeli 'La Bataille des vins'. Cypriot brandy and *zivania* (an eau-de-vie of the same family as grappa and *raki*) are not so old and have only local fame.

The Wider Diaspora

Greeks have travelled by sea and established trading colonies at strategic points abroad ever since ancient times. There was a strong Greek presence, and some continuity of settled Greek communities, in Italian coastal cities from ancient and medieval times to the Renaissance. With the Ottoman conquest and in the centuries that followed, many of the Greek families who were able to travel had found safety and prosperity abroad, whether in the Balkans, Italy or Western Europe. Typically, these families retained their foothold in Greece, the islands, Smyrna or Constantinople; for most of them this was not simply exile or emigration, but more a continuation of the old trade and colonization impulses in a new political context.

So the Greek war of independence, which broke out in 1821 and resulted in international recognition of independent Greece in 1832, did not cause the modern Greek diaspora but strengthened it. Greeks of the diaspora, from their refuges abroad and with the help of political sympathizers (Lord Byron being the most notable of many), were able to offer powerful support to those in old Greece who were fighting and eventually defeated the Ottomans.

Greece and Cyprus, even when independent, have not been noted for their prosperity. From the nineteenth to the twenty-first centuries Greeks abroad have been as necessary to these homelands as ever, and geographically the diaspora now spans the world. Among the new nineteenth-century Greek 'colonies' were Alexandria and London, from both of which the liberal government of Eleftherios Venizelos drew financial and political strength in the early twentieth century. Among the greatest centres of the

An old label for the most medieval of Cypriot wines, the sweet and heavy Commandaria.

twentieth-century Greek diaspora are New York, Montreal and Sydney; it is no surprise that the most flamboyant of Alexis Tsipras's ministers in 2015 worked for many years in Sydney and has dual Australian citizenship.

'We talked about the aubergines: we talked about the *imam bayıldı*,' said Hélène Venizelos in her memoir, recalling her first meeting with her future husband. As a rich heiress in a Greek family based in Smyrna and London, she was among the hosts of a dinner given in 1913 by the London Greek community, at which Eleftherios Venizelos was guest of honour.[17] She is telling us that Greek, or at least Constantinopolitan and Smyrniot, food was served in Greek diaspora society even at the highest and most cosmopolitan level. But it was not until the second half of the twentieth century that Greek and Cypriot restaurants made their mark among non-Greek diners and gastronomes.

And then they really did. In New York the Livanos family, migrants from Greece in the 1950s who at first ran diners and restaurants of little ethnic distinction, came together in the last few years of the twentieth century with the young chef Jim Botsacos, who, though he belonged to a long-settled family of Italian and Greek origin, had so far cooked American and French. Together they created Molyvos, named after the family's town of origin (ancient Methymna on Lesbos), and it scaled the heights of culinary reputation: there is scarcely a more famous Greek restaurant anywhere.[18] They didn't hesitate to go Italian simultaneously, with Abboccato, founded in 2004 and almost equally successful; Nick Livanos is now a stalwart of the Culinary Institute of America. Michael Psilakis works harder for his publicity and reaps his reward with frequent television exposure and a Michelin star, albeit for a restaurant that closed soon afterwards.[19] The one New York Greek restaurant that has threatened to overshadow Molyvos is, in truth, Canadian: Costas Spiliadis, a Greek of Montreal, founded his first Milos in his home city and has boldly spread the Melian empire from London to Las Vegas (this without mentioning his Mediterranean yacht). Australian Greek chefs are just as ambitious, and the *Daily Telegraph*, lionizing Peter Conistis, went so far as to claim that his 'new venture Alpha is a monument to everything that's great about Greeks in Australia'. If this sounds like hyperbole, that's because it is, but Alpha is part of the Hellenic Club, whose revitalization could almost truthfully be described as 'a gift to the city from the Greek community'.[20] Conistis in Sydney and Livanos in New York belong in a history of Greek food: they have spread its reputation beyond the gastronomes, and beyond the fashionable and confused dining habits of great cities.

SIX

A Culinary Geography, Part II: Within Greece

The Greek mainland was conquered piecemeal by the Ottomans in the fifteenth century. Thessaloniki fell to them in 1430. Lesbos became an Ottoman possession soon after 1453, Rhodes not until 1522. Genoese Chios held out until 1566, its irreplaceable supply of mastic keeping Genoa prosperous all that time. Venetian Crete was not conquered by the Ottoman Empire until 1669.

The Greek mainland was reconquered as independent Greece grew step by step from south to north, beginning small and poverty-stricken in 1832. Thessaloniki remained in Ottoman hands until 1913, when it was snapped up by the Greek army. After the First World War Greece was awarded western Thrace and unwillingly had to give up hope of Constantinople.

The islands had various fates as Ottoman power declined. Rhodes and the Dodecanese underwent a strange episode of Italian rule from which they were extracted in 1947. Crete also came to the attention of foreign powers (as they called themselves) who tried weakly to oversee its autonomy and eventually in 1913 allowed Greece to take it over. As for the Ionian islands, Ottoman rule hardly touched them at all. From the medieval lordships they passed to Venice, then, in the late eighteenth century, with Napoleon's annexation of that city, to France and afterwards Britain. The British proved incompetent rulers of this unusual territory and were persuaded to give it up to independent Greece in 1864. This, then, is the piecemeal origin of modern Greece, united by its majority population, not by history, not by geography.

Ever since the fifth century BC, and indeed long before, Greece has been a landscape of extreme variation, an unending series of microclimates and microhabitats that have produced remarkably varied foods and food customs. Why does Siphnos abound in cooks? asks Patrick Leigh Fermor.

Why were the distillers of Constantinople mostly from Tsakonia?[1] No mere chapter can ask, let alone answer, all such questions, but this chapter will display some of the endless geographical variety of Greek food, largely through the eyes of medieval-to-modern observers.

IONIAN ISLANDS

We begin in the far west, with the island chain that was never part of the Ottoman Empire: Venice ruled instead. The Septinsular Republic, French and briefly Russian, gave way to the oddly named United States of the Ionian Islands, a forgotten corner of the British Empire, acquired by independent Greece in 1864. Why the British were interested will soon become clear. So the distinctive foods and drinks of the Seven Islands are in small proportion British, in large proportion Venetian, and in even larger proportion traditional and native (to each island singly, because each is different).

The Venetians and British together shifted the islands towards monoculture, with scant regard for their descendants' carbon footprint. Ever since those days Corfu is olive-green with olive trees and Kephallenia, Ithake and Zakynthos grow far more currants than any Greek islander could want. Writing of Zakynthos (Zante) George Wheler, a traveller of the late seventeenth century, explained how and why the latter trade had developed:

Two near-monocultures of the Ionian islands: the olive groves of Corfu . . .

... and the currant vineyards of Zakynthos. In the foreground the just-picked currants are drying in the sun.

This is now the chief island from whence the currans come, whereof we make so many pleasant dishes here in England. They borrowed their name from Corinth . . . They grow not upon bushes, like our red and white currans, as is vulgarly thought, but upon vines, like other grapes; only their leaf is something bigger and the grape much smaller than others . . . In August when they are ripe they are laid thin on the ground until they are dry: then are they gathered together, cleaned, brought into the town, and put into warehouses they call seraglios, into which they are poured through a hole above until the room be filled up to the top . . . When they barrel them up to send into these parts, a man getteth into the vat with bare legs and feet, and as they are brought and poured in he still keeps a stamping and treading of them down to make them lie close together . . . The English have the chief trade here, and good reason they should, for I believe they eat six times as much of their fruit as both France and Holland do. The Zantiots . . . have been persuaded that we use them only to dye cloth with, and are yet strangers to the luxury of Christmas pies, plum-potage, cake and puddings.[2]

Preparation for the olive harvest: mats are spread under the trees.

Wheler adds that Zakynthos could fill five or six vessels a year with its currants (compressed by the method that he so enticingly describes), Kephallenia three or four, and Ithake two. He notes also the olive oil produced by several of the islands, Corfu, Kephallenia and Zakynthos again, where they made an 'abundance of excellent oil, but it is not permitted to be exported by foreigners . . . only what the island can spare is sent to Venice'. As this detail shows, the olive oil monoculture, unlike that of currants, was intended purely to supply the mother city with what it needed. There was plenty of olive oil in southern Italy, but it was not under Venetian control as the Ionian islands were. Visitors to Crete, another former Venetian possession, are often told (and who would dare to argue?) that much of that island's matchless olive oil is, even now, dispatched to Italy and sold as Italian.

Long after the Venetians left, Corfu is still notable for the olive groves that they planted. The first Baedeker guide to Greece, in 1894, noticed of Corfu that 'the olive-trees, which are allowed to grow without pruning, here attain a height, beauty, and development elsewhere unparalleled in the Mediterranean, if indeed in the world. They blossom in April, and the fruit ripens between December and March.'[3] Others agree that there is no pruning, and also that the fruit is not knocked down with sticks, as was traditional elsewhere in Greece. 'Women should be beaten like an olive-tree,' one of Lawrence Durrell's mythologized informants in *Prospero's Cell* observed, 'but in Corfu neither the women nor the olive-trees are beaten – because of the terrible laziness of everyone.'[4]

These two Ionian cash crops, currants and olives, were not entirely alien to the agriculture that they replaced. There had been olives already, though not the serried rows that the Venetians planted; before the currant vine came along there had already been wine grapes, as there still are, of numerous, ancient and interesting varieties, producing a surprising range of wines untasted elsewhere. These vines are still purely local from root to fruit, because the western mainland districts of Greece and the Ionian islands beyond them have never been touched by phylloxera. So Wheler was right to say that Kephallenia was fruitful in 'excellent wines, especially muscatels (which we call Luke Sherry)' and that Zakynthos 'affords other vines that yield good, though very strong, wine . . . the red wine endures the sea very well, but the muskatels [sic], not, though they are very delicious, and in great plenty here'.[5] Corfu was also 'fertile in wine' according to Wheler and many others. Durrell's reader need not conclude, though some perhaps do, that the writer's enthusiasm for the wines of his adopted island was excessive. He found good wines at Kastellani, better still near Palaiokastritsa and near Chamos, and in the mountains 'a wine that bubbles ever so slightly; an undertone of sulphur and rock. Ask for red wine at Lakones and they will bring you a glass of volcano's blood.'[6] The description convinces Miles Lambert-Gócs, who in *The Wines of Greece* identifies this as 'a very dry red wine made from the *martzaví*', the same grape known on Leukas as *vertzamí* and the same that is called *marzemino* in Tuscany; it was surely introduced by the Venetians.[7]

Perhaps Durrell's mentor, the Armenian poet Kostan Zarian, literally did spend 'nearly two years . . . making an exhaustive study of the island wines' of Corfu.[8] There is great depth in Ionian wines, from Corfu all the way south to Zakynthos, where a poem written as early as 1601 catalogued 34 varieties, including these:

> Grapes on Zakynthos are the *kozanitis*,
> *Mygdali, fleri, razakia, chlora* and *moronitis* . . .
> Others are the very beautiful *robola* and *aïtonychi*,
> *Moschato, ambelokoritho, ftakilos* and *xyrichi* . . .
> After all those comes the *skylopnichtis*,
> But the most famous of all is the red *roïditis*.[9]

Grapes and olives were already among the fruits for which Corfu was famous 2,700 years ago, when the *Odyssey* was composed – assuming that the mythical island, Scherie, of that poem is the real Corfu. Odysseus in the orchards of Alkinoos (as quoted on page 32) saw pears, pomegranates, apples, figs, olives and grapes. In 1682 Wheler found Corfu 'fertile in wine and oil and all sorts of good fruit'. He noticed orange and lemon trees, and was given a present of large green figs, which he describes carefully, 'having in the middle a round lump of jelly, of the bigness of a nutmeg, very delicious, and refreshing in the heats of summer'.[10] After remarking on the olives and vines, the Baedeker guide of 1894 notes that 'the oranges, lemons, and figs are of excellent quality,' adding, with slight exaggeration and a silent nod to the *Odyssey*, that they 'afford several harvests in the course of the year'.[11] Durrell hears 'the oranges dropping from the trees in the orchard – dull single thuds upon the mossy ground –' and notes a 'cloud of almond-trees' and the sour cherries from which the fruit drink *vyssinada* is made.[12] Could this possibly have been the 'water with berries in it' that Prospero offered and Caliban refused on Shakespeare's fictional Adriatic island in *The Tempest*?[13]

On Zakynthos, long before, Wheler had noticed the citrons, oranges, lemons and especially the peaches, 'extraordinary good and big'. But most of all he admired 'the best mellons (I dare confidently say) in the world', whose pale green flesh 'has a perfumed taste and smell, as if they were seasoned with ambergrease'.[14]

In their cooking as well as their crops, the Ionian islands show a little British and a great deal of Italian influence. In the mid-nineteenth century, when the United Kingdom was ruling the Ionian islands, Corfu somehow became enamoured of that peculiarly British flavour, ginger beer. Edward Lear, who once wrote of himself 'He cannot abide ginger-beer,'[15] nevertheless urged a friend to visit him on Corfu and promised to feed him on 'ginger-beer and claret and prawns and figs'.[16] 'Dropping down through the silver olive-groves' of Corfu in 1937, Durrell and his friends arrived at 'a small tavern . . . where Edwardian ginger-beer, made after an Edwardian recipe, is served in little stone bottles with a marble for a cork'.[17] Its local name was, and still is, *tsitsimbira*. But Durrell's story that when William Gladstone bowed to kiss the hand of the bishop of Paxos the resulting banging of heads was soothed by a shared ginger beer . . . is apocryphal.

On these islands, *horta* – wild greens – are sautéed with paprika, garlic and tomato paste rather than plain-boiled as elsewhere. This is a richer and more complex cuisine than that of the Aegean islands. British influence is seen not only in ginger beer (to be sipped while watching a game of cricket on the esplanade at Corfu) but in a pudding or two, the bread pudding from Ithake *boutino* (but this might have travelled via

Sofrito

Sofrito is one of the traditional meat dishes of the Ionian islands. Found also in Venetian stronghold towns such as Nafplio and Monemvasia on the Peloponnese, this style of cooking, making a quick sauce in the pan with the meat juices, is uncommon elsewhere and is a direct influence of the Venetian occupation, via the bourgeoisie of these ports and islands.

4 thin veal escalopes
plain flour, enough to coat the veal
a knob of butter
2 tbsp olive oil
2 cloves garlic, crushed
white wine vinegar
stock, vegetable or light chicken
a handful of flat-leaf parsley, finely chopped
salt and pepper

Season the escalopes well on both sides and then dredge them in the flour, pressing to adhere.

Heat half of the butter and 1 tbsp oil in a large frying pan and sauté two of the escalopes until nicely coloured. Turn and continue to fry for a couple more minutes. Then remove the veal, add the rest of the butter and oil to the same pan and repeat with the rest of the meat. This ensures the meat is well browned but not cooked through.

Return all of the veal to the frying pan together with the garlic and stir gently for a minute before increasing the heat, pouring over the vinegar and stock, and bringing to the boil. Reduce the heat again, and leave to bubble for ten minutes until the sauce has reduced and thickened. Add the parsley to the veal, stir again and serve hot.

Serves 4

Italy), and the steamed pudding from Corfu, *poutinga* (a name that surely was copied from English lips). *Minestra*, a very Italian word for a soup, becomes *manestra* in these islands, a paprika-and clove-seasoned broth which on serving is sprinkled with cheese to melt over the surface, a practice uncommon elsewhere in Greece. *Pastafrola*, a thick-based jam tart with a lattice-patterned top, *pastaflora* in ordinary Greek, finds its roots in the Ionian islands – imported from Italy. *Polpettes*, the meatballs of Kephallenia and Corfu, are Italian *polpette*, 'meatballs, rissoles,' from *polpa*, 'flesh'. A cockerel or meat ragout saucing a long tubular pasta, *pastitsada*, can be compared with Italian *maccheroni pasticciati*, macaroni cooked with cheese, butter and meat gravy; it is quite different from the *pastitsio* (another Italian name) known all over Greece, the carbohydrate-lover's version of *moussaka*. As is already evident, Italian influence is found not only in dishes but in their names: the Corfiot fish soup *bourdeto*, from Italian *brodetto*, 'broth, fish soup'; pan-fried veal in a sharp sauce, *sofrito*, from Italian *soffritto*, 'lightly fried'; *stoufado*, meat or poultry stewed with onions, directly from Italian *stufato*, 'stew' (the usual word elsewhere is *stifado*). *Aliada*, the garlic sauce of the Seven Islands, the preferred relish for *bakaliaros*, salt cod, is Italian *agliata*, from *aglio*, 'garlic'.

THE PELOPONNESE

The southern third of the Greek mainland peninsula, attached to the rest by the isthmus of Corinth, was divided under the later Byzantine Empire between Greek and French rule. An imperial viceroy ruled the southeast from Mistra, near ancient Sparta, while the Latin principality of Achaea, facing westwards, had a port city, Glarentza, long since forgotten but lying not far west of Patras, a major modern port and the third city of Greece. The Peloponnese, also known by its medieval name, Morea, is a mountainous peninsula with, at its centre, the inaccessible region of Arkadia. Mindful of ancient myths such as that of the Erymanthian boar, and of classical huntsmen such as Xenophon, travellers have looked here for forests and game, and have found them. 'The best woods I saw in Peloponnesus are those of Achaia,' wrote Francis Vernon in 1676, 'abounding with pines and wild pear, ilex and esculus-trees, and, where there runs water, with plane-trees.'[18] Achaia, properly speaking, is the northern edge of the peninsula, and Erymanthos is a part of the mountain range that divides it from Arkadia. On those slopes, reported Leake in 1830, deer had become rare, but 'the roebuck (*zarkadi*) and the wild hog (*agriochoiros*) are frequently seen.'[19] Further east, at Stymphalos, where deer and hares were common, Leake paused at a spring where local people 'wait in summer to shoot the deer (*elaphia*) when they come here to drink, the other springs and waters of the mountain being then dry. My guides describe the deer as being sometimes as large as an ox, and as having long branching antlers, which are renewed every year.' His attention turned from hunting to gathering, Leake saw 'some bushes of wild gooseberry . . . with the fruit just formed; it is called *louloustida*: the children, they say, come in the season and gather the fruit.'[20] South again, and 'wild strawberries are found plentifully in the eastern Laconic mountains', east of Sparta, that is.[21]

The Peloponnese was not all woods and mountains. In 1676 Bernard Randolph had listed 'the merchandises of the Morea', including olive oil, honey, butter, cheese, raisins, currants, figs, wines, wheat, barley, rye and oats.[22] The oil, said Leake in 1830, went to Italy, just as it did from the Ionian islands. Leake adds maize and rice to Randolph's list, along with two other unexpected exports, '*kedrokouki* or juniper berries, which are sent to England' and pine nuts, harvested near Patras from 'a thick forest of *strofilia*, *Pinus pinea*, the species of pine which produces the esculent seed eaten like almonds, and often used as a substitute for them in Greek cookery'.[23] In the nineteenth century figs were typically dried and threaded onto rushes for long-distance trade, much as they were in classical times. This is still occasionally done today. The rye was grown in mountainous districts unsuited to other grain crops, and in general, throughout the peninsula, the choice of crops and the time of sowing and harvesting perforce depended on the extremely varied local geography, water resources and microclimate. Randolph was still able to give a Peloponnesian farmers' calendar, however:

> In the month of December they begin to make oil, continuing it till the beginning of March or according as the quantity of olives is. February, March and April are for making butter and cheese, also for shearing their sheep. May and June is the time for cutting their corn. In June and July they are employed in gathering mulberry leaves to feed their silkworms. August, September and October are for gathering and drying their currants, figs, raisins . . . and tobacco; also for making their wine and taking up their honey and wax.[24]

Set beside the Ionian Sea in its western coastal plain, Patras is praised by every observer of recent centuries for its gardens, which gave the place 'a very agreeable aspect' (says Leake with a sting in his tail) 'when seen at such a distance as does not betray the misery of the greater part of the habitations'.[25] Randolph, 150 years earlier, had listed orange, lemon, citron, pomegranate, apricot, peach, plum, cherry and walnut in those orchards. 'Apples and pears they have not many,' he adds:[26] in southern Greece apples find the lowlands too hot for comfort and prefer mountain villages. The citrons were among the best of the Turkish Empire, wrote Vernon, and his contemporary Wheler went at breakfast time to visit 'the garden called Glycada where those delicious citrons grow'. He describes them lovingly.

> The biggest are as large as two or three fair limons, and the white within the rind is very well tasted, but the little juice it hath in the middle is sour . . . The good man that kept the garden made us a present of oranges, limons, citrons, pomegranates and walnuts in a handsome basket covered with nosegays of violets. Whereupon, sending for bread and pitch-wine, for which Patras is celebrated, we drank our morning's draught and our friends' good healths, wishing them as good wine and cheer but not so far from their homes to drink it. The oranges here are much the same with Sevil oranges for taste and shape.[27]

Wheler's pitch-wine is, of course, retsina. The insatiable British demand for currants eventually led to widespread planting of this aberrant grape variety on the Greek mainland, especially around Patras. Increased production, dependent on trade, which could decline as easily as it could increase, led to a couple of interesting experiments. 'They sometimes make wine from them, as an experiment, but it is too rough. It can turn into very good eau-de-vie, however,' wrote Jacob Spon in 1678.[28] Any taster who has wondered whether Greek brandy was formulated in a galaxy far, far away should consider whether the explanation for its oddity is simpler: a basis of currant wine? In any case, the experimenting did not stop there. The market for Patras currants probably faltered at the moment when the enterprising Bavarian Gustav Clauss, contemporary of the brewer Johann Georg Fuchs, came to Patras to make wine and eventually created his port-and-sherry avatar Mavrodaphne. One of its constituent grapes is *mavrodaphni*; the other is *korinthiaki*, the currant.

Leake, a lateral thinker, noticed one good thing that the currant vine had done. The wine made at Patras is better than that in many other places, he argues, because although hill slopes are better for wine, lowland plains are all too easy for vine-growers. At Patras, where currants occupy the lowlands, the wine grapes are perforce planted 'on the rugged hills', where Leake tasted wine 'which was not inferior to port'.[29] It must have been the traditional, pre-Clauss *mavrodaphni*; those who want to taste its like today must find the Mavrodaphne of Kephallenia if they can.

The southwestern quarter of the Peloponnese is the ancient region of Messenia. Here in the Mycenaean period was the palace of Nestor, or, at least, a vast ruined palace so called by archaeologists. Here in classical times was the port of Methoni, a Venetian outpost whose medieval name was Modon. Pilgrim ships put in here on their way to the Holy Land. It was a good place for food: 'Bread and meat are cheap,' according to a narrative of 1480, 'but the wine is so pitchy as to be undrinkable.'[30] The table wines were indeed resinated, as Pietro Casola confirms a decade later: 'The wines are made strong by the addition of resin during the fermentation, which leaves a very strange aroma which I dislike: they say that the wines would not keep otherwise.'[31] Felix Faber, a contemporary, described the local trade in pork:

> The people from the galleys buy them, kill them, singe off the bristles, discard the heads and intestines, cut out and reject the bones from the meat. They keep only the bacon, and they put all the fat from two or three pigs into the gutted body of one, seal up the belly firmly with a needle, and take it back to their galleys and back home to Venice . . . Sausages are also plentiful there: they are sold by the cubit.[32]

There was veal, beef, mutton; there was chicken, but expensive; there were figs, plums and above all oranges, plentiful and cheap. 'Anyone can buy a basketful of good quality oranges for five or six marks, 20 or 30 for a denarius. The galleys were full of these fruits: everyone bought a basket for himself, even we pilgrims,' writes Faber, though he did not know why this fruit was so valuable to those on a long voyage.[33]

Two great medieval wines were exported from Modon. One style was malmsey; the other was known in trade as *vin de Romanie*, Rumney wine or Rumney of Modon. The pilgrims describe them lovingly, making no link between these and the table wine they disliked. 'What shall I say of the wine that is made there?', writes Faber again. 'I take pleasure even in thinking about it.'³⁴

Another Venetian enclave, Koroni, once exported olive oil. Modon and Koroni are now both insignificant in trade, supplanted by Kalamata, the city at the head of the Gulf of Messenia which was already a major centre in the early nineteenth century. Leake describes a fair every Sunday at which maize, wheat, barley, oil, figs, cheese and butter, cattle and other livestock, produced locally, were sold. The figs, 'inferior only to those of Smyrna,' were packed in *tzapeles*, small wicker baskets.³⁵ Half of them were exported to Trieste, a shipload a year to Malta, the remainder to Greece and Albania. It is surprising to find no mention of olives, since the name of Kalamata is now synonymous worldwide with fine, fat, purple olives, harvested young

Olives for sale at a city market. In the left foreground are *tsakistes*, harvested green, 'smashed' and flavoured with garlic and herbs. You can almost taste the *freskies glykopikrides*, 'fresh bitter-sweet', to their right. These, like others further back, come from the Chalkidiki peninsula of Macedonia. Some others again, red-brown in colour, are from Kalamata in the Peloponnese: *psiles*, slim and cheap, to the left, and *hondres*, big, fat, unbearably succulent, the most expensive of all, over to the right.

and quickly cured. But olive oil is rightly mentioned: there was good oil from the Mani peninsula, exported via Kalamata to Russia and Italy.

The best oil of the region came to Kalamata from around Mistra and Sparta in Lakonia, the southeastern Peloponnesian region, not far distant from Kalamata though separated from it by Mount Taygetos. West and south one comes to the old fortified port Monemvasia, the same that gave its name to malmsey wines; the sweet wine tradition, long dormant here, is at last being revived. Northward is the mountainous district of Tsakonia, origin of several families of distillers. Northward again, Nauplion (Nafplio, briefly the capital of Greece) is noted for *tsakistes*, 'smashed' green olives flavoured with garlic and herbs, quite different from those of Kalamata. In this same northeast Peloponnesian region, around Nemea to the south of Corinth, some of the best red wine of Greece is made. The variety, *agiorgitiko*, 'St George's', is very local and apparently very old.

Returning to the far south, not far on from Kalamata but endowed with all the mystery of remoteness for everyone else, traditional and fiercely independent, rocky, barren and proud of it, the Mani peninsula is Greece to an extreme. The antiquarian Cyriac of Ancona, who visited in the fourteenth century, observed an event that might as well have been described by Pausanias more than a millennium earlier:

> They showed me a place bounded by natural stones where every year the young men engage by ancient custom in a competition, for which their prince provides the prizes: a men's footrace over a distance of five furlongs, which they run barefoot, dressed only in a linen tunic. Whoever comes in first is given ten bronze *hyperpera*, and after that all the others, in order of finishing, a little cash or a quantity of goat meat. None goes unrewarded – the prince gives an onion to the last-comer, which makes him the object of mockery.[36]

The Mani had few visitors in the six centuries between Cyriac and Leake, or, at least, few wrote about it. Those youths who raced were lucky: there was little meat in the daily diet. 'Except on the great feasts, none but the richest . . . kill mutton or poultry: an old ox no longer fit for the plough, or a sheep or fowl already at the point of death, they sometimes indulge in.'[37] Cheese and garlic, beans, 'lean wheat' and maize bread were the principal foods, said Leake, adding, though, that the produce of one coastal village was quails and 'Frank figs' or prickly pears; this cactus was grown round the villages for the sake of the fruit. A few figs and grapes and some vegetables were all that the gardens produced. Women sowed and harvested the wheat: they 'collect the sheaves at the thrashing floor, winnow it with their hands, and thrash it with their feet, and thus their hands and feet are covered with a dry cracked skin, as thick as the shell of a tortoise'.[38] There was no flowing water; farms and villages had cisterns for rainwater, with 'an arched covering of stone, with a little wooden door kept constantly locked'.[39] Life was hard, but Leake's hosts did not complain. They boasted of the sweetness of their mutton, and that they could sometimes sell wheat to Kythera and cattle at Kalamata, and that when things went well they needed to buy nothing but wine and cheese. Besides oil, they exported the famous honey of the Mani:

> The hives are made of four slates set up on the edges, with other pieces for the roofs and floors. In some of the stands there are eight or ten hives in a row, and two or three stories of hives, so that at a distance the structure looks like a wall built of very large stones: the junction of the slates is cemented with plaster.[40]

There was one other export: 'Salted quails, put into bags of lamb-skin, are carried to Constantinople and the Islands.'[41] This was a famous resource. From at least the fifteenth century, when pilgrim narratives mention it, quails on their annual migration have rested on rocky coasts in the Mani and the offshore island of Kythera before and after their crossing of the Mediterranean. More than anywhere else they gather at a remote rocky harbour and headland near Cape Matapan known by its Italian name, Porto delle Quaglie, 'Port of the Quails'. It lent its name to a nearby monastery, where, as we shall see later, Leake was rewarded for his difficult journey with agreeable lodging, a salad for his dinner, and the finest Maniate honey.

ATHENS

Greatest city of ancient Greece, cultural centre of Roman Greece, backwater of the Ottoman Empire, capital of independent Greece since 1834, the now vast and untidy metropolis of Athens is, unavoidably, the centre of the Greek food trade. At the city's centre rises its Central Market, where the fish is as varied and as highly prized as it was in Athens as known to Archestratos and the comic poets in the fourth century BC. The great covered market was built in 1886. Crowded from dawn until mid-afternoon, it houses butchers and fishmongers in all their rich

Athens before the Central Market was dreamed of. The Bazaar of Athens, as painted by
the Irish artist Edward Dodwell in 1821. The viewpoint is just outside what is now
Monastiraki metro station.

variety, jostling with other food trades, many of which also cluster in
colonies in the surrounding streets, which are busy day and night: fruit
and vegetables close at hand, dried fruits, cheese, oils, salt meats and
salt fish, herbs, spices and much else.

Athens to early modern travellers was a leisurely provincial town, but
even then 'all sorts of provisions are good cheap here, whether corn, wine,
oil, mutton, beef, goat's flesh, fish or fowl; especially partridges and hares
are in great abundance here', wrote Wheler in 1682.[42] Randolph added
that the town was surrounded by small villages, 'where are very pleasant
gardens which afford all sort of fruit and saleting, having walks round
them covered with vines'. The red grapes, he continued, 'are not ripe till
September, then they cut them off and hang them up in their houses for
winter'.[43] These were the table grapes of seventeenth-century Athens, while
Randolph's 'saleting' is salad greens.

The local wine of Attike, the region of which Athens is the capital, is
retsina. This was already the best retsina in Greece in the 1930s, when Patrick
Leigh Fermor was promised a fine meal with 'some retsina you'll like . . . a
whole demijohn from Spata in Attica . . . I've put a couple of bottles in the
well to get cold.'[44] He knew *why* it was the best, attributing its quality to the
closeness of the vineyards to the pine forests of Attica and southern Euboia.[45]
Retsina was already appreciated 250 years earlier, when Wheler admitted

Hare or Rabbit

Lagos in Greek means hare, which was a popular game meat in classical times. The physician Anthimos gives an early Byzantine recipe with early health advice attached:

> Hares, if they are quite young, can be eaten with a sweet sauce including pepper, a little cloves and ginger, seasoned with costus and spikenard or bay leaf. Hare is an excellent food, good in cases of dysentery, and its bile can be taken, mixed with pepper, for earache.[46]

> Hare is still a good catch for hunters, but rabbit (unknown in ancient Greece) is now common, and *lagoto*, literally 'stewed hare', in the world of supermarkets and meat counters has become stewed farmed rabbit or, commoner still, pork. Only the name remains the same.

> The use of vinegar may be ancient or it may be the Balkan influence of the Arvanites, the southern Albanian settlers who migrated in the fourteenth to seventeeth centuries to Thessaly and the Peloponnese.

that 'their wine also is very good here, but they put a little pitch in it to preserve it, which is not very pleasant until one is used to it.'[47] The retsinas of Attike, of Boiotia to the northeast and of the big island of Euboia to the northwest now enjoy separate 'district' appellations, with many tiny 'area' appellations including Spata, but the best retsina is the retsina you like best.

An alien, north European beverage threatened the popularity of local retsina in newly independent Athens under its first monarch, Bavarian Otto. The story of this introduction begins with Adolph von Schaden, whose little book of 1833 encouraged Bavarians to follow their prince and set up in business in Greece, noting incidentally that although there was no Bavarian beer to refresh a thirsty Teuton, there was at least Italian beer and English porter. That was soon no longer true: by the late 1830s Athens had a beer garden, *Zum grünen Baum* ('The Green Tree'), complete with stone tankards and noisy German drinking songs. 'How necessary it is to

Stewed hare is given a Cretan flavour in Nikos Kazantzakis's novel *Freedom and Death* (1953). Captain Michales (a character based on the author's father) rides to overcome his despair for Crete under Turkish occupation:

He felt hungry and dismounted at the widow's inn. The owner came – a gay, capable widow, rank and fat. She smelt cool, of onions and caraway seeds. Captain Michales looked past her: he did not like coquettish women, waggers of buttocks . . .

'We don't see you often!' said the widow, and winked at him artfully. 'If you're not fasting, I've hare stewed with fresh onions and caraway seeds.'

She bent down to get him a dismounting-stool, and the cleft of her hospitable bosom was visible, downy and cool.

'You should eat meat, Captain Michales,' she said, giving him another wink. 'You're on a journey, and it's no sin.'

the Bavarian's soul,' a German professor wisely observed, 'that even here, on the edge of the Orient, he can get his native beer.'[48] The next step followed in 1850. Johann Georg Fuchs, son of a Bavarian mining engineer, noted the rapidly spreading popularity of this un-Greek beverage and began to brew it himself. In 1864 his son Johann Ludwig built a big brewery at Kolonaki in what were then the outskirts of Athens, and captured the national market with the help of a royal warrant and a monopoly. The brand name Fix, the Greek form of the ancestral surname Fuchs, is conveniently memorable (and has been rescued from disappearance at least twice). The monopoly having been lost, a family quarrel resulted in the founding of the rival Alpha brewery by Karolos Ioannou Fix, Johann Ludwig's third son. Among Greeks there are faithful followers of each brand; foreigners in Greece find it harder to distinguish them, but also find it hard to live without beer. In the 1930s the Bristolian professor Humphrey Kitto carefully recorded

Lagoto – *Peloponnesian Rabbit*

1 rabbit, cut into eight pieces

1½ tbsp tomato purée

a pinch of sugar

a small cinnamon stick, a bay leaf, a couple of cloves

250 g shelled walnuts, roughly chopped

250 ml good olive oil

3 slices stale sourdough bread, crusts removed

60 ml red wine vinegar

60 ml dry red wine

4–6 cloves garlic, to taste

salt and pepper

Wipe the rabbit pieces well. Heat a little of the oil in a large casserole pan and brown the rabbit, in batches.

Return all the meat to the pan together with the tomato purée and a pinch of sugar, and pour in enough water to just cover. Add the spices, bring to the boil then turn down the heat, cover and leave to simmer for 30–40 minutes.

While the rabbit cooks, wet the bread and squeeze it dry. Put it into the bowl of a food processor and, with the motor running, pour in the oil slowly, then the vinegar and the wine. When it is all incorporated, add the garlic and walnuts and process until you get a textured but homogeneous paste.

When the rabbit is tender and the pan juices good and savoury, pour in the bread-walnut paste and tilt and swirl the pan to distribute. Leave to heat through and serve, hot or warm, with sautéed potatoes or *chilopites* – wide egg noodles common throughout Greece but a speciality of the Peloponnese.

Serves 4

that Megalopolis in Arkadia 'is supplied with the admirable Fix beer from Athens'. Ancient Greeks had been known to boast that they were 'men, not drinkers of a barley brew',[49] but those, Kitto observed, were the days before Herr Fuchs and his brewery. 'Those towns in Greece where ice-cold Fix can be got should be marked on the maps in red,' he advised.[50]

Another great local product is, as it was two thousand years ago, the honey of Mount Hymettos. It has the colour of naphtha, the Turkish traveller Evliya Çelebi begins unattractively, but is so fragrant that it suffuses the brain with the odour of pure ambergris and musk.[51] More adventurous in this case than Çelebi, Wheler visited the beekeepers and describes how they made their hives ' like our common dust baskets, wide at the top, and narrow at the bottom', plastered with clay inside and out, with flat sticks laid across the top to which the bees attached their combs. The swarms were artificially divided in spring, says Wheler, by moving some of the sticks to new baskets. The combs on the outermost sticks of each hive were harvested in August, leaving the innermost to feed the bees in winter. The method required no smoke, a rare thing in Wheler's time, and so the honey had no flavour of smoke and the bees were not injured by sulphur.[52]

As the capital and for a long time the only considerable city of independent Greece in the late nineteenth and early twentieth centuries, Athens, if anywhere, was where restaurants were able to flourish. Always modest, and no worse for it, is the Damigos family taverna, Bakaliarakia, occupying a basement room in the heart of Plaka, under the almost equally venerable Brettos distillery. Bakaliarakia was founded in 1864 and named after its staple Norwegian salt cod, and what else should the wine be if not Attic from Mesogia, the neighbourhood of Athens? It is surrounded now by other restaurants – Plaka is full of them – but similarly modest establishments with almost equally venerable histories are few: Platanos and Psaras both not far away, Ideal near the university, Sigalas further off but worth finding in Keramikos.

Historic photographs surround the diners at Bakaliarakia. So they do at Athinaikon, though this has become a far more grandiose establishment than the modest *ouzeri* that was founded in 1932 and the respectable *ouzomezedopoleio* 'ouzo-and-mezedes tavern' that succeeded it. Vassilenas in Piraeus, founded in or about 1920, has likewise transferred a long history into a handsome new interior, its prices raised to match, its food said to be none the worse.[53] As for Dionysos, founded in the early 1960s, it has been from the beginning as proud of its architecture as of its cuisine: the view of the Akropolis is stunning and much admired by the international politicians who eat there. Some newer establishments draw on the style and substance of the international Greek restaurant circuit and look the part; others, following a more traditional pattern, bring regional and island cookery to the ever-greedy capital, which thrives on it. The restaurant business in Athens naturally reflects the increasing mobility of Greeks, generation after generation, yet it lives on the family links that they retain. Because of these links the food and wine of all Greek regions, from Thrace and Epiros to Crete and the Dodecanese, and from the diaspora, can be found in the big city by those who look patiently.

CENTRAL GREECE

Travelling west of Athens and crossing the mountains, one reaches the north shore of the gulf of Corinth, where Leake wandered among foothills 'clothed with oaks and planes, festooned with wild vines', where carob and Christ's thorn, covered in blossom, were 'mixed with the aromatic shrubs with which Greece so eminently abounds, and peopled with nightingales singing in the deep shade'.[54] West again, overlooking the gulf from a considerable height, is the ancient sacred site of Delphi, which Francis Vernon is said to have been the first of modern travellers to discover and identify. He found it 'very strangely situated on a rugged hill', high above the sea but far below the peak of Parnassos. 'It seems very barren to the eye, but the fruits are very good . . . the wines are excellent, and the plants and simples which are found there very fragrant and of great efficacy.'[55] Vernon's 'plants' are wild greens as food; his 'simples' are medicinal herbs, the two categories overlapping for him as they would have done in ancient times. Vernon might have noted sheep's milk cheeses, *formaella* and feta. His wines, local to Delphi, were the wines of Arachova in eastern Boiotia, once excellent, now hard to find: Arachova has turned its attention to olive oil, and there are fine olives from nearby Amphissa.

Far to the west again, north of Patras and looking out across the Ionian Sea to Ithake and Kephallenia, are a series of towns on the western Greek coast, significant for food and in trade, occasionally prominent in history. Byron died at Mesolongi in 1824, too young to see Greece regain the independence for which he had romantically struggled, too early to experience the horrors, the famine, the cannibalism of the siege in 1826.[56] Octavian defeated Mark Antony and Cleopatra at Actium in 31 BC, founding, in a sense, the Roman Empire; founding also the town of Nikopolis ('city of victory') named below. Not far east at Lepanto, whose proper Greek name is Naupaktos, the Europeans (some of them) defeated the Turks, ensuring that the Ionian islands would remain securely outside the Ottoman Empire.

The ancient Greek city at the strategic southwestern corner of the mainland was Kalydon. It was hardly famous, yet according to the

Botargo (*avgotaracho*), grey mullet roe, prepared at Mesolongi, where Byron died and the best Greek botargo is produced.

geographer Strabo it was 'once a showpiece of Greece' and a regular fair was held there.[57] Archestratos, the gastronomic poet, mentions Kalydon more often than almost any other city, and it is tempting to wonder whether, in a lost passage of his poem, he might have praised (or vituperated) the great marine delicacy that is traditionally produced on this coast, the salted, conserved roe of the grey mullet, known to gastronomes as botargo.

It is made, writes the sixteenth-century ichthyologist Ludovicus Nonnius, 'from the eggs of the grey mullet commonly called *cephalus* in their two neat sacs, mixed with the blood of the same fish and with salt'.[58] The making of botargo is described by Leake, who encountered the manufacture at a small Greek seaport ('the Forty Saints'), which is now Saranda in Albania, close to the ruins of the Graeco-Roman city of Buthrotum. His host's house, at once customs office, fish shop and smokery, was notable for its odour:

> At one end is a hearth, but no chimney, the smoke serving, as it effects its escape through the tiles, to cure the botargo, or roes of the mullet, which, enclosed in the natural membrane as extracted from the fish, are suspended to the rafters, and after the smoking will be dipped in melted wax. The *kephalos* is produced in abundance in all the lagoons and lakes of Greece,

Spetsofaï *from Mount Pelion*

Spetzes (literally 'spices') are the Pelion dialect word for the small hot peppers so popular in northern Greek and Balkan cuisine. Originally they would have been the main ingredient of the simple peasant dish called *spetsofaï*. Gradually, as tastes and lifestyles have changed, meat has been used in larger pro-portions, in this case the cumin- and paprika-spiced sausages of Thessaly. In shepherd communities mutton would be the sausage filling, but pork is now usual.

Spetsofaï is one of the better-known Greek dishes outside the country, and one of the few that use sausages as a com-ponent. (Greek sausages are flavoursome enough to need no accompaniment other than lemon and bread to mop up the fatty, savoury and lemon-spiked juices). This recipe makes enough for four people, with bread and a wedge of hard yellow cheese like *kefalograviera* and perhaps a shredded lettuce salad, or for more than four as one among several *mezedes*.

Spetsofaï, named after the chilli peppers ('spices') that give the dish its bite.

Spetsofaï

olive oil

500 g sausages (if not Greek, perhaps Italian or even
merguez)

1 large onion, sliced

4 sweet red peppers, cut into thick strips

1 small red chilli, chopped, with seeds removed if preferred
— or a good pinch of chilli flakes

3 small ripe tomatoes, coarsely grated (plum tomatoes would
be ideal)

a pinch of sugar

salt, pepper, cumin and a little paprika

In a large frying pan, heat a slick of oil (not too much, because
the sausages should be fatty enough) and fry the sausages till
coloured nicely and mostly cooked through. Remove them
from the pan, leaving behind the oil and sausage fat. Put the
pan back on the heat and fry the onion, peppers and chilli over
a lowish heat until they have softened and the water released
from the peppers has evaporated.

Add the tomatoes, the sugar and the other seasonings to
taste, and cook until the sauce thickens. Slice the sausages into
thick, bite-sized chunks and return them to the pan to finish
the cooking. *Spetsofaï* should be eaten hot from the pan.

---

which like that of Buthrotum have a communication with the
sea; and the botargo is a great resource to the Greeks during the
severer fasts, when only a bloodless fish diet is allowed.[59]

Botargo today still comes in the same yellow wax coating. As Leake
explains in a footnote, the name derives via Byzantine Greek *augotari-
chon* from an ancient Greek term that meant literally 'pickled eggs'. The
exact ancient term is not recorded, but there is a hint of it in Coptic, the
language of medieval Egypt, in which botargo is *butarikh*, a term clearly
borrowed from Greek; and another hint of it in Athenaios, who quotes
a dietary writer asserting that 'salt fish roe', *ta ton tarichon oa*, is hard to

digest.[60] So it may be, but, believe me, it's well worth the trouble. Slice the botargo paper-thin, Diane Kochilas advises, and peel off the wax. Sprinkle, perhaps, with freshly ground pepper, a drizzle of olive oil, a little fresh lemon juice. That's all.[61]

Among the harbours on this northwestern coast, between Mesolongi and lost Kalydon to the south and now-Albanian Saranda to the north, is Preveza, forgotten today, once a Venetian possession. It always had a rural air, the houses dispersed over a large area, each with a garden and orchard attached containing fig, walnut and apricot trees and culinary herbs. Apart from botargo, olive oil used to be the main export, as at so many Venetian harbours: it went to feed the insatiable Italian market. 'The best oil is made from olives gathered by hand,' Leake reports, 'though these do not yield half so much in quantity as the fruit which falls from the tree.' Wheat and barley were not sown under the olive trees for fear of exhausting the soil and injuring the crop; 'Vines are supposed not to have the same effect, and are sometimes planted among the trees.' Fish is plentiful and good, as it had already been in Archestratos' time, along this coast, in the gulf of Ambrakia, and in the coastal lagoons as far south as Mesolongi:

> Shell-fish, eels, and grey mullet, are caught – the two latter in the lagoon of Nicopolis. Of shell-fish there is an inexhaustible supply in the shallows around the strait and near the town; a great quantity of these is sent to the islands in the time of Lent. Occasionally also an immense number of eels from the lagoons of Arta suddenly make their appearance in the harbour of Prevyza. This...probably occurs only when in migrating to the sea from their breeding-places in the rivers and lagoons of the gulf they meet with a storm.[62]

Northern Greece

Northern Greece, west of the Pindos mountain spine, is very different from the centre and south. Hills and mountains are not absent, notably Olympos and Pelion along the Aegean coast, but this is in large part wheat and cattle country. It once housed a seemingly inextricable mixture of peoples: Greeks in the Thessalian plain and along the northern coast; southern Slavs (Bulgarians and Macedonians) immediately inland; Turks and other Muslims in considerable numbers; Vlachs or Aromunians on the Pindos slopes and northeastwards. Thessaloniki, now the metropolis of the Greek north, was once a great Jewish city and at the same time the cradle of the Young Turk movement: Atatürk, founder of the modern Turkish state, was born there in 1881.

Thessaly, prehistoric and classical and modern, bred cattle. Ancient Thessalians, fairly or unfairly, were famous as heavy, dull beef-eaters, and one of the favourite everyday dishes of modern Thessaly is tripe, of which there is plenty wherever there are plenty of cattle. The most typical product of the Pelion region is the sausage-based *spetsofaï*, whose main ingredient is traditionally the *loukaniko* sausage of Pelion, made of mutton or goat meat. But there are other products too. Tyrnavos is noted for its ouzo and for its wild annual carnival, at which no small quantity of ouzo is consumed (see page 257).

Farsala above all is the place for halva. Its special version of this Middle Eastern sweet is celebrated with an annual festival and sold at fairs and markets all over Thessaly under the names *farsalinos, panigiriotikos* (fairground halva) and *sapoune*, with a nod to its soapy texture. With its cornflour basis, Farsala halva is indeed different from the two better-known styles of halva, both of them already popular in early modern Constantinople: the light, sweet cake-like confection made from semolina and the heavier, almost crunchy block based on sesame, which is the best-known halva internationally.

In the northern mountains that divide Thessaly from Macedonia is Siatista, praised in the nineteenth century for its mutton, 'fed on the delicate herbage of this limestone mountain', and for its abundance of game, notably hares, 'so numerous, that when the snow lies upon the vineyards . . . it is a common custom to go in pursuit of them without dogs, and to kill them with sticks, half famished as they then are, and unable to run.'[63] Siatista was once a great wine-producing district, in spite of winter snows and unpredictable autumns. This was 'some of the best wine in Rumili', according to Leake, though mostly sold locally in Thessaly and Macedonia. The stoniest soils were said to produce the best wine; as elsewhere, a dry year would reduce the quantity but improve the quality. He most admired the *elioumeno* or 'sun-dried' wine from white and red grapes that were 'left for eight days in the sun, or for six weeks in a covered building, after which the produce is a white sweet wine of strong body and high flavour':

> The Siatistans keep their wines three, four, five years, and sometimes more. Each considerable proprietor has a wine-press, and there are cellars under all the larger houses, exhibiting the agreeable spectacle of butts arranged in order, as in civilized Europe.

The 'sour black' Xynomavro grape variety, as used for Siatista and some other
northern Greek red wines.

Siatista also produced a wine called *apsithino*, flavoured with wormwood, which was 'laid among the grapes when placed in the press. This
wine is sweet and high flavoured, but not the better for the wormwood.'[64]
Leake might have said exactly the same of Martini, had he known it,
because what he is describing is vermouth. The wine-cellars of Siatista can
still be admired, says Miles Lambert-Gócs; the 'sun-dried' wine described
by Leake is still made but not marketed. It is a version of *liasto* or raisin
wine, and among the finest in Greece:

> Well-ripened grapes are spread in the sun for about a week, or
> else in airy rooms for about six weeks. The grapes are crushed and
> passed through pouches of clean goat's wool. The must is then put
> to ferment in small casks, sometimes of chestnut and sometimes
> of *robolo*, a local pine-wood – although it does not give a piny
> flavour to *liasto*. After ten to fifteen days, the casks are closed and
> fermentation goes on for a further twenty-five to thirty days, at
> which time cold weather intervenes to impede the progress of
> the yeasts until about May the following year. Fermentation then
> recommences, and is allowed to come to a halt naturally when
> the wine has reached 15–16% alcohol.[65]

As Lambert-Gócs observes, the common modern name *liasto* has the
same literal meaning as Leake's *elioumenon*, 'sunned'. The process that gives
the wine its name, the partial sun-drying, is very ancient: Hesiod described
it around 700 BC. The season he prescribes, speaking of a much warmer
site in central Greece, is mid-September:

When Orion and Sirius reach the middle of the sky,
And rosy-fingered Dawn observes Arcturus,
Then, Perses, bring your grape harvest in.
You must show them to the sun ten days and ten nights;
For five more, shade them; on the sixth
Draw off into jars the gifts of joyous Dionysus.[66]

The principal grape variety of Siatista is the northern Greek classic Xynomavro, 'sour black'. It's better than it sounds, and is also the main variety in the flourishing Naoussa district, not very far off, northeast of Kozani and west of Thessaloniki, where the wines are still most reliably and classically good.

Another resource of rural Macedonia, hardly familiar in most of southern Greece, is its freshwater fish. The great rivers of the north are rich in them: long ago at Neolithic Kryoneri, on the banks of the Strymon, grey mullet were taken alongside carp, tench, catfish (*Silurus glanis*) and eels, and the descendants of these eels were still admired and enjoyed in classical times. At that period lake Volvi (Bolbe), dividing the Greek peninsula of Chalkidiki from the Macedonian hinterland, was famous for its perch. More recently lake Kastoria and the Prespes lakes on the Albanian border, remote and hardly familiar to classical Greeks, have been renowned for carp, tench, eel and catfish, and the Macedonian river Aliakmon for its trout.

In much of this northern region of Greece travellers have been conscious, more than elsewhere, of the mountain peoples as quite distinct from the Greeks of the lowlands. Some have been seasonal transhumant pastoralists and some still are, most especially in the northwestern region

River fish for sale at Thessaloniki market.

189

Milk: From Shepherds to City-dwellers

In a goat-herding community, *galatopita* was an economical treat. Some recipes want filo (*phyllo*) pastry as cover or wrapping. If the milk is good and sweet enough the filo is not necessary, but it makes the pieces easily transportable — useful to shepherds.

Other recipes substitute wheat flour for semolina, but in the mountains of Macedonia cornmeal is what was available. Sometimes a simple sugar syrup, perhaps flavoured with orange or lemon, is poured over the pie while it is still warm from the oven, making it more luxurious, and in modern times vanilla is widely used as a flavouring. 'Galakto pastries make a tasty breakfast treat but are also served by Greek Jews after special dairy meals, such as on Shavuot, when the rectangular shape of individual small pies resembles the stone tablets of the law that Moses formed on Mount Sinai,' writes Gil Marks.[67]

A similar recipe is used (often without eggs) for the cream filling in *bougatsas*, popular in Serres and Thessaloniki and available all over Greece. *Bougatsa* is literally the filo (it is Turkish *poğaça* which in turn comes from Latin *panis focacius*, 'oven bread', via Italian *foccacia*) because originally there was no filling, and still today the filo is as important as what is inside. The cream

of Epeiros. Apart from their back-and-forth spring and autumn migrations, they have driven their herds and flocks over very long distances for sale to city-dwelling eaters of meat. They have ways with milk. And they have been prominent in the political and commercial development of independent Greece.

Already in the mid-sixteenth century Pierre Belon, crossing the Strymon by the road bridge that carried the ancient Via Egnatia, encountered 'shepherds who were roasting whole sheep, except the head, to sell to travellers':

> They had spitted them on willow poles, having taken out the entrails and sewn up the belly. No one who did not see it would believe that such a huge mass of flesh could be cooked by roasting ... These shepherds cut up the mutton when it was cooked and sold the pieces to travellers. We camped under the willows at the end of the bridge,

filling is most widespread, though in the north *bougatsas* are also sold with a cheese or a minced meat filling, which would be called *tyropita* or *kreatopita*, 'cheese pie, meat pie', elsewhere. Most shops now use mass-produced filo but the best *bougatsas* use handmade filo; skilled bakers make their filo by holding it by the edges and throwing it repeatedly as though it were a fishing net, enlarging the dough sheet each time.[68]

Context is everything. *Bougatsa* is to be eaten with a small fork on the way to work, standing in a breakfast bar, drinking coffee, watching the morning news and discussing the latest tax increases and wage cuts with friends. There is no better city breakfast.

Galaktoboureko, a Greek custard pie, its name half-Turkish and half-Greek, its historical origin still uncertain.

to rest our horses, and bought some of this meat, which we found tastier than if it had been cooked in pieces.[69]

So there was nothing strange in the fact that shepherds and sheepdogs from the Greek and Balkan mountains took part with all the rest in the great procession of the guilds at Constantinople – shepherds who looked on their dogs as companions and did not mind eating out of the same dish.[70] There was nothing strange in Leake's observation at the Aitolian town of Stratos of a drove of three hundred Wallachian oxen, every one of which was white, passing through 'to be shipped for the Islands'. They had travelled all the way from southern Romania, but in addition large herds and flocks were brought every year from the Pindos mountains to feed through the winter in the plains of Akarnania and Aitolia.[71] Soon afterwards Leake was exploring those mountains, and near Syrrako, a Vlach

Galatopita – *Milk Pie*

750 ml fresh milk (a mix of cows' and goats' milk if you like)
225 g caster sugar
150 g fine semolina
100 g butter, cubed, plus extra for greasing
finely grated zest of one small orange
2 eggs
ground cinnamon

Preheat the oven to 180°C and butter a 20 cm by 30 cm dish.

In a saucepan, heat the milk and sugar. As it reaches boiling point, pour in the semolina in one go, stirring with a wooden spoon. Continue to stir and cook the mix until it thickens slightly. Remove from the heat and add the butter, using a whisk to combine. Then add the eggs one at a time, whisking well, and the orange zest. Pour the mixture into the buttered dish and bake for 30 minutes, until a thin crust has formed and it is browned and set.

Leave to cool before cutting into squares or diamond-shaped pieces and sprinkling with cinnamon. Serve at room temperature, preferably the same day, or store in the fridge.

township, found himself 'suddenly in a thick forest of linden, maple, cherry, horse-chestnut, oak, elm, ash, beech, sycamore, and hornbeam, mixed with cornel, holly, elder, hazel, and a variety of plants of lower growth'. At the foot of a steep descent was a rushing stream, a tributary of the Arachthos, with deep pools abounding in trout 'most commonly taken by means of quicklime thrown into the head of the pool, which soon brings the intoxicated fish to the surface'.[72]

The Vlachs speak a language akin to Romanian, and Leake elsewhere gives a sentence (taught him by Greeks) to demonstrate the 'vocality' of this language: *oáo aué oí auá*, which, as he explains, corresponds to Greek *auga staphylia probata edo*, 'I eat eggs, grapes, sheep.' Using these words a party of Albanian or Greek shepherds could order a dinner when arriving at a Vlach village.[73] But not all of Greece's modern transhumant

Sweet Bougatsa

1 litre creamy milk
180 g semolina
200g sugar
3 tbsp butter, cut into cubes
6 sheets filo pastry
melted butter
icing sugar and ground cinnamon, for dusting

Heat the milk, semolina and sugar in a pan and when thick add the butter. Beat well and don't allow the mixture to boil. Leave it to cool down completely: it should be thick enough to spread.

Brush a sheet of filo with butter, then lay another sheet over it. Spread the cream filling on the centre of the filo in a rectangle. Fold the edges over to cover the filling as though wrapping a present. Repeat this process with another two sheets, and then again, until the *bougatsa* is a neat package. Brush the top liberally with more butter and bake at 180°C for 30–40 minutes. Petros at Dodoni in Thessaloniki takes them out of the oven when they are nearly done and pricks them all over with the point of a sharp knife.

Remove from the oven and leave to cool a little before cutting into four pieces. Dust with icing sugar and cinnamon and serve cut into small squares.

Dodoni, probably the best place to get Thessaloniki's favourite breakfast.

The city market at Thessaloniki, second only to that of Athens.

Among the dried beans at the Thessaloniki market, side by side, are seen chickpeas and lentils from Drama; behind them, purple kidney beans and white *gigantes*, 'giant beans', from Prespes; behind these, imported rice. Apart from the rice, no imports are visible.

pastoralists were Vlach. The Greek-speaking Sarakatsani, among whom Patrick Leigh Fermor was invited to a wedding feast in Thrace in the 1930s, had a similar nomadic lifestyle.[74] The description has reminiscences of the dinners in the *Odyssey* (which Leigh Fermor knew well):

> Low circular tables, all ready laid with glasses and with communal dishes of roast and steaming lamb skilfully hacked from the carcases turning outside and sprinkled with rock salt, were being moved in and wedged among the company ... glass jugs of wine were beginning to travel from hand to hand overhead ... we could

hear the crash of cleaver on block and the crunch of hewn bones as a sinewy nomad toiled like a headsman to keep pace with two hundred magnificent appetites. Nothing accompanied this delicious roast except for cross-sections of dark and excellent bread … hot from the domed ovens outside … Strangers, on occasions like these, are the objects of eager solicitude: special titbits, forkfuls of liver and kidney, and yet more recondite morsels are constantly being proffered and helpings of brain are delved from heads which have been bisected lengthwise.

Guests tried to avoid the sheeps' eyes, Leigh Fermor admits, but they were 'highly prized by mountaineers'.[75]

The whole of the north comes together at Thessaloniki, already nine hundred years ago a good place for food and the site of an annual fair, the greatest in Macedonia, held outside the city gates and beginning six days before the feast of St Demetrios (26 October); it attracted not only Bulgarians and Vlachs but Catalans, Italians and French.[76] The people of the first Crusade arrived joyfully in 1097 at 'Thessalonica, rich in all things and populous', and there, pitching their tents outside the city, they feasted

Chillies continuing the drying process, and meanwhile attracting customers, in Thessaloniki market.

Pilgrim stamp of St Isidore, whose tears were, according to legend, the first drops of mastic. This was a souvenir sold to medieval pilgrims who visited Chios.

happily for four days.[77] Ninety years later the Normans of Sicily besieged and captured the city, but they, according to bishop Eustathios, were not uncritical. They spurned the exotic spices and the well-aged wine – which was too dry for them – but gorged on pork, beef and garlic.[78] It was after this that the Jews arrived, refugees originally from Spain and Portugal, and made of Thessaloniki one of the greatest of Jewish cities. They are gone, but it has been said that the typical Jewish food of early twentieth-century Thessaloniki sounds very like the city's typical food today.[79] It is great now not only for its central market district, rebuilt after the great fire of 1917 and second only to that of Athens, but also for its food shops and restaurants, many of which cluster nearby, such as Ragian with its unique Pontic specialities; and for *bougatsa* and coffee, the perfect Thessaloniki breakfast; and for its fortifying *salepi*, still sold as a hot drink by itinerant vendors as it has been for hundreds of years (see page 248).

Aegean Islands

Every Aegean island has its history of foreign domination, and each island is different in its food specialities, from the ouzo of Lesbos to the mastic of Chios.

Chios, a big, mountainous island very close to the Asia Minor coast, was already a land of luxury in classical times, producing not only the best of all wines but its golden lightly dried figs and its irreplaceable mastic, the aromatic resin of a local variety of the lentisk tree, *Pistacia lentiscus* var. *chia*. Although it is mentioned by several ancient authors, especially for its medicinal uses, no writer had described the mastic harvest before the indefatigable Cyriac of Ancona, who was on Chios in January 1446, rode through the 'remarkably green, precious groves of mastic' and examined the famous trees that produced the valuable substance. He saw drops of glistening mastic seeping from the 'tearful but joyous trunks' and, gathering some in his hand, reflected that Chios was the only island in the world where this tree grew.[80] It was by that time one of the principal sources of wealth of the Genoese, the medieval possessors of Chios (they called the island Scio), and a legend had grown up that the first droplets of mastic were the tears of St Isidore of Chios, tortured and killed for his Christian faith.

Not many years later the Genoese Christopher Columbus, with first-hand knowledge of the mastic monopoly, searched for mastic among other aromatics when exploring the West Indies and, with his unquenchable optimism, believed that he had found it. He was wrong, and it is still true today that mastic resin is produced only on Chios. Many later travellers describe the harvest, the trade and the uses of mastic. The trees 'would give scarcely any resin if they were not given the necessary care', says Belon.[81] Richard Pococke is the best observer of the harvest:

> On the ninth of July they make holes in the rind across the trunk
> ... They sweep the ground, and throwing water on it, tread it even
> to make a smooth floor; in three days the gum begins to run, and
> they let it lie and dry for about eight days; it is then hard enough
> to handle, and they take it up; it continues running all the month
> of August.[82]

Turkish ladies chewed mastic 'as an amusement, and also to whiten their teeth', Pococke explains. So did the girls of Chios, according to Antoine Des Barres: 'They offered me some, and I refused, saying that I never took tobacco in any form. They burst out laughing, and told me that what they were chewing was mastic ... they said it was very healthy.'[83] He did not believe them, but the Scot William Lithgow was wiser: 'The medicinable masticke', he called it, and it now has many health uses.[84] Mastic liqueur is suddenly popular in Greece, but mastic ouzo, an unsweetened spirit, is known to few who are not Chians. Mastic is also put in bread, Pococke adds, 'and is said to have a very good taste'.[85] It does.[86]

Chios and its northern neighbour, Lesbos, were celebrated in antiquity for their wines, but no longer. Lesbos, the island of eleven million olive trees, produces, alongside its olive oil, what many agree to be the best ouzo

Wall painting from the Minoan town of Akrotiri (Santorini). If the figure is a fisherman the fish could be imagined at a larger scale; if he is a god, all bets are off. They are *Coryphaena hippurus*, which have the confusing English name dolphinfish but are now better known by the Hawaiian name, mahimahi, and they are good to eat.

of Greece. The distilleries cluster at the small town of Plomari on the south coast, and Lesbos ouzo is never better than when accompanying the salted sardines of nearby Kalloni.

South of Chios is Samos; northwest of Lesbos are Tenedos (now Turkish) and Lemnos. Samos and Lemnos are rightly proud of their sweet muscat wine. The best of Lemnos can stand beside the muscat of Pantelleria, than which there is none better. Tenedos, too, grew muscat grapes not long ago: its 'chief export is good wine and brandy',[87] writes Pococke, and Antoine Galland agrees. As to Samos, the naturalist Joseph Pitton de Tournefort in the early eighteenth century considered the muscat grapes the best fruit of the island, adding that the wine would be good 'if they knew how to make and keep it; but the Greeks are dirty, and also they cannot be persuaded not to put water into it'.[88] It has improved: aged Samos muscats, the Nectar and the Old Nectar, are quite remarkably aromatic.

Belon visited Lemnos around 1550 and saw no muscat grapes, but noted that 'water is very carefully conserved because they work hard on their gardens, keenly growing onions and garlic ... and paying great attention to the cultivation of cucumbers, which are as tasty as can be. They eat them with bread, without oil or vinegar':

Revithada – *Chrisoula's Chickpeas*

500 g dried (not canned) chickpeas
3 or 4 garlic cloves, peeled, either left whole or cut in half
(these will melt into the sauce)
2 bay leaves
2 bushy sprigs of fresh rosemary, about 6 cm long
2 medium onions, thickly sliced
150 ml fruity olive oil
salt and pepper
juice of about ½ lemon per serving
bread, to serve

Soak the chickpeas overnight in plenty of water. Drain and rinse them, and put them together with the garlic, bay leaves and rosemary in a large ovenproof dish to which you have a tight-fitting lid. Cover with the sliced onions, salt and pepper and water, then pour over the olive oil. Make sure the lid fits well: cover with a double layer of aluminium foil if in doubt. Leave in the oven to bake at 150°C for at least four hours – five will not hurt.

Serve with plenty of lemon juice squeezed over, bread to mop up the juices, and perhaps hard *kefalotyri* (or a sharp Lancashire cheese). *Revithada* is a perfect match for hot and crispy fried squid, but Chrisoula serves it with octopus in red wine (see page 66).
Serves 6–8

When a friend visits the garden the owner will choose a cucumber, holding it upright in his left hand, and peel it lengthwise down to the stem, letting the peel fall down over his hand like a star. Then he will cut it in quarters and present one to each person. They eat it without any other relish ... This is the height of politeness among them, as with us might be the sharing of a fine pear.[89]

Thus each island can be praised for making the best use of its own water and its own soil to produce the vegetables and fruits that succeed

Island Flavours, Wild and Tame

On the islands, by the middle of spring, the bitter winter greens have grown woody and are not for the pot. From March, spinach and chard, refreshingly sweet after the unrelenting bitterness of winter, are ready to take their place. Then briefly *kalfa*, *Opopanax hispidis*, is in season. The plant begins to sprout after the first autumn rains. All winter it is left to grow: the sprouting rosette of leaves is not eaten but the flower shoot is. For about two weeks in May, when the shoots are no longer than 10 centimetres and still tender, they are picked from the wild. The look and even the taste is reminiscent of asparagus, though *kalfa* is softer and has a more rounded flavour. In that short period tavernas will serve family-picked *kalfa*, but it has no English name and rarely appears on menus: it has to be asked for.

Chickpeas are far from wild. Grown in Thessaly since the fourth millennium BC or before, they are an important staple food in regions (such as the Aegean islands) where there may be practically no summer rains, because chickpeas rely on winter moisture, retained in the soil, to grow and ripen.

Kalfa: in its short season, better than asparagus. Strip the tougher skin from the base of the shoots, then boil them carefully to tenderness, mindful of the delicate tips. Serve warm with lots of olive oil or a mild mustard dressing.

Chrisoula's *revithada*.

Traditionally *revithada* is cooked in large earthenware pots (the island of Siphnos in the Cyclades has good natural clay deposits and is famous for the production of these pots, called *skepastaria* or *pilina*), which are taken to the village baker's oven on Saturday evening. *Revithada*, like some other dishes, is left to cook slowly overnight in the residual heat after the bread-baking, to be collected on Sunday after mass, ready for lunch. This is still common practice in many rural communities, and visitors to a bakery on Sunday mornings will most likely be greeted with a row of cooking pots by the door, waiting for their owners. The pots are often sealed with a simple paste of flour and water to ensure that none of the precious liquid which sauces the chickpeas is lost to evaporation during cooking. This method of cooking turns the result into a velvety, nutty, cohesive stew.

Rosemary grows easily in Greece, but not everyone uses it in *revithada*: some find the flavour too strident. The quality of the olive oil is of the utmost importance: this is where the dish gets its flavour. The 'cream' of the chickpeas is the layer of cara-melized, oily onions that stays on top during cooking, and, if not stirred in when served, is a treat on its own.

perfectly. Becalmed offshore somewhere in the Dodecanese, Lithgow in the early seventeenth century saw a man and two women swimming out to the ship 'more than a mile away', carrying baskets of fruit to sell. They would not board, but floated on the surface 'above an hour', chatting and bargaining with the passengers.[90] The cuisine of the modern Dodecanese sometimes betrays old trading contacts. In Olympos on Karpathos, remote though it is, breads and cheese tarts are flavoured with an aromatic blend of coarsely crushed coriander seeds (locally grown), ground allspice, cinnamon, cloves, cumin, black pepper, and mastic or aniseed.[91]

The figs of Naxos were enjoyed by Lord Charlemont in 1749 ('those of Marseille . . . are insipid compared to them') and they are still as good.[92] 'Tomatoes grew anywhere out of the bare white ground . . . small, but of a splendidly rich flavour,' writes Humphrey Kitto of his visit to Santorini around 1930. Vines have thrived there (or at least lived and fruited) for over two thousand years, clustered in the hollows of the windswept slopes, in local varieties including Assyrtiko which is praised for its resistance to phylloxera; and many people think the resulting raisin wine or *visanto* or *vin santo* is rather good. Kitto, however, found it to be 'a red wine rather like the famous Mavrodaphne, that is to say, dilute sherry-and-treacle'.[93] The Dutch travellers Egmont and Heyman report enthusiastically on Melos (where, irrelevantly, the women had 'the worst character of any in the whole archipelago in respect to chastity'):

Delivery of fresh vegetables to a restaurant on Market Street, Paroikia, Paros.

It abounds with provisions of the most delicate kind, as partridges, turtle-doves, beccafigoes, ducks, &c.; delicious fruits, as
melons, figs, grapes, &c.; and fish equally good. Its wine is also
excellent . . . they make excellent cheese from goats milk.[94]

Thus, too, each island and each Aegean microclimate can be examined
and evaluated for its wild resources – the mountain herbs, the aromatic
shrubs and the wild fruit trees whose special value has already been discovered or awaits discovery one day. Wheler reported that on the small island
of Delos, site of the ruined ancient sanctuary of Apollo, 'groweth lenticus,
or the mastick shrub, in great plenty, wild, upon which I observed tears
of mastick, which made us believe that if it were cultivated here as well as
at Scio it might bear as well as there'.[95] One might think the same of the
mountainous Karaburun peninsula of Turkey, which looks like a twin of
Chios at the same latitude and with the same climate, and once produced
wine not so very different from Chian; but the lentisk, so far, has yielded
a useful supply of mastic in none of these places.

Many will single out Santorini, devastated by the eruption of 1629–7
BC and thus uniquely preserving something of the prehistoric context of
its local foods, the beehive, the store of *fava Santorinis*, the wall paintings
of the saffron harvest, the goats entombed in their pens by volcanic ash.

We praise the mushrooms of Paros; Lambert-Gócs has warm words for
the mushrooms of Samos and Ikaria. Leigh Fermor wondered why Siphnos
abounds in cooks. He raised the question because Nikolaos Tselementes,
whom he not unreasonably calls the Greek Mrs Beeton, came from Siphnos,
or at least his family did.[96] Indeed, the first cookbook published in Greece (in
1828, four years before Greek independence was internationally recognized)
appeared in the nearby island of Syros.

Each island has its cakes and sweetmeats. Kalymnos was known in
ancient times and is still known for its honey, but for the best honey-and-
sesame sweets, so much appreciated by classical Greeks, try Karpathos, or
Kasos, or again Kythnos, or even tourist-heavy Ios; for sugar-coated almonds,
Anafi, they say. Each of the islands can be separately praised for its interpretation of those foods and drinks that need not vary but in fact always do.
Local producers have their local markets even in these. The ouzo of Paros is
unlike the ouzo of Naxos, a mere forty minutes away by ferry. The cheeses of
Naxos are remarkable when aged, and the Chian *kopanisti* at its mouldy best
is incomparable. The table olives of Chios, notably the *chourmades*, 'dates', are
like no others, but that is true too of the *throumbes*, 'tree-ripe olives', of Naxos.

CRETE

The geography of Crete alone is as varied as that of many independent countries. (For a while, around 1900, it almost was an independent country.) Its food, too, has been enormously varied. The mountainous west had its orange and lemon orchards, its meat dishes, its butter and cheese, and its liking for rice; the centre its wine of the Peza and Archanes appellations; the rocky east its fish, its preference for bulgur wheat and for spices. Intensive tourism and commercial pressure have brought radical change, but many Cretans retain their rural links and something of their traditional ways of eating.[97]

For wild edible plants and their health-giving properties, no island is more renowned than Crete. Its herbs were already prized under the Roman Empire. They are no longer important in the pharmacopoeia as they once were. Nowadays, nonetheless, the 'Cretan diet', very sparing in meat, rich in wild greens, generously seasoned with Cretan olive oil and washed down with Cretan wine, is reputed to be the best variant of the 'Mediterranean diet'. Cretans live long on it, even if not quite as long as Ikariots.

Around the entrance to the covered meat and fish markets on Athinas Street in the central Athens district of Monastiraki, and at open-air markets all over Greece, can still be found *horta*-sellers, squatting on a folding camp-stool, with a couple of plastic bags stuffed with freshly gathered wild greens. Tavernas often list *horta* as a vegetable dish, and some will specify which kind is on offer (most likely *radikia*, or on Crete *stamnagathi*). Increasingly, *horta* are also sold by greengrocers and in specialist supermarkets. *Kafkalithres*, *vlita* and *vrouves* are among those that command premium prices. In November 2014, in one popular Athens supermarket, wild Cretan greens fetched more than €4 a kilo – five times the price of a romaine lettuce.

Crete, of course, has no monopoly. 'Here are some fine fields of wheat,' Leake narrates during his journey across Lakonia, 'which women are now clearing of weeds. As we pass, one of our party asks them what they are doing. *Botanizomen* is their Laconic answer.'[98] Laconic indeed: it takes five words to say the same thing in English, 'we are gathering wild greens.' It is telling, incidentally, that Leake uses the term 'weeds'. In her text for this book Rachel more than once used the same word, and Andrew edited it out before realizing that she has Leake on her side.

Crete now produces very little of the strong, sweet wines for which the Byzantine Greeks and the people of medieval Europe paid high prices. The island shows its Venetian heritage – Venice ruled Crete for a longer period than did the Ottoman Turks – in recipes and in the names of foods.

Waterfront tavernas at Rethymno, Crete.

Medieval travellers most often called Crete *Candia*. Unprepared to take interest in the herbs, they noted the wine first ('the famous Cretan wine which is exported to the whole world',[99] 'the best Malvasy, Muscadine and Leaticke wines, that are in the whole Universe'[100]), then the cheese, then the fruit.

The anonymous author of a pilgrim narrative of 1480 faced a problem: Cretan wine was so fiery that it had to be mixed with three parts of water.[101] This is corroborated by Felix Faber, who travelled in the same year and 'saw several pilgrims standing swaying at the edge of the sea, hesitating about stepping into the boat, because the sweet and pleasant Cretan wine, taken copiously, induces dizziness'.[102] The observation is explained by Pietro Casola, ten years later, who found at Rethymno that if you asked for table wine you would be served malmsey. He also observed that the vines were ground-trained, 'left trailing on the ground as we leave melons and water-melons'.[103]

Horta – *Wild Herbs of Crete and Greece*

A mixture of different greens is best: dandelions, *zochos* and *radikia* are very bitter, wild lettuce almost excessively so; knapweed is savoury and *podarakia* has a juicy, succulent quality, but both are hard to eat in large quantities. Some common kinds are listed below.

When collecting, try to cut the plant so that the leaves are still attached at the base but the root is left in the ground to sprout again. Clean, trim off the root and any small brown leaves, and rinse off any grit under running water. Put into a large basin or sink with a few dashes of vinegar and soak with plenty of water. Leave standing in the water for an hour or so, then lift out of the basin with your hands and put in a colander. Rinse the basin and repeat the soaking twice. Grit, even if caught in tight folds, will thus eventually sink to the bottom to be removed. Then boil for about 25 minutes in plenty of water until completely soft and most of the bitterness has gone. Don't pour the water out of the pan (which risks redistributing any residual grit), but hook the *horta* out of the water with a fork. It doesn't do to steam wild greens, nor to leave them crunchy. Test for tenderness by gently squeezing the base of one clump: if it gives under your fingers the *horta* are ready. Allow to cool; pour lemon juice and olive oil generously over the greens when serving.

Knapweed and *petromaroulo*, a wild lettuce, encountered in the wild.

Agria sparangia (wild asparagus, *Asparagus* spp.) is found for only two or three weeks between March and May, depending on weather conditions each year. It always grows close to a water source: in more arid districts one hunts for it in dry river beds. Grilled in a dry pan or incorporated into a simple omelette, it can be served as a *meze* to accompany *tsipouro*.

Agrioradiko, pikralida, pikromaroulo, antidi (wild chicory and endive, *Cichorium* spp.) comes in many kinds, some more bitter than others, throughout Greece. *Stamnagathi* (spiny chicory) is unique to Crete and is now so sought-after that it has been taken into cultivation.

Chamomili (camomile, *Matricaria chamomilla*) is collected in the spring, when the daisy-like flowers carpet the ground and fill the air with their unmistakable fragrance, and then dried for year-round consumption. It is a common herbal infusion in Greece, where the folk saying is *Ta niata theloun erota kai oi geroi chamomili*, 'Youngsters need love, old men need camomile tea.'

Chirovoskos, karyda (knapweed, *Centaurea* spp.), with its savoury taste, is good mixed with bitter greens in a boiled salad.

Kafkalithra (close to chervil, *Tordylium apulum*) is among the commonest aromatic winter *horta*. Young leaves are collected and used with other, more bitter greens.

Lapatho (dock and sorrel, *Rumex* spp.) is found in abundance close to nettle patches – which is a good thing. As many as 25 species grow in Greece; they flourish from winter until late spring. Young shoots are eaten raw and mature leaves are boiled. The flavour is reminiscent of vinegar.

Molocha (mallow, *Malva* spp.): tender leaves are boiled with other greens or used, as in a recipe from the Dodecanese, in place of ancient fig or modern vine leaves as the wrapping for *dolmades*.

Myroni (*Scandix pecten-veneris*) was known to the ancient Greeks as *skandix*. The young leaves of this winter green are used in small quantities as an aromatic together with other more bitter plants.

Petromaroulo, agriomaroulo (wild lettuce, *Lactuca serriola*) is distinct from the wild chicories mentioned above but is treated in the same way, as part of a mix of greens in a boiled salad. This is a very common winter green all over Greece.

Taraxako (dandelion, *Taraxacum officinale*) is used raw in salads or boiled with other greens throughout the winter months and throughout Greece and Cyprus.

Tsouknida (nettle, *Urtica dioica*) is not so common on the dry southern Aegean islands, but is among the favourite winter greens on the mainland, particularly in the north. Pontic Greeks make great use of nettles in fritters and soups, such as *kinteata*, a thick broth of nettles and spearmint, spiced with red chilli flakes or paprika and thickened with cornmeal and *korkoto* (husked and cracked wheat).

Vlita (blite or amaranth leaves, *Amaranthus blitum* and relatives) is found all around the Mediterranean in well-watered fields, gardens and fallow land during the long summer months. In the Mani and on Crete it is often cooked with *ambelofasoula* (young black-eyed peas), tomatoes and onions. Elsewhere, it is boiled and served as a cooked salad dish beside the meat or on its own. The taste is juicy and fresh, not at all bitter like winter greens. If bought in the market, trim the ends of the stalks and de-string the rest as one would with celery, then boil for 25 minutes or until tender.

Vrouves (mustard greens, *Hirschfeldia incana, Sinapis alba, S. nigra*) were noted under this Greek name by Pierre Belon at the vegetable market in Constantinople. Some kinds are highly prized, others rejected as tough and un-aromatic.

Zochos (smooth sow-thistle, *Sonchus oleraceus*) and *agriozochos* (literally 'wild sow-thistle', *Urospermum picroides*) are two of the most widespread and widely collected ('cultivated, waste and fallow ground, field margins, meadows, roadsides, olive groves, vineyards, ditches':[104] that's practically all of Greece) from November to March or early April. Always boiled, on their own or with other winter greens, drenched in lemon juice and olive oil, these two are often found on taverna menus.

Wild greens are an essential element of the real Mediterranean diet.

Cretan malmsey and muscat, like other Greek wines intended for long-distance export, were specially treated. Belon's description shows that two fortified wine traditions – the *solera* method used for sherry, and the 'cooking' undergone by Banyuls and Maury – have their ancestry in medieval Greece. The best Cretan malmsey was exported from Rethymno, Belon confirms, and 'the more it travels the better it is', as was said in due course of Madeira.[105]

Cretan wine is now remarkably varied (but then it's a big island). The eastern district of Siteia makes most of the sweet wine, which is red and based on the old *liatiko*, 'July', variety. There is dry red from the central districts of Archanes and Peza, south of Heraklio. There is good wine at Kissamos in the far west. But it is very hard to find any of the malmseys or muscats for which medieval and early modern Europeans paid so highly.

The most plentiful fruits of Crete are listed as early as 1323 by the Irish pilgrim Symon Semeonis: pomegranates, citrons, figs, grapes, melons, watermelons and cucumbers.[106] Belon, on his scientific mission to the

East, stopped first in Crete, noticing that the climate and spring water encouraged vegetable gardens and orchards, planted with almonds, olives, pomegranates, jujubes and figs, but especially orange, citron and lemon trees. He is the first to remark on the pressing of oranges and lemons and the sale of their juice to Constantinople 'because the Turks make much use of it in their cooking instead of verjuice: hence it is sold retail in the same shops that sell salt fish and fish sauce'.[107] As for the raisins, the best of them are the sultanas for which Crete is still famous and in honour of which Siteia at the eastern end of the island now holds an annual festival. Medieval and modern writers rarely mention quinces, though these were the fruits for which Chania (Kydonia) had been famous in classical times. In that neighbourhood they have given ground to oranges, but Crete still has some quinces, as Xan Fielding found in the 1940s on the occasion when his breakfast turned out to be tea followed by *tsikoudia* with quinces.[108]

The olive oil of Crete, a high-profile export now, is mentioned only by relatively recent sources: Ellis Veryard in 1701 and Richard Pococke in 1743 (perhaps because until 1668, when Crete was Venetian, oil went as a matter of course to Venice). Honey is mentioned earlier: it was the clearest and purest of any, resembling white muslin, writes Evliya Çelebi, and was 'renowned and exported to all countries'.[109] Honey, Fielding adds, was the pride of Agia Roumeli at the foot of the Samaria gorge: offered the chance of ridding their village of lice by allowing their fields to be sprayed with DDT, they chose to retain their vermin rather than risk their bees.

That is why Fielding was able to enjoy 'the *spécialité de la région*: cream-cheese pancakes soaked in honey'.[110] This brings us to butter and cheese from goats' and sheep's milk. They could well be the oldest of all Cretan food products if the reason suggested in Chapter One for the spread of Neolithic human settlement to the high plateaus happens to be correct. Butter of Chania and Rethymno is turned into *staka*, cooked and with flour added, and *stakovoutyro*, butterfat used in cooking and baking, both distinctive.[111] An equally unique, creamy, semi-soft cheese is *anthotyro*, 'flower of cheese'. Several medieval authors remark that Cretan cheese was loaded in quantity on to the ships in which they travelled. Crete produced at least as much sheep's milk as wine, writes Pietro Casola, and a great many cheeses were made; it was a pity they were so salty. 'I saw great warehouses full of them, some in which the brine was two feet deep, the large cheeses floating in it. They told me that the cheeses could not be preserved in any other way, being so rich.'[112]

SEVEN

Food of Recent Greece

The physical geography of Greece has changed in the last 17,000 years. The waters have advanced. The Aegean is a sea of many small islands, not of a few big ones. The islands, in common with mainland hill and mountain slopes, are not forested as they once were. The drier Greece becomes, the less likely it is that the forests will regenerate.

Many other changes to the landscape, like the deforestation, have happened under human control – if control is the word to use. Terraces cover hillsides, sometimes to a great height: perhaps intensely cultivated, perhaps abandoned, but what is abandoned may be brought into use again, as is happening now on Naxos, for example.

Olives and wild vines once took a modest share of the sunlight. Olives now almost define Greek landscapes. Like the terraces on which many of them grow, some olive trees are carefully tended, some forgotten, but many of the forgotten ones live on and can be reclaimed. Vines, in their weedy way, take over landscapes too, ground-trained as many are, sprawling across rock-strewn fields. Lush orchards, dark green with citrus leaves, occupy irrigated lower slopes and valley bottoms.

The detritus of human activity spreads far wider than it should. It's not just buildings in use, but buildings that won't ever be finished and buildings that have had their day; empty buildings carpeted in concrete, unlike older ruins, where fig trees and caper bushes can flourish within the walls. It's also roads that are needed and roads that aren't needed and roads whose construction destroyed far more of the living landscape than was necessary; it's rubbish dumps and rubbish that didn't ever reach a dump.

COOKBOOKS AND COOKS

The Aegean island of Syros, though neutral in the revolutionary struggle, was serving as a refuge for revolutionaries, an embryonic national capital, at the moment when Greece's first cookbook was published there in 1828. The anonymous author's stated aim was to bring Italian cookery to Greeks, but by 'Italian' Western is meant: of the eight sweets two are English, bread-and-butter pudding and rice pudding. The next Greek cookbook dates from 1863 and is also largely foreign in inspiration. Compiled by Nikolaos Sarantis and published in Constantinople, the overt aim of *Syngramma magirikis* (Manual of Cookery) was to describe French cuisine to a bourgeois readership of Greeks of the city, whose traditional cooking was, to our tastes, considerably more interesting. And yet, in a strange gesture to Greek independence (a gesture that in Constantinople was surely subversive), Sarantis named three dishes after revolutionary naval commanders, Miaoulis from Euboia, Sachtouris from Hydra and Kanaris from Psara.[1] The last of these had wreaked revenge on the Ottoman navy for the 1822 Chios massacre, had afterwards served as Greek prime minister and was still an active politician when Sarantis's book was published.

The next in the series of Greek cookbooks is the *Odigos Magirikis* (Guide to Cookery) of the celebrated Nikolaos Tselementes, Siphnian by parentage, born in Athens in 1878. Tselementes trained as a cook in Vienna. Convinced that Greek food must drop all eastern influences, he steered his readers towards the sweetness and spicelessness of Central-to-Western Europe. 'This culinary traitor exiled olive oil and garlic, banished traditional Greek herbs and spices, ushered in butter, cream and flour,' Jonathan Reynolds wrote trenchantly in 2004, but in Tselementes's own time 'upper-middle-class Greeks, not unlike Chekhov's Russians, clamored for this new sophistication, and the resulting bland, bloated, blubbery cuisine spread through a country yearning to be more European.'[2] The cookbook sold in successive editions to a whole generation of new and aspiring housewives, and it spread across the world in translation. As Aglaia Kremezi points out, those few of Tselementes's recipes that are most authentically Greek come from his Siphnian heritage, including *skaltsounia*, honey-and-cheese pastries. But his everlasting memorial is *moussaka*, a dish with a complex history. Its name is 'the Arabic word *musaqqā*, which means "moistened"', the Arabist Charles Perry explains, 'referring to the tomato juices.' In the Middle East it is a cold dish of fried aubergines dressed with a rich tomato sauce, the kind of thing that Greeks would call pseudo-*moussaka* and reserve for fast days. In Turkey it became a casserole of sliced aubergine and meat; so it would have been in Greece, too, if Tselementes had not added the béchamel topping.[3]

Modern Writers and Chefs

Artemis Leontis in *Culture and Customs of Greece* spins Tselementes positively as one of the 'forces pushing towards the definition of a national Greek cuisine'. He 'removed improvised variations and exotic flavors'; he '"upgraded" recipes by adding French culinary techniques to create a reproducible set of recipes'. But those scare quotes are a sting in the tail. Rather late in the day, from the 1980s onwards, Leontis continues, Greeks became aware of the contribution that the Asia Minor refugees had made 'with some of the exotic "Turkish" spices that Tselementes had sought to expunge', and perhaps through this recognition began to value their own local food traditions, which they had gone some way towards forgetting.

At the same time the new food experts began to attain celebrity. 'Their ethnographic approach to cooking has expanded Greeks' imaginative grasp of what they can do with basic, seasonally fresh ingredients, time-tested techniques, and their own creative engagement', thus at last undoing most of Tselementes's work.[4] In restaurants in Greece now the food will be better and fresher than it would be in most countries to the north and west – Greek restaurateurs are beginning to be proud of the fact – and the dishes will often betray their regional origins even in Athens, perhaps especially in Athens, because, as James Pettifer writes, 'Athens is a city of strangers . . . Greek loyalty is ultimately to the birthplace, even if this is an inhospitable rocky island in the Aegean or a poverty-stricken mountain village in Thessaly.' These links are if anything stronger, he continues, because during the repeated privations and famines that modern Athens has suffered, with malnutrition and deaths from starvation during both world wars, those who still had connections with the countryside and perhaps retained land where food could be grown were somewhat luckier.[5] No wonder some abandoned terraces are now being farmed once again.

Athens may be the publishing and broadcasting metropolis and perennially a magnet for writers and celebrities. But the would-be successors of Tselementes, the food writers and personalities of today, would be much poorer if they lacked connections with the regions, the diaspora and the world beyond.

Two restaurant chefs, out of many, to begin the examples. Rightly and appropriately, Lefteris Lazarou prides himself on his seafood cookery,

Chrisoula's Moussaka

5 medium or large aubergines
salt, olive oil

For the filling:
150 ml olive oil
1 large onion, chopped
½ kg minced beef
½ kg minced fatty pork
150 ml dry red wine
1 tbsp tomato purée, or 1 kg fresh blended fresh tomatoes
1 generous tsp ground cinnamon
no more than ¼ nutmeg, freshly grated
1 coarsely grated carrot (optional, but it complements the
tomatoes' acidity)
55 g grated cheese – *kefalotyri*, mature Cheddar or Gruyère
salt and pepper

For the béchamel:
1½ litres full-fat milk
140 g plain flour
50 g coarsely grated cheese – *kefalotyri* or mature Cheddar
1 generous tbsp unsalted butter
¼ nutmeg, freshly grated
3 eggs, lightly beaten

For the finished dish:
a little butter
grated cheese
fine breadcrumbs

First prepare the aubergines: top and tail and slice lengthwise
into 1 cm strips. Place in a colander and sprinkle with salt
(which will eventually be washed away). Leave to drain overnight, pressed down with a saucer.

Dry the aubergines with kitchen paper. Then either fry in hot olive oil and drain, or (as Chrisoula does) lay out on aluminium foil, brush with oil and bake in a scorching hot oven. Turn once; remove when cooked through but still firm enough to hold their shape. Leave the aubergines aside while preparing the meat filling (at this stage they can be left to cool, wrapped well, and frozen, for making *moussaka* in the winter, when there are no tasty fresh aubergines).

For the meat, heat the oil in a large saucepan and fry the onion for a few minutes over a medium heat to soften but not colour. Add the mince and lightly brown before pouring in the red wine and leaving to bubble for 5 minutes. In summer, if you have flavourful tomatoes, blend a kilo of ripe but firm fruits, drain briefly and add to the mince. In winter, substitute with 1 tbsp of good-quality tomato purée and 335–450 ml water to make up for the missing juice. Either way, leave to simmer for 5 more minutes, sprinkle in the cinnamon and grate over the nutmeg. Add pepper and cook together, breathing in the aromas. At this point grate the carrot into the mix. Leave to simmer over a low to medium heat for 30–45 minutes.

The sauce should be slightly undercooked, as it will bake further in the oven, but it should not be so wet as to make a sloppy dish. (This same basic sauce can be cooked longer and served with spaghetti as a typical Greek *ragu* or as the filling of *pastitsio*.)

Add a mean amount of salt towards the end of the cooking: Chrisoula advises that the meat will 'seize' or toughen if salted too early. When ready, remove the pan from the heat and stir in the grated cheese, which will increase the salt but also add depth to the taste.

The béchamel can be prepared while the meat simmers. In a large pan, begin to heat the milk over a medium heat. Add the flour, cheese, butter, nutmeg, a good seasoning of pepper and some salt. Leave this to cook, whisking only occasionally, while the mince bubbles. It will eventually begin to thicken: remove from the heat when it has the consistency of thick double cream. Let the sauce cool for a few minutes before whisking in the eggs (which 'fix' the béchamel, making it easier to cut neat slices next day).

Now assemble the dish. Lightly butter a 40 cm diameter round dish – or large rectangular baking dish – and put a layer of aubergines in the bottom. Sprinkle over a small handful of cheese, then spoon a thin covering of mince over that. Repeat the layers once or twice more until all the ingredients are used up. If the meat filling is rather wet – in the summer, with fresh tomatoes, it may be – sprinkle a small handful of fine bread-crumbs over each meat layer to soak up the excess liquid. Some tavernas add more breadcrumbs as a cheap meat substitute; the practice has a firm basis in tradition, especially on the islands where meat (even for a festival dish) was scarce. Finish the *moussaka* by spooning over the béchamel sauce: if poured it could spoil the careful composition underneath. Add another handful of grated cheese and fine breadcrumbs. Bake the majestic dish for 1 hour or so at 200°C. It will emerge blistered and coloured in places and will smell amazing.

In an ideal Greek world, leave to cool to a warm room temperature before serving – or, better, until the next day. Serve with a plain chopped green salad of lettuce and rocket and some chunks of *kefalotyri* or mature Cheddar, and bread.

Chrisoula's moussaka.

praising the special qualities of Aegean salt, which gives local fish an incomparable flavour. He trained as a ship's cook, like his father. After 22 years in that trade he decided to open a restaurant 'that didn't move'. Founder of Varoulko in his native Piraeus, he has been a judge on the Greek version of *Masterchef* and a guest of the Culinary Institute of America. He claims the first Michelin star awarded for Greek cuisine.

Christoforos Peskias belongs to the oldest Greek diaspora, that of Cyprus. He studied in Boston, worked as a chef in Kephisia near Athens, trained in Chicago and finally returned to Athens to found the restaurant that (for want of a better name) he calls πbox. 'We eat what we are,' he says philosophically, and claims to work with the classics of Greek cookery, deconstructed.[6]

Ilias Mamalakis, not a restaurant chef (though he has been a restaurant consultant), is a native of Athens. Author and radio and TV personality, game-show host, judge on the Greek *Masterchef*, he is a cheese-lover, a Slow Foodie and – no mean achievement – a French gastronomic academician.

Vefa Alexiadou, doyenne of all these celebrities and described in a British newspaper as 'Greece's answer to Delia Smith', born at Volo in Thessaly, reached classic status with a TV series in the form of a recipe competition that gathered thousands of traditional dishes from all over the country: 'Some would even send me the original manuscript in their grandmother's handwriting.'[7] Vefa's daughter Alexia, born in Thessaloniki, chef and culinary writer in her own right and editor of the cookery section of the daily newspaper *Ta Nea*, died suddenly in 2014.

Another major figure is Stelios Parliaros. He has diaspora heritage, having been born in Constantinople. He trained in Paris and Lyon as a confectioner and it is for his sweets, 'sweet alchemy' as he likes to call them, that he is best known as author of recipe books, as teacher, and as journalist on the vanished daily *Eleftherotypia* and on *Kathimerini*. This leads us to other writers and journalists. Diane Kochilas, TV cook in Greece and consultant chef in the United States, comes from an Ikarian family, was born in New York, but now lives and teaches cookery on Ikaria. Aglaia Kremezi studied in London, wrote for the Sunday edition of *Eleftherotypia*, and now lives and teaches cookery on Kea. The food historian Mariana Kavroulaki, whose links are with Crete, edits the cookery section of *To Vima* and runs symposia on Greek gastronomy. Linda Makris and Diana Farr Louis are Americans who married Greeks and Greece: Makris wrote for the English edition of *Kathimerini*, while Louis wrote for *Athens News*, another lost newspaper, and is co-author of the cleverly titled *Prospero's Kitchen*, on Ionian island cooking.

MAKING A MEAL

After all, Greece has been the target for travellers for a long time. Ancient Romans came to Athens to study philosophy and rhetoric and perfect their Greek. Medieval backpackers like St Willibald, and economy-class pilgrims like Symon Semeonis, toiled along Greek roads or landed at Greek harbours on their way to the Holy Land. Crusaders came this way and some of them outstayed their welcome. Antiquarians like Cyriac of Ancona hunted for ruins and inscriptions; naturalists like Pierre Belon found long-forgotten plant species. All of them had something to say about the food, both good and bad.

Greek food shows extreme geographical variation – it must, because of Greece's uniquely varied geography – but historically there has been surprising continuity in the foods that people eat, the ways they prepare them and how they go about enjoying them. We have surveyed the prehistoric Greek foods for which archaeologists could find evidence: fruit, vegetables and herbs by way of the seeds; fish from the bones (though these are too easy to miss and were rarely found in older excavations); shellfish from the shells; meat from animal bones; bread and cheese and wine and olive oil to the extent that evidence of their making can still be recognized. For classical Greece we had the evidence of the texts that people wrote about what they ate. When they were speaking generally there was a tendency to mention bread and wine and olive oil, meat and fish – the meat because feasts centred on it, the fish because money was spent on it, bread and wine because they were always there, olive oil because it was so useful and so valuable. We may have suspected that meat is more prominent in the evidence, both prehistoric and classical, than it was in real everyday life: occasional pieces of evidence focusing on the lifestyle of poorer people directed our attention to fruit, vegetables, bread and perhaps cheese.

Bread and wine and olive oil as necessities, vegetables and fruit and cheese as their usual companions, fish when possible, meat much more rarely: this, not so very different after all from what the classical sources say, is what recent travellers to Greece have learned all over again. 'Wine and bread appeared to be the staple food of the people,' wrote Isabel Armstrong in 1893 in her memoir *Two Roving Englishwomen in Greece*. She and her companion travelled on the mainland and therefore saw little of fish, but meat of almost any kind, they found, would have to be ordered in advance, 'and the traveller does not generally stay long enough in a place to benefit from the execution of a lamb'. Eggs she noted as an occasional luxury; coffee too, something they might have had more readily had they been men and therefore welcomed at *kafenia*. But what kinds of meat? 'Until we went to Thessaly I do not remember seeing a cow in Greece, but there were sheep and goats in abundance, and so milk and cheese could be had: butter was an extravagance that we only tasted in Patras, Athens and Volo.'[8] Greece at the time when these Englishwomen roved did not extend north of Thessaly. Macedonia and Thrace were solid Ottoman provinces, and a ten-year-old boy who would eventually be called Atatürk was growing up in Thessaloniki. In that northern region, mostly annexed by Greece in 1913, meat – beef in particular – was a much more regular part of the diet. So was butter, largely replacing the olive oil that is an everyday necessity in southern Greece. And it is no surprise that the pies made with filo pastry, which are so familiar all over Greece, are at their best and most varied in the north. There, too, pies are more meat-filled than anywhere else – because even where farmers keep large herds and flocks, meat cannot in reason be cheap, and pastry makes minced meat go a long way.

Whatever they might find when they reached their evening resting place, travellers in Greece of the recent past had no expectation of a meaty midday meal. The Irish painter Edward Dodwell, who was in Greece around 1805, was advised to carry food with him because if he stopped at villages to look at ruins and inscriptions he would find nothing to eat but bread and cheese. His party therefore took along coffee, tea, sugar, raisins, figs, olives, caviar and halva; for those who can't afford or don't care to carry caviar on a long hike he recommends botargo, itself by no means cheap, but probably easier to find in northwestern Greece. The olive he rightly describes as 'an excellent food and a good substitute for meat'; the same might be said of caviar and botargo. He considered halva (he calls it *kalbaz*) a substitute for butter, which is one way of looking at it.

Dodwell had a feeling that readers would ask why cheese was not included among his supplies. 'The cheese', he excuses himself, 'is made of goat's or sheep's milk, and being extremely salt, is not suited to our palates.' He also had a problem with Greek wine, 'frequently so resinous and pungent that as a substitute we were obliged to take *raki*, a strong spirit extracted from the stalks of vines taken from the wine presses,' and that is certainly a good reason for drinking *raki*.[9] Expecting to find bread on his way, Dodwell carried none. Leake, having no food at all with him, asked in a village in Lakonia for the makings of a lunch and was supplied with eggs, wine and wheat bread; his Greek guide, though, had to make do with 'cold bean porridge of yesterday, which, being a solid mass, is sliced and eaten with salt and vinegar'.[10] But what if there is no village? Pierre Belon, on his visit to Mount

Dodwell's Meal at Salona

Edward Dodwell, travelling in northwestern Greece, was invited to a meal by the bishop of Salona (ancient Amphissa) in 1805. He describes the scene fully in his *Classical and Topographical Tour in Greece* (1819) and illustrates it in *Views in Greece* (London, 1821). This may be the first time the text and illustration have been printed side by side:

> Nothing could be more miserable! He lives with all the simplicity of the primitive Christians; there was nothing to eat, except rice and bad cheese; the wine was execrable, and so impregnated with rosin, that it almost took the skin from our lips! An opportunity however was now offered us of seeing the interior of a Greek house, and of observing some of the customs of the country. Before sitting down to dinner, as well as afterwards, we had to perform the ceremony of the *cheironiptron*, or washing of the hands: a tin bason is brought round to all the company, the servant holding it on his left arm, while with the other hand, he pours water from a tin vessel on the hands of the washer, having a towel thrown over his shoulder, to dry them with.
>
> We dined at a round table of copper tinned, supported on one leg or column. We sat on cushions placed on the floor; and our dress not being so conveniently large as that of the Greeks, we found the greatest difficulty in tucking our legs under us, or rather sitting upon them, as they do with perfect ease and pliability. Several times I was very near falling back, and overturning the episcopal table, with all its good things. The Bishop insisted upon my Greek servant sitting at table with us; and on my observing that

Athos around 1550, was guided by a young monk from one monastery to the next. In crossing the mountain on one occasion they missed the path. They had brought no food with them and it was eventually too late to reach their destination that evening, but they came to a rivulet teeming with freshwater crabs. Their guide 'ate them raw and assured us they were better raw than

it was contrary to our customs, he answered, that he could not bear such ridiculous distinctions in his house. It was with difficulty I obtained the privilege of drinking out of my own glass, instead of out of the large goblet which served for the whole party, and which had been whiskered by the Bishop, and the rest of the company, for both the Greeks and Turks use only one glass at meals.

After dinner, strong thick coffee, without sugar, was handed round: the cup is not placed in a saucer, but in another cup of metal, which defends the fingers from being burnt, for the coffee is served up and drank as hot as possible.[11]

In the illustration Dodwell can be seen nursing his personal glass. Next to him is his guide, Dr Andrea Cattani of Kephallenia; facing him is his servant, with whom he would have preferred not to share a table. A Greek visitor is making obeisance to the bishop.

Edward Dodwell, meal with the bishop of Salona (ancient Amphissa) in 1805.

cooked. We ate them with him, and did not remember ever having tasted meat that was so delicious and savoury, whether because of our pressing hunger or because this food was so new to us.'[12]

The provisions enumerated by Dodwell make some sense as nourishing snack foods, but the list has a luxurious feel to it. It contrasts strongly with the impromptu lunch enjoyed by Xan Fielding after some hours' scrambling down the Samaria gorge in western Crete: cheese, raw onions and *paximadia* ('home-baked rusks with a satisfying nutty flavour, but so hard that they have to be soaked in water before being eaten').[13] Fielding, journeying about 130 years later than Dodwell, relied on his Greek companions to know what food to carry and to spend no money on it.

So did Patrick Leigh Fermor at about the same date. This, then, is a typical supper in a cave in Crete under German occupation: a stew of beans, lentils, snails and herbs, eaten in spoonfuls from a single tin dish, accompanied by 'that twice-baked herdsman's bread that must be soaked in water or goats' milk before it is eaten' (*dakos* or *paximadia* again). Leigh Fermor and his comrades toasted goats' cheese on the points of their daggers and drank from flasks of *raki* sent up from the village below.[14]

Finding a Meal

What if invited to a meal? If in a monastery, as it frequently would be for travellers even of the very recent past, 'the worst was the food and the filth,' wrote Edward Lear, who from his peaceful retreat on Corfu had determined to visit and paint the monasteries of Mount Athos. He did not admire the 'minced-fish and marmalade masticating' monks. But this emerges from a private letter.[15] Travellers reporting on visits to Greek monasteries have generally, in print, expressed pleasure at their reception and at the food they got, simple though it usually was. Leake, at the Virgin of Porto delle Quaglie, enjoyed 'by far the most agreeable lodging I have met with in Mani', and a very healthy supper:

> On the eastern side a spring issues from the side of the hill, and falls over several terraces of garden ground on the side of the mountain, which are grown with olives, caroubs, and cypresses, mixed with a few orange-trees. The garden furnishes me with a salad for dinner, and the stores of the convent some of the choicest Maniate honey.

Leake's Greek guides had earned a hot meal, so they got bean soup and salted olives.[16] Those olives will recur.

George Wheler in 1682 notes a monastery breakfast 'with bread and honey and olives, good wine, and *aqua vitae*' (an early mention of what later writers know as *raki*) which the abbot allowed himself to enjoy with

The kitchen gardens of Iviron monastery ('of the Iberians', from what is now Georgia). The monastery gardens of Athos have hardly changed since Vasilii Barski sketched them in 1744.

his guests in 'a kind of buttery' after morning service. This was near Livadia in Boiotia, and Wheler went on to dine with three hermits living under Mount Helikon. Their usual food was bread and herbs, their drink water, and even those were enjoyed only on four days of each week. On festival days Wheler's host might eat a little honey; wine he would taste only at communion. His two neighbours had a garden 'well planted with beans and pease, and another just by it furnished with four or five hundred stocks of bees'. Wheler was entertained with 'a plate of delicate white honeycombs, with bread and olives, and very good wine', dining 'with far greater satisfaction than the most princely banquet in Europe could afford us'.[17]

Pierre Belon visited several of the monasteries of Mount Athos, and was invited to share a Lenten dinner. The abbot 'served us rocket, celeriac, heads of leek, cucumbers, onions and nice little green garlic shoots. We ate these herbs raw, without oil or vinegar. That is their regular diet,' Belon observes, but he was additionally offered black conserved olives, biscuits (*paximadia*, not bread, because there had been no baking) and wine.

> During a fast they can eat all kinds of crabs, sea-squirts and shell-fish such as mussels and oysters . . . They always start their meals with raw onions and garlic; their main dishes are salted olives and broad beans soaked in water, and they finish with rocket and

cress . . . It is not only the monks who choose to live like this but the priests and other churchmen of Greece and also the common people, who during their fasts would not eat fish with blood, or meat, or any other inappropriate food even if they were to die for lack of it.[18]

Belon's sea-squirts will be explained below. Monastery olives are a staple in reality as they are in these narratives. Nothing was in commoner use than conserved olives, Belon writes elsewhere, and these were quite different from the olives familiar in France, being 'black, ripe, and kept without any sauce, like dried prunes'.[19] Wheler, 125 years later, agrees: pickled olives were the Lenten mainstay, 'not pickled green as in these parts but when they are full ripe and full of oil. They eat them with vinegar, being very nourishing and wholesome food and very grateful to the stomach.'[20] Another 125 years takes us to Dodwell: 'When the olive ripens, it grows black, and falls from the tree; it is then eaten, with bread and salt, without any preparation.'[21] Those olives, like the vegetables and herbs, came from the monasteries' communal kitchen gardens, and Belon adds that some monks had their own little gardens too. The Russian monk Vasilii Barskii, who made sketches of the monasteries of Mount Athos during his visits there in 1725 and 1744, was particularly careful to draw these kitchen gardens and the monks at work in them. Monastic gardeners did not grow much cereal, Belon observes; they had vines, olive trees, figs, onions, garlic, broad beans and vegetables, and exchanged their surplus with sailors who brought them wheat. They also gathered bayberries, pressed them for oil,

Formerly a monastery staple noted by every traveller, *hamades* are olives gathered when already fully ripe, either fallen or about to fall, and conserved in salt.

and sent it for sale in the Balkans.[22] Meat being entirely ruled out, they kept no domestic animals and did not even catch wild birds, but some monks passed their time in sea fishing, Belon observes; sure enough, Barskii depicts a monk of Esphigmenou fishing with a rod, and another in a rowing boat spearing an octopus with a trident.[23]

Several writers were impressed by the vast wooden casks in which wine was stored in monastery cellars. Iakobos, sacristan of Iviron on Athos, was luckily free to show Cyriac of Ancona the monastery cellars:

> In the absence of the Georgian abbot of Iviron, Gerasimos, who was on a diplomatic mission to the Turk, it was the sacristan him-self who showed me all the important holdings of the monastery including three ancient wine casks, huge in size, for we measured the first one that he showed us, full of wine, as twenty feet long and ten feet in diameter.[24]

Wheler had a similar experience: when it came to the cellars, it was not the abbot but a monk who had served as interpreter, 'a young father that spake very good Italian, being a native of Zant' (Zakynthos), who took him to see the stocks of wine and olives, 'which they preserve in the longest casks I ever saw, several of them I measured near twenty foot long'.[25] Leake was more impressed by the cellars at the cave monastery Megaspelio, near Kalavryta, cooled in summer by its thick walls and by the water trickling down the rock, than by the flavourless and diluted red wine that the casks contained.[26]

Although meat was unavailable on Athos and ruled out for monks elsewhere, some monastery guests were lucky enough to get some. Wheler reported a most hearty and Christian welcome: a lamb was killed for the party, and the meal included rice, chickens, good olives, cheese, bread and wine.[27] The two roving Englishwomen, visiting St Basil's monastery at Meteora, also benefited from the slaughter of a lamb and were encouraged to share the titbits from the head. One of the two, braver (I believe) than Patrick Leigh Fermor on a similar occasion, accepted the most honourable portion of all, an eye. Rice, pickled cabbage, yoghurt and cheese were also on the menu. The abbot took no meat for himself, but did not go as far as to object when others transferred the meat from their overloaded plates on to his.[28]

It was good, then, to be invited to a meal even by hosts who were pre-vented by religious rule from being as generous to themselves as they were

Sketch of the *xenodochion* (inn) and the rival Hotel Olympia, *c.* 1890, where Edith Payne and
Isabel Armstrong first encountered yoghurt ('very sour clotted cream'); from Armstrong's
Two Roving Englishwomen in Greece (1893).

to their guests. Better still, logically and in reality, is to be invited home,
and this thought is the starting point for Lawrence Durrell's nuanced
answer to the general question of whether Greek food is good. If the real
test is what the Greeks ate at home, then he allows no doubt that they eat
well, they choose well, they cook well. Invited to a private house or to some
family festivity, one would be astonished at the variety and tastiness of the
food. But it takes a lot of preparation, Durrell adds: 'Always in the background there is the hovering figure of grandma who has been up since four
to start cooking for the feast.' The very tastiest and the most varied foods
tend to be encountered at the beginning of a good Greek meal, served
briefly, successively, individually in small quantities as *mezedes*, 'starters'
so to speak; understandably so, Durrell adds, when the food is likely to be
enjoyed outdoors, shaded by a vine.[29] In proper Greek dining, main courses
gradually follow in the same way and in similar variety, very much in the
Chinese fashion, and this is quite different from the sequential meal with
long gaps between courses that the French prefer and from the rushed
series, over and done with as soon as possible, that the English thrive on.
A good Greek meal is shared by a party – larger, ideally, than the three or
four or five that Archestratos considered to be an absolute maximum – and
takes a long time.

Conviviality being a precondition in good Greek dining, the pleasure
to be gained from a restaurant meal depends on a complex negotiation:
what food there is, what the cook can do with it, what the party brings to
the restaurant and what the restaurant gives to the party. The negotiation
may be doomed. 'It is impossible to get a decent boiled egg in the country;

no one has the faintest idea what three and a quarter minutes really are,' Humphrey Kitto averred.[30] He may have been right at that, but he would have done better not to worry about it. Durrell similarly lost his sense of humour over food that was not served even reasonably warm; Fielding was fated never to get used to Cretan village cooking, which, he admitted, would be tolerable if the food were served hot, 'but it never is';[31] while Leigh Fermor tells a story of ordering fried eggs and chips and waiting half an hour while they were cooked and allowed to cool. 'Hot food is bad,' the café owner told him. 'It makes people ill.'[32]

Since good Greek food depends on the place and the season – and on chance – good restaurants will be inconsistent. 'Dinner was always a surprise,' the two roving Englishwomen found, 'the menu varying from three to six courses.'[33] They were lucky. Kitto while in Tsakonia was sometimes satisfied with one: 'Nothing to be got today. Would you like an omelette?'[34]

Kostas Prekas's shop on Syros is famous far beyond the island for its range of traditional products from all over Greece. He sells his own sun-dried tomatoes, salted capers and other conserves.

There is an art to being satisfied, and it is easily learned. Kitto learned it, not long after Tsakonia, on the day when he found 'a second breakfast . . . a vast dish of fried liver and tomatoes in the restaurant-half of a butcher's shop'.[35] 'You get over your first vexation rapidly' (Lawrence Durrell might have been responding to Kitto) 'and sink into a resigned mood where you accept whatever comes with equanimity – and so much is really good that does come.'[36] Durrell at this point names some of the very best: lobster or crayfish on Hydra, *sofrito* on Corfu (see recipe on page 169), *soutzoukakia* (spitted entrails) on Rhodes. Accepting what comes with equanimity means being ready to wait for those great dishes until they happen to present themselves, and enjoying the fried liver at the butcher's meanwhile. This, in a sense, was what the two Englishwomen did on their first evening at Olympia, when 'dinner turned out much better than we expected':

> The soup was strong – we pronounced it excellent – though it cannot be denied that it would have had a very soothing effect on a troubled sea; then came lamb cut about in various curious forms and served à la discretion, followed by cutlets that explained the former dish; a sort of very sour clotted cream and oranges brought the repast to an end. The resinous wine of the country, both red and white, was quite drinkable, dry and exceedingly wholesome.[37]

This, also, is exactly what Felix Faber did. We return to the fifteenth century and to Candia (Heraklion) on Crete, where he arrived one evening by ship as one of a miscellaneous party of German pilgrims, 'nobles, priests, and monks', on their way to the Holy Land:

> We found no inn save one that I am sorry to say was a brothel, which was kept by a German woman . . . As soon as we entered she cleared her house and put all of its rooms at our service. She was a well-mannered, respectful, and discreet woman, and obtained all that we needed in great quantity, and we had a glorious supper with Cretan wine, which is what we know as malmsey. That day we had ripe grapes, black and white, in great plenty.[38]

Durrell gives another useful pointer: 'One must work to find one's own palatable restaurant in whichever place one is.'[39] Four hundred and fifty years after Faber, forty years before Durrell wrote, Fielding worked away at this task in Chania at the western end of Crete, and settled on a nameless harbour tavern:

> There was no menu; one only had to lift the lids of the copper cauldrons bubbling over charcoal braziers to see, quite literally, what was cooking. The food was sometimes excellent and always unpretentious: young octopus stewed with tomatoes and olives; sucking-pig cooked in the same way; cod-steaks with *skordalia*, the Cretan equivalent of Provençal *aioli*; veal-steaks grilled, or grilled red-mullet; sometimes only soup, lentil or chick-pea or bean with . . . my favourite 'volcanic' salad.[40]

The Raw Materials: Fruit and Vegetables

Fruits are among the first foods named in Greek poetry and they are the stuff of poetry even now. We have seen that the *Odyssey* evoked an orchard in Phaiakia, a fictionalized Corfu, stocked with six fruit species.[41] In medieval literature, in a speech of welcome to Princess Agnes of France, Archbishop Eustathios described the emperor Manuel, who used marriage alliances as a means to shore up Byzantine defences, as an orchardman bringing young fruit trees from north, south, east and west to plant them in Constantinople. A funeral lament recorded in modern Mani adopts the same image:

> Death planned to make an orchard.
> He dug it and prepared the ground to plant trees in it.
> He plants young maids as lemon-trees, young men as cypresses,
> He planted little children as rose-trees all around,
> And put the old men, too, as a hedge around his orchard.[42]

The orchards of Greece have become ever more varied. Olives, grapes and figs, already being cultivated several thousand years ago, were joined towards the end of the prehistoric period by the apples, pears and pomegranates listed in the *Odyssey*, along with plums, quinces and walnuts. The classical period added cherries, peaches, apricots, pistachios and citrons. Then came lemons, bitter and sweet oranges and most recently kiwi fruit. They have all found their place in Greek food: lemons, for one, it is now hard to imagine doing without. And yet the wild fruit species known to the earliest human inhabitants of Greece, some of them occasionally grown

Not beautiful, not good to eat, but very aromatic, the citron (*Citrus medica*) was the first of the citrus fruits to reach the Mediterranean, soon after Alexander the Great's time. It is grown in Greece now and gives its distinctive flavour to an island liqueur, *kitron Naxou*.

in gardens, some never yet taken into cultivation, are still found in the forests. One such is the strawberry tree (arbutus), noticed by Leake in wild country in the Peloponnese, discussed on Corfu in Durrell's hearing for a curious property attributed to its fruit: 'I wonder', his friend Theodore Stephanides is quoted in *Prospero's Cell* as saying, 'if you have remarked that arbutus berries are among the things which can also intoxicate?'[43] Biologist, radiologist and poet, Stephanides long afterwards published his personal observations on Greece, its natural history and its food, and gave chapter and verse for that unexpected assertion:

> In September and October the arbutus, sometimes called strawberry trees, are heavy with their clustered orange-red fruit, each the size of a large cherry, which can be made into a delicious jelly having a delicate strawberry aroma. If eaten raw on an empty stomach, these berries produce a kind of intoxication resembling drunkenness. On the Macedonian front, during the First World War, I once saw a whole working-party of some fifty men reduced to a state of hilarious inebriation from its effects.[44]

Among cultivated fruits the grape is never forgotten as a source of wine, but it is possible to overlook the pleasure of eating fresh grapes in season. It was to supply table grapes to Athens markets that vines used to be grown at Ambelokipi, 'vine gardens', now an inner-city district and a metro station known to those who travel to and from the airport. There Bernard Randolph (quoted more fully on page 177) walked through 'very pleasant gardens which afford all sort of fruit and saleting, having walks round them covered with vines'.[45] It was for the supply of table grapes after the usual season that big shady plane trees once flourished beside the river at Platanias, 'the plane trees', west of Chania on Crete. They were admired by Richard Pococke in 1743:

> They are very high, and make a most beautiful grove; vines are planted at the bottom of them, which twine about the trees, and are left to grow naturally without pruning; and being backward by reason of the shady situation, do not ripen till the vintage is past; they hang on the trees till Christmas, and bring in a very considerable revenue.[46]

The same trees and the same vines, by now 'of a size unknown in France or Italy, the thickness of many of their stems being that of an ordinary man's waist', were praised by Robert Pashley in 1837 as 'one of the objects best worth viewing by those who visit Khaniá'. Edward Lear, Pashley's most assiduous reader, made his way there in 1864 'along refreshing nightingale-haunted green lanes', but he came too late: the vines were dead and the plane trees, now useless, had been felled.[47]

Arbutus or strawberry tree, *Arbutus unedo*. The small white flowers, unripe and ripe red fruit are all visible in October.

Naxian and Greek Salads

We follow the course of a torrent overhung by plane
trees and full of oleanders, and so enter an Arcadian
valley with two villages. The larger of these, Melanes,
a half-hour east, is our destination. Still following
the watercourse, with an occasional pool and abundant planes, we rise over an outcrop of white marble
to the village. It is on the south side of the gorge,
whereas the far famed *peribolia* (gardens), which had
invited this hot journey, are on the other . . . My
guide has deliberately misled me in order to visit his
own home at my expense; for the village café, with its
pretty hostess Kaliope, seems to be among his family
affairs. But one might easily have found a worse place
for a hot noon-day: there was cool shade, fresh eggs,
good bread, figs to melt in one's mouth, delicious
grapes, and Naxian wine . . . Upon this feast, topped
off with good Turkish coffee and a short siesta, I am
half ready to forgive the young rascal.

So wrote J. Irving Manatt, an American living on Andros
but here visiting neighbouring Naxos, in his book *Aegean Days*
(1914). Those 'far famed *peribolia*' are virtually unchanged and
still well tended today, a hundred years later, and Melanes is
still a good place for lunch. A long, hot and ultimately satisfying walk on Naxos in early November led us from lushly
terraced valleys dotted with watermills to a steep donkey track

Fruit is occasionally mentioned in Greek narratives of festivity;
vegetables almost never. No one boasts of them. Yet their importance is
evident, especially in everyday food (meat being always a luxury), especially for poorer people (meat and fish being expensive), especially for
poor people living in country districts if they have the space and time to
tend a kitchen garden. A poor old woman in an ancient comedy listed
the mainstays of her life, including beans, lupin seeds, turnips, black-
eyed peas and *bolboi*.[49] Cabbage, lettuce, chicory, turnip and beet were

among olive groves, a rocky pass leading to an ancient half-finished *kouros* statue lying where it broke and was abandoned 2,500 years ago, and to an elusive ancient aqueduct entrance. And then the gardens that Manatt wrote of, steeply terraced on one side of the valley, curling around, and with no easy way down or across the stream. And once crossed, more orchards and kitchen gardens and finally Melanes itself and the taverna O Giorgos. We ate sweet cucumbers, their own, the first of the season — a whole plate of them — peeled and sliced the thickness of a couple of euros; and *anthotyro*, again their own, fresh white cheese skimmed from the top of the milk — the really creamy milk that is only possible after the early autumn rain has produced fresh green shoots for the goats to graze on — dressed with oil and eaten with bread.

The classic 'Greek salad' of a thousand menus is tomato, cucumber, onion, green pepper, feta cheese, olives and oregano. But Greek salads are manifold: sensible combinations of good ingredients, dressed with a limp wrist, consumed with a generous amount of country or sourdough bread. John Fowles suggests one: 'We had lunch, a simple Greek meal of goat's milk cheese and green pepper salad with eggs, under the colonnade.'[48] Tomatoes are the basis of many, but they must be good: from the end of July until October they can be tart, sweet, even reminiscent of strawberries in their remarkable range of flavours. Add at will red onion, cucumber, capers, green peppers, red peppers, white salty cheese like feta or *myzithra*, soft purslane leaves, oregano, and so on.

known to classical Greeks; broad beans, peas, lentils and chickpeas had been familiar for thousands of years. They were even potential staples if wheat and barley fell short, but, if there was bread, the pulses would commonly serve as main dish. In medieval Lakonia, Cyriac of Ancona reported, 'their meals consist of split beans seasoned generously with oil, and their loaves are made from barley.'[50] Even for such basic foods one depended on a peaceful environment and on access to water for irrigation, as observed by Leake, whose travels through Greece took place

Watermelon and Feta Salad

For two people: a wide slice of watermelon, perhaps
300 g, rind removed and the flesh cut into large chunks
150 g feta cheese, roughly crumbled over the melon
black pepper
a little olive oil and a lot of bread

Eat, spitting out the seeds.

Watermelon goes even better with *touloumisio*, hard goats' milk
cheese with a honeycomb-like texture, matured in a goat's
stomach, but that is difficult to find.

at the beginning of the nineteenth century, in the last few years before
Greece gained its independence from the Turks:

> The summer productions of the garden . . . which depend on
> irrigation, such as gourds, cucumbers, badinjans [aubergines],
> water-melons, &c. are too dear for the poor, or rather are not
> to be had, as gardening, the produce of which is so liable to be
> plundered, can never flourish in a country where property is so
> insecure as in Turkey.[51]

In this brief list Leake includes two species – gourds and watermelons
– that were already available in ancient Greece but are scarcely even mentioned in classical literature. Between them he names cucumbers and
aubergines, both of which are now known to have been introduced in
Byzantine times. He might have added spinach, likewise; and tomatoes,
quite a recent arrival, indispensable today; he might have added onions
and garlic, and of course leeks, which were so quietly significant in classical
times that a vegetable bed was literally called a leek-bed, *prasion*. They are
still significant now, as in another poetic lament from Mani. 'I was in a
garden and among my herbs,' the mourner weeps. 'I picked the parsley and
pulled up the leeks . . . The parsley is my tears, the leeks are my sorrow.'[52]
Pulses and some others are likely enough to make a *meze* or side dish, such
as the *gigantes* of so many restaurant menus; vegetables can be baked in a

Peloponnesian Orange Salad

Skin a couple of large, thick-skinned oranges — the thick-skinned ones are good for eating — by topping and tailing them, then running a sharp knife down the length in curves, between the flesh and the pith. Slice the oranges into rounds and arrange on a plate with as much of their juice as you can catch. Finely chop a couple of spring onions and sprinkle them over the oranges. Crumble over the top some soft, sharp, white goats' or sheep's cheese: *xinomyzithra*, for example. Finish with a few red chilli flakes. Dress with a little oil but no vinegar.

Naxos Potato Salad

500 g boiled Naxian potatoes, cut into large bite-sized pieces
a couple of plum tomatoes, quartered
½ red onion, sliced
½ tbsp salted capers, drained and soaked
olive oil, vinegar to taste, a little salt
(capers are already very salty)

The potatoes of Naxos, buttery with the perfect combination of flouriness and waxiness, are equally good in salads and as the accompaniment to a roast. The menu of Meze Meze in Naxos town offers 'potato salad' and 'Naxos potato salad': choose the latter. In Lefkes on Paros (visible from Naxos town), potato salad would be different: potatoes and caper leaves dressed with oil.

pie, spinach (*spanakopita*) and even lettuce (*maroulopita*); and sappy and juicy fresh vegetables will feature in the 'Greek salad' of restaurant lunches, not forgetting those that Xan Fielding preferred in his 'volcanic salad': 'garlic and raw onions, red and green and orange peppers and – as a cooling element – half a dozen little pear-shaped winter tomatoes'.[53]

Also belonging to the vegetable kingdom are aromatic herbs and spices, those that the Byzantines and the Turks who followed them used in food for their health and pleasure, in the tradition that the Asia Minor Greeks retained and the independent Greeks almost forgot, and would have forgotten if Nikolaos Tselementes had had his way. It was not to be: Greek food now makes good use of aromatics, and Artemis Leontis neatly tabulates the ones that often seem to go together: 'lemon and dill, lemon and olive oil, vinegar and olive oil, vinegar and honey, vinegar and garlic, garlic and oregano, garlic and mint, tomatoes and cinnamon, tomatoes and capers, anise (or ouzo) and pepper, orange and fennel, allspice and cloves, pine nuts and currants, *mahlepi* and *mastiha*.'[54] Later arrivals from east and west brought the cloves, lemon, orange, tomatoes and allspice, but some of those combinations are already familiar from ancient cookery.

THE RAW MATERIALS: FISH AND MEAT

For those living near the sea, shellfish and other invertebrate seafood is important in spring for exactly the same reason as the wild greens. For those who keep to the traditional rules, fish as well as meat is forbidden during fasts but 'fish without blood' is permitted. Hence the great effort put into seafood cuisine at medieval Constantinople; hence the comprehensive interest in modern Greece in the unfishy things that come out of the sea, cuttlefish and squid, crab and lobster and crayfish and shrimp. And the octopus: 'The octopus is to be beaten with twice seven blows,' according to the Greek proverb, because it will be very hard to eat unless thus tenderized.[55] And the sea urchin, which Xan Fielding learned to enjoy at his favourite taverna in Chania, in taste 'a mixture of grit, slime and iodine: the very essence of the sea': hedgehog-like on the outside, hence its name, but very different on the inside. He would watch the purple spines still moving even when the body was bisected and the deep orange 'contents' – the ovaries – were scooped out on to a crust of bread. Fielding wanted to drink white wine with this luxurious *meze*, but his host insisted on ouzo.[56] And the sea-squirt, the only 'fish without blood' mentioned in the *Iliad*, carefully described by Aristotle because no other living thing is quite like it (it is not so much an animal as a microcosm) and recommended by Archestratos for purchase at Kalchedon opposite Byzantion. Sea-squirt, modern Greek *fouska*, ancient *tethyon*, is to be cut in half and the soft yellow interior ('like scrambled egg', says Alan Davidson) eaten raw.[57] Let it be seasoned with lemon juice; or else with the aromas recommended by the ancient seafood writer Xenokrates, but necessarily using asafoetida in place of the vanished *silphion*: '*Sea-squirt.*

It is cut and rinsed and seasoned with *silphion* from Kyrene and rue and brine and vinegar, or with fresh mint in vinegar and sweet wine.'[58]

Ever since the people of Franchthi cave went hunting for tunny, the Aegean has been famous for its fish. And ever since the invention of coinage, Greeks have been ready to pay good money for good fish. These riches have extended along the Dardanelles (Hellespont), into the Sea of Marmara (Propontis), and to the very shores of Constantinople. The Propontis has been no less productive in seafood than any region of good pasture is in animals, Pierre Belon observed, adding that 'the whole population of Turkey and Greece favours fish over meat as food.'[59] With a very long coastline, a high proportion of inhabitants living close to the sea, and some excellent city markets, Greece is unique in its special focus on marine gastronomy. 'They fish with a little light in their boat, which the fishes seeing follow, which the fisherman perceiving presently strikes the fish with a trident,' wrote Wheler in 1682.[60] Much Aegean fishing is on a very small scale, but stocks are declining and the industry is under deadly threat as governments encourage unsustainable methods with one foot and stamp out local traditions with the other.[61]

Whether sold at the harbourside or at a market, when it reaches a kitchen the fish is likely to be cooked as simply as Archestratos recommended, and perhaps using exactly the same recipe. The perfect way to deal with each species, once devised, has no need to change. Faced with a fish he did not know, Fielding was taught the three lines of verse that define the appropriate punning recipe Σκάροι στη σχάρα (*skaroi sti schara*, wrasse on the grill):

> My name is *skaros*, cook me on the grill
> And dish me up in oil and vinegar:
> Then you can eat me up, my guts and all.[62]

That was a fish for which ancient Romans paid high prices, but their poet Martial was a choosy eater: 'Its guts are good: the rest tastes cheap.'[63]

If you order fresh fish in a restaurant (frozen fish must not be sold as fresh), you will point to the fish you fancy and pay for it by weight, remembering, if you wish, the many discussions on the ancient Athenian stage concerning the high price of fish. The fresh fish will probably not be enumerated on the menu: how could it be? No one can know what will arrive each day. It depends on the fishermen and also on the fish. As a mere hint of the potential variation, Diane Kochilas provides a brief fish calendar for northwestern Greece: 'Bream (*tsipoures*) are at their peak in September. The small ones, known as *ligdes*, are preserved lightly in salt and olive oil.'[64]

Meat is the luxury that humans hardly deserve. What excuses the people of prehistoric Greece made for killing their farm animals we cannot fully know, but we do know that some feasted at sanctuaries, thus bringing gods into it. This is certainly what classical Greeks did: an animal was sacrificed – in all senses of that word – and nearly all its meat was shared among the human participants in the ritual, leaving very little for the gods to whom it was offered. This is the background to the Byzantine and modern Greek approach to meat: common enough now on restaurant menus, but not always available when expected; much commoner in modern life than it was in the past, but eaten by most Greeks in much smaller quantities than by northern Europeans, because meat (especially

Wall painting of the Last Supper, Vatopedi monastery, Mount Athos, *c.* 1312.

Miran, the most popular charcuterie in the Monastiraki district of Athens and a long-established landmark. *Soutsouks* and *pastourma* are hanging from the ceiling.

lamb) is still the sacrificial food, even though the god has changed and the philosophy of religion too.

Killing an animal produces a lot of food, from the muscle meat, which may well be roasted, to the head, which will provide special delicacies, to the innards, which are converted into all kind of picturesque and tasty products. Once the animal has been killed all except the muscle meat will eventually be eaten without any celebration or ritual. But roast meat makes a celebration, whether it is the dinner offered to guests in the ancient *Iliad* and *Odyssey*, or the Easter lamb or wedding feast of modern Greece, or a more modest celebratory meal. At major events it may still be the men who do the roasting, as it was in the epics, but not always. 'There's a marvellous leg of lamb in here,' Patrick Leigh Fermor's temporary companion told him, patting his rucksack. It was from a three-month-old spring lamb, and to be roasted by his landlady, 'all wrapped up in grease-paper . . . she pokes whole garlic cloves right down between the meat and the bone.' Duly roasted and unwrapped, the golden-brown leg of lamb would be 'blistering and bubbling with juice and surrounded by a brood of spitting potatoes', all redolent of garlic, thyme and rosemary.[65]

Minced meat may go into economical dishes such as *soutzoukakia* or *keftedes*, or it may be extended further into pies, for meat, too, is among the potential fillings of the pies produced with local variants in every part of Greece.

Or into sausages. Many butchers in Greece make their own, mainly from pork, but also beef and lamb, or a mix of meats, and the recipes vary from region to region and butcher to butcher. People can travel a long distance to a favoured sausage-maker. Varying natural resources and a long history of population exchange result in sausages from the northernmost regions differing substantially from the south. In Thrace and Greek Macedonia the aromatics are similar or identical to those used in the neighbouring Balkan countries of Bulgaria and former Yugoslav Macedonia. Hot red chilli peppers (known as *boukovo*), whether fresh or dried and flaked, are used liberally, together with ground cumin, allspice and black pepper. At Kozani in central Macedonia sausages are coloured a deep orange with the saffron stamens that take their name from the area, *krokos Kozanis*; around the Naoussa region east of Thessaloniki, where there is still a semi-nomadic Vlach minority, they are made with a mix of a little pork meat and fat and the goat meat so readily available in shepherd communities. The sausages of Trikkala in Thessaly are sweetened with leeks. Further south, and in the Peloponnese, winter savory and orange peel are preferred aromatics, as they are in the Maniot *singlino* (discussed shortly); the nearby Lakonian plain is famous for its orange crop, the largest in the Peloponnese. Island sausages are variously aromatic with local herbs: garlic is added on Syros together with fennel seeds, as also on Tinos; aniseed on Paros and on Andros, where the sausages are then preserved in lard and used to make a type of frittata, *fourtalia*. Winter savory and thyme scent Mykonos sausages. In western Crete oregano, thyme and cumin are mixed with the mince, which is then soaked in red wine for up to a week before encasing. Sausages in Cyprus often contain coriander seed, common in Cypriot cuisine but virtually unused in the rest of Greece, and they are again soaked in red wine for several days before being encased.

On Corfu, in the Ionian islands as well as on Crete and in parts of the Peloponnese, a version of the Venetian *boldon* or blood sausage is found, spiced with garlic, cinnamon, cloves and nutmeg. The *bourdouni*, brought by Venetians to Corfu, is made with calf's blood and pig's fat. It may well be traceable to ancient Greek blood sausages, in which case, via the Roman and then the Venetian kitchen, it has returned to its motherland. Mariana Kavroulaki points out that although blood in food is outside the culinary mainstream, many such dishes of medieval or older origin are still found across Greece; but replacing blood with lung and spleen is common.[66]

These sausages, for the most part, are lightly air-dried or smoked and consumed 'fresh' – within a few weeks of production. Alongside them there is a strong tradition of preserved and cured meats: in a peasant or semi-nomadic community, before refrigeration, there had to be means of preserving meat for long periods after the slaughter of an animal.

If there is one item of charcuterie repeated throughout Greece, it is salted and smoked pork, usually tenderloin. Traditionally, after the family pig was slaughtered at Christmas and the perishable delicacies such as the liver, heart and spleen had been consumed, the leftover meat would be preserved for the remaining winter months and beyond. Tenderloin is an ideal cut for smoking and serving thinly sliced as a *meze* for ouzo or *tsipouro*. The name and the flavourings vary but the method endures. On Tinos and Andros it is commonly found flavoured with fennel seeds, black pepper and allspice; on Syros spiced with pepper, allspice, cinnamon and cloves; and on all three islands it is marinated in red wine.

On Santorini and Crete the Byzantine name *apokti* survives for a variant in which the pork loin is unsmoked and marinated in vinegar. It is trimmed, salted for a day, steeped in vinegar for three days, then patted dry, rubbed with cinnamon and left thus for about six hours so that the spice adheres to the meat: 'Then it is rubbed with ground black pepper, dried savory and more cinnamon and hung to dry for several weeks.'[67] Out of this grew the Cretan *apaki*: the tenderloin is again soaked in vinegar but then smoked for several days and flavoured with ground cumin and herbs such as sage, thyme and savory.[68]

The Corfiot *nouboulo* is smoked over an aromatic fire of sage, bay, myrtle, oregano and almond husks, and in the Mani region of the Peloponnese the now very fashionable *singlino* is smoked over sage or cypress branches. Here the predominant flavouring – as with the sausages of that region – is orange peel, and the loins are salted and pressed with mountain sage branches before smoking. These days, as traditional methods and regional specialities heve regained popularity, many of these once obscure preparations can be bought in supermarkets, vacuum-packed, sliced and ready for the *tsipouro meze*.

The north of Greece differs in the methods of preservation and in the main ingredient, preferring fried beef or goat (although pig is commoner than it once was) stored in lard or oil. The *kavourmas* or *kaparnas* of Thrace is usually beef, which is salted, cooked in oil with herbs for six hours or so

The best-known Greek cheese is surely feta. The best Greek feta is barrel-matured.

Myzithra is one of the widespread class of whey cheeses, traditionally a means of making the fullest possible use of the food value of the milk. *Yiayia*, 'granny', stirs the whey as it coagulates.

Cretan *graviera*. The name is borrowed from Gruyère, but in its regional Greek incarnations the product has become very different: a small wheel of typically very hard sheep's-milk cheese.

until the fat is rendered out, rolled into thick sausage shapes and stored much like a French *confit*. *Soutzouk*, the dense, salami-like sausages found all over the Balkan region, take their name from the Turkish word for sausage – which is what they are, although pressed and dried for preservation.

Throughout the north, from Macedonia eastwards, is found *pastourma*, the dried and cured beef known all over the Eastern Mediterranean in former Ottoman countries. It is beef or occasionally camel, which some say makes the best *pastourma* of all and which can be found in the centre of Athens in specialist delicatessens. As a complete contrast, an Italian-style salami – fatty pork with plenty of seasoning and garlic – was introduced by immigrants from Burano in the Venetian gulf to Leukas in the eighteenth century, and is now also made in Crete, Thasos and Eurytania.

THE RAW MATERIALS: BREAD AND CHEESE

In farming terms meat, the death of the animal, weighs against milk, a recurrent food source if it can be conserved. Leake took a close interest in the farming economy and gives an outline of the milk business. 'A good ewe', he begins, 'gives at every milking a pound of milk, of which are made butter, cheese, misithra, and yaourt.' He then explains the making of the first three, one leading to the next. For butter the milk was left for twenty-four hours to become sour and then churned in a narrow cask with a stick to produce butter. The remaining liquid (buttermilk) was mixed with an equal quantity of milk: this mixture (*tyrogalo*), warmed, with salted rennet added, would produce cheese, whose making he then describes. The remaining liquid this time (*nerogalo*, 'milk-water') had a further use:

> *To make misithra.* The *nerogalo* . . . is placed upon the fire: about a tenth of milk is added to it, and after a short boiling the misithra is collected on the surface. Goat's milk makes the best misithra, even though the butter has been extracted from it.[69]

Myzithra is thus a whey cheese and a Greek version of ricotta, as the Dutch travellers Egmont and Heyman noticed on their visit to Kythera, then a Venetian possession where Italian was spoken: 'Its most remarkable commodity is a kind of cheese, called *ricotta*: it is made of goats' milk boiled.'[70] French travellers similarly equate *myzithra* with *recuite*, a product once typical of Savoy.

Yoghurt is described with puzzlement even in the writings of recent travellers: it is hard to remember now how unfamiliar it used to be. Many were faced with it for the first time in Greece, such as the two roving Englishwomen of 1893, who spoke of 'a sort of very sour clotted cream,'[71] and Lawrence Durrell in 1945, whose glossary includes the line '*Yaourti*: a sort of junket of curdled milk sprinkled with cinnamon.'[72]

The cheese of Greece is more varied, and often better, than any but very recent visitors have been able to see: the best cheeses too rarely reach the most discriminating consumers. Some are unusual indeed, such as the sea-washed *melipasto* of Lemnos. Some are both good and well-known, none more so than brined and barrel-aged feta, a traditional Middle Eastern style of cheese which in Greece is made from sheep's milk or with up to 30 per cent goats' milk. Imitation being the best form of praise, Greek feta is imitated elsewhere in the world, and until recently the imitations could legally be called feta. In the European Union, since a legal battle with Denmark was settled in 2002, only the Greek product can have this name. Many other Greek cheeses now have appellations of origin, but none of those others is as famous ouside its own region as Greece's best-known cheesemaker, the Sphakiot (of southwestern Crete) Barba Pantzelios, known not for his cheese but for the epic poem he composed in 1786, the *Song of Daskalogiannis*, celebrating the bravery and death of a rebel who fought the Turks.

Bread has been baked in Greece for at least seven thousand years, and the bread ovens of classical Athens were famous in their time; it was surely the first city in the world where money could be used to buy bread. Good Greek bread now, raised bread, is the body of many a simple meal and the accompaniment to nearly every restaurant meal. But there are others too – the hard *paximadia* that have played such a part in history, and the ring-shaped *koulouria* that are bought in such quantity in city streets as a quick breakfast. As with meat, beliefs and rituals surround bread, and special breads are often baked for special occasions: Christmas and Easter, engagements and weddings and the birth of a child. Bread in the morning, cakes in the afternoon, but Greek cakes are very different from bread, in a tradition that is easily assumed to be Turkish (most of the names are Turkish, *kadaifi, baklava*) but has pervasive similarities with what we know of classical and Byzantine patisserie. Certainly this tradition is very different from that of northern Europe, most obviously, perhaps, because the cakes – most cakes – come soaked in honey. So, it appears, they always did. 'Eat the best honey fresh. It is not only pleasant to eat, but prolongs life,' the Byzantine farming manual *Geoponika* wisely advises, adding that the ancient philosopher Demokritos, asked how men could ensure health and long life, replied: 'By treating their outsides with oil and their insides with honey.'[73] As to the olive oil, it is used less to treat the outside these days – soap has replaced it for that purpose – but it remains the staple of the Greek kitchen and, today, of the Mediterranean diet. Table olives are sold at markets in many varieties and styles and in great quantities. And market sales are only a partial reflection of the significance of olives and olive oil, because many country people have their own olive trees, from which they supply family and friends as well as their own households.

The Accompaniments

'Water is best,' the classical poet Pindar famously wrote.[74] Water has always been important in Greece. George Manwaring, who was in Zakynthos around 1598, asked his host's servant for a cup of water. 'The merchant, hearing me, told me I should drink wine so much as I would, for his water was dearer unto him than his wine.'[75] Ancient Greeks were careful to evaluate the quality of the water from different springs, using criteria that are obscure to us. A long catalogue of springs is found in the *Deipnosophists*, including one 'very drinkable and with a wine-like flavour: local people are said to go to it for their drinking parties . . . I weighed the water from the Corinthian spring Peirene,' a speaker adds, 'and found that it was lighter than any other in Greece.'[76] This special expertise was retained into recent times. Water of Lake Kastoria in Macedonia (covered with a green surface, hot, turbid and by no means tasteless, according to Leake) was preferred by local people in the nineteenth century to that of local springs, which they considered heavy.[77] Even in the 1930s 'the Greek countryman is a connoisseur of waters as some Westerners are of wines,' writes Kitto. 'Your guide will tell you not to drink at this spring: the water is poor and thin . . . better wait half an hour when you will reach a spring whose water is much lighter.'[78]

Tea and chocolate have never made much impression in Greece – 'tea' will sometimes be understood as meaning not the Chinese camellia leaf (called 'European tea') but a local herbal infusion. Coffee is different. As was demonstrated by Antoine Galland, the first European expert on the history of coffee, it began its world conquest from the southern shores of the Red Sea around the tenth century, is catalogued from that date onwards by Arabic medical authors, but took a long time to catch on as a hot drink. It became known in Greece during the seventeenth century. Greece retains the customary Turkish or Greek or Middle Eastern style. 'Coffee they drink any time but at meal, and is the usual entertainment when any come to visit them,' George Wheler wrote briefly in 1682.[79] In 1894 the first English edition of Baedeker's *Greece* gave excellent practical advice, still valid:

> The coffee is generally good, but it is invariably served in the Oriental manner, i.e. in small cups with the grounds. As a rule it is already sweetened (*gliko*), but the visitor may order *metrio* with little sugar or *scheto* with no sugar . . . It should be allowed to cool and 'settle' and then drunk carefully so as not to disturb the sediment at the bottom.

Served with a glass of cold water, Greek coffee is a breakfast drink, a drink offered at home to guests and a staple of the old-fashioned *kafenia*. Baedeker describes these too: 'Cafés (*kafenia*) of all kinds abound in Greece, from the wretched wooden shed of the country-village up to the Athenian establishments handsomely fitted up in the Italian style.'[80] Those Athenian establishments, where politicians once crossed the paths of poets, are now disappearing fast, supplanted by modern international coffee shops, where the fashionable coffees are frappé and freddo.[81] The country *kafenia* remain, not all of them quite as wretched as Baedeker thought, places where old men gossip endlessly, women generally having better things to do.

The traditional *salepi* seller, as described by Theodore Stephanides and immortalized in the folk art of Karipi street in Thessaloniki . . .

. . . and his modern replacement among the evening crowds on Aristotle Square.

These newfangled stimulants have failed to drive *salepi* off the market. As Durrell's friend Theodore Stephanides explains, this is the dried, ground bulb of the lax-flowered orchid (*Orchis laxiflora*) and other species, making a glutinous opalescent liquid, sweet and insipid but fortifying when taken very hot with a flavouring of ginger or cinnamon. Until the early nineteenth century it was sold in London under the name 'saloop'. Much more recently the *salepijis* was a familiar figure in Thessaloniki, 'with his ornate brass urn slung to his back, the long curved spout jutting over his right shoulder . . . he would take a glass from one of the compartments of his broad leather belt and fill it with a dextrous bend of his torso at the waist,' thus offering his client a courtly bow as well as an invigorating drink. Still widely consumed in Turkey and still popular in Thessaloniki, *salepi* is now sold from a wagon in which the beverage is kept hot. The use of *salepi* was first noted, in a discussion of sexual stimulants, by Theophrastos around 310 BC.[82] The seventeenth-century trade in Constantinople is described by Evliya Çelebi:

> The *salep* is commonly called 'fox's testicle', and grows on high mountains such as the Olympus of Bursa . . . It grows like an onion, and when dried is ground to a powder, cooked with sugar like a jelly, and sold in cans heated by fire. They cry, 'Take salep, seasoned with rosewater: rest for the soul, health for the body!' It is a fortifying and invigorating beverage, and sharpens the eyesight.[83]

Alcohol touches the Greek palate in three forms above all: beer, spirits, wine. The invasion of beer was discussed above (page 179). Except in the strictest fasts of the strictest believers, wine, not water, is the drink that accompanies a meal, and so it has been since prehistoric times. Classical Greeks were closely interested in the making of their wine and choosy as to its origin and quality. The procedure is hinted at briefly in Odysseus' exploration of Phaiakia:

> And there his fruitful vineyard is planted,
> Where a drying platform on an open ground
> Is baked by the sun, and where they are gathering and
>   treading.[84]

These lines, like Hesiod's already quoted (page 188), already suggest the making of wine from semi-dried grapes, *liasto* in modern terms, slow to ferment and with residual sweetness, good for its keeping qualities. As to the treading, Leake talks of vineyards with 'a square vat of masonry built in the field for treading the grapes, after which operation the juice, in skins, is carried into the villages'.[85] As to fermenting and maturation, a change took place in medieval times quite slowly and irregularly from earthenware *dolia* half-buried to wooden casks. William Lithgow found *dolia* still used in Cyprus in the seventeenth century:

> They have no barrels, but great jarres made of earth wherein their wine is put . . . These jarres are all inclosed within the ground save onely their mouthes, which stand always open . . . whose insides are all interlarded with pitch to preserve the earthen vessells unbroke a sunder, in regard of the forcible wine, yet making the taste thereof unpleasant to liquorous lips.[86]

Yet, as we have seen, visitors to monasteries much earlier than this had found huge old casks in their cellars, filled with monastery wine.

Modern Greek wines are struggling to recover the good name they had in the Roman and medieval West, although the vineyards that declined in the last Ottoman centuries have in many cases revived, and modern bottling and modern transport allow their products to travel over long distances. For the first time Greek dry reds and whites, which formerly would never have been exported further than Italy, cross the world. The appellations spread across Greece from Kephallenia to Lemnos and Rhodes and Sitia of Crete; from Naoussa in Macedonia to Mantinea in the Peloponnese, which, even according to one of the more fastidious Corfiots in Durrell's *Prospero's Cell*, is 'not a very bad wine as wines go'.[87] Local grape varieties have never lost their eminence; they really suit the landscapes and microclimates of Greece, and few do well elsewhere (muscat, *monemvasia* and *liatiko* being the exceptions to this rule). Some good wine is even made on the eastern shores of the Aegean, though it has only a limited market in its native Turkey.

Wine is made by many Greeks on a small-to-medium scale. Much of it is not bottled and never enters commerce: it is for households, extended households and restaurants run by the extended household. Some of the worst, the strangest and the best wine that you will drink in Greece is served in a carafe, costs you very little, and was made in the family. A larger such operation, verging on the commercial, is described by Durrell on a large family estate in central Corfu, where careful attention was paid each

Moustalevria – *Grape Must Pudding*

As Lawrence Durrell describes it, *moustalevria* is 'that delicious
Ionian sweet or jelly which is made by boiling fresh must to
half its bulk with semolina and a little spice. The paste is left
to cool on plates and stuck with almonds; and the whole either
eaten fresh or cut up in slices and put away in the great store
cupboard.'[88] It was normally made after the grape harvest in
the autumn as a good way of using leftover grape must. In
the days before cheap chocolate and sweets it was a children's
favourite. It is now not so easy to find a bakery that makes it:
creamy, sugary cakes and tarts are too popular.

5 water glasses grape must (about 800 ml)
1 water glass cornflour (200 ml)
1 branch citronella
a couple of handfuls skinned, whole almonds (75 g)
sesame seeds and ground cinnamon

Mix together one glass of must and the cornflour. In a large
saucepan bring the remaining must and the citronella to the
boil before pouring in the must-cornflour mixture. Simmer,
stirring frequently, until the mixture thickens and becomes
creamy in texture.

Cool slightly before stirring in the almonds (they can be
omitted for a smooth texture). Pour into serving glasses (such
as whisky glasses) or bowls and sprinkle with sesame seeds and
cinnamon. Serve at room temperature.

year to the harvesting and vinification of the *robola*, one of the classic and
historic grapes of the Ionian islands – and, once the wine was safely on its
way, to the making of *moustalevria*.

SPIRITS AND *MEZEDES*

Setting aside the occasional fashion for liqueurs, the spirits Greeks
drink are the unflavoured *tsipouro* (or *raki*, or in Crete *tsikoudia*) and

Selection of Greek ouzos. Visible to the eye of love are at least three brands from Lesbos (Mini, Arvanitis and Varvagiannis) and even the Psihis mastiha ouzo from Chios. Sans Rival, once a prize-winning brand, too sweet for modern tastes, still sells to tourists but is not visible at this market stall.

the anise-flavoured ouzo. Joseph Pitton de Tournefort's description of Crete, published in 1717, includes what may be the first mention of *raki* by name:

> The eau-de-vie, *raki*, which is drunk on Crete and all over the Levant is detestable. To make this liquor one adds water to grape marc: after fifteen to twenty days' steeping it is pressed with heavy stones. The first half of the resulting *piquette* is distilled, the remainder discarded. They would do better to discard the lot.[89]

Recent travellers, such as Xan Fielding, are less inclined to complain, whether they find *tsikoudia* served as a breakfast or offered to visitors alongside dessert – 'mountains of walnuts, cascades of pomegranates, chains of dried figs'.[90] *Raki* under its various names is often home-distilled. Ouzo, by contrast, is made all over Greece by small commercial distillers, who have a faithful local market. Under better-known names it is marketed nationwide. It is a very similar drink to the pastis of France and to some other Mediterranean spirits, all originally popular not just because anise tastes good but because it has real benefits as a digestive. Like those other spirits, owing to the chemical properties of anethole, ouzo turns milky when water is added, but no one will protest if you drink it without water, which is not the case with pastis.

Ouzo, the typical Greek aperitif, is often drunk alongside *mezedes*, as are *tsikoudia* and other spirits. While the leg of lamb is roasting Patrick Leigh Fermor's host opens a bottle of ouzo, a now old-fashioned favourite brand, Sans Rival from Tyrnavos; he slices sausage, cheese, spring onions and botargo and sprinkles salt over radishes and 'giant olives' in a saucer as *mezedes* to accompany the ouzo.[91] Alongside cafés and restaurants, which happily serve it, there are establishments whose sole purpose is to offer ouzo and its accompaniments, *ouzeria* (a name that emphasizes the ouzo) and *mezedopoleia* (emphasizing the *mezedes*). The word *meze* is in its immediate origin Persian: in that language it means 'taste' or 'a titbit', which already foreshadows its development in Turkish into the name for a collection of foods, snacks as one might call them in English, that precede a meal and typically accompany spirits. The *meze* habit, spreading from Thessaloniki and the north, has reached every corner of modern Greece. They are varied, strong-flavoured and savoury, 'refined yet elementary' in Aglaia Kremezi's words, the ingredients varying from everyday and basic to unexpected and a little rare.[92]

SPOON SWEETS

The history of Greek spoon sweets has hardly been traced, but somewhere in their prehistory lie the *kydonata*, 'quince conserve or marmalade', and the *karydaton*, 'walnut conserve', of the Byzantine Empire. It is clear from George Wheler's descriptions, which are among the very earliest, that sugar syrup, honey and grape syrup, *petimezi*, were alternatives in the making of early spoon sweets: 'They preserve fruits with new wine boiled to syrup, honey, and sometimes sugar.' Wheler returns to the subject when describing Chalkis:

> Here also they make sweetmeats of all sorts of fruits, quinces, pears, plums, nuts, walnuts and almonds. For sugar they use wine boiled to a syrup, and make them grateful enough to the taste; yet I believe they would hardly please some of our nice ladies, unless, perhaps, because they were far fetched.[93]

About this same period Evliya Çelebi lists the sugar-workers of Chios (an island famous today for its spoon sweets) among the trade guilds of Constantinople, so it is no surprise that Egmont and Heyman, in the 1750s, were welcomed to Chios with 'sweetmeats, coffee, sherbet, rose-water, and perfumes'.[94] From the beginning of the nineteenth century the ritual as described becomes recognizable: 'On entering a house you first are presented with a pipe, then coffee, and sometimes a spoon full of citron and a bowl of water,' writes the American financier Nicholas Biddle. Citron peel is indeed one of the traditional ingredients for a spoon sweet. Far to the east, at Konya in central Anatolia, Leake was welcomed with coffee, sweetmeats, sherbet and perfumes.[95] In the 1890s the two roving Englishwomen at Andritsena were presented with a tray on which were two kinds of preserve in glass jars, tumblers of water and tiny cups of coffee: 'The light coloured jam that we tasted was something like pear marmalade, and strongly to be recommended.'[96]

In Corfu in the 1930s Durrell encounters the 'submarine', which is the particular application of the same general ritual to a sweet paste flavoured with mastic. He makes the whole thing clear:

> The waiter darts across to them from the tavern with the 'sub-marine' – which consists of a spoonful of white mastic in a glass of water. Nothing more or less. The procedure is simple. You eat the mastic and drink the water to take the sweetness out of your mouth.[97]

The submarine or *ypovrikio* was fairly new in Durrell's time, but it was already a favourite among children lucky enough to get it. It still is, but has now reached the status of a traditional and endangered pleasure. Those who pay the bill now need to be reassured that the teaspoonful of mastic or vanilla or fruity spoon sweet, in its glass of water, is not so wickedly sugary that it must be forbidden.[98]

WINTER SUSTENANCE

Food is not available unchangingly through the year. If supermarkets try to make it appear otherwise, they will eventually fail. In Greece most foods are in some way seasonal. The vegetables that Byzantine Greeks were advised to eat for health's sake in January are the cabbage, turnips and carrots they had stored for winter, and the recommended fruits were dried fruits, nuts, pomegranates (because they store well) and pears (because some varieties do not ripen till early winter). Of course they were to look out for 'green olives in brine' in March, because early olives cured over the winter would be ready for eating in March. Naturally they were to inhale the scent of aromatic flowers in April, eat red cherries in June and pick sweet apples in September.[99]

Beyond this pure seasonality, the Christian calendar is studded with festivals throughout the year, enthusiastically celebrated with rituals whose roots go back to a period before Christianity existed. These rituals (some popular almost everywhere, others purely local) appear to have specific purposes that also are independent of Christianity: whatever the current religion, such rituals ensure suitable weather and a regular seasonal cycle, and those things in turn ensure that there will be food next year. Naturally, then, Greek festivals, especially during winter and spring, are closely tied to food.

Panagia Polysporitissa is celebrated on 21 November. In Christian terms it is the feast of the presentation to the Jewish Temple of the Virgin Mary, the *Panagia* or 'all-holy'. Cereal grains and pulses of many kinds from the recent harvest are boiled together and blessed in church, and then eaten by those who are now planting seeds for next year, in hope of a good crop. The word *polysporitissa*, 'to whom many seeds are offered', now attached to the Virgin Mary, hints at pre-Christian origins: classical Greeks also cooked multiple seeds together each year to offer them to Demeter, the goddess of the cereal harvest.[100]

Although there is meat at the centre of modern Christmas meals, no single animal is embedded in tradition as the one to be killed: instead the traditional focus of Christmas and New Year food is on special bread and elaborate cakes. In Greece this focus begins with *kourabiedes*, little shortbread cakes of flour, butter and sugar, often flavoured with almonds, sometimes with orange water and even with brandy, that helped many to get through the pre-Christmas fast days. *Kourabiedes* have a long and largely non-Christian history, traceable to the *ghraiba* and *qurabiya* of Arab, Persian and Turkish cuisine, and possibly beyond.[101]

Christopsoma, 'Christ's breads', are baked for Christmas itself and appear to continue the pagan custom of offering bread and cakes to the gods. Often spiced, they are shaped as or decorated with religious symbols (sometimes a cross or a figure of the baby Jesus), snakes and other images of fertility and prosperity; they may have walnuts or eggs embedded in them, and symbolism is attributed to those as well. *Christopsoma* and

Vasilopita, the indispensable New Year's cake, always decorated, sometimes iced.

other traditional Christmas foods are made for giving and sharing, with strangers, with beggars, with neighbouring households, with children. The Cappadocian Greeks boiled beef and rice, or made *cherse* with meat, cracked wheat, onions and butter, or sweet *ashure* soup with walnuts, and distributed these on Christmas morning to neighbours or to the poor. But yoghurt, after many days of fasting, was as welcome as any bread or meat.[102]

Everywhere in Greece *vasilopita* is eaten at New Year. It aims to confirm fertility and good fortune for the coming year. Traditional recipes are surprisingly varied, savoury as well as sweet, but a sweet cake is becoming the new tradition (see recipe on page 258).

Winter, as it draws to its end, leads into the period of *Apokries*, 'carnival', that immediately precedes Lent. Food may be offered to the dead, who are said to wander among the living at carnival time. Doubtless they enjoy as much as others the smell of roast meat and fat that is redolent of *tsiknopempti*, 'Smoky Thursday', when so much roast beef is consumed that the whole week seems to be named after it: *Kreatini*, 'Meat Week'. It is followed by *Tyrofagou*, 'cheese-eating', when meat is forbidden in

Lenten Tahini Cake

Containing no eggs, oil or butter, tahini cake is one of the most popular Lenten pleasures, to be enjoyed any time from Clean Monday until Big Friday.

150 g tahini, shaken well if the oil has separated
170 g water
200 g soft brown sugar
250 g plain flour
½ tsp baking powder
¼ tsp ground cloves
sesame seeds

Preheat the oven to 170°C. Line the base of a 20-cm-square cake tin and oil the base and sides.

With a stiff whisk or metal spoon, in a large bowl mix the tahini, water and sugar together. Sift in the flour and baking powder and mix till combined.

Pour the mixture into the prepared cake tin, smoothing down the top. Sprinkle all over with sesame seeds and bake for 45–50 minutes. If the cake starts to brown too much, cover it loosely with foil. Test with a skewer or knife, which should come out clean. The cake will have a softly dense and moist texture.

Leave to cool in the tin before cutting into squares.

preparation for Lent but cheese is still allowed, Then, eleven days after Smoky Thursday, comes *kathara deftera*, 'Clean Monday', the first day on which the full Lenten restrictions apply: no meat, no fish, no oil, no eggs or milk products. Much can be made of shellfish and crustacea, however, as the medieval abbots already knew. *Lagana*, an unleavened bread whose name already occurs in classical texts, is eaten on Clean Monday.[103]

At Tyrnavos in Thessaly an unusually liberated festival is held on Clean Monday, which surely helps to relieve Lenten gloom and probably contributes to the town's fertility. The food basis of the festival is (correctly for the season) spinach soup prepared and served without oil. There are phallic

Easter: Feast and Fast

A whole lamb or kid, to be eaten on Easter Sunday, is jointed and roasted in the oven overnight or cooked over a special bar-becue pit, large enough for this purpose and therefore used only on this one annual occasion. Smaller, but still large, skewers and individual steaks and cutlets can be cooked over one charcoal grill, as here by the grill master of a restaurant. The meat is cut off the skewers to order.

Maundy Thursday is the day for painting hard-boiled eggs – almost always red, though some like multi-coloured. They first appear on the table after midnight in the night of Saturday/Sunday to precede the fast-breaking feast of *mageiritsa* (a thick soup of lamb or kid intestines and herbs). The eggs are bashed one against another: if your eggshell doesn't break, you win.

Easter in modern Greece: meat sizzling . . .

. . . and red-painted eggs.

Vasilopita

Vasilopita is the traditional New Year's cake, and every taverna will offer a slice to customers after midnight or on New Year's Day. Now often cake-like, *vasilopita* used to be more like an enriched bread, resembling *tsoureki* or brioche. This recipe, based on one by Stelios Parliaros (see page 217), will suit a smaller family with a twenty-first-century cranberry obsession.

75 g each dried cranberries and stoned prunes, chopped
100 ml brandy, Cognac or Metaxa
125 g butter, at room temperature, plus
extra for greasing
125 g sifted icing sugar, plus extra for dusting
125 g ground almonds
3 large eggs, lightly beaten
125 g plain flour sifted with ½ tsp baking powder
a coin or token, *flouri*, to drop into the mix

Soak the chopped cranberries and prunes in the brandy for several hours, or overnight. Then purée the mix in a blender. Cream the butter with the sifted icing sugar and the ground almonds.

Gradually incorporate the fruit purée, then the eggs, beating well after each addition.

Fold in the flour and baking powder with a metal spoon and pour the mix into a 20-cm-diameter round cake tin which has been buttered and lined. Drop in the *flouri* and press it under the surface. Bake for 45 minutes at 170°C.

processions, sexual horseplay, obscene and suggestive songs and jokes, and a great deal of drinking of *tsipouro*. The spinach soup, *bourani*, has a history of its own unconnected with Christian fasts. It is certainly the descendant of Arabic *buraniya* (which is also known in Andalusia as *alboronia*), a dish that is said in medieval sources to be named after and to have been invented by Buran, wife of the ninth-century caliph al-Ma'mun.[104]

Greek Easter most often falls in early April. The great forty-day fast of Lent, which immediately precedes it, accounts for March, which explains why the Byzantine dietician Hierophilos recommended no meat in March. If he had, his readers would rarely have been able to eat it. In the early nineteenth century Leake was crossing the southern Peloponnese in early spring; his guide at that moment was an old man who 'walks so fast that my horse can hardly keep pace with him [and] has lived for the last month, being Lent, upon scarcely any thing but bread and onions'.[105] As Leake explains elsewhere, the search for 'esculent wild herbs' was especially necessary in Lent because so many other foods were ruled out.[106] For the same reason, Dodwell confirms, the discovery of a plant that Greek country people did not previously know to be edible and health-giving would be important to them. He claimed to have contributed to the repertoire himself. At the Kastalian spring at Delphi he found watercress growing along the banks and picked some for his dinner. 'The poor people' asked him if this plant was medicinal, and he replied that it was good to eat: 'The next morning, I met a party of the villagers returning from the spring, each with a provision of the newly-discovered vegetable. They ... told me they should for the future give them the name *phrankochorton*, or the Frank's Herb.'[107]

Normally, however, the strictness of Lent is relieved by at least one great festival of the Christian church, that of the Annunciation, celebrated unvaryingly on 25 March. On this day, even if it falls in Lent as it usually does, observant modern Greeks allow themselves fish cooked with and served with olive oil. Medieval monks did so too: the rules of Byzantine monasteries are definite and detailed as to what may and may not be eaten on this one occasion, permitting fish (unless the Annunciation coincides with Holy Week), allowing a larger helping of wine, and even encouraging the leftovers to be eaten, with more oil, next day.

Easter preparations begin on Holy Thursday, when eggs are painted red and sweet Easter bread is baked. *Lampropsomo*, 'bright' or 'Easter bread', also *tsoureki* (an Arabic and Turkish name), is rich in eggs and butter, unlike any Lenten food, and is decorated with shapes of spring flowers, leaves, crosses and snakes – but there are many other traditional forms. On Easter Saturday the breads and the eggs are blessed, and children give some to their godparents.

On that day too, older Greeks may remember lamb intestines being washed at the communal water tap before being plaited into a broad, slippery braid, which, flavoured with oregano, plenty of salt and pepper, would be roasted in the baker's oven; but more often nowadays the intestines go

Kokoretsi, the entrails and offal of the Easter lamb, cooked on a spit. A family Greek Easter celebration in Dallas, Texas.

into *kokoretsi*. Lamb or goat kidneys, liver, heart, lungs and a good amount of residual fat and caul fat are skewered on a long metal spit and wrapped in the intestines as if one were winding an elongated ball of wool. This is cooked over coals for hours, perhaps over a specially made barbecue pit, alongside the whole lamb or kid, also on a spit. Slow cooking, regular basting with a herb-sprig brush and constant rotating of the spit result in an unforgettable fast-breaking feast. But, to be precise, the long fast is traditionally broken in three steps: first, after midnight on Easter Sunday, with *magiritsa* (the name is Greek, 'the cooked dish'), a soup made from the kidneys and other offal and thickened with rice; then around midday *kokoretsi* (the name is apparently Albanian) as a first course while the lamb or kid is still roasting; then, finally, the roast meat.

In medieval Constantinople there was disagreement in monastic rules as to when the Lenten fast should be broken, and some considered that a midnight meal would weigh too heavily on monkish minds and stomachs. Others allowed a full meal, but with mulled wine spiced with cumin to reduce flatulence.[108] On Easter Sunday, so a Muslim hostage remarked, not water but sweet spiced wine flowed from the fountain on the route of the solemn procession from the Great Palace to Agia Sophia:

> On the festival day this tank is filled with ten thousand jars of wine and a thousand jars of white honey, and the whole is spiced with a camel's load of nard, cloves and cinnamon . . . When the Emperor leaves the Palace and enters the church he sees the statues and the spiced wine that flows from their mouths and their ears, gathering in the basin below until it is full. Each person in the procession . . . gets a brimming cup of this wine.[109]

Immediately after Easter the dead may once again be invited to join the festivity. At the village of Olympos on Karpathos on White Tuesday (two days after Easter Sunday), women place dishes of food beside the graves in the village cemetery, such as *kollyba* (one more mixture of multiple seeds, nuts and fruit), cakes, wine, orange juice, cheese, sweets and fruit, and the priest says a prayer over each grave.[110]

Conviviality

Beyond a certain point the food doesn't matter, after all. A half-loaf of bread, a hunk of cheese and a bottle of retsina confer as much pleasure as one person can reasonably expect, given a long morning's walk and a long way still to walk in the afternoon. So much for one person. More than one person participates in practically all the meals described in this book. An exception, possibly, is the meal sketched by Hesiod in what may be the oldest surviving text in Greek literature, about 700 BC, as at noon he sits in the shade of a rock, facing the west wind, reflecting that July is the season when 'goats are fattest and wine is best and women are lustiest and men are weakest', and enjoys creamy barley-mash and the last milk of the goats and forest-fed veal and fiery wine.[1] He is alone, it seems. Another example is Liutprand's meal in Constantinople in AD 968: too cross to dine at the Palace, he stumps home to his lodgings and eats what the emperor has sent after him to cheer him up, a fat kid stuffed with garlic, onion and leeks, dressed with *garos*.[2] If he, too, is dining alone his melancholy is better understood.

Nearly every other Greek meal in this book involves two at least and is all the better for it. Cyriac of Ancona, Pierre Belon and almost all the other early travellers give an occasional hint that they are travelling in company, even if they hardly ever name any names. The hint is usually given when a meal is described: on Mount Athos the abbot 'served *us* rocket', leek, cucumbers, onions and green garlic,'[3] on Chios '*we* passed lightheartedly through those remarkably green, precious groves of mastic,'[4] in Thrace '*we* camped under the willows . . . and bought some of this meat,'[5] at Candia '*we* were kindly used . . . especially by the gentlewomen, who oftentimes did make us banquets in their gardens with music and dancing,'[6] at Rethymno '*we* made a lunch of . . . red mullet, eggs, bread and cheese and *stupendous*

The 'Eurytios krater', Corinthian, *c.* 600 BC, is one of the oldest Greek depictions of a banquet. In this incident from myth, Herakles pays a visit to Eurytios his sons, and his daughter Iole. It will end in tears, but that is not shown here. Iole servesand father, sons and Herakles recline (below). In a separate scene, young men roast the meat.

wine,[7] and at Mesolongi '*we* scarcely touched our luncheon octopus, swallowing glass after glass of cold Fix beer.'[8] The two exceptions stick out like sore thumbs: Antoine Des Barres and William Lithgow travelled alone; Des Barres was laughed at by the girls of Chios[9] and Lithgow took them for whores.[10] Neither was at ease.

When there are two there is company and comfort; already there is difference between them, as it may be Leake's guide in the Mani who gets bean soup while Leake has salad and honey, and both are happy.[11] There may be more than two, of course. The emperor John VIII Palaiologos,

The 'Hospitality of Abraham' in a late 14th-century Byzantine icon. In this scene, as it was gradually developed by Greek artists, both host and hostess wait at table. There is a special reason: their guests are the Holy Trinity. The source is Genesis 18.

picnicking near Florence, ate alone (as an emperor unluckily has to do, having no equals) and cleaned the salad himself, but then took only as much as he wanted and sent the dishes along to his companions under the trees.[12] At a Cretan monastery Lear's Greek servant George Kokalis was not so happy as his Turkish guide: 'poor George has been obliged to eat fasting food, the pilaf and eggs going to the Turk.'[13] Dining with the bishop of Salona, Edward Dodwell has his own jealously guarded glass, his guide and servant sharing the general drinking bowl (see box on page 220).

Hospitality, *philoxenia*, has been at the centre of Greek food ever since the *Dinner* of Philoxenos (whose name, strangely, encapsulates the concept). When there are two or more the roles of host and guest must be filled. A mere guide may play host, as did those bold sacristans who, unlike their abbots, would show guests the monastery cellars; as did the young monk who, having led Belon's party astray on the mountain paths of Athos, knew where to find river crabs to be eaten raw.[14]

The host's role is to be fair, ceremonious and generous. When Achilles and his friend Patroklos entertained guests in the *Iliad*, Achilles roasted the meat (often a male role), Patroklos served bread in baskets, and Achilles himself served the meat.[15] 'In Greece,' wrote the classicist John Myres in 1901, 'this is still done with great ceremony, and beforehand. The host stands, and picks over the whole dish of bits, putting fair equivalents towards each of the guests, before helping on to the plates.'[16] So even if he has only one guest: Patrick Leigh Fermor's host held the joint upright in the pan, sliced away helping after helping, and heaped the two plates in turn.[17] Eumaios in the *Odyssey*, as liberal as only a pig-farmer can be, sacrificed two piglets, singed them, chopped them, skewered and roasted them:

> He set them before Odysseus, hot, on their skewers; he sprinkled white barley-meal on; he mixed honey-sweet wine in a mug, and himself sat down facing him, and to encourage him said: 'Eat now, stranger, what servants have to eat: piglets, because the fat porkers are eaten by those suitors!'[18]

Generosity need not be in any way political, but it may be. Odysseus, spinning a tale, explains how he gathered a band to go fighting at Troy: 'They dined on me six days before we sailed.'[19] Leake quotes a much more recent ballad from the Mani in which Tzanet Bey Grigorakis was celebrated for similar hospitality: a bell marked the hour of supper at his palace at Gythio; all who heard it entered, ate at his table, and went away satisfied.[20]

The role of guest is usually easy to play. 'Stranger,' says Eumaios to the disguised Odysseus, 'it would not be right for me, even if one worse than you should come, to slight a stranger: before Zeus everyone is a stranger and a beggar.' One of the more thoughtful of Penelope's suitors gives an even stronger reason not to spurn a stranger: he might be one of the gods. They, disguised as strangers, 'all take existence and wander through cities, observing the bad and the good that mortals do'.

Eumaios honoured the wandering stranger (not knowing, though readers do, that it is his old master, Odysseus) 'with the long chine of the white-tusked boar'.[21] As generous a host as Eumaios was the abbot (*igoumenos*) of the monastery visited by Isabel Armstrong and Edith Payne in 1853. Meat being off the menu for monks, he had profited by their visit to arrange a meal of lamb, 'jerking bits of meat on to our plates whenever he thought we were within a measurable distance of finishing', not knowing, but surely guessing, that some of it would come back to him:

> The more we protested we did not want any, the more delighted he grew and insisted that we must eat it. When he turned to those on his left I always took the opportunity to quietly transfer to his plate all the choice morsels he had put on mine; this I discovered was a delicate attention which he quite appreciated, although it was not etiquette to appear to notice it.[22]

When guests are being entertained, women in the household have more to do than to sit at the table. Even if men have roasted the meat, women do nearly all the rest. We can begin 2,700 years ago with the *Odyssey*. When the goddess Kalypso says goodbye to Odysseus she packs his lunch (a skin of wine, a skin of water and food in a leather bag). Nausikaa's lunch, when she goes down to the beach to wash clothes, is packed by her mother in a hamper, with wine in a goatskin. Later Nausikaa tells Odysseus that when he reaches her home he must go straight to her mother, who will be 'sitting at the hearth in the glow of the fire, spinning her sea-purple wool . . . and there is my father's chair, leaning against her, where he sits and drinks his wine like a god'; by dinner time, if there were guests, women would not be so visible, but after the meal the maids would re-emerge to clear the dinner-things. Eumaios, as servant in a different household, remembered such an evening, 'chatting in front of the mistress and finding everything out and eating and drinking and taking a little back to the farm for myself'. With no guests, at a supper for two, it is simpler but the roles are still to be played. Thus when Odysseus and Kalypso dined for the last time, she serves him yet they eat together: 'she put out every food for him, to eat and drink, that mortal men eat; she was sitting facing godlike Odysseus, and house-girls put out ambrosia and nectar for her; and they set their hands to the food laid out ready'.[23]

In classical Athens, as can now be seen from Menander's rediscovered comedy *The Bad-tempered Man*, it was not so different. Women and slaves make nearly all the decisions about the big family meal – when it was to take place, what animal was to be sacrificed, where and to which god – yet the women hardly speak on stage, the lunch under discussion is the men's lunch, and the named host and guests are men. The women eat before, or after, or aside: there is hardly a word to tell us. At the supper and dancing afterwards (it has turned into a wedding, which can happen more quickly in comedy than in life) the men and women are in separate groups, visible to one another.[24] 'I told you,' the host tells the cook at another comedy wedding, 'four tables for the women and six for the men.'[25] 'Married women do not go to dinners with their husbands,' according to an Athenian legal speech, 'nor do they care to dine with men of other families.'[26] True: the women in Menander's play manage to enjoy themselves without quite doing that.

In Crete under the Venetians and the Turks it was still not very different. 'Women never take part in their banquets,' writes Pierre Belon, 'and are not present when they drink and eat in company.'[27] Richard Pococke, two centuries later, agrees: 'The women never sit down to eat with men that are not of the house, and though they are not so strict as the Turks, yet they rarely come into the rooms where any strangers are.'[28] At the dinner celebrating Eleftherios Venizelos's farewell to his native Crete to become a Greek politician in 1913, the only toast he proposed was 'to the last-comers, who are not the least!' It was to the women (one of whom was his mistress Paraskevoula Blum), because the women did not appear at the tables – no, not even the guest of honour's best friend – until they had prepared the sweets.[29]

The role-playing tends to differentiate men and women, but it does not prevent both from taking part. On Chios in the seventeenth century the French ambassador the marquis de Nointel gave an elaborate entertainment 'to the ladies'. Men were present too, but there was proper distinction:

> There were three rows of benches, covered with Turkish carpets, on which the ladies were seated, so that they could all without inconvenience see M. de Nointel's table and could themselves easily be seen (several among them were well worth looking at). In the middle of the circle of ladies there rose more than eight feet

In ancient Greece men rarely saw women drink wine (at celebrations the two sexes usually ate separately), but felt sure they did when no one was watching. On this pot a housewife is imagined taking advantage of her guardianship of the cellar.

high a rustic rock made of comfits, sugar sweets, marzipans and fruits, from which three springs welled up, one of lemonade, one of orangeade, and one of Cordova water. Four little cupids were continually serving spoon sweets, fruits and drinks to the ladies. Behind this circle there was a basin ... from whose centre sprang a jet of wine which reached a great height and lasted throughout the entertainment.[30]

The divine participates in Greek feasting and probably always has. God may be acknowledged nowadays, in the simplest way perhaps, by the sign of the cross, the thumb and two first fingers conjoined to honour the Trinity, the cross-bar going from right shoulder to left. Bread, as symbol of the Eucharist, will probably be treated ceremoniously: a loaf brought to the table unbroken (so it is in almost all Greek restaurants) for the host to break; leftover fragments perhaps kissed and stored away.[31] In monasteries greater ceremony was observed. After the meal George Wheler saw a piece of bread and a cup of wine brought to the abbot's table for him to consecrate and then carry around the refectory, the bread first, from which each monk took a morsel, then the cup of wine, from which each took a sip.[32]

God (classical Greeks might have said 'gods' or 'a god') enjoins fasting at certain times, feasting at other times. The wedding in *The Bad-tempered Man* was preceded – was caused, in fact – by a family sacrificial feast to the god Pan. Sacrifices of oxen to Zeus, king of the gods, are described in the *Odyssey*, and these also were feasts for the worshippers, not just for the god:

> When the thighs were burnt up and they had tasted the vital parts, they cut up the rest and stuck it on spits and roasted it, holding the sharp spits in their hands ... So, when they had roasted the upper flesh and pulled it from the spits, they sat and ate.[33]

The old gods did not always want meat. The classical traveller Pausanias was anxious to visit Phigalia in the Peloponnese to see the famous and already ancient shrine of Demeter, goddess of the cereal harvest. Entering the grove of oaks, he offered on the table before the cave mouth, in accordance with the rule, 'the fruit of cultivated trees, especially the grape, and also honeycomb' with oil poured over.[34]

The fasts of the Orthodox calendar have served to distinguish Greeks not only from Western guests, whose churches were less demanding, but from the Turks who lived among them and whose fast during Ramadan imposed different rules. In Nikos Kazantzakis's *Freedom and Death*, Nuri Bey brings a partridge to share with Captain Michales – 'I thought we could eat it together and remember old times':

> 'I'm not eating, it's a fast day for us,' he answered.
>   Full of regret, Nuri Bey took him by both hands. 'If I'd known,' he said, 'by Mohammed, I'd have got you some black caviare.'[35]

That was no throwaway line: Captain Michales would have been perfectly entitled to eat the caviar. When Belon visited Lemnos he was given a simple dinner by the island's Turkish governor ('The first dish was of raw cucumbers without vinegar or oil . . . with no other seasoning but salt; after that we had raw onions and fresh sturgeon, and beside this there was a soup of *trachanas*, and honey and bread'), but because the group included some Greek Christians there was also wine, which the host himself, as a Muslim, would not drink.[36]

Past and Future

Some long-established expatriate Greek communities (in Georgia, southern Russia, Romania, southern Italy and Sicily) are almost unseen by the world at large. Others, of more recent origin, are very well known. There is now a third diaspora: Greeks of working age with skills to sell go to work abroad, sometimes for many years, yet they maintain links with their families and their native towns and islands, and eventually return. As the Greek economy stumbles on, this diaspora of the third kind continues and increases.

It is partly because of these diasporas that Greek food has its strong international image: thanks to them, others have learned to know it and demand it. Greece has been for many centuries a goal for travellers, and more recently Greece and Cyprus have been tourist destinations. This, too, has helped to make Greek food known abroad, though not sufficiently admired. Travellers sometimes found poor food hospitably given to them by people who had hardly the resources to feed themselves; food that was so far from their everyday experience that they could not learn to enjoy it (retsina); food that was so famous that they could not look beyond it (the honey of Mount Hymettos). Tourists find food that is cleverly shaped to their expectations by Greeks, many of whom have lived abroad, who have

Food is essential: street food at a wet and wintry demonstration in front of the parliament building in Syntagma ('Constitution') Square, Athens, 2015.

seen at first hand what foreigners like but scarcely know the full range of the best Greek food of today. The grandchildren of the forced migrants of 1923 continue to enrich the food traditions of Greece, but tourists, unless they are also fearless explorers, see nothing of this.

Always one of the poor countries of southern Europe, and now deep in debt, Greece has necessarily accepted the new colonialism of the North. It has destroyed large tracts of its coastline in welcoming cheap holiday-makers; it has sold large parts of itself to multinationals, which are currently living on their fat while local businesses are bankrupted; it has embraced European protected designations and geographical labels, though they freeze and bureaucratize ideas that should develop creatively with their markets. And whatever the immediate outcome, Greece is thrown back on its own resources. This is easier for those whose extended families are partly rural, since food and wine produced on the farm are for the family first. But in Athens, above all, there are many who have no such links, no safety net, when driven into poverty as many are. Greeks are likely to be resourceful in redeveloping, helped perhaps by online marketing, which can ensure the survival of good local foods and small-scale businesses.

The growing fashion for the use of local products ought to work in favour of traditional Greek food habits, but fashion is not the same as what most people unthinkingly do or want to do. In that unfashionable daily reality there are three big threats from the globalized world to the local use of local products: any product from anywhere can market itself as well as the next; long-distance transport of foods pretends to be far cheaper than it truly is; and as people become more rootless they want local products less. Greek food can possibly withstand even these threats better than some, because the Greek way of living can possibly hold out better than some. Greeks have historically been good at maintaining their culture. They have exported themselves for millennia, retaining Greekness and the desire to go on retaining it, a fact demonstrated in their enjoyment of good Greek food.

So, will there still be good local Greek food, good Greek cuisine and Greeks who enjoy these things, fifty years from now? The roots of Greek food tradition appear strong even now. The tastes experienced by those who lived in Franchthi cave, in Akrotiri on Thera, in classical Athens, in medieval Constantinople and in Greece under Genoese, Venetian and Ottoman rule have all lived on, so far, as parts of that tradition. Spring lamb, enjoyed by Greeks long before there was a Christian Easter to justify it, belongs to that tradition. So does the fine fish of the Aegean, for which ancient Athenians paid through the nose just as do modern Greeks in fish tavernas. So do the cheeses and wines; so do those recent exotic invaders, the oranges of Chania and the tomatoes of Thera; so do the breads and the two-thousand-year-old *paximadia* and the honey-soaked cakes; so do the incredibly invigorating *salepi* of Thessaloniki, the masticha and the spoon sweets of Chios and the well-rounded ouzo of Lesbos. This tradition will somehow continue to flourish.

References

ONE: Origins

1 Out of several interpretations of the Atlantis myth, this is not the most popular
  – but it could still be true.
2 Lawrence Durrell, *Prospero's Cell* (London, 1945), pp. 23–5.
3 'These changes must to some extent be attributed to the activities of prehistoric
  people,' says Sytze Bottema (p. 46), writing of the spread of styrax and terebinth
  as well as olive: Sytze Bottema, 'The Vegetation History of the Greek Mesolithic',
  in *The Greek Mesolithic: Problems and Perspectives*, ed. N. Galanidou and C. Perles
  (Athens, 2003), pp. 22–50.
4 P. Warren, *Myrtos: An Early Bronze Age Settlement in Crete* (London, 1972),
  pp. 255–6.
5 J. Aegidius van Egmont and John Heyman, *Travels* (London, 1759), vol. I, p. 255.
6 Winifred Lamb and Helen Bancroft, 'Report on the Lesbos Charcoals', *Annual
  of the British School at Athens*, XXXIX (1938/9), pp. 88–9.
7 F. Fouqué, *Santorin et ses éruptions* (Paris, 1879), pp. 98–129; *une espèce de pois
  encore cultivés dans l'île, où ils sont connus sous le nom d'arakas*, p. 120; *une matière
  pâteuse*, p. 128.
8 Anaya Sarpaki and Glynis Jones, 'Ancient and Modern Cultivation of *Lathyrus
  clymenum* L. in the Greek Islands', *Annual of the British School at Athens*, LXXXV
  (1990), pp. 363–8.
9 Warren, *Myrtos*, pp. 255–6.
10 *Odyssey* 2.337–343.
11 Nikos Kazantzakis, *Καπετάν Μιχάλης*, in Jonathan Griffin, trans., *Freedom and
  Death* (Oxford, 1956).
12 Valasia Isaakidou, 'Cooking in the Labyrinth: Exploring "Cuisine" at Bronze
  Age Knossos', in *Cooking Up the Past: Food and Culinary Practices in the Neolithic
  and Bronze Age Aegean*, ed. C. Mee and J. Renard (Oxford, 2007), pp. 5–24,
  at pp. 8–9.
13 Fouqué, *Santorin et ses éruptions*, p. 128.
14 Athenaios, *Deipnosophistai*, in *Athenaeus: The Learned Banqueters,* ed. and trans.
  S. Douglas Olson (Cambridge, MA, 2006–12), 111a.
15 Martial, *Epigrams*, in *Martial*, ed. D. R. Shackleton Bailey (Cambridge, MA,
  1993), Book 14 no. 22; Andrew Dalby, *Empire of Pleasures* (London, 2000), p. 151.
16 Pausanias, *Guide to Greece*, in Peter Levi, trans., *Pausanias: Guide to Greece*
  (Harmondsworth, 1971), 8.1.5. The oracle, of which this is only a part, is: H. W.
  Parke, D.E.W. Wormell, *The Delphic Oracle* (Oxford, 1956), II, p. 15. *Phegos* is
  Valonia oak, *Quercus macrolepis*.
17 *Homeric Hymn to Demeter*, 480–82.
18 Herodotos, *Histories*, 8.55.

19 Apollodoros, *Mythology*, in *Apollodorus: The Library*, ed. J. G. Frazer (London, 1921), Book 3 ch. 14, quotation abridged.

20 *Odyssey*, 7.112–21.

21 This phrase is a literary pun. The Homeric epics have the recurring formula 'oxen and fat sheep', using an archaic word for sheep, *mela*. In later Greek the same word meant 'apples'.

22 Athenaios, *Deipnosophistai*, 650c.

23 *Epitome of Athenaios*, in S. Douglas Olson, ed. and trans., *Athenaeus: The Learned Banqueters* (Cambridge, MA, 2006–12), 49f.

24 Mariana Kavroulaki, 'Pomegranates', at http://297315322.blog.com.gr.

25 Dioskourides, *Materia medica*, in *Pedanii Dioscuridis Anazarbei de materia medica libri quinque*, ed. M. Wellmann (Berlin, 1907–14), Book 5 ch. 20.

26 Ibid., 5.21.

27 Athenaios, *Deipnosophistai*, 374d; Aristophanes, *Birds*, 485.

28 Theognis, *Elegies*, in Dorothea Wender, trans., *Hesiod: Theogony, Works and Days; Theognis, Elegies* (Harmondsworth, 1973), ll. 863–4; *Epitome of Athenaios*, 57d.

29 Oreibasios, *Medical Collections*, in Mark Grant, trans., *Dieting for an Emperor: A Translation of Books 1 and 4 of Oribasius' Medical Compilations* (Leiden, 1997), Book 4 ch. 6.

30 Herodotos, *Histories*, 9.82.1–3.

31 Athenaios, *Deipnosophistai*, 82f.

32 Pliny, *Natural History*, in *Pliny: Natural History*, ed. H. Rackham et al. (Cambridge, MA, 1938–63), Book 15 section 41.

33 Theophrastos, *History of Plants*, in Arthur Hort, ed. and trans., *Theophrastus: Enquiry into Plants* (Cambridge, MA, 1916–26), 4.4.7.

34 Nikandros, *Theriaka*, in *Nicander*, ed. A.S.F. Gow and A. F. Scholfield (Cambridge, 1953), l. 891.

35 al-Istakhri, *Kitāb al-Masālik wa'l-Mamālik*, in *Viae regnorum descriptio ditionis Moslemicae*, ed. M. J. De Goeje (Leiden, 1927), p. 173.

36 Jacques de Vitry, *Historia Orientalis et Occidentalis*, in *Iacobi de Vitriaco . . . libri duo* (Douai, 1597), p. 86.

37 H. Winterwerb, ed., *Porikologos* (Cologne, 1992), l. 6.

38 Ibid., 4.

39 *Scholia on Nikandros' Alexipharmaka*, in *Scholia in Theocritum; Scholia et paraphrases in Nicandrum et Oppianum*, ed. F. Dübner and U. C. Bussemaker (Paris, 1847), l. 533. The commentator thinks the bitter orange, *nerantzion*, is the same as the ancient *melon Medikon*. A nice idea but mistaken: the latter was the citron.

40 Aglaia Kremezi, 'Greece: Culinary Travel: Ionian Islands', at www.epicurious.com/archive.

41 Aglaia Kremezi, 'Tomato: A Latecomer that Changed Greek Flavor', *The Atlantic* (July 2010).

42 Strabo, *Geography*, in *The Geography of Strabo*, ed. H. L. Jones (London, 1917–32), 15.1.18.

43 Quoted in Athenaios, *Deipnosophistai*, 153d.

44 W. M. Leake, *Travels in the Morea* (London, 1830), vol. I, p. 309.

45 Ibid., p. 337.

46 Diogenes Laertios, *Lives*, in *Diogenes Laertius: Lives of Eminent Philosophers*, ed. R. D. Hicks (London, 1925), Book 1 ch. 81.

47 Plutarch, *Banquet of the Seven Sages*, in *Plutarchi Chaeronensis scripta moralia*, ed. F. Dubner (Paris, 1846–7), ch. 14.

two: Classical Feasts: The First Gastronomy

1 *Odyssey*, 4.620–24.

2 Ibid., 9.219–23.

3 Ibid., 9.244–9.

4 Ibid., 4.220–21.

5 See Mariana Kavroulaki, 'Mixing the Kykeon', at http://297315322.blog.com.gr.

6 *Iliad*, 11.624–41.

7 *Odyssey*, 10.233–6.

8 For a recent study of modelled pottery of this tradition see Louise Steel, 'The Social World of Early-middle Bronze Age Cyprus: Rethinking the Vounous Bowl', *Journal of Mediterranean Archaeology*, XXVI (2013), pp. 51–73.

9 Hesiod, *Works and Days*, in M. L. West, trans., *Hesiod: Theogony and Works and Days* (Oxford, 1999), ll. 582–96.

10 *Epitome of Athenarios*, in *Athenaeus: The Learned Banqueters*, ed. S. Douglas Olson (Cambridge, MA, 2006–12), 30f.

11 Athenaios, *Deipnosophistai*, in *Athenaeus: The Learned Banqueters*, ed. and trans. S. Douglas Olson (Cambridge, MA, 2006–12), 138d.

12 Ibid., 462c.

13 Ibid., 65c and 370d.

14 Ibid., 399d.

15 Ibid., 228c.

16 Ibid., 313f.

17 Hesiod, *Works and Days*, 640.

18 Athenaios, *Deipnosophistai*, 293a.

19 Ibid., 295d.

20 Ibid., 322c; the first speaker responds with a full recipe.

21 Pliny, *Natural History,* in *Pliny: Natural History*, ed. H. Rackham et al. (Cambridge, MA, 1938–63), Book 19 section 39.

22 *Geoponika*, in Andrew Dalby, trans., *Geoponika: Farm Work* (Totnes, 2011), Book 20 ch. 46. *Garos* can be made in suitable conditions with due care, but these recipes are not recommended for casual experiment.

23 Pierre Belon du Mans, *Les Observations de plusieurs singularitez et choses memorables trouvées en Grèce, Asie, Judée, Egypte, Arabie et autres pays étranges* (Paris, 1555), 1.75.

24 Athenaios, *Deipnosophistai*, 302e.

25 *Epitome of Athenaios*, in Olson, *Athenaeus: The Learned Banqueters*, 54f.

26 Columella, *On Agriculture*, in *Lucius Junius Moderatus Columella: On Agriculture*, ed. Harrison Boyd Ash, E. S. Forster and E. H. Heffner (Cambridge, MA, 1941–55), Book 10, ll. 105–6.

27 *Epitome of Athenaios*, 64e.

28 *Apicius*, in *Apicius*, ed. and trans. Christopher Grocock and Sally Grainger, (Totnes, 2006), Book 7 ch. 12.

29 *Odyssey*, 13.412.

30 H. W. Parke and D.E.W. Wormell, *The Delphic Oracle* (Oxford, 1956), vol. II, pp. 1–2.

31 *Epitome of Athenaios*, 28a.

32 Ibid., 27e.

33 Athenaios, *Deipnosophistai*, 540d.

34 *Epitome of Athenaios*, 29e.

35 Athenaios, *Deipnosophistai*, 321c.

36 *Epitome of Athenaios*, 4e.

37 Athenaios, *Deipnosophistai*, 101c.

38 Ibid., 311a.

39 See Mariana Kavroulaki, 'Ovens', at http://297315322.blog.com.gr.

40 Athenaios, *Deipnosophistai*, 111f.

41 *Epitome of Athenaios*, 64a.

42 Athenaios, *Deipnosophistai*, 92d.

43 Oreibasios, *Medical Collections,* in *Oribasii Collectionum medicarum reliquiae*, ed. Ioannes Raeder (Leipzig, 1929), Book 2 ch. 58.

44 Athenaios, *Deipnosophistai*, 92d.

45 Catullus, in *Catulli carmina*, ed. R.A.B. Mynors (Oxford, 1958), fragment 1.

46 Athenaios, *Deipnosophistai*, 278a.

47 Ibid., 116f.

48 *Apicius*, 9.10.8.

49 Plato, *Gorgias*, 518b.

50 Athenaios, *Deipnosophistai*, 325f.

51 Ibid., 324a.

52 Ibid., 516c.

53 Athenaios, *Deipnosophistai*, 146f, 642f. Some editors reject the identification with Philoxenos of Kythera and call this poet Philoxenos of Leukas.

54 *Epitome of Athenaios*, 6d.

55 Athenaios, *Deipnosophistai*, 643d.

56 Ibid., 499c.

57 Ibid., 75e.

58 Ibid., 647b.

59 Ibid., 130c.

60 *Souda* s.v. 'Paxamos'. See the online edition at www.stoa.org/sol.

61 Galen, *Handy Remedies*, in *Claudii Galeni opera omnia*, ed. C. G. Kühn (Leipzig, 1821–33), vol. XIV, p. 537.

62 Athenaios, *Deipnosophistai*, 689c.

63 Oreibasios, *Medical Collections*, in Mark Grant, trans., *Dieting for an Emperor: A Translation of Books 1 and 4 of Oribasius' Medical Compilations* (Leiden, 1997), Book 1 ch. 3.

64 Galen, *On the Properties of Foods*, in O. Powell, trans., *Galen: On the Properties of Foodstuffs* (Cambridge, 2002), 1.3.1–2.

THREE: Roman and Byzantine Tastes

1 *Apicius*, 2.4, in *Apicius*, ed. and trans. Christopher Grocock and Sally Grainger (Totnes, 2006), pp. 153–5.

2 Horace, *Epistles*, in *Horace: Satires, Epistles and Ars Poetica*, ed. H. R. Fairclough (London, 1924), Book 2 epistle 1, ll. 32–3.

3 *Anthologia Palatina*, in *The Greek Anthology*, ed. W. R. Paton (London, 1916–18), Book 11 no. 319.

4 *Geoponika*, in Andrew Dalby, trans., *Geoponika: Farm Work* (Totnes, 2011), Book 15 ch. 7.

5 Macrobius, *Saturnalia*, in *Macrobius: Saturnalia*, ed. Robert A. Kaster (Cambridge, MA, 2011), Book 7 ch. 12.

6 *Aetna*, in *Minor Latin Poets*, ed. J. W. Duff and A. M. Duff (Cambridge, MA, 1935), ll. 13–14.

7 Apuleius, *Metamorphoses*, in Sarah Ruden, trans., *Apuleius: The Golden Ass* (New Haven, CT, 2011), Book 1 ch. 5.

8 Pliny, *Natural History*, in *Pliny: Natural History*, ed. H. Rackham et al. (Cambridge, MA, 1938–63), Book 14 section 54; compare *Odyssey*, 9.39–42. Odysseus, like Mucianus, sometimes embellished the truth.

9 Horace, *Odes*, in *Horace: Odes and Epodes*, ed. Niall Rudd (Cambridge, MA, 2004), Book 1 ode 27, ll. 1–2.

10 Galen, *On Antidotes*, in *Claudii Galeni opera omnia*, ed. C. G. Kühn (Leipzig, 1821–33), vol. XIV, pp. 4–79; A.-M. Rouanet-Liesenfelt, 'Les Plantes médicinales de Crète à l'époque romaine', *Cretan Studies*, III (1992), pp. 173–90; Myrsini Lambraki, *Τα χορτά* (Chania, 1997).

11 Strabo, *Geography*, in *The Geography of Strabo*, ed. H. L. Jones (London, 1917–32), 14.1.35.

12 Galen, *Therapeutic Method*, in Kühn, *Claudii Galeri opera omnia*, vol. X, p. 830.

13 Horace, *Satires*, in *Horace: Satires, Epistles and Ars Poetica*, Fairclough, Book 2 satire 8, l. 52. Two thousand years later, aged Assyrtiko vinegar, made from a single Greek grape variety, would fetch high prices.

14 Pliny, *Natural History*, Book 14 section 78.

15 *Geoponika*, 8.24.

16 Theophrastos, *On Odours*, *Theophrastus: Enquiry into Plants*, ed. and trans. Arthur Hort (Cambridge, MA, 1916–26), ch. 10.

17 Theophrastos, *History of Plants*, in Hort, *Theophrastus* 9.20.1.

18 Tāyan-Kannanār, *Āgam*, 149.7–11, in Pierre Meile, 'Les Yavana dans l'Inde tamoule', *Revue asiatique*, CCXXXII (1940/41), pp. 85–123.

19 *Periplous*, *The Periplus of the Erythraean Sea*, ed. and trans. Lionel Casson (Princeton, NJ, 1989), ch. 56.

20 Athenaios, *Deipnosophistai*, in *Athenaeus: The Learned Banqueters*, ed. and trans. Douglas Olson (Cambridge, MA, 2006–12), 90f.

21 Plutarch, *Symposion Questions*, in *Plutarch's Moralia*, ed. E. L. Minar et al., vol. IX (Cambridge, MA, 1969), Book 8 ch. 9.

22 Dioskourides, *Materia Medica*, in *Pedanii Dioscuridis Anazarbei de materia medica libri quinque*, ed. M. Wellmann (Berlin, 1907–14), Book 2. ch. 160.

23 Quoted in Strabo, *Geography*, 15.1.20.

24 Galen, *On Antidotes*, vol. XIV, pp. 63–5; translation after Casson, *Periplus*, p. 244.

25 *Prodromic Poems*, 4.174–6, in *Πτωχοπρόδρομος*, ed. Hans Eideneier (Heraklio, 2012).

26 Psellos, *Poem on Medicine*, in *Psellus: Poemata*, ed. L. G. Westerink (Stuttgart, 1992), ll. 208–10.

27 Simeon Seth, *Alphabetical Handbook of the Properties of Foods*, in *Simeonis Sethi Syntagma de alimentorum facultatibus*, ed. B. Langkavel (Leipzig, 1868), p. 33.

28 Ibid., p. 125.

29 Pollux, *Onomastikon*, in *Pollucis Onomasticon*, ed. Ericus Bethe (Leipzig, 1900–37), Book 6 ch. 57.

30 Xan Fielding, *The Stronghold* (London, 1955), p. 115.

31 *Book of the Eparch*, in *The Book of the Eparch*, ed. I. Dujcev (London, 1970), ch. 18.

32 *Prodromic Poems*, 4.17 (ms. g) and 4.80.

33 Prokopios, *On the Wars*, in *Procopius*, ed. H. B. Dewing (London, 1914–40), Book 3 ch. 13.

34 Prokopios, *Anekdota*, in G. A. Williamson, trans., *Procopius: The Secret History* (Harmondsworth, 1966), ch. 6 section 2.

35 *Geoponika*, 18.19.

36 Simeon Seth, *Alphabetical Handbook*, p. 75.

37 Liutprand of Cremona, *Antapodosis*, in F. A. Wright, trans., *The Works of Liudprand of Cremona* (London, 1930), Book 6 ch. 8–9.

38 Ahmad ibn Rustih, *Kitab al-a'lah al-nafisa,* in *Ibn Rustih: Kitab al-a'lak an-nafisa*, ed. M. J. De Goeje (Leiden, 1892).

39 Liutprand, *Antapodosis*, 6.8–9.

40 William of Rubruck, *Report*, in P. Jackson, trans., *The Mission of Friar William of Rubruck* (London, 1990), ch. 9.

41 Evliya Çelebi, *Seyahatnâme*, in Alexander Pallis, *In the Days of the Janissaries: Old Turkish Life as Depicted in the Travel-book of Evliyá Chelebí* (London, 1951), p. 95.

42 Simon Malmberg, *Dazzling Dining: Banquets as an Expression of Imperial Legitimacy* (Uppsala, 2003).

43 Liutprand of Cremona, *Antapodosis* and *Embassy to Constantinople*, in Wright, *The Works of Liudprand of Cremona*, ch. 1.

44 W. M. Leake, *Travels in the Morea* (London, 1830), vol. II, p. 276.

45 Allan Evans, ed., *Francesco Balducci Pegolotti: La pratica della mercatura* (Cambridge, MA, 1936), pp. 33–47.

46 Ioannes Choumnos, *Letters,* in *Monemvasian Wine – Monovas(i)a – Malvasia*, ed. Ilias Anagnostakis (Athens, 2008), p. 131.

47 Anagnostakis et al., *Ancient and Byzantine Cuisine.*

48 Ilias Anagnostakis et al., *Ancient and Byzantine Cuisine* (Athens, 2013), p. 181.

49 *Prodromic Poems*, 4.172–88.

50 Pero Tafur, *Travels and Voyages*, in Malcolm Letts, trans., *Pero Tafur, Travels and Adventures, 1435–1439* (London, 1926), p. 141.

51 Cyril of Skythopolis, *Life of St Sabas*, in *Kyrillos von Skythopolis*, ed. E. Schwartz (Leipzig, 1939), pp. 130–31.

52 Liutprand, *Antapodosis*, 5.23. Unlike Liutprand, Byzantine chroniclers attribute to Romanos a more sententious observation, quoting Isaiah 1:2: 'I have nourished and brought up children, and they have rebelled against me.'

53 Anna Komnene, *Alexiad*, in E.R.A. Sewter, trans., *The Alexiad of Anna Comnena* (Harmondsworth, 1969), 3.1.1.

54 Leontios of Neapolis, *Life of St John the Almsgiver*, in E. Dawes and N. H. Baynes, trans., *Three Byzantine Saints* (London, 1948), Book 2 ch. 21.

55 *Prodromic Poems*, 4.394–412.

56 Unfortunately the only available recipe strays into fantasy. 'After all these dishes have been served comes in a nice *monokythron*, slightly blackened on the top, preceded by its aroma . . . Four hearts of cabbage, fat and snowy white; a salted neck of swordfish; a middle cut of carp; about twenty *glaukoi* [an unidentified fish]; a slice of salt sturgeon; fourteen eggs and some Cretan cheese and four *apotyra* and a bit of

Vlach cheese and a pint of olive oil, a handful of pepper, twelve little heads of garlic and fifteen chub mackerels, and a splash of sweet wine over the top, and roll up your sleeves and get to work – just watch the mouthfuls go.' *Prodromic Poems*, 4.201–16.

FOUR: An Empire Reborn

1 Liutprand of Cremona, *Embassy to Constantinople*, in F. A. Wright, trans., *The Works of Liudprand of Cremona* (London, 1930), ch. 11.

2 Ibid., p. 20.

3 Ibn Battuta, *Travels*, in H.A.R. Gibb, trans., *The Travels of Ibn Battuta AD 1325–1354* (Cambridge, 1958–71), p. 504.

4 Anna Komnene, *Alexiad*, in E.R.A. Sewter, trans., *The Alexiad of Anna Comnena* (Harmondsworth, 1969), 10.11.3–4.

5 *Life of St Theodore of Sykeon*, in E. Dawes and N. H. Baynes, trans., *Three Byzantine Saints* (London, 1948), ch. 3, 6. Andrew Dalby, *Siren Feasts: A History of Food and Gastronomy in Greece* (London, 1996), pp. 195–6.

6 *Timarion*, in Barry Baldwin, trans., *Timarion* (Detroit, MI, 1984), ch. 2.

7 *Pilgrimage of St Willibald*, in W. R. Brownlow, trans., *The Hodoeporicon of Saint Willibald* (London, 1891), p. 256.

8 Michael Choniates, *Letters*, in *Michael Akominatou tou Khoniatou ta sozomena*, ed. S. P. Lampros (Athens, 1879–80), vol. II, p. 194.

9 Anthony of Novgorod, *Pilgrim's Book*, in M. Ehrhard, trans., 'Le Livre du pèlerin d'Antoine de Novgorod', *Romania*, LVIII (1932), pp. 44–65, at pp. 63–4.

10 Claudian, *Against Eutropius*, in *Claudian*, ed. M. Platnauer (London, 1922), Book 2, ll. 326–41.

11 Benjamin of Tudela, *Itinerary*, in Marcus Nathan Adler, trans., *The Itinerary of Benjamin of Tudela* (London, 1907), p. 23.

12 Ibn Battuta, *Travels*, pp. 506–8; Gibb, pp. 430–432.

13 Allan Evans, ed., *Francesco Balducci Pegolotti: La pratica della mercatura* (Cambridge, MA, 1936), pp. 33–47.

14 *Anthologia Palatina*, in *The Greek Anthology*, ed. W. R. Paton (London, 1916–18), Book 9 no. 650.

15 *Book of the Eparch*, in *The Book of the Eparch*, ed. I. Dujcev (London, 1970), ch. 19.

16 Pero Tafur, *Travels and Voyages*, in Malcolm Letts, trans., *Pero Tafur: Travels and Adventures, 1435–1439* (London, 1926), p. 141.

17 Niketas Choniates, *Chronicle*, in Harry J. Magoulias, trans., *O City of Byzantium: Annals of Niketas Choniates* (Detroit, 1984), p. 57.

18 Ahmad ibn Rustih, *Kitab al-a'lah al-nafisa*, in *Ibn Rustih: Kitab al-a'lak an-nafisa*, ed. M. J. De Goeje (Leiden, 1892).

19 Simeon Seth, *Alphabetical Handbook of the Properties of Foods*, in *Simeonis Sethi Syntagma de alimentorum facultatibus*, ed. B. Langkavel (Leipzig, 1868).

20 Ibid., ch. 85.

21 Liutprand, *Embassy to Constantinople*, 11.

22 Eustathios, *Capture of Thessaloniki*, in John R. Melville Jones, trans., *Eustathios of Thessaloniki: The Capture of Thessaloniki* (Canberra, 1988), ch. 136–7.

23 Choniates, *Chronicle*, p. 594.

24 Cyriac of Ancona, in *Cyriac of Ancona: Later Travels*, ed. and trans. Edward W. Bonar (Cambridge, MA, 2003), pp. 342–5.

25 Ibid., pp. 254–5, 262–3. The phrases are synonyms, used in letters to different recipients, for one of whom Cyriac inserted the classical Greek word.

26 There was in recent times a small production of caviar in Greece: see Marina Kavroulaki, 'Fish Roe', at http://297315322.blog.com.gr.

27 Michael Apostolios, *Letters*, in *Lettres inédites de Michel Apostolis, publiées d'après les manuscrits du Vatican; avec des opuscules inédits du même auteur*, ed. Hippolyte Noiret and A. M. Desrousseaux (Paris, 1889), p. 77.

28 Ludovicus Nonnius, *Ichtyophagia sive de piscium esu commentarius* (Antwerp, 1616), p. 176.

29 Pierre Belon du Mans, *Les Observations de plusieurs singularitez et choses memorables trouvées en Grèce, Asie, Judée, Egypte, Arabie et autres pays étranges* (Paris, 1555), Book 1 ch. 75.

30 George Wheler, *A Journey into Greece* (London, 1682), pp. 203–4.

31 Antoine Galland, *Smyrne ancienne et moderne*, in *Le voyage à Smyrne: un manuscrit d'Antoine Galland* (1678), ed. Frédéric Bauden (Paris, 2000), p. 149.

32 Evliya Çelebi, *Seyahatnâme*, in Alexander Pallis, *In the Days of the Janissaries: Old Turkish Life as Depicted in the Travel-book of Evliyá Chelebí* (London, 1951), pp. 88–9.

33 Patrick Leigh Fermor, *Roumeli: Travels in Northern Greece* (London, 1966), p. 186 footnote. The wise reader believes nearly everything Leigh Fermor says, likewise Lawrence Durrell below.

34 Galland, *Smyrne ancienne et moderne*, p. 144.

35 Ibid., pp. 137–8.

36 Ibid., p. 119. *Verdea* was once a popular north Italian wine style; wine called *verdea* is now made in the Ionian islands.

37 Ibid., p. 149.

38 *Timarion*, 2.

39 Menander Protector, *History*, in *The History of Menander the Guardsman*, ed. and trans. R. C. Blockley (Liverpool, 1985), fragment 10.3.

40 Ibn Battuta, *Travels*, p. 488.

41 Manuel Palaiologos, *Letters*, in *The Letters of Manuel II Palaeologus*, ed. and trans. George T. Dennis (Washington, DC, 1977), letter 16.

42 Manuel Palaiologos, *Dialogues with a Muslim*, in *Manuel II. Palaiologos: Dialoge mit einem Muslim*, ed. and trans. Karl Förstel (Würzburg, 1995), ch. 10.

43 Giovanni de' Pigli, in Ilias Anagnostakis et al., *Ancient and Byzantine Cuisine* (Athens, 2013), pp. 169–73.

44 Belon, *Observations*, 1.59.

45 Ibid.

46 Bernard Randolph, *Present State of the Morea* (London, 1689), pp. 18–19. The now-forgotten English term 'wine cute' is a version of French *vin cuit*.

47 Belon, *Observations*, 3.29.

48 Ibid.

49 W. M. Leake, *Travels in the Morea* (London, 1830), vol. 1, pp. 17–18.

50 J. Aegidius van Egmont and John Heyman, *Travels* (London, 1759), vol. 1, p. 68.

51 Michel Baudier, *Histoire générale du Serrail*, in B. de Vigenère, trans., *Histoire générale des Turcs, contenant l'Histoire de Chalcocondyle* (Paris, 1662), vol. II.

52 Evliya Çelebi, *Seyahatnâme*, in J. von Hammer, *Evliya Efendi: Narrative of Travels* (London, 1834–50), vol. 1 pt 2, p. 148.

53 Belon, *Observations*, 3.32.

54 Ibid.

55 Felix Faber, *Evagatorium*, in *Fratris Felicis Fabri Evagatorium*, ed. Cunradus Dietericus Hassler (Stuttgart, 1843–9), vol. I, p. 165.

56 *Geoponika*, in Andrew Dalby, trans., *Geoponika: Farm Work* (Totnes, 2011), Book 3 ch. 8.

57 Belon, *Observations*, 1.59.

58 Charles Perry, 'Trakhanas Revisited', *Petits Propos Culinaires*, 55 (1997), pp. 34–9; William Woys Weaver, 'The Origins of Trachanás: Evidence from Cyprus and Ancient Texts', *Gastronomica*, II/1 (Winter 2002), pp. 41–8; Mariana Kavroulaki, 'Trachana Soup' and 'Xinohondros' at http://297315322.blog.com.gr; Aglaia Kremezi, 'Greece: Culinary Travel: Ionian Islands', at www.epicurious.com/archive.

FIVE: A Culinary Geography, Part I: Beyond Greece

1 Kritoboulos of Imbros, *History*, in Charles T. Riggs, trans., *Kritovoulos: History of Mehmed the Conqueror* (Princeton, NJ, 1954), 5.9.3.

2 Evliya Çelebi, *Seyahatnâme*, in Alexander Pallis, *In the Days of the Janissaries: Old Turkish Life as Depicted in the Travel-book of Evliyá Chelebí* (London, 1951), pp. 83–4.

3 Ibid., pp. 86–7.

4 George Wheler, *A Journey into Greece* (London, 1682), pp. 203–4.

5 *Geoponika*, in Andrew Dalby, trans., *Geoponika: Farm Work* (Totnes, 2011), Book 12 ch. 1.

6 Pierre Gilles (Petrus Gyllius), *De Bosphoro Thracio* (Lyon, 1561).

7 Pierre Belon du Mans, *Les Observations de plusieurs singularitez et choses memorables trouvées en Grèce, Asie, Judée, Egypte, Arabie et autres pays étranges* (Paris, 1555), Book 3 ch. 51.

8 Evliya Çelebi, *Seyahatnâme*, in J. von Hammer, *Evliya Efendi: Narrative of Travels* (London, 1834–50), vol. I pt 2, p. 137.

9 Çelebi, *Seyahatnâme*, in Pallis, *In the Days of the Janissaries*, pp. 138–9.

10 Ibid., pp. 142–3.

11 Ibid., pp. 143–4. *Kalikanzaros* is a confused reference to All Saints' Day.

12 Çelebi, *Seyahatnâme*, in von Hammer, *Evliya Efendi*, vol. I pt 2, p. 250. Evliya's modern readers suspect that his show of ignorance is a pretence.

13 Richard Pococke, *A Description of the East* (London, 1743), vol. II pt 2, p. 38.

14 Antoine Galland, *Smyrne ancienne et moderne*, in *Le Voyage à Smyrne: un manuscrit d'Antoine Galland (1678)*, ed. Frédéric Bauden (Paris, 2000), pp. 146–9.

15 Ibid.

16 Mariana Kavroulaki, 'A Taste of the Past: Pastirma', at http://297315322.blog.com.gr.

17 Andrew Dalby, '"We Talked About the Aubergines": International Diplomacy and the Cretan Diet', in *Vegetables: Proceedings of the Oxford Symposium on Food and Cookery*, ed. Richard Hosking (Totnes, 2009).

18 Jonathan Reynolds, 'Greek Revival', *New York Times* (4 April 2004).

19 Elisabeth Saab, 'Michael Psilakis' Quest to Make Greek Go Mainstream', *Fox News* (19 December 2013).

20 'Sydney Confidential', *Daily Telegraph* (3 August 2013).

SIX: A Culinary Geography, Part II: Within Greece

1 Patrick Leigh Fermor, *Roumeli: Travels in Northern Greece* (London, 1966), pp. 184–5.

2 George Wheler, *A Journey into Greece* (London, 1682), pp. 42–3.

3 Karl Baedeker, *Greece* (Leipzig, 1894), p. 10.

4 Lawrence Durrell, *Prospero's Cell* (London, 1945), pp. 44–5.

5 Wheler, *Journey into Greece*, pp. 35, 44.

6 Durrell, *Prospero's Cell*, p. 20.

7 Miles Lambert-Gócs, *The Wines of Greece* (London, 1990), pp. 224–7.

8 Durrell, *Prospero's Cell*, p. 14.

9 Quoted in Lambert-Gócs, *The Wines of Greece*, p. 207; he gives a complete translation.

10 Wheler, *Journey into Greece*, p. 32.

11 Baedeker, *Greece*, p. 10.

12 Durrell, *Prospero's Cell*, pp. 20, 78.

13 Shakespeare, *The Tempest*, 1.2.335–6; Durrell, *Prospero's Cell*, p. 80.

14 That is, ambergris. Wheler, *Journey into Greece*, p. 44.

15 Edward Lear, 'How Pleasant to Know Mr Lear!', in *Edward Lear: The Complete Verse and Other Nonsense*, ed. Vivien Noakes (London, 2001), p. 429.

16 Edward Lear, letter to Chichester Fortescue, in *Edward Lear: The Corfu Years*, ed. Philip Sherrard (Athens, 1988), p. 131.

17 Durrell, *Prospero's Cell*, pp. 85–6, cf. p. 49.

18 Francis Vernon, 'Observations', *Philosophical Transactions of the Royal Society*, XI (1676), pp. 575–82, at p. 580.

19 W. M. Leake, *Travels in the Morea* (London, 1830), vol. II, pp. 233–4.

20 Ibid., vol. III, p. 108.

21 Ibid., vol. II, pp. 517–18.

22 Bernard Randolph, *Present State of the Morea* (London, 1689), p. 17.

23 Leake, *Travels in the Morea*, vol. II, p. 144.

24 Randolph, *Present State of the Morea*, pp. 18–19.

25 Leake, *Travels in the Morea*, vol. II, pp. 140–41.

26 Randolph, *Present State of the Morea*, pp. 18–19.

27 Wheler, *Journey into Greece*, pp. 295–6.

28 Jacob Spon, *Voyage d'Italie, de Dalmatie, de Grèce et du Levant* (Paris, 1678), vol. I, pp. 111–12.

29 Leake, *Travels in the Morea*, vol. II, pp. 153–4.

30 *Le Voyage de Hiérusalem,* in Ch. Schefer, ed., *Le Voyage de la saincte cyté de Hierusalem* (Paris, 1882), p. 47.

31 Pietro Casola, *Pilgrimage*, in M. M. Newett, trans., *Canon Pietro Casola's Pilgrimage to Jerusalem in the Year 1494* (Manchester, 1907), p. 194.

32 Felix Faber, *Evagatorium*, in *Fratris Felicis Fabri Evagatorium*, ed. Cunradus Dietericus Hassler (Stuttgart, 1843–9), vol. III, pp. 336–7.

33 Ibid.

34 Ibid.

35 Leake, *Travels in the Morea*, vol. I, pp. 346–8.

36 Cyriac of Ancona, in *Cyriac of Ancona: Later Travels*, ed. and trans. Edward W. Bodnar (Cambridge, MA, 2003), pp. 322–5. Quotation abridged.

37 Leake, *Travels in the Morea*, vol. I, pp. 309–10.

38 Ibid., p. 337.

39 Ibid., p. 319.

40 Ibid., p. 281.

41 Ibid., pp. 241–2.

42 Wheler, *Journey into Greece*, p. 352.

43 Randolph, *Present State of the Morea*, p. 21.

44 Leigh Fermor, *Roumeli*, p. 210.

45 Ibid., pp. 184–5.

46 Anthimos, *Letter on Diet*, see *Anthimus: De observatione ciborum: On the Observance of Foods*, ed. and trans. Mark Grant (Totnes, 1996), ch. 13.

47 Wheler, *Journey into Greece*, p. 352.

48 Josef von Ow, *Aufzeichnungen eines Junkers am Hofe zu Athen* (Pest, 1854), vol. I, p. 84.

49 Aischylos, *Suppliants*, 952–3. The words were spoken pointedly to travellers from Egypt, where, as ancient Greeks knew, beer was the usual beverage.

50 H.D.F. Kitto, *In the Mountains of Greece* (London, 1933), p. 95.

51 Evliya Çelebi, *Seyahatnâme*, in Alexander Pallis, *In the Days of the Janissaries: Old Turkish Life as Depicted in the Travel-book of Evliyá Chelebí* (London, 1951), p. 146.

52 Wheler, *Journey into Greece*, pp. 412–13.

53 'How to Eat Well in Athens', *New York Times* (14 January 2011).

54 W. M. Leake, *Travels in Northern Greece* (London, 1835), vol. I, p. 164.

55 Vernon, 'Observations', p. 581.

56 Sources quoted by Mariana Kavroulaki, 'The Only Food They Had Was the Spring Swallows', at http://297315322.blog.com.gr.

57 Strabo, *Geography*, in *The Geography of Strabo*, ed. H. L. Jones (London, 1917–32), 10.2.3.

58 Ludovicus Nonnius, *Ichtyophagia sive de piscium esu commentarius* (Antwerp, 1616), p. 176.

59 Leake, *Travels in Northern Greece*, vol. I, pp. 9–10.

60 Athenaios, *Deipnosophistai*, in *Athenaeus: The Learned Banqueters*, ed. and trans. S. Douglas Olson (Cambridge, MA, 2006–12), 121c.

61 Diane Kochilas, *The Glorious Foods of Greece* (New York, 2001), p. 113.

62 Leake, *Travels in Northern Greece*, vol. I, pp. 176–82.

63 Ibid., p. 307.

64 Rumili, more often spelled Roumeli, is a name for the European provinces of the Ottoman Empire. Leake, *Travels in Northern Greece*, vol. I, p. 306.

65 Miles Lambert-Gócs, *The Wines of Greece*, p. 133. Quotation abridged.

66 Hesiod, *Works and Days*, in M. L. West, trans., *Hesiod: Theogony and Works and Days* (Oxford, 1999), ll. 609–14.

67 Gil Marks, *Encyclopedia of Jewish Food* (Hoboken, NJ, 2010).

68 For the *bougatsa* of Crete, which has its own well-deserved fame, see Mariana Kavroulaki, 'Cretan Food Markets', at http://297315322.blog.com.gr.

69 Pierre Belon du Mans, *Les Observations de plusieurs singularitez et choses memorables trouvées en Grèce, Asie, Judée, Egypte, Arabie et autres pays étranges* (Paris, 1555), Book 1 ch. 60.

70 Çelebi, *Seyahatnâme*, pp. 137–8.

71 Leake, *Travels in Northern Greece*, vol. I, pp. 142–3.

72 Ibid., p. 273.

73 Ibid., pp. 280–81.

74 Aglaia Kremezi finds them now settled on the slopes of Parnassos, and where better? 'Greece: Culinary Travel: Athens and Central Greece', at www.epicurious.com/archive.

75 Leigh Fermor, *Roumeli*, pp. 15–16.

76 *Timarion*, in Barry Baldwin, trans., *Timarion* (Detroit, MI, 1984), pp. 4–5.

77 Bartolf of Nangis, *History of the Franks who Stormed Jerusalem*, in *Recueil des historiens des croisades: Historiens occidentaux* (Paris, 1866), vol. III, pp. 487–543, at p. 493.

78 Eustathios, *Capture of Thessaloniki*, in John R. Melville Jones, trans., *Eustathios of Thessaloniki: The Capture of Thessaloniki* (Canberra, 1988), ch. 136, 137.

79 Claudia Roden, *The Book of Jewish Food* (New York, 1996); Diane Kochilas, *The Glorious Foods of Greece* (New York, 2001), p. 202.

80 Cyriac, *Later Travels*, pp. 212–15.

81 Belon, *Observations*, 2.8.

82 Richard Pococke, *A Description of the East* (London, 1743), vol. II pt 2, pp. 3–4.

83 Antoine Des Barres, *L'estat présent de l'Archipel* (Paris, 1678), pp. 93–5.

84 William Lithgow, *The Totall Discourse, 1632* (Glasgow, 1906), p. 92.

85 Pococke, *Description of the East*, vol. II, pt 2, pp. 3–4.

86 Dimitrios G. Ierapetritis, 'The Geography of the Chios Mastic Trade from the 17th through to the 19th Century', *Ethnobotany Research and Applications*, VIII (2010), pp. 153–67.

87 Pococke, *Description of the East*, vol. II pt 2, p. 22.

88 J. Pitton de Tournefort, *Relation d'un voyage du Levant fait par ordre du Roy* (Paris, 1717), vol. I, p. 409.

89 Belon, *Observations*, 1.31.

90 Lithgow, *Totall Discourse*, p. 158.

91 Aglaia Kremezi, 'Greece: Culinary Travel: Aegean Islands', at www.epicurious.com/archive.

92 Quoted in W. B. Stanford and E. J. Finopoulos, eds, *Travels of Lord Charlemont in Greece and Turkey* (London, 1984).

93 Kitto, *In the Mountains of Greece*, p. 145.

94 J. Aegidius van Egmont and John Heyman, *Travels* (London, 1759), vol. I, p. 69.

95 Wheler, *Journey into Greece*, p. 61.

96 Leigh Fermor, *Roumeli*, pp. 184–5.

97 Mariana Kavroulaki, 'Recording Food Culture of Amari Valley', at http://297315322.blog.com.gr.

98 Leake, *Travels in the Morea*, vol. I, p. 325.

99 Symon Semeonis, *Pilgrimage*, in *Monemvasian Wine – Monovas(i)a – Malvasia*, ed. Ilias Anagnostakis (Athens, 2008), p. 131.

100 Lithgow, *Totall Discourse*, p. 71.

101 *Le Voyage de Hiérusalem*, p. 51.

102 Faber, *Evagatorium*, vol. I, p. 49.

103 Casola, *Pilgrimage*, p. 202.

104 Marjorie Blamey and Christopher Grey-Wilson, *Wild Flowers of the Mediterranean* (London, 2004).

105 Belon, *Observations*, 1.19.

106 Semeonis, *Pilgrimage*, p. 131.

107 Belon, *Observations*, 1.5.

108 Xan Fielding, *The Stronghold* (London, 1955), p. 230.

109 Çelebi, *Seyahatnâme*, p. 146.

110 Fielding, *The Stronghold*, p. 75.

111 Mariana Kavroulaki, 'How to Make Your Own Butter', at http://297315322.blog.com.gr.

112 Casola, *Pilgrimage*, p. 202.

SEVEN: Food of Recent Greece

1 Mariana Kavroulaki, 'English Desserts' and 'Admiral's Miaoulis Sea Bass', at http://297315322.blog.com.gr.

2 Jonathan Reynolds, 'Greek Revival', *New York Times* (4 April 2004).

3 Aglaia Kremezi, '"Classic" Greek Cuisine: Not So Classic' and 'Tomato: A Latecomer that Changed Greek Flavor', *The Atlantic* (July 2010).

4 Artemis Leontis, *Culture and Customs of Greece* (Westport, CT, 2009), pp. 93–4.

5 James Pettifer, *The Greeks: The Land and People since the War*, 2nd edn (London, 2012), ch. 12.

6 'Interview with Lefteris Lazarou' and 'Interview with Christoforos Peskias', at www.exero.com.

7 Quoted in Lena Corner, 'Vefa Alexiadou: Meet Greece's Answer to Delia Smith', in *The Independent* (16 July 2009).

8 Isabel J. Armstrong, *Two Roving Englishwomen in Greece* (London, 1893), pp. 1–3.

9 Ibid., pp. 143–4.

10 W. M. Leake, *Travels in the Morea* (London, 1830), vol. I, p. 110.

11 Edward Dodwell, *A Classical and Topographical Tour through Greece* (London, 1819), pp. 155–7.

12 Pierre Belon du Mans, *Les Observations de plusieurs singularitez et choses memorables trouvées en Grèce, Asie, Judée, Egypte, Arabie et autres pays étranges* (Paris, 1555), Book 1 ch. 47.

13 Xan Fielding, *The Stronghold* (London, 1955), p. 64.

14 Patrick Leigh Fermor, *Roumeli: Travels in Northern Greece* (London, 1966), pp. 130–31.

15 Edward Lear, letter to Chichester Fortescue, in *Edward Lear: The Corfu Years*, ed. Philip Sherrard (Athens, 1988), p. 89.

16 Leake, *Travels in the Morea*, vol. I, p. 305.

17 George Wheler, *A Journey into Greece* (London, 1682), pp. 323–6.

18 Belon, *Observations*, 1.48.

19 Ibid., 1.35.

20 Wheler, *Journey into Greece*, pp. 323–4.

21 Dodwell, *Classical and Topographical Tour*, pp. 143–4.

22 Belon, *Observations*, 1.49.

23 Ibid., 1.38; Vasilii Barskii, *Travels*, in *Vasilii Barskii: Ta taxidia*, ed. Pavlos Mylonas et al. (Thessaloniki, 2009), pp. 414–15.

24 Cyriac of Ancona, in *Cyriac of Ancona: Later Travels*, ed. and trans. Edward W. Bodnar (Cambridge, MA, 2003), pp. 122–5, cf. p. 421.

25 Wheler, *Journey into Greece*, pp. 323–4.

26 Ibid., pp. 176–7.

27 Ibid., pp. 323–4.

28 Armstrong, *Two Roving Englishwomen*, pp. 250–51.

29 Lawrence Durrell, *The Greek Islands* (London, 1980).

30 H.D.F. Kitto, *In the Mountains of Greece* (London, 1933), p. 121.

31 Fielding, *The Stronghold*, p. 125.

32 Leigh Fermor, *Roumeli*, p. 149.

33 Armstrong, *Two Roving Englishwomen*, p. 27.

34 Kitto, *In the Mountains of Greece*, p. 103.

35 Ibid., p. 123.

36 Durrell, *Greek Islands*.

37 Armstrong, *Two Roving Englishwomen*, p. 22. The 'very sour clotted cream' is evidently yoghurt.

38 Felix Faber, *Evagatorium*, in *Fratris Felicis Fabri Evagatorium*, ed. Cunradus Dietericus Hassler (Stuttgart, 1843–9), vol. I, pp. 167–8.

39 Durrell, *Greek Islands*.

40 Fielding, *The Stronghold*, p. 135. The 'volcanic salad' ingredients are listed on page 235 of this book.

41 *Odyssey*, 7.112–21.

42 Gareth Morgan, 'The Laments of Mani', *Folklore*, LXXXIV (1973), pp. 265–98, at p. 268.

43 Lawrence Durrell, *Prospero's Cell* (London, 1945), p. 112.

44 Theodore Stephanides, *Island Trail* (London, 1973), p. 101.

45 Bernard Randolph, *Present State of the Morea* (London, 1689), p. 21.

46 Richard Pococke, *A Description of the East* (London, 1743), vol. II pt 1, pp. 243–4.

47 Edward Lear, *Cretan Journal*, in *Edward Lear: The Cretan Journal*, ed. Rowena Fowler, 3rd edn (Limni, Evia, 2012), p. 41 and note 42. In a note that he wrote later about the disappearance of these vines, Lear blamed 'the vine disease two years earlier', but if he meant phylloxera by this, 1862 was too early for phylloxera in any part of Greece. According to Miles Lambert-Gócs, *The Wines of Greece* (London, 1990), p. 14, phylloxera had not reached western Crete at the time of writing.

48 John Fowles, *The Magus*, revd edn (London, 1977).

49 *Epitome of Athenaios*, *Athenaeus: The Learned Banqueters*, ed. and trans. S. Douglas Olson (Cambridge, MA, 2006–12), 54f.

50 Cyriac, *Later Travels*, pp. 322–5.

51 Leake, *Travels in the Morea*, vol. I, pp. 258–9.

52 Morgan, 'The Laments of Mani', p. 269.

53 Fielding, *The Stronghold*, p. 135.

54 Leontis, *Culture and Customs of Greece*, p. 94.

55 *Souda s.v. poulypous*, see the online edition at www.stoa.org/sol.

56 Fielding, *The Stronghold*, p. 156.

57 Alan Davidson, *Mediterranean Seafood*, 2nd edn (Harmondsworth, 1981).

58 Xenokrates, in *Xenokratous kai Galenou peri tes apo ton enydron trophes*, ed. Adamantios Korais and Georgios Christodoulos (Chios, 1998).

59 Belon, *Observations*, 1.72.

60 Wheler, *Journey into Greece*, p. 352.

61 Editor: How do you encourage something with your foot? Authors: You put your foot in it.

62 Fielding, *The Stronghold*, p. 12.

63 Martial, *Epigrams*, 13.84.

64 Diane Kochilas, *The Glorious Foods of Greece* (New York, 2001), p. 126.

65 Leigh Fermor, *Roumeli*, pp. 200, 210–11.

66 Mariana Kavroulaki, 'Blood in Food', at http://297315322.blog.com.gr.

67 Kochilas, *Glorious Foods*.

68 Mariana Kavroulaki, 'Cured Lean Pork: A Byzantine Tradition' and 'Cretan Food Markets', at http://297315322.blog.com.gr.

69 Leake, *Travels in the Morea*, vol. I, p. 17.

70 J. Aegidius van Egmont and John Heyman, *Travels* (London, 1759), vol. I, p. 66.

71 Armstrong, *Two Roving Englishwomen*, p. 22.

72 Durrell, *Prospero's Cell*, p. 139.

73 *Geoponika*, in Andrew Dalby, trans., *Geoponika: Farm Work* (Totnes, 2011), Book 15 ch. 7.

74 Pindar, *Olympian Odes*, in *Pindar*, ed. W. H. Race (London, 1997), ode 1, l. 1.

75 George Manwaring, *A True Discourse of Sir Anthony Sherley's Travel into Persia*, in *The Three Brothers: Travels and Adventures of Sir Anthony, Sir Robert and Sir Thomas Sherley in Persia, Russia, Turkey and Spain* (London, 1825), p. 28.

76 *Epitome of Athenaios*, 42f.

77 W. M. Leake, *Travels in Northern Greece* (London, 1835), vol. I, pp. 326–7.

78 Kitto, *In the Mountains of Greece*, p. 122.

79 Wheler, *Journey into Greece*, pp. 203–4.

80 Karl Baedeker, *Greece* (Leipzig, 1894), p. XXIV, slightly abridged.

81 Theodora Matsaidoni, 'Historic Cafés in Athens Completely Gone' (2014), at http://greece.greekreporter.com.

82 Stephanides, *Island Trail*, p. 7; Andrew Dalby, 'The Name of the Rose Again; or, What Happened to Theophrastus on Aphrodisiacs?', *Petits Propos Culinaires*, 64 (2000), pp. 9–15.

83 Evliya Çelebi, *Seyahatnâme*, in J. von Hammer, *Evliya Efendi: Narrative of Travels* (London, 1834–50), vol. I pt 2, p. 155.

84 *Odyssey*, 7.122–6.

85 Leake, *Travels in the Morea*, vol. I, p. 102, cf. vol. II, pp. 279–80.

86 William Lithgow, *The Totall Discourse*, 1632 (Glasgow, 1906), pp. 163–4.

87 Durrell, *Prospero's Cell*, p. 112.

88 Ibid., p. 128.

89 J. Pitton de Tournefort, *Relation d'un voyage du Levant fait par ordre du Roy* (Paris, 1717), vol. I, p. 89.

90 Fielding, *The Stronghold*, p. 127.

91 Leigh Fermor, *Roumeli*, p. 210.

92 Aglaia Kremezi, 'Greece: Culinary Travel: Macedonia and Thrace', at www.epicurious.com/archive.

93 Wheler, *Journey into Greece*, pp. 203–4, 458.

94 Egmont and Heyman, *Travels*, vol. I, p. 258.

95 R. A. McNeal, *Nicholas Biddle in Greece: The Journals and Letters* (University Park, PA, 1993); W. M. Leake, *Journal of a Tour in Asia Minor* (London, 1824), pp. 47–8.

96 Armstrong, *Two Roving Englishwomen*, p. 74.

97 Durrell, *Prospero's Cell*, p. 49.

98 Nelli Paraskevopoulou, 'Ένα «υποβρύχιο», παρακαλώ!' at www.womenonly.gr.

99 Hierophilos, *Dietary Calendar*, in Andrew Dalby, *Flavours of Byzantium* (Totnes, 2003).

100 The story of the Presentation, which is not biblical, is told in the apocryphal Infancy Gospel of James. Mariana Kavroulaki, 'Ensuring Abundance of Food', at http://297315322.blog.com.gr; Evy Johanne Håland, 'Rituals of Magical Rain-making in Modern and Ancient Greece: A Comparative Approach', *Cosmos*, XVII (2001), pp. 197–251, at pp. 205–8.

101 Charles Perry, at www.anissas.com/medieval-virgins-breasts; Mariana Kavroulaki, 'O kourabiedes!', at http://297315322.blog.com.gr.

102 Eleni Stamatopoulou, ed., Χερσέ βασιλόπιτες και άλλα. Το μικρασιάτικο τραπέζι του δωδεκαημέρου (Athens, 1998).

103 Håland, 'Rituals of Magical Rain-making', pp. 209–20.

104 Mariana Kavroulaki, 'Bourani: A Celebration of Fertility', at http://297315322.blog.com.gr; Manuela Marín, 'Sobre Buran y buraniyya,' in *al-Qantara*, II (1981), pp. 193–207; Tor Eigeland, 'The Cuisine of al-Andalus', *Saudi Aramco World* (September 1989).

105 Leake, *Travels in the Morea*, vol. III, p. 173.

106 Ibid., vol. I, pp. 258–9.

107 Dodwell, *Classical and Topographical Tour*, pp. 173–4.

108 John Thomas, Angela Constantinides Hero, eds, *Byzantine Monastic Foundation Documents* (Washington, DC, 2000), pp. 1701–9.

109 Ahmad ibn Rustih, *Kitab al-a'lah al-nafisa*, in *Ibn Rustih: Kitab al-a'lak an-nafisa*, ed. M. J. De Goeje (Leiden, 1892).

110 Håland, 'Rituals of Magical Rain-making', p. 221.

EPILOGUE: Conviviality

1 Hesiod, *Works and Days*, in M. L. West, trans., *Hesiod: Theogony and Works and Days* (Oxford, 1999), ll. 582–96.

2 Liutprand of Cremona, *Embassy to Constantinople*, in F. A. Wright, trans., *The Works of Liudprand of Cremona* (London, 1930), ch. 20.

3 Pierre Belon du Mans, *Les Observations de plusieurs singularitez et choses memorables trouvées en Grèce, Asie, Judée, Egypte, Arabie et autres pays étranges* (Paris, 1555), Book 1 ch. 48.

4 Cyriac of Ancona, in *Cyriac of Ancona: Later Travels*, ed. and trans. Edward W. Bodnar (Cambridge, MA, 2003), pp. 212–15.

5 Belon, *Observations*, 1.60.

6 George Manwaring, *A True Discourse of Sir Anthony Sherley's Travel into Persia*, in *The Three Brothers: Travels and Adventures of Sir Anthony, Sir Robert and Sir Thomas Sherley in Persia, Russia, Turkey and Spain* (London, 1825), p. 29.

7 Edward Lear, *Cretan Journal*, in *Edward Lear: The Cretan Journal*, ed. Rowena Fowler, 3rd edn (Limni, Evia, 2012), p. 59.

8 Patrick Leigh Fermor, *Roumeli: Travels in Northern Greece* (London, 1966), p. 162.

9 Antoine Des Barres, *L'estat présent de l'Archipel* (Paris, 1678), pp. 93–5.

10 William Lithgow, *The Totall Discourse, 1632* (Glasgow, 1906), pp. 92–3.

11 W. M. Leake, *Travels in the Morea* (London, 1830), vol. I, p. 305.

12 Giovanni de' Pigli, in Ilias Anagnostakis et al., *Ancient and Byzantine Cuisine* (Athens, 2013), pp. 169–73.

13 Lear, *Cretan Journal*, p. 43.

14 Belon, *Observations*, 1.47.

15 *Iliad*, in Martin Hammond, trans., *Homer: The Iliad* (Harmondsworth, 1987), Book 9, ll. 202–17.

16 J. L. Myres, in *Homer's Odyssey*, ed. D. B. Monro (Oxford, 1901), vol. II, p. 39.

17 Leigh Fermor, *Roumeli*, pp. 210–11.

18 *Odyssey*, 14.73–81.

19 Ibid., 14.249–51.

20 Leake, *Travels in the Morea*, vol. I, p. 333.

21 *Odyssey*, 14.56–8, 17.483–7, 14.437–8.

22 Isabel J. Armstrong, *Two Roving Englishwomen in Greece* (London, 1893), p. 251.

23 *Odyssey* 6.303–9, 15.376–9, 5.194–201.

24 Andrew Dalby, *Siren Feasts: A History of Food and Gastronomy in Greece* (London, 1996), pp. 2–11.

25 Athenaios, *Deipnosophistai*, in *Athenaeus; The Learned Banqueter*, ed. and trans. S. Douglas Olson (Cambridge, MA, 2006–12), 644d.

26 Isaios, *On Pyrrhos's Estate*, in *Isaeus*, ed. E. S. Forster (London, 1927), ch. 14.

27 Belon, *Observations*, 1.4.

28 Richard Pococke, *A Description of the East* (London, 1743), vol. II pt 1, p. 266.

29 Andrew Dalby, *Eleftherios Venizelos: Greece* (London, 2010), p. 54.

30 Des Barres, *Estat présent de l'Archipel*, pp. 113–24.

31 Leigh Fermor, *Roumeli*, p. 130 footnote, cf. p. 210. In restaurants today the usual way is to slice the loaf, but not all the way through.

32 George Wheler, *A Journey into Greece* (London, 1682), pp. 323–4.

33 *Odyssey*, 3.461–72.

34 Pausanias, *Guide*, in Peter Levi, trans., *Pausanias: Guide to Greece* (Harmondsworth, 1971), Book 8 ch. 42.

35 Nikos Kazantzakis, *Καπετάν Μιχάλης*, in Jonathan Griffin, trans., *Freedom and Death* (Oxford, 1956).

36 Belon, *Observations*, 1.27.

Bibliography

Further Reading

Anagnostakis, Ilias, ed., *Monemvasian Wine – Monovas(i)a – Malvasia* (Athens, 2008)

—, et al., *Ancient and Byzantine Cuisine* (Athens, 2013)

Blamey, Marjorie, and Christopher Grey-Wilson, *Wild Flowers of the Mediterranean* (London, 2004)

Bottema, Sytze, 'The Vegetation History of the Greek Mesolithic', in *The Greek Mesolithic: Problems and Perspectives*, ed. N. Galanidou and C. Perles (Athens, 2003), pp. 22–50

Bozi, Soula, *Καππαδοκία, Ιωνία, Πόντος. Γεύσις και παραδόσις* (Athens, 1997)

—, *Μικρασιατική κουζίνα* (Athens, 2005)

—, *Πολίτικη κουζίνα* (Athens, 1994)

Brewer, David, *Greece: The Hidden Centuries* (London, 2010)

Brubaker, Leslie, and Kalliroe Linardou, eds, *Eat, Drink, and Be Merry . . . Food and Drink in Byzantium: In Honour of Professor A.A.M. Bryer* (Aldershot, 2007)

Campbell, J. K., *Honour, Family and Patronage* (Oxford, 1964)

Dalby, Andrew, *Flavours of Byzantium* (Totnes, 2003)

—, *Food in the Ancient World: From A to Z* (London, 2003)

—, trans., *Geoponika: Farm Work* (Totnes, 2011)

—, *Siren Feasts: A History of Food and Gastronomy in Greece* (London, 1996)

Davidson, Alan, *Mediterranean Seafood*, 2nd edn (Harmondsworth, 1981)

—, and Tom Jaine, eds, *The Oxford Companion to Food*, 2nd edn (Oxford, 2006)

Eideneier, Hans, ed., *Πτωχοπρόδρομος* (Heraklio, 2012)

Fowler, Rowena, ed., *Edward Lear: The Cretan Journal*, 3rd edn (Limni, Evia, 2012)

Gerasimou, Marianna, *Η οθωμανική μαγειρική* (Athens, 2004)

Graham, J. Walter, 'A Banquet Hall at Mycenaean Pylos', *American Journal of Archaeology*, LXXI (1967), pp. 353–60

Grant, Mark, trans., *Dieting for an Emperor: A Translation of Books 1 and 4 of Oribasius' Medical Compilations* (Leiden, 1997)

Halstead, P., and J. C. Barrett, eds, *Food, Cuisine and Society in Prehistoric Greece* (Oxford, 2004)

Hamilakis, Y., and S. Sherratt, 'Feasting and the Consuming Body in Bronze Age Crete and Early Iron Age Cyprus', in *Parallel Lives: Ancient Island Societies in Crete and Cyprus*, ed. G. Cadogan et al. (London, 2012), pp. 187–207

Harvey, David, and Mike Dobson, eds, *Food in Antiquity* (Exeter, 1995)

Hitchcock, L. A., R. Laffineur and J. Crowley, eds, *Dais: The Aegean Feast* (Liège, 2008)

Hort, Arthur, ed. and trans., *Theophrastus: Enquiry into Plants* (London, 1916–26)

Isaakidou, Valasia, 'Cooking in the Labyrinth: Exploring "Cuisine" at Bronze Age Knossos', in *Cooking Up the Past: Food and Culinary Practices in the Neolithic and Bronze Age Aegean*, ed. C. Mee and J. Renard (Oxford, 2007), pp. 5–24

Kochilas, Diane, *The Glorious Foods of Greece* (New York, 2001)

Kremezi, Aglaia, '"Classic" Greek Cuisine: Not So Classic' and 'Tomato: A Latecomer that Changed Greek Flavor', *The Atlantic* (July 2010)

—, *The Foods of the Greek Islands* (New York, 2000)

—, 'Nikolas Tselementes', in *Cooks and Other People: Proceedings of the Oxford Symposium on Food and Cookery, 1995*, ed. Harlan Walker (Totnes, 1996), pp. 162–9

Lambert-Gócs, Miles, *The Wines of Greece* (London, 1990)

Lambraki, Myrsini, *Τα χορτά* (Chania, 1997)

Leigh Fermor, Patrick, *Roumeli: Travels in Northern Greece* (London, 1966)

Leontis, Artemis, *Culture and Customs of Greece* (Westport, CT, 2009)

Louis, Diana Farr, *Feasting and Fasting in Crete* (Athens, 2001)

—, and June Marinos, *Prospero's Kitchen: Island Cooking of Greece* (New York, 1995)

Luard, Elisabeth, *European Peasant Cookery* (London, 2007)

Lyons-Makris, Linda, *Greek Gastronomy* (Athens, 2004)

Malmberg, Simon, *Dazzling Dining: Banquets as an Expression of Imperial Legitimacy* (Uppsala, 2003)

Marks, Gil, *Encyclopedia of Jewish Food* (Oxford, 2010)

Matalas, Antonia-Leda, and Mary Yannakoulia, 'Greek Street Food Vending: An Old Habit Turned New', *World Review of Nutrition and Dietetics*, LXXXVI (2000), pp. 1–24

Mee, C., and J. Renard, eds, *Cooking Up the Past: Food and Culinary Practices in the Neolithic and Bronze Age Aegean* (Oxford, 2007)

Megaloudi, Fragkiska, *Plants and Diet in Greece from Neolithic to Classic Periods: The Archaeobotanical Remains* (Oxford, 2006)

Motzias, Christos, *Τι έτρωγαν οι Βυζαντινοί* (Athens, 1998)

Nikitas of the Holy Mountain, *Παραδοσιακές Αγιορειτικές συνταγές* (Thessaloniki, 2013)

Olson, S. Douglas, ed. and trans., *Athenaeus: The Learned Banqueters* (Cambridge, MA, 2006–12)

Palidou, Paraskevi, *Βίβλια μαγειρικής ως πήγες της ιστορίας της διατρόφης στην Ελλάδα* (Athens, 2005)

Pallis, Alexander, *In the Days of the Janissaries: Old Turkish Life as Depicted in the Travel-book of Evliyá Chelebí* (London, 1951)

Papanikola-Bakirtzi, Demetra, *Food and Cooking in Byzantium* (Athens, 2005)

Papoulias, Th., *Τα φαγώσιμα χορτά* (Athens, 2006)

Perry, Charles, 'Trakhanas Revisited', *Petits Propos Culinaires*, 55 (1997), pp. 34–9

Pettifer, James, *The Greeks: The Land and People since the War*, 2nd edn (London, 2012)

Pittas, George, *Kafenia in the Aegean Sea* (Lefkes, Paros, 2012)

Powell, O., trans., *Galen: On the Properties of Foodstuffs* (Cambridge, 2002)

Prekas, Kostas, *Tastes of a House in Syros* (Ermoupolis, Syros, n.d.)

Roden, Claudia, *The Book of Jewish Food* (New York, 1997)

—, *Mediterranean Cookery* (London, 1987; new edn, 2006)

Rouanet-Liesenfelt, A.-M., 'Les Plantes médicinales de Crète à l'époque romaine', *Cretan Studies*, III (1992), pp. 173–90

Salaman, Rena, *The Cooking of Greece and Turkey* (London, 1987)
—, *Greek Food* (London, 1993)
Sarpaki, Anaya, and Glynis Jones, 'Ancient and Modern Cultivation of *Lathyrus clymenum* L. in the Greek Islands', *Annual of the British School at Athens*, LXXXV (1990), pp. 363–8
Sherrard, Philip, ed., *Edward Lear: The Corfu Years* (Athens, 1988)
Sherratt, Susan, 'Feasting in Homeric Epic', *Hesperia*, LXXIII (2004), pp. 301–37
Simeonova, Liliana, 'In the Depths of Tenth-century Byzantine Ceremonial: The Treatment of Arab Prisoners of War at Imperial Banquets', *Byzantine and Modern Greek Studies*, XXII (1998), pp. 75–104
Skarmoutsos, Dimitris, *64 εδώδιμα* (Athens, 2011)
Spintheropoulou, Charoula, *Οινοποιήσιμες ποικιλίες του Ελληνικού αμπελώνα* (Loutrouvio, Corfu [2000?])
Stamatopoulou, Eleni, ed., *Χερσέ βασιλόπιτες και άλλα. Το μικρασιάτικο τραπέζι του δωδεκαημέρου* (Athens, 1998; 2nd edn, 2002)
Steel, Louise, 'The Social World of Early-middle Bronze Age Cyprus: Rethinking the Vounous Bowl', *Journal of Mediterranean Archaeology*, XXVI (2013), pp. 51–73
Stocker, Sharon R., and Jack L. Davis, 'Animal Sacrifice, Archives, and Feasting at the Palace of Nestor', *Hesperia*, LXXIII (2004), pp. 179–95
Τα αυτοφυή μανιτάρια της Πάρου (Naoussa, Paros, 2011)
Thomas, John, and Angela Constantinides Hero, eds, *Byzantine Monastic Foundation Documents* (Washington, DC, 2000)
Valamoti, Soultana Maria, 'Ground Cereal Food Preparations from Greece: The Prehistory and Modern Survival of Traditional Mediterranean "Fast Foods"', *Archaeological and Anthropological Sciences*, III (2011), pp. 19–39
Weaver, William Woys, 'The Origins of Trachanás: Evidence from Cyprus and Ancient Texts', *Gastronomica*, II/1 (Winter 2002), pp. 41–8
Wilkins, John, and Shaun Hill, trans., *Archestratus: The Life of Luxury* (Totnes, 1994)
Wright, James C., 'A Survey of Evidence for Feasting in Mycenaean Society', in *The Mycenaean Feast*, ed. J. C. Wright (*Hesperia*, LXXIII, 2004), pp. 133–78
Yotis, Alexander, *Ιστορία μαγειρικής και διατρόφης*, 2nd edn (Athens, 2003)
—, E. Kalosakas, and A. Panagoulis, *Greek Culinary Tradition: The Past Lingers On*, 3rd edn (Athens, 2007)
Zen, Ziggy, *The Ten Unexpected Greeks Just Arrived for Dinner Cookbook* (2001)
Zohary, Daniel, and Maria Hopf, *Domestication of Plants in the Old World: The Origin and Spread of Cultivated Plants in West Asia, Europe and the Nile Valley*, 3rd edn (Oxford, 2001)

Websites

Kavroulaki, Mariana, 'History of Greek Food', at http://297315322.blog.com.gr
Kochilas, Diane, at www.dianekochilas.com
Kremezi, Aglaia, at www.aglaiakremezi.com
Mamalakis, Ilias, at www.eliasmamalakis.gr
Parliaros, Stelios, at www.steliosparliaros.gr
Sotiropoulos, Sam, at http://greekgourmand.blogspot.com

Acknowledgements

We have acknowledged, in text, footnotes and bibliography, as much as we can of the specific assistance we have had from others. For some recipes we have friends to thank: Chrisoula at Lefkes, Linda at Marina Café, Alexia at Prodromos, Manolis at Kolymbithres, Vangelis Chaniotis in Paroikia, Dieter and Hedi from Vienna. Special thanks to Theofilos Giorgiadis and Eleni Georgiadou who taught us so much about the foods of the Pontos, to Manolis Panorios and Manolis at Lefkes, and to Linda Makris and Diana Farr Louis for help in several ways. Our gratitude for their help and patience to Martha Jay, Harry Gilonis and Michael Leaman at Reaktion Books.

Our thanks, last and not least, to Maureen who lives with one of us and to Kosta who lives with the other.

Photo Acknowledgements

The authors and publishers wish to express their thanks to the following sources of illustrative material and/or permission to reproduce it. Some locations of artworks are given here for reasons of brevity.

Archaeological Museum, Thessaloniki: pp. 72, 82; from Isabel J. Armstrong, *Two Roving Englishwomen in Greece* (London, 1893): p. 226; Sebastian Ballard: pp. 10, 11; from Pierre Belon, *Observations de plusieurs singularitez et choses memorables, trouvées en Grèce, Asie, Iudée, Egypte, Arabie, et autres Pays Étranges ...* (Paris, 1553): p. 129; Benaki Museum, Athens: p. 264; Bibliothèque Nationale de France, Paris: pp. 52 (Cabinet des Médailles), 129; Bodrum Sualtı Arkeoloji Müzesi, Bodrum, Turkey: p. 61; photo Cobija: p. 146; from William Curtis, illustration for *The Botanical Magazine, or, Flower-garden Displayed ...*, vol. VIII (1794): p. 23; photo Ian Dagnall/Alamy Stock Photo: p. 8; photos by, or courtesy of, Andrew Dalby: pp. 121, 238, 264; photos by, or courtesy of, Rachel Dalby: pp. 15, 16, 18, 26, 28 (top), 32, 41, 62, 66, 72, 81, 82, 83, 92, 101, 109, 116, 118, 120, 133, 141, 143, 144, 152, 153, 159, 166, 174, 189, 193, 194, 195, 200, 201, 206, 209, 216, 227, 239, 242 (foot), 247, 251, 255, 257; from Edward Dodwell, *Views in Greece, from Drawings by Edward Dodwell, Esq. FSA. &c.* (London, 1821): pp. 177, 221; photo Valery Fassiaux: p. 52; Getty Villa, Malibu: pp. 48, 49, 86, 267; from Vasilii Grigorovich-Barskii, *Vtoroe Poseshchenie Sviatoi Afonskoi Gory Vasiliia Grigorovicha-Barskago* [1774] (St Petersburg, 1887): p. 97; photo Martin Henke: p. 127; from the *Illustrated Times*, 19 September 1868: p. 160; photos JPS68: pp. 160, 161; photo Karaahmet at English Wikipedia: p. 126; photo Library of Congress, Washington, DC (Prints and Photographs Division): p. 142; photo Мико: p. 188; Musée du Louvre, Paris: pp. 45, 46, 51, 263; Museo Archeologico Nazionale di Napoli: p. 67; National Archaeological Museum, Athens: pp. 28 (foot), 114, 198; photo Marie-Lan Nguyen: p. 67; Österreichische Nationalbibliothek, Vienna: p. 71; photo Peter Pearsall/U.S. Fish and Wildlife Service: p. 88; photo Peter H. Raven Library, Missouri Botanical Garden, St Louis: p. 23 (courtesy the Biodiversity Heritage Library); Rethymno Archaeological Museum, Rethymno, Crete: p. 17; photo Sailko: p. 71; photos Bibi Saint-Pol, pp. 46, 51; Walters Art Museum, Baltimore: p. 196; photo Zde: p. 17.

Bernard Gagnon has published online the images on pp. 24 and 110 under Creative Commons Attribution-Share Alike 4.0 International, 3.0 Unported, 2.5 Generic, 2.0 Generic and 1.0 Generic licenses; Badseed has published online the image on p. 184, Dietrich Krieger that on p. 35, and Nikater that on p. 205 under Creative Commons Attribution-Share Alike

Index

The New Times Nature Diary

The New Times Nature Diary

Derwent May

Illustrated by Richard Blake

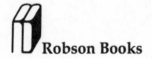

Robson Books

First published in Great Britain in 1993
by Robson Books Ltd, Bolsover House,
5-6 Clipstone Street, London W1P 7EB

**British Library Cataloguing in Publica-
tion Data**
A catalogue record for this title is available
from the British Library.

ISBN 0 86051 850 7

Set in Palatino by Spectrum Typesetting
Printed and bound in Great Britain by W.B.C.
Print and W.B.C. Bookbinders, Bridgend, Mid-
Glamorgan

Preface

Nature Notes by DJM first appeared in *The Times* on 11 July 1981. After a few erratic weeks, they settled down as a regular Monday morning feature, and have not missed a week since. They are always 200 words long, and were conceived as practical bulletins about what readers could see if they went out in the country that morning. They are not about a particular locality, but generally refer to what can be seen in the south of England, with regular forays to other parts of Britain like the east coast or the Scottish moors. Readers in the north usually find that birds are singing and wild flowers coming into bloom a week or more later – though there are exceptions like this year (1993) when the chaffinches were singing in Scotland before they began in the south.

This book is based on the Nature Notes, though the entries for each week are rather longer than the newspaper bulletins. Drawing on the records of the whole twelve years, they aim to give an unfolding portrait of a typical year. Every year is different, of course, so I have had to make certain decisions: I have given the year a short cold spell in January, a sunny spring, neither unduly early nor unduly late, and a fairly long, colourful autumn. Other years may prove better or worse. I have tried not to wax sentimental about nature in these notes, but sought to be vivid and precise in my descriptions.

My thanks to the Editor of *The Times* for allowing me to reprint them, and to my son, Orlando May, who put the manuscript on to the word processor, and edited it meticulously as he did so.

DERWENT MAY

1 January – 7 January

The mild New Year has set birds singing vigorously. Wood-pigeons take up their territories and coo regularly in the morning, though they flock again in thousands to roost at night. Song thrushes, wrens, robins and hedge-sparrows can be heard at any time of the day. There is a murmur of song occasionally from the goldfinch flocks, though many British goldfinches have left for France and Spain; those which remain feed from dead thistle-heads on the ground, or on the standing teasels in a damp corner of an allotment. They are the only finches with beaks long enough to reach the teasel seeds, which lie at the bottom of prickly tubes. Linnets produce their twangy song in a small chorus; they feed on the ground on the fallen seeds of persicaria.

Among the bare trees in parks and gardens, Algerian oaks still have bright green and yellow leaves on them. On the roadside, the pale green spikes of cuckoo pint are already several inches high, and unfolding to reveal themselves as arrow-shaped leaves. The heart-shaped leaves of jack-by-the-hedge, or garlic mustard, are also coming through, while small cow parsley leaves form thick carpets. Male buckler fern is battered but still green in the ditches. On dead tree stumps, candle-snuff fungus lifts its forked grey branches.

Otters are still active on streams and rivers; they go upstream at night to fish, or to catch an unwary rabbit or vole, then back to their lair in the river bank at dawn. Badgers should be asleep, deep underground, but a spell of weather like this brings them out to grub for a few acorns or beetles.

8 January – 14 January

Mistle thrushes are singing, a hectic trumpeting from the swaying tops of the trees. Black-headed gulls are showing the first traces of spring plumage, as the dark patch behind their eyes starts to spread into a facial mask. Herring gulls are courting and quarrelling in the sky: they stretch out their necks and emit wild, yelping cries. But winter immigration continues: this is the peak time for pochards, many of which have flown in from Russia. They are vigorous diving ducks, with red heads and grey backs.

Normally they live on large, shallow waters, where they can take seeds and vegetation from the mud at the bottom. Bearded tits from East Anglia or Holland are appearing in reed beds further west; they flit over the reeds for a moment with a pinging call, like a delicate glass being struck, then drop back into deep cover.

In low-lying pastures there are mixed flocks of jackdaws and common gulls. When alarmed they rise in a confused cloud, but quickly separate out. The black jackdaws wheel and dive low over the fields, their loud clacking cries sounding like a roar of applause, while the white gulls glide silently above them.

Snowdrops are out in sheltered spots; on river banks, the fragrant pink buds of winter heliotrope are opening. The leaves of Oxford ragwort are pushing up hard, and a few precocious plants are already in flower. Violet leaves are coming through in the woods; new ivy leaves have fine, pale veins. Earthworms are busy dragging dead leaves into their holes for food; blackbirds stand in line on a lawn, looking for the worms.

15 January – 21 January

Frost and snow drive birds to new feeding grounds. More tawny owls have come into the towns: they hoot and call all night as they search for sparrows roosting in the shrubberies. In this weather they can also be seen feeding by day. Short-eared owls move in from the east coast and are found beating up and down the river valleys. Redwings and fieldfares also flock westward; the redwing's thin note and the fieldfare's chuckling cry are heard in the treetops in city parks. Blackbirds and song thrushes scuffle among the leaves under the hedges where seeds and insects are still to be had. Unusual visitors come to well-stocked bird-tables: lesser redpolls, nuthatches and great spotted woodpeckers. Hunger is stronger than fear in many species, and robins venture in through open kitchen doors.

The loudest singers now are great tits, which can be heard even on very cold mornings if the air is still. Wrens are singing, but in a distinctly subdued way.

Wind blows the brown keys off the ash trees. Some of the sparse colour in the wintry fields comes from the white willow and the crack willow, whose young shoots are a pale olive-yellow. Water voles are normally nocturnal, but on very cold days they will come out of their holes to sit on river banks and feed in the sun. The small tortoiseshell butterflies that came out of hibernation in many places in the mild days of Christmas are now either dead or sleeping again in dark corners of garden sheds.

22 January – 28 January

The thaw may have come just in time to save the lives of many birds. But there have been serious losses. Mallard and tufted duck swimming in the last unfrozen corner of a pond have finally been frozen into the ice. Many redwings and fieldfares have been found dead or dying. Small birds find their food supplies barred to them: insect pupae in cracks in the bark are frozen over, slugs and springtails that live in the dead leaves are buried under snow, worms stay well below the hard surface of the ground. Coal and marsh tits often store seeds for the winter under moss or behind bark – but in these conditions they cannot get to them.

Waxwings have come in from Scandinavia: they roam about the countryside in search of rose-hips and cotoneaster berries, often in flocks. Long-tailed ducks from the Arctic have been feeding close in to the seashore on the east side of Britain: outside Edinburgh, on the Firth of Forth, they can be seen from the Corporation buses.

A few barren strawberries are in flower. Under weeping willows, the ground is strewn with silvery leaves, which did not fall until the snow came. On tree trunks, the powdery algae that live in the rain channels are jade-green in the sunlight. The crusty grey and yellow lichens also thrive in winter, when there are no leaves on the trees, and the light can get to them.

Song thrushes have begun to sing again after the cold spell: their clear, flute-like notes, often repeated several times, are usually followed by some brief, muttered gabbling. Woodpigeons have also resumed their song, a gruff pattern of long and short coos that is never varied. They have also begun their soaring spring display flights. Some collared doves are heard singing even on the coldest days. Magpies are chattering around their old nests: they steer themselves through the branches with their very long tails, which swell out in the middle like a rubber pipe with a bulge in it. Greenfinches are calling with a long, slurping sound in the treetops; they will soon be in full song. Skylarks are singing over the meadows where lapwings are feeding among the growing grass.

In woods, winter aconites are coming into flower, though the petals do not open until the temperature is more than 10°C. The yellow flowers have a ruff of leaves beneath them. On hornbeam trees the long spiky buds are chequered brown and green, and yew trees have small yellow flower buds among the needles. Rosettes of dandelion leaves, like long green fishbones, are bursting out at the foot of walls.

Silverfish, which belong to a group of wingless insects called the bristle-tails, are active at night in kitchens and on open hearths. House-crickets are sometimes heard chirping in old buildings, but are much rarer than they used to be. Male winter moths are out flying when the evenings are mild and dry: they are pale brown with dark brown bands on their wings, and settle in a triangular shape. The almost wingless females live on orchard tree trunks.

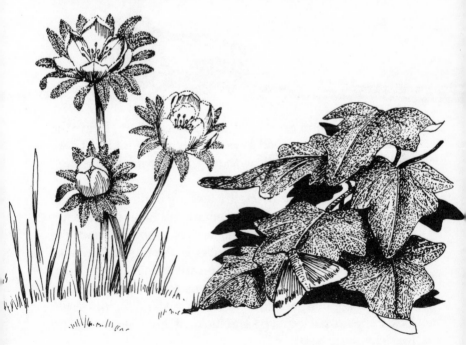

5 February – 11 February

The first oystercatchers are returning to the Scottish moors from the western shores of England, but large flocks still remain on the estuaries, feeding mainly on cockles and mussels. They are large, black-and-white birds that fly fast, piping loudly, up and down the beach; and with their long, red beaks they can break their way into most shellfish.

Small parties of turnstones often feed near them, lifting the pebbles and the seaweed as they search for winkles. These birds will stay till April or May, then return to the high Arctic.

Jack snipe from the Arctic are feeding in the mud among low water plants. They have a remarkable habit of bouncing up and down, as if on springs, as they probe for food: the motion probably disturbs creatures in the mud and makes them easier to find. The jack snipe are usually solitary, but one or two common snipe sometimes feed near them: they are noticeably larger, and walk about steadily, while the jack snipe, its back curved and its head down, moves along like a bobbing beetle.

In the oak woods, jays are collecting the remaining acorns; on a sunny day they chase each other through the trees in a long line. Song thrushes are already prospecting for nesting sites in the bare hedges. Partridge coveys are breaking up, and the paired birds are settling in their territories.

In the West Country, some sweet violets are in flower, and their heart-shaped leaves are opening everywhere in the south. A few hawthorn bushes are showing small leaves: it is the same bushes that shoot early every year. By roadside ditches, the coarse, toothed leaves of hogweed are dominating the other spring growth.

12 February – 18 February

Blue tits are pairing. The two birds fly about excitedly, leapfrogging over each other in the twigs, with blue tits from neighbouring territories sometimes joining in the chase. Linnets are singing regularly again; the flocks are breaking up, and some mated pairs are returning to the gorse and bramble heaths where they will nest. Among the teal flocks, the drakes are challenging one another: they rise up in the water with their beaks bowed, then throw their heads sharply back. Meanwhile the females paddle restlessly around them, with thin, trilling quacks.

There are still many cormorants inland on lakes and rivers. Though they spend much of their time almost submerged under water, with only their heads and long beaks above the surface, they are also very competent perching birds. In the London Docklands, they land with ease on the tops of high cranes, and in some parts of Britain they roost in large numbers on suspension bridges. On the coast, gannets are returning to their breeding sites after a winter far out at sea: they sweep over the waves like giant gulls, their tails as sharply pointed as their beaks. They usually dive for fish at an angle to the sea, closing their wings just before they crash into the water.

Dark red flowers are opening on the bare twigs of the elm trees. On purple osiers by the riverside, silver catkins are opening: they have a reddish glow at the centre. On some crab-apple trees there are already a few pale green leaves, and young hornbeam buds are turning green. The first lesser celandines are in flower in sheltered places.

19 February – 25 February

Great crested grebes are back in full plumage, with dark ear-tufts and handsome chestnut ruffs. Their spring courtship displays are also beginning: the pair face each other on the water and waggle their heads with ear-tufts lifted and ruffs spread out. Between these head-shaking bouts, both of them engage in a ceremonial preening of their wings; when they move apart, they continue to call to each other with a sharp barking cry.

Chaffinches are singing again in most parts of the country. The male chaffinches have acquired bright blue heads and pink breasts; some are just trying out the first few notes of their song, some already have the full run of notes and the flourish at the end. Yellowhammers are singing in hedgerow trees; when approached, they flick their tails nervously and flit along the hedge tops. Their heads are primrose yellow. Some fieldfares have left for Holland and Sweden, but many are still feeding out in the middle of large fields; in the late afternoon, small flocks of them warble together in the treetops.

Snowdrops are growing in dense masses; they look like white waterfalls on the woodland banks. The three petals of the outer bell are now opening, and revealing the green-streaked inner petals. Some low-growing plants of wild angelica have gone on flowering throughout the winter; while on elder trees new buds are opening among the last traces of last year's leaves. Yellow catkins are swinging freely on the hazels.

26 February – 4 March

The noticeable new feature of the countryside is the blackbird song. The rich, leisurely fluting can be heard everywhere at dawn and dusk. It has an odd ventriloquial quality: sometimes it seems to come from the branches of a tree, but one looks for the singer in vain till he hops out from under some shrubs on the ground. Pairs of mallards are walking about awkwardly on the river banks, with the drake's head shining like green velvet; they are looking for safe nesting places under the hedges. On the east coast, winter migrants are beginning to leave: hen harriers that have been hawking on the marshes are drifting back to the Continent, Brent geese are deserting the estuaries and heading for Arctic islands.

More lesser celandines are coming into flower: the leaves lie flat on the ground and the buttery yellow stars stand above them. Flowers are growing thicker on the gorse bushes. There are new pink flowers on the red dead-nettles, and the first primroses are out. On crab-apples, the buds are like small crimson cherries, but will open to form white flowers.

Many badgers have come out of hibernation, and some of the sows are gathering moss and grass for that part of the underground set where the cubs will be born. Rabbits are already breeding. Frogs have practically disappeared from some eastern counties, but where they are still numerous they are gathering in ponds and pools to croak and mate. Some have already laid their jelly-like clumps of spawn.

5 March – 11 March

Flocks of redwings are singing in the treetops: a rambling, chattering song that has little resemblance to the true spring song that they will switch to when they return in the next few weeks to Sweden or Iceland. Soft calls, like lip-smacking, come from cypresses and gorse bushes where long-tailed tits are looking for nest sites. Lapwings are tumbling above the ploughed fields with plaintive cries. Coots collect pond weed from underwater but come to the surface to eat it: other coots often try to steal it. Now that the males are starting to compete for nesting places, there are more fights than ever.

On the moors, curlews are beginning their display flights: they rise steeply, but hang on quivering wings as their bubbling cry rings out faster and faster, then glide

down into the heather again. Lacking song perches in open country, this is their way of announcing that they own the territory around them.

The sallow trees are a mass of gold and silver catkins, and the first flowers, the colour of pure, pale white linen, are opening on the blackthorn bushes. Early wood anemones sprinkle the ground in dark woods: their six-petalled white stars are surrounded by fern-like leaves with a rich parsley smell. Daisies are multiplying on damp lawns, among lesser celandines that are already beginning to fade.

Male hares are starting to fight over mates: they rear up on their hind legs and box with each other, or jump over a rival and kick him from above. Bumble bees circle the new primroses, and bluebottles buzz against the window panes.

12 March – 18 March

Sparrow hawks are soaring over their territories, or calling with a shrill lamenting sound among the trees. This is the only time of year when they are so vocal and conspicuous; normally they glide silently along the woodland edges as they hunt for titmice and chaffinches.

Great spotted woodpeckers are drumming in loud bursts on dead branches. This is a warning to rivals not to enter the drummer's territory; but if one ventures in the occupant will attack it, flying up at it fiercely from below. Green woodpeckers do not usually drum, though they sometimes tap on a tree trunk when excited; they threaten intruders by ruffling up the red feathers on their crown, and rocking their head vigorously from side to side as they hang on the bark.

Reed buntings are beginning their jangling song in the osiers; the whole head is black in the males, apart from a white moustache and a white collar, and they have a rich chestnut-and-black mantle, like a fine rug. Goldcrests are singing in the conifers, a thin reeling song with a little explosion at the end of each phrase.

Dog's mercury grows in carpets in the woods; its tiny green flowers might easily be mistaken for seeds. Nearer the wood's edge, the first mauve flowers of ground ivy are coming out. The yellow colt's-foot is in flower on dusty roadsides, and the first marsh marigolds are opening by the streams. Vipers are coming out of hibernation, and black ants are on the move again. The first brimstone butterflies are careering along the woodland rides.

19 March – 25 March

Siskins are lingering in southern England because of the cold weather in the north. There are still plenty of seeds for these small, green finches in the black cones on the alders, where they hang upside down to extract them. Some of the males have started singing without waiting to return to their breeding territories: they have a thin, sweet song, with curious buzzing notes in it.

Many other birds are getting ready to nest. Kingfishers are inspecting holes in river banks; starlings are going in and out of holes in trees; coots are beginning to pluck at reeds, though not seriously starting to build yet. Drake Canada geese have a call that is almost like a song, a repeated set of rising and falling trumpet notes, uttered on the ground with head held high: when the pair flies up, their honking sounds like deep groans.

Wrens are singing higher in the trees and their song can be heard a quarter of a mile away. Chaffinches are singing energetically, and also making a distinctive call like a stone splashing into water. Little owls are yelping in the fields.

Everywhere hawthorn leaves are opening, in bunches like little green whisks. On the sallows, leaves are coming out on the twigs among the silver and gold catkins. On the black Italian poplars, there are brilliant red catkins, like fat caterpillars, which come tumbling down in the wind. On horse-chestnuts, the opening leaf buds are a pale papery green.

26 March – 1 April

The first chiffchaffs are back from the Mediterranean: their clinking song rings out from the treetops. Newly arrived sand martins flutter and dart over lakes and rivers, where most of the early flying insects are to be found; they will not move on for another week or two to the sandy cliffs where they will make their nest holes.

Wheatears stop to feed on playing fields on their way to the rocky moors where they will breed; they are restless birds, bobbing, flicking their wings, and running fast to pick up an insect they have seen in the grass.

Shelduck are appearing on lakes and reservoirs as they

head back to the sandy coasts. They are like small black-and-white geese, with an orange band across the chest; the drakes have a bright red beak with a knob at the base. Mallards have begun nesting, and some are sitting on clutches of 11 or 12 olive-grey eggs.

Many hedges are a foaming white sea of blackthorn flowers; on some bushes the leaf buds are also opening. Other white spring flowers that are already out are greater stitchwort, cow parsley and wild strawberry. Dandelions are in flower everywhere, and in dry, stony places the lesser dandelion is to be found, with its smaller flower heads and sharp-toothed leaves. On sallow bushes the golden male catkins are now a decaying mass of threads, while the fertilized female catkins are long and green.

2 April – 8 April

Millions of willow warblers and sedge warblers that have been making their way up through France are poised to invade Britain. Willow warblers are very similar in appearance to the chiffchaffs that were arriving last week, but they have red legs, not black, and their song is unmistakable: a rippling cadence of notes like water trickling over a rock. The sedge warblers are furtive birds that sing from thick bushes at the edge of ponds and ditches – a babbling song, in which sweet notes alternate pell-mell with harsh, grating sounds.

In lambing fields, mixed flocks of magpies, jackdaws, rooks, and woodpigeons gather to feed around the sheep. In the woods, cock pheasants press their tails on the earth and flap their coppery wings, as they send their explosive trumpet-calls over the dry bracken. Moorhen are fighting on the ponds, rearing up and striking at each other with their green feet. Starlings and house sparrows stuff their beaks with white feathers as they begin to nest.

The half-open leaves on the horse-chestnuts are like small green parachutes; some have already been blown down by the wind. Forsythia has woven itself into some hawthorn hedges, and its spiky yellow flowers mingle with the bright green shoots. Bulbous buttercups are opening in the meadows, and goldilocks – the only woodland buttercup – in copses and under hedges. On still or slow-flowing water, the pale white flowers of water crowfoot tremble just above the floating leaves. Grey squirrels are beginning to mate; when they are alarmed on the ground they move off in a cautious series of bounds and motionless tableaux.

Blackcaps dart energetically through the treetops, singing every time they pause with a sustained rich jangle of harsh and melodious notes. Rooks, long-tailed tits, song thrushes and hedge sparrows all have eggs in the nest. Usually the hen bird lays one egg a day until the clutch is complete, and then begins incubating. A hard frost may addle the unattended eggs of an incomplete clutch, but once incubation has begun the eggs are not so likely to be affected by cold weather, as the female only leaves the nest to feed for very short periods. In the case of rooks, the male actually brings food to the female on the nest; while the domed nest of the long-tailed tit gets extra heating at night, when the male comes inside to roost on top of the female.

Over the lakes where tufted duck are gathering, a sweet, musical murmur is heard from the drakes courting the brown females. The last of the wintering teal are going north to the moors.

The second wave of trees is coming into leaf after the horse-chestnuts and hawthorns: there are small translucent leaves on the limes, there is a sprinkling of leaves along the elm twigs, and the pink sycamore buds are bursting. The silver birch woods are dusted with pale green. Stubby plants of yellow Oxford ragwort are coming into flower on the roadside. Stinging nettles are ankle-high, often growing among goose-grass and red dead-nettle.

Cuckoos are back, calling tirelessly across the fields. Nightingales sing in the copses by day and night. But not all singers in the dark are nightingales: robins and wrens can also be heard in the small hours. Carrion crows have eggs in their conspicuous treetop nests; the male keeps the female company, and feeds her with large insects while she incubates. Woodpigeons sit among the cherry blossoms, and peck at the sprouting leaves: they often tumble off the thin twigs. On the Suffolk lagoons, avocets are back. They became extinct in Britain in 1844, but since 1947 they have slowly established themselves again. They are noisy black-and-white birds that scoop the water from side to side with long, upturned bills. On marshes and moors, red-shanks are trilling and yodelling.

White wood anemones carpet the sunny banks; wood-sorrel crowds around the tree stumps in shady beech-woods. The first bluebells are opening among their long, slender leaves. Bugle is appearing on the roadside, its powder-blue flowers half-hidden by its purplish leaves. Wood-spurge grows thick in southern woodlands; it has bright green cups with smaller, stemmed cups rising out of them. The watery lilac blossoms of cuckoo-flower, or lady's smock, are waving on long stems in damp meadows. On the river banks, horsetails are pushing up through the grass: they look like spiky brown thimbles on top of a pink stem.

On sunny woodland edges, speckled wood butterflies have emerged. They have a flickering, erratic flight, and are often first noticed because of their shadows on the ground.

23 April – 29 April

More nesting is under way. Blackbirds and song thrushes are on eggs in their deep nests, with just their beaks and tails showing above the rim. They sit tight, but fly off with a skittering cry if an intruder comes too close. Wrens are building: the cock bird makes several domed nests of grass and leaves, and the hen chooses one of them and lines it with soft feathers. She usually lays six minute, red-spotted eggs. New arrivals from the south include house-martins, wheeling and braking above the house tops and making a clicking note like a magic-lantern lecturer calling for his slides to be changed. The first grasshopper warblers are back: they have become much more common in neglected, bushy patches of countryside in the last few years. On the moors, blackcock gather for their annual 'lek;' a communal ritual of fighting and mating: the males spread their tails in a broad fan, and jump up and down in front of their rivals.

A few wrynecks are coming into south-east England. Although this bird is a woodpecker, it looks like a small striped thrush; it perches across a branch, continually twisting its head to look in every direction, then runs up a sloping bough and turns to sit across it. When it flies on, it flirts its tail in the air before settling once more. It draws attention to itself by its shrill call – 'ki-ki-ki-ki', like a very loud-voiced nuthatch.

Nearly all the trees are now coming into leaf. On the larches there are fresh green leaves and red female flowers. The new bright green leaves of the lime trees hang like small medallions, while on sycamores long flower spikes are already cascading under the leaves. On young hornbeams, the green turned-down leaves look like small birds' feet. In northern hedgerows bird-cherry is opening: this is a light, airy tree, with widely spaced branches on which feathery fingers will soon appear and turn into white blossom.

Swallows are back around the barns where they will nest: the males chase each other in the sky, sometimes swerving to pick up a fly while still in hot pursuit. The first wood warblers are arriving; they sing in the translucent green tops of the beeches, with a shivering call and an occasional trill like a nightingale's. Tree pipits are back, singing at the woodland edges and in parkland. They flutter up from a perch, then lift their wings and tail so that they look like shuttlecocks, and float down singing loudly until they are back on their perch again. Whitethroats have returned to the lanes; they also sing in the air, fluttering up from a hedge making their scratchy song, and dropping down jerkily as though they were on an elastic string.

Young coots are out on the water: they leave the nest three or four days after hatching, but return to it at night. They are quite unlike their parents, with bright orange heads and white-tipped beaks. Some robins are already feeding young in the nest. The first greenfinches are building in thick evergreens; the males are singing noisily, soaring through the sky on a wild, erratic course.

Under lime trees the ground is littered with pink bud scales as the luminous green leaves grow larger. Many horse-chestnut trees are in full leaf with pyramids of white flowers now opening on every branch. The pink and white blossom of the crab-apples is already falling in the rain. In the copses there are sheets of bluebells. The bell-shaped flowers of snake's-head fritillary nod in the wind in wet meadows and sometimes on damp lawns: some flowers are deep purple with flickering lighter patches, some are pale purple, some are almost pure white.

7 May – 13 May

The last summer visitors are coming in: swifts are screaming across the sky and garden warblers are singing deep in rhododendrons or honeysuckle. Flocks of sand-martins are digging out nest holes, wherever they can find undisturbed cliffs of sand or gravel. They buzz in front of the cliff face like brown insects. Whinchats have arrived on the moors; they bob on top of the gorse bushes, with short bursts of song like a rapid robin. A few pairs of marsh harriers are back on the Suffolk coast: they sweep across the reed beds on massive wings, suddenly turning and pouncing on a frog or a moorhen.

Olive-green oak leaves are coming out, with catkins dangling by them: among the catkins there can sometimes be found what looks like a redcurrant, which is the home of the grub of a gall-making wasp called the spangle gall. A wedge of crinkled leaves and catkins is breaking out of the thin, spiky buds of the beech trees, and the bronze bud-scales flutter to the ground.

Fragrant white flowers are opening on the rowans, but like hawthorn flowers they have an acrid smell mingled with their sweetness. Fields of oilseed rape are a sheet of yellow flowers, with the buzz of honeybees coming from every part of it. Cowslips are abundant in some meadows. Holly blue butterflies are out in the woods: when they settle they show their distinctive silvery underwings. A common moth just now is the silvery-brown brindled beauty; its twig-like caterpillars are also appearing on apple trees and willows. Black ants are exploring gaps under larder doors.

14 May – 20 May

Turtle doves have returned from tropical Africa; they sing their purring song deep in the blackthorn hedges. Spotted flycatchers that wintered in the same regions as the turtle doves are back in gardens and churchyards; their thin song is seldom heard, but they are conspicuous as they dart into the air for an insect, then swoop back to the wall or tombstone on which they were perching.

In town and country, the air is full of blackbird song, especially towards evening: a lazy-sounding song of a few rich, fluting notes followed by a tired whisper. It can be drowned by the calls of young starlings that have now left the nest and fly after their parents from tree to tree begging to be fed.

White and green are now the prevailing colours in the
countryside, as more hawthorns come into flower, spreading their scent far around them, and the cow parsley grows
thick and tall. There are also small rosettes of white flowers
on the wayfaring trees. The last of the trees have come into
leaf: ash trees have spiky shoots of new leaves between
the crimson flowers, while plane trees have young leaves
tinged with bronze. There is a moment in mid-May when
the foliage of the trees is at its fullest and freshest green.

The untidy pink flowers of ragged robin are in bloom in
wet meadows while on dry roadsides mallow is opening.
The tall spotted orchids are coming out here and there in
southern England; early purple orchids, with their smell of
tom-cats, are already common throughout most of Britain.
Three species of white butterfly are on the wing: the large
and small cabbage whites, and the dainty green-veined
white. Ragged-looking comma butterflies settle on sunny
hedges; common blues flutter restlessly over heathland.

49

21 May – 27 May

Blackbirds and song thrushes are still singing vigorously; a male blackbird will sometimes sing with his beak full of insects on his way to feed his young. Green woodpeckers are nesting; they bore a new hole in a tree each year, a foot or more deep, and lay their translucent eggs on woodchips at the bottom.

Ringed plovers are nesting on shingle beaches: they have four blotchy eggs arranged like a cross in a hollow. Near them, solitary bar-tailed godwits feed in the shallow water: these are birds who have left it too late to go up to the Arctic to breed, and will have a lazy summer in Britain.

On the black Italian poplars, the young leaves glitter like copper in the sun. Horse-chestnuts are already like hills of darkening foliage and white blossom. In limestone country, the spurred purple flowers of the wild columbine are appearing. Wild grasses are growing tall, with meadow foxtail grass already three feet high and its silky spikes dipping in the wind. In meadows where cuckoo-flower is blooming, there are many delicate orange-tip butterflies.

Caterpillars of the gold-tail moth are common on hawthorn hedges. They are red, black and white, with poisonous spines; the moth they will turn into is pure white, with a golden tuft at the stern. Fox cubs are out of their earths, and playing above the ground; the vixen will stay with them till autumn.

28 May – 3 June

On the moors, female cuckoos sit on walls and bushes, looking out for meadow pipits' nests in the grass. During the afternoon, the cuckoo will glide down to a pipit's nest, remove an egg, and lay one of her own in its place. Her offspring will later throw out the other eggs, and any nestlings that have hatched before it. Most cuckoos lay about a dozen interloping eggs in a season.

In the Outer Hebrides, corncrakes are back; until the grass and corn grow taller, they stay in the beds of yellow-iris leaves, climbing up on stones to make their loud, grating call resound over the islands. Great northern divers are still making their way up western coasts: at high tide they come in closer to the shore, where their massive bills and brilliant spangled backs can be clearly seen. Oyster-catchers are displaying excitedly on the rocks: they point their long red bills downwards and pipe loudly to drive an intruder away. A few are already nesting in shallow scoops in the meadow grass.

Bluebells are dying, and the first petals are falling from the snowy hawthorn bushes. After blackthorn in April and hawthorn in May, the third white flower to dominate the hedgerows is the dog-rose: early individuals are already coming out, and they will be at their best by the middle of June. They have large, floppy petals, often flushed with pink. The meadows are full of buttercups; red campion is already tall in the woods and on chalky hillsides the wayfaring trees are a dense mass of woolly green leaves and creamy flower-rosettes.

55

4 June – 10 June

Birds are at all stages of nesting. Most of these summer broods, hidden in deep foliage, will survive, though the rain has washed out the nests of some blackbirds and song thrushes. Garden warblers and blackcaps are sitting on their mottled eggs in loose, grassy nests, usually in brambles or honeysuckle. There are bright green young in the domed nests of the willow warblers – they crouch on a soft bed made of two or three hundred feathers, sometimes with their tails in the entrance. The adult willow warblers will try to lure a cat or human away, calling with a pleading note, and trailing a wing as if it were broken.

Young blue tits are calling from their nests deep inside lamp posts. Rooks have already fledged, and young and old fly in circles, cawing, high above the rookery. Young carrion crows are out in the fields; they hop heavily after their parents, still expecting to be fed. Lapwing chicks turn up their tails and bury their beaks in the grass when their parents fly overhead, giving the alarm: the young birds are richly mottled to match their surroundings, but when they run their white collars are conspicuous.

Many June flowers are already abundant. Poppies and ox-eye daisies are thick in the grass. In the cow parsley family, or umbellifers, pignut is out; it is distinguished by its sparse, spiky leaflets just under the white flowerhead. Yellow rocket grows in big clumps on the banks of rivers. The first cat's-ears are opening – solitary dandelion-like heads on a long bare stalk.

Red deer calves call plaintively for their mothers while they are still dark-furred and wet, lying at the foot of a tree. But they will soon be running in their dappled coats with the hinds.

11 June – 17 June

On northern moors, dunlins are singing their high trilling song, like the vocal equivalent of shimmering heat. They sing both on the ground and in the air, and sometimes local skylarks imitate them very accurately. The neat nest of these small wading birds is hidden in a tussock of grass near water; once the young are fledged, they quickly return to the coast.

Snipe often breed on the same moors, though their range extends to boggy places throughout the south of England as well. They are also aerial performers – not singing, but diving down with their outer tail feathers spread to produce a bleating noise as the air rushes through them. Whinchats nesting on the moors make sharp, scolding noises on the tops of the gorse bushes as they wait to take food to their young.

Honeysuckle is in bloom, smelling sweetest in the twilight; after it has been pollinated by moths, its white or pink flowers turn orange. Bugle covers the woodland floor with misty blue patches; in the shadiest parts of the wood, yellow pimpernel is in flower. On chalk hills there are fragrant orchids which have a long purple spike of flowers, and pyramidal orchids which are more tent-shaped, with a disagreeable smell. On lime trees, flower buds are growing out of the papery wings that will eventually carry the seeds away: the little cluster of knobs on stalks looks like the model of a molecule. The first meadow brown butterflies are flying along roadsides, the males chocolate-coloured, the females predominantly orange.

18 June – 24 June

Birds have a busy, preoccupied air; most of them are feeding hungry nestlings or fledgelings. Finches have begun a second brood: goldfinches build again in the swaying outer branches of fruit trees, linnets in thick bramble hedges. Tawny owls range far at night to gather mice and beetles, and are heard hooting in unexpected gardens. The young owls in the nest hole pipe loudly, sometimes beginning to call even before they have broken out of the egg. The robin's song begins to falter; the wren's voice dominates the countryside.

Midsummer flowers are out in profusion. Greater stitchwort sprinkles the ground with white among the young bracken plants; it will die as the bracken canopy closes over it. The purple flowers of tufted vetch twine round the grasses; grass vetchling, with its long thin leaves, is almost undetectable in the meadows, until its deep crimson flower opens on the stem. Poppies and ox-eye daisies fall with the first hay. On woodsides there are tall stands of pink foxglove. Deeper beneath the trees, there are starry white clusters of sanicle.

Water crowfoot covers the ditches with flowers and leaves. Yellow flag stands in clumps on the lakesides; out in the water, yellow water lilies stick up at odd angles on their stems, like the head and neck of some small lake monster. On beech trees the last dry nutshells of last autumn tremble and fall, while the new fruit swells, green and hairy, on the same twig. In cornfields, harvest mice have young in their nests, which are beautifully woven balls of grass, suspended between the stalks.

61

25 June – 1 July

Oak woods are full of blue tit and great tit families, feeding on the caterpillars. Sometimes a blue tit will haul up a dangling caterpillar by its own silk thread. Young cuckoos are out of the nest, but still pursuing their foster-parents with loud chirpings; when they have been fed, they often peck at the robin or meadow pipit that has adopted them. The adult cuckoos are silent, and lead a solitary life in the treetops; in a month they will be gone.

Young downy white gannets are growing in their nests on island cliffs, but some will die from a new hazard. The nests are usually made of seaweed, but gannets also pick up coloured nylon threads from fishing nets and weave it in with the other material. Subsequently it gets tangled round the legs of both nestlings and adults. In the Channel Islands, winter sorties have been made by helicopter to remove the tons of nylon on the ledges. Shags are nesting in similar rocky places; the pale brown nestlings put their heads right down their parents' throats to feed. The adult shags are already losing the curly black tuft on their crown that gives them their name.

Most duck are going into 'eclipse', when the brightly coloured males look more like the females. Drake shovelers lose all their brilliant green, white and chestnut and turn into a muddy purple; drake pintails lose their fine neck pattern. They will all resume their distinctive plumage in the autumn.

Giant hogweed is in some places ten foot high, and in recent years has often formed populous colonies. These small forests are dangerous, since touching the plant in sunlight brings up blisters. The first blossoms are appearing on brambles and attracting crowds of butterflies. Red flowers hang from the stems of many stinging nettles, and dogwood flowers have opened in the hedges. Stoat families hunt in packs and take many young rabbits.

2 July – 8 July

Skylarks are still nesting in the corn: many females are sitting on a second clutch of eggs, while the males sing high overhead. When they come down to ground and run along a field path, they look like small game-birds; when they skim over the waving barley, with their long wings and hesitant wing-beat they seem like brown swallows.

Corn buntings are singing in hedgerow trees or on electricity cables over the fields: they have a short, jangling song, which they deliver with head thrown back and thick beak open wide, as if they were snarling. Some males have several mates, and survey their various nests from their high vantage-point, without helping the females with the nestlings.

At field-edges, the first scabious flowers are opening: they are like jewelled mauve pincushions. Nipplewort is in flower: its small yellow blossoms close quickly when the sun goes in. Hedge bedstraw is coming out everywhere, with its innumerable tiny stars: sometimes it is like a thin mist in the grass, sometimes it grows in large, creamy-looking masses. In chalky places, the ragged purple flowers of greater knapweed are abundant and almost always have a bee sipping at them. There are still a few seedheads of goat's-beard on the roadsides: they look like crystal globes, and when they break up the seeds float away on large parachutes.

Ringlet butterflies are just emerging: they are chocolate-coloured above, but when they settle on bramble or thyme they close their wings and patiently allow an observer to see a line of ringed eye spots on their underwings. Frothy blobs of cuckoo-spit are seen on many plants, especially privet and goose-grass: inside each capsule of foam is a green spittlebug nymph, feeding on the sap.

9 July – 15 July

Young magpies already have tails as long as their parents', and are very pugnacious: they will run at a flock of pigeons and send them flying. But they still beg for food, calling harshly and fluttering their wings. Goldfinches come down on to railway lines to eat the seeds of the Oxford ragwort growing between the rails. House-martins fly tirelessly round the roof-tops; the glossy-blue parent birds have been joined by the juveniles, who have a distinctly browner tinge. All the family roosts in the small mud nest at night. Collared doves are still soaring and gliding in sexual display, but it is a rather half-hearted performance compared with the bold and noisy soaring and swooping of the woodpigeons. On northern moors, twites are nesting in the heather or gorse: they are like small grey linnets with pale bills, and the male has a pink rump. They fly as fast as linnets, singing as they go.

The ground is sticky under the lime trees: the minute aphids that feed on the leaves coat them with a honeydew that slowly drips off. Ladybirds come to the limes to feed on the aphids and bees come for the rich nectar in the flowers. Under horse-chestnut trees, the grass is covered with embryo fruit that has been knocked off by the thunderstorms. Three spectacular wild flowers are just coming out: nettle-leaved bellflower with its white buds and spiky violet trumpets, and the two finest willowherbs – rosebay willowherb in pale pink spires, and great hairy willowherb, or 'codlins and cream', in purple-pink clumps that are often six feet tall.

Painted lady butterflies have come up from the Mediterranean: they fly in sweeping zigzags along the lanes, then settle on a sunny patch of ground and fan their white-streaked orange wings.

16 July – 22 July

Birds lie on their sides and rest in very hot weather: a blackbird has been seen lying with its head resting on a small stone. In gardens, the noisiest birds are families of spotted flycatchers; they call continually with a sharp, high-pitched note as they dart through the top branches of the limes and ash trees to snap up flying insects. The first waders are beginning to come down from the north and are appearing on the estuaries. Greenshank step delicately along the edge of muddy pools on their long green legs; when they fly up, they give a triple, yodelling cry. Whimbrel sometimes feed near them. Common sandpipers bob at the edge of lakes and streams, then fly off across the water on flickering wings. Little ringed plovers gather in deserted gravel pits, where they run rapidly across the sandbanks.

Most trees are now a much darker green, and leaves are withering in the drought on some horse-chestnuts. But on rowan trees fresh green leaves are sprouting at the end of the shoots, as the berries turn scarlet. On oak trees, the acorns are growing plump, but are still hard and green.

Hedge woundwort and stinging nettles grow over the woodland paths. The purple flowerheads of lesser knapweed or hardheads attract small skipper butterflies, which rest with their rear wings flat and their orange forewings held upright.

Two plants which have yellow flowers on spikes are now common: the sweet-scented great mullein, which has thick, downy grey leaves, and agrimony which is shorter and more wiry. Long beak-like seed-pods are appearing among the electric blue flowers of meadow crane's-bill. In sunny places the first blackberries are ripe.

23 July – 29 July

Most summer bird song is coming to an end; but skylarks are still singing high above the ripening wheat, and the yellowhammer's song chimes on through the long, hot afternoons. Goldfinch families are very noticeable in the trees; they all have flashing gold wing-bars, and the parents have a shining red, white and black face. Robins look worn and battered with the effort of feeding their young, who can be heard hissing deep in the hedges.

The flowers of high summer are in full bloom everywhere. By the roadside, there are tall mallows, bushes of hedge bedstraw and the yellow ladders of melilot. Dry, chalky places are overgrown with the dark yellow flowers of St John's wort and pale pink centaury. Rosebay willowherb makes patches of shocking pink among the bracken. The soft young heads of teasel are guarded by a ring of curved silver spears. The petals of the dog roses have fallen, but green hips are swelling beneath the star-shaped sepals.

There are thick clusters of flowers by the edge of ponds: the handsome purple spires of marsh woundwort, tall clumps of great hairy willowherb, and low tangles of white and pink yarrow. Chicory grows in dry places, its misty blue flowers lined all the way up the long stalk; the large yellow flowers of bristly oxtongue open among the prickly, white-wealed leaves. Black-and-orange caterpillars of the cinnabar moth strip the ragwort plants almost bare.

30 July – 5 August

Some birds are still tending their young. On grassy heaths, meadow pipits make an insistent call like a cricket chirping, as they wait nervously to take food to their nestlings; a few females are still incubating a late clutch of mottled chocolate-brown eggs. Around the Scottish coasts, eiderduck are swimming with flotillas of ducklings; they make a noisy party, with the females continually grunting and growling, and the young piping shrilly. Puffins are feeding their solitary nestlings, deep in sandy burrows; if the mouth of the burrow collapses, the adults whirr the sand out in a brown cloud. Fulmars also have a single chick in their cliffside nests. The parents fish out at sea, gliding on stiff wings; when they come back, the cliffs echo with murmurs and rattling cries from the nests.

The nut-shaped yellow flowers of hop trefoil are common in the long grass. Tufted vetch already has black seed pods, which reveal a silver lining when they split open. The greenish-white flowers of traveller's joy are sprawling over the hedges. Wild basil, which has bright pink flowers and faintly aromatic leaves, is common under hedges; and in some chalky lanes there are banks of lesser calamint, a small, pale purple flower that sends waves of fragrance across the road. Wild carrot is out at the edge of fields: it has flowers like small white saucers, with a tangle of feathery bracts beneath them.

Spindle trees are showing small green seeds which look like four-pointed club-heads; whitish-green hazel nuts are fattening in their leafy sockets, but they will not be ripe for a month or more. Conkers are swelling in their spiky green cases.

6 August – 12 August

Most of the barley has been harvested, and where the stubble is being ploughed flocks of black-headed gulls are foraging in the newly turned earth. The first wheat is being cut, and house sparrows come into the fields to pick up split grain. Kestrels have finished breeding; the young birds swell the numbers hunting along the motorway verges.

On the Scottish moors, families of red grouse are joining up in small parties; when they rise from the heather they give a cackling cry, and whirr into the distance, tilting from side to side. On Scottish coasts, more curlews are coming down to feed along the shoreline; and in sheltered pools behind the sand-spits there are often quite large gatherings of red-breasted mergansers.

Foxglove is abundant. On the moors it grows with the yellow tormentil; lower down it is found with rosebay willowherb and red campion. In the west of England, the small white spires of wall pennywort stand among their round leaves in shady lanes, and English stonecrop, with its starry white petals and red stems, grows among the rocks where the sheep feed. Cow-wheat is common at the shady edges of oak woods: its lipped yellow flowers all face the same way on the stalk, and it feeds on the roots of trees and other plants. Bilberries are ripening everywhere on the hillsides; some are already fat and juicy.

Young frogs have dispersed and are foraging for insects in the thick grass, but they will return to their native ponds to breed next spring.

13 August – 19 August

Yellow wagtails have finished nesting in the fields, and begin to flock together in reed-beds at dusk. They will soon be leaving for west Africa. Swifts career in wild screaming-parties round roofs and steeples: on a cool morning, with a favourable wind, they will suddenly disappear, bound for South Africa. Lapwings are beginning to arrive from the Continent: the first flocks consist mainly of young birds who have set off ahead of their parents.

Herons still stand on their nests, though their young are fully grown and can only be distinguished by their grey heads and rudimentary crests. Sometimes a flock will set off to feed together; they call to each other with a duck-like quack, rather than the usual deep honk of a solitary bird. Starlings wheel in the air like swallows, in pursuit of flying ants. Blackbirds are moulting: they look like worn velvet cushions.

Yellow toadflax is bright on the roadsides; lilac flowers are appearing on the burdocks. Wild strawberries can be picked in dry woods. The drooping purple cones of buddleia are found growing wild on railway embankments and waste land: they attract enormous crowds of insects, especially peacock and small tortoiseshell butterflies, bumblebees, and drone flies, which are a long-tongued species of hoverfly. Other kinds of hoverfly (of which there are over 200 varieties) are busy feeding in the convolvulus, or licking up the honeydew left by aphids on the leaves of flowers. Yellow underwing moths flash their lower wings as they fly along a hedge, but vanish when they settle, their dull upper wings merging with the twigs and leaves.

77

20 August – 26 August

The first robins are singing again as they take up their autumn territories. This autumn song is thinner and less varied than the spring song which begins at the end of December. As well as the males, some females are now establishing territories, but they will abandon them and join up with a male in the new year. Great tits are also singing intermittently: in these late summer days there is often a short burst of aggression and competition before the tits join up in their winter feeding flocks.

Jays occasionally produce a curious song, muted screams mixed with magpie-like chattering and musical notes. Collared doves are still singing energetically on television aerials in village high streets. On coastal mudflats, shelducks are fussily escorting their broods of ten or twelve young. The grey-capped juveniles, almost as big as their parents, walk in a long line; the two parents, honking nervously, walk either side of them.

Burnet saxifrage is in bloom: this is one of the most delicate of the 'umbrella' flowers, and is distinguished by the very small leaves at the top of the stalk and the large ones at the bottom. Tansy is out, with its button-like yellow flowers and lemon scent. Dry grass is everywhere dotted with small dandelion-like flowers: this is autumnal hawkbit, which has a rosette of small jagged leaves at its base. Most hawthorn berries are still apple-green, but some have a dark-red flush.

Gatekeeper butterflies chase each other over marjoram and knapweed; wall browns settle on dry paths. On downland by the coast, grayling butterflies are on the wing. When they alight, they close their dappled orange wings, and tilt them towards the sun, so that they do not cast a shadow by which predators might detect them.

27 August – 2 September

Swallows are gathering in twittering flocks on telephone wires or the warm tiles of farm buildings; sometimes they all fly up from the roof in an obscure panic, but quickly return again. After a few days of excitement like this they set off on migration for South Africa.

Sedge and reed warblers have deserted the lakesides and ditches; tree pipits have left the woodland edges. Willow warblers are moving south on a broad front. All these species are now *en route* for tropical Africa, with thousands crossing the English Channel every day. Chiffchaffs are also leaving, but most of them will go no further than the Mediterranean – and they will be among the first spring migrants to return next year, at the end of March.

On many lime trees, a whole branch is turning yellow, while the rest of the tree remains quite green; on the hornbeams, individual leaves are changing colour all over the tree, giving it a dappled look. Some birches have turned completely. Among the dead purple stalks of cow parsley, its dainty autumn relative, upright hedge parsley, is flourishing with many white and pink flowers. Badgers are busy extending their underground sets before the cold weather comes. Wasps are feeding on fallen fruit and jammy knives, but for the larvae in their nests they take back meatier food and can be seen biting off the wings and legs of a daddy-long-legs, or crane fly, before flying away with the body. On the moors, millions of bees are feeding on the heather, and produce a seamless humming that extends for miles.

3 September – 9 September

Curlews are at the height of their migration on the shores and estuaries; both their ringing 'cur-lee' call and their bubbling summer trill are heard along the water's edge. Some house martins are moving south, but many can still be seen feeding out in the fields: they swoop over the heads of grazing cattle which have disturbed the insects in the grass. In the woods, mixed flocks of tits are forming: the coal tits are particularly noisy and active, hovering and darting among the twigs, and bursting into loud, plangent calls. The staccato whistling of nuthatches can be heard again, with one bird joining in after another until the treetops seem to be full of echoing typewriters. Great spotted woodpeckers are looking very bright after moulting, barred black and white above and scarlet under the tail; at this unhurried time of year for resident birds, they like to sit for long periods on the very pinnacle of a fir tree, looking around them.

Everywhere in the countryside there is a glimmer of autumn reds. Hawthorn bushes are laden with crimson berries, while the clusters of black elderberries are surrounded with vinous red leaves. On brambles, the ripening berries are a glossy red and some of the leaves are scarlet. The lower leaves of docks are also turning bright red. Rosebay willowherb is going to seed, and wasteland is covered with the white, fluffy spires. In the fields, much of the stubble has now been ploughed in; where it remains, grass, thistles, fat hen and scentless mayweed are all pushing up between the fading, yellow lines.

Brown aeshna dragonflies, the largest of the common dragonflies, dart and glide over the water, hunting until it is almost dark.

10 September – 16 September

Hobbies are small, scythe-winged hawks, that catch their prey on the wing; some are still at their nesting sites on heaths or lonely farmland, others are heading south catching house martins or dragonflies wherever they can. They fly very fast – now overhead, now far away, their plaintive calls fading.

On ploughed fields, there are small flocks of skylarks; and much larger flocks are starting to come in from the Continent. Many of the immigrants will move on to southern Europe, but the British skylarks will stay near their territories and resume song occasionally between now and Christmas. Meadow pipits are also arriving on the east coast. The pipits and the larks call as they fly, and can be heard passing through the sky at night almost anywhere in England. Whinchats are coming down both east and west coasts; they are quick, restless birds with a bold white eyestripe, which stop to feed in bushes in neglected fields. Eventually the whole European population will be settled for the winter in tropical Africa.

Leaves are yellowest on the elder trees. Limes, elms and horse-chestnuts are also beginning to turn. Many sycamore leaves are framed in brown. On hazel bushes, green nuts sit side by side with tiny, hard catkins that will dangle long and loose in the spring. There are black berries on the dogwood bushes, and yellow fruit litters the ground beneath crab-apple trees. Under oak trees there are many half-eaten acorns dropped by woodpigeons and grey squirrels. Small tortoiseshell butterflies are abundant; red admirals are starting to join the peacocks on the buddleias.

17 September – 23 September

Moorland birds on their way south are appearing in unexpected places; ring ousels – like blackbirds with a white gorget – stop to feed in the early morning on golf courses; merlins pursue skylarks and waders along the shore.

Great black-backed gulls from Norway are already well distributed along the east coast. They are enormous, fierce birds, and though they live largely on herrings, they have been known to kill lambs, cats and moles. They are mainly distinguished from lesser black-backed gulls by being larger, and by their white or pinkish legs. Lesser black-backs, which have yellow legs, are only just beginning to come down from their northern breeding grounds. They are often found on fields inland when migrating; they roost on reservoirs and fly out in the half-light of dawn.

In marshy places the leaves of great water dock – up to a yard long – can still be seen. Water mint remains in flower and gives off a sweet scent when crushed under foot. The large pink flowerheads of hemp agrimony are looking grey and dusty as they turn to seed.

In damp fields, yellow flowers continue to bloom on silverweed, though its leaves are not as glittering as they were earlier in the year; and fleabane is still flowering abundantly. On heathland, harebells are still in bloom: they have long, spiky sepals at the base of the lilac flowers. They often grow near sweet-smelling mats of wild thyme, which also still has plenty of small pink flowers. The snapdragon-like flowers of yellow toadflax are abundant in grassy places; this is a tenacious plant, and if dug up can grow again from a small scrap of root left behind. Small heath butterflies are on the wing, mingling in some places with a late brood of meadow browns.

24 September – 30 September

Tree sparrows are flocking; the two sexes have the same plumage, like neat male house sparrows with a smudge on the cheek. Starlings are roosting communally again, both in dense woods and on city buildings. Most of these are British birds, but they will soon be joined by vast flocks of winter visitors from Germany and Poland. Wrynecks are now appearing in the eastern counties on their way south; they feed on the ground as well as in the treetops. Manx shearwaters have left their nesting holes and have spread all round the coast, where they skim with stiff wings over the waves. Practically all of them will move on to more southern waters. Kittiwakes are also appearing everywhere offshore; they are dainty gulls with a soft, dark eye, and will stay throughout the winter.

Some horse-chestnut trees have red or yellow crowns, though boys knocking down the conkers find that they are still white, or only streaked with glossy brown. Hawthorn trees also have many red patches, and Lombardy poplars are flecked with pale yellow. Golden rod is in flower on railway embankments; nipplewort is still common on roadsides, and daisies continue to open on lawns. In many places mushrooms and blackberries are at their best. Garden spiders are building large webs, which glitter when the morning mist collects in droplets on them. In the evening caddis flies swarm over ponds; there are almost 200 species in Britain, most with lacy wings and long thread-like antennae.

91

1 October – 7 October

Teal are coming in from Germany and Denmark; they haunt the edges of lakes where there are reeds growing in the water. Sometimes they dabble, sometimes they swim a long way with their heads beneath the surface. The speculum on their wing is a glittering green; the drakes also have a comma-shaped green band across the eye. Snipe from the same part of Europe often feed near them on the mud: they probe deep with their long beaks, sucking up worms without raising their heads. Last chiffchaffs are singing in the sunshine, before they leave for the Mediterranean.

Conkers and horse-chestnut leaves are falling together, producing the first rich, musty smells of autumn. Lime and birch leaves are coming down in the wind. There are dangling green seed-pods among the pink flowers on Himalayan balsam: when the pods are touched they split open and leap in the air, sometimes two or three feet high, scattering the brown seeds. Wild Michaelmas daisies are found in extensive clumps on waste ground, looking like gigantic heather.

On garden walls, ivy-leaved toadflax is still in flower, and the yellow blooms of the ivy itself are full of nectar – the last feeding place of wasps and hoverflies before they die. The crackling leaves at the bottom of hedges are full of life, as slugs and snails go down from the branches, and ground beetles hunt for ants and the minute springtails. Female glow-worms shine at night: the winged males glimmer feebly. Late moths include the angle shades, whose fine green and chestnut markings blend with the dying leaves, and the merveille du jour, whose pale green wings match the lichen on the oak trunks.

8 October – 14 October

Fieldfares are back from the north of Europe: the first nervous one announces itself with a harsh chatter in the sky, then the surrounding hedges or treetops are seen to be full of them. Their blue-grey heads and rumps contrast strikingly with their chestnut backs. Black-headed gulls are now back inland in vast numbers; many of them roost at night on the reservoirs.

Young sparrow hawks are moving out of their parents' territories. They dart through the tops of the fir trees, snatching up small birds; sometimes they soar on rounded wings, surveying the land below. Buzzards are wandering afield; occasionally they pass over cities, very high in the sky. Kingfishers are leaving the rivers where they nested in the banks, and appearing on new waters. Blackbirds are gorging themselves on fallen apples. Apart from robins and wrens, there is little song: a brief outburst from a great tit or coal tit, the raucous cooing of a late collared dove. A few goldfinches and skylarks are also singing again – but this autumn burst of song will not last long.

There are thick drifts of yellow leaves under the black Italian poplars. Oaks and ash trees are still very green. The dry, white stalks of dead hemlock stand in clumps, with a few tall plants still bearing green leaves and white flowers. Wild angelica has large, dark brown seedheads; its shrivelling leaves retain their curious double form, with a fleshy bracket clasping the stem, and a second, fern-like leaf growing out of it.

As autumn progresses, most birds are noisiest around dusk. House sparrows roost in huddled flocks in evergreens or under the roofs of houses, and chirp together loudly for up to an hour before they sleep. Blackbirds come to the edges of their territories and challenge each other with loud, chinking cries as the light fades; afterwards, if there is not much thick cover to be had, they too will gather together to roost. Hedge sparrows that have spent the day on their own call to each other with thin cries, and often roost in pairs. Robins generally sleep alone in fir trees or thick ivy.

Some young woodpigeons are only just leaving the nest, the last fledgelings of the year. They have white wing-bars like their parents, but not the white bar on the neck. A few woodpigeons are still singing, but they will not be heard regularly again until January. They have an almost invariable song of short and long cooing notes, which could be represented as 'Take two books with you, take two books with you, dolt' – the 'two books' being the most emphatic notes.

Hornbeams are rapidly losing their leaves, but on many the boughs are still crowded with hanging orange clusters of seeds, like frilly-edged lanterns. On ash trees there are patches of paler green or yellow, but most of the leaves will stay bright green until they fall.

There are bead-like streams of brilliant red berries where the black bryony has coiled round the stems of other plants or along wires; the leaves have often withered or gone. There are also shining red berries on the unrelated white bryony, which climbs with the help of small tendrils, not by twining itself round supports. The berries of both bryonies are very poisonous.

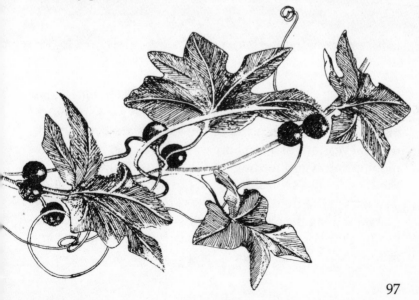

Pied wagtails are running about on farmhouse roofs, and
occasionally singing on the crest; they have a short, babbling song, in which many of the sounds are like slurred,
musical versions of their sharp call-note. Lesser redpolls are
moving south and feeding on the catkins of silver birches:
they sometimes send showers of the winged seeds floating
down from the trees. Hen harriers are appearing on lonely
marshes along the east coast: they sweep low over the land
hunting for voles and snipe, and often sleep in small, communal roosts in reed-beds or long grass.

Most of the waders that come down the British coasts on their way further south have now passed through; those that remain will spend the winter here. They include up to half a million dunlin which have been coming in from Russia and Scandinavia (while the birds that bred on our own moors have left for Africa). The dunlin feed on the shoreline in large flocks; in flight, hundreds of them will twist and turn simultaneously at great speed and, as they land again, they all lift their wings high for a moment before settling down.

Leaves are showering down from the trees in the wind and scampering across open spaces, especially the large leaves of planes and Norway maples. Beech leaves are bronze and gold; they are mostly holding firm on the trees still. In the hedges, dogwood leaves are like purple smoke among the browns and greens; sometimes a nearby ditch is full of small dogwood saplings as well. Wild angelica is still in flower in damp places, its tall red stems swaying in the wind; there are also a few flowers left on yarrow and red clover.

29 October – 4 November

The last of the Arctic terns are passing along the coast: they dip through the mist, calling harshly. Some will go as far south as the Antarctic Circle. Golden plovers feed with the lapwings out on the arable fields. When they all rise, the lapwings spread out with slow, heavy wingbeats, but the golden plovers rapidly find each other, and the flock cuts sharply through the sky. Redwings from Scandinavia are back in Britain for the winter; they are like song thrushes with a bright red underwing which is very conspicuous when they fly up. Feeding on the berries in hawthorn hedges, they often use a call like the clucking note of blackbirds, but with a strong nasal twang to it; migrating overhead at night they utter long, thin cries. Song thrushes and mistle thrushes are singing again: some of the song thrushes sing more quietly than in the spring, but the mistle thrushes bugle as loud as ever from the swaying treetops.

On roadsides in the south, there is a late flowering of bristly oxtongue: every part of this plant is covered with rough hairs, except for the pale yellow flowerheads. Elm hedges are sprinkled with a brighter yellow, and oak leaves are shrivelling. Bracken is turning brown and gold. Beech-nuts and sweet chestnuts litter the woodland floors, not yet hidden by fallen leaves.

In oak and beech woods, cep mushrooms, also known as penny-bun boletus, are growing large, with white flesh and sticky chestnut caps. Nearby there sometimes grows the brown-stalked bitter boletus. Money-spiders are on the move, floating through the air on threads of silk: on warm, dry days they sometimes descend in vast numbers on fields and gardens, covering the grass with their gauzy webs.

5 November – 11 November

Wild geese are back from their summer breeding-grounds in Greenland and the Arctic. They fly strongly in V-shaped skeins, different birds taking it in turn to lead. In England, the most commonly seen are white-fronted geese, with their conspicuous white faces; they roost on estuaries or floodwater, and fly in to feed on the clover and winter wheat. Pink-footed geese are commoner in the north; and on the west coast of Scotland, especially on the island of Islay, enormous flocks of the black-and-white barnacle goose come in, yapping like dogs. Brent geese are flocking into the estuaries of south-east England: they are smaller, darker birds, but also have a barking cry. They feed, mainly by day, on the long, green underwater ribbons of eel-grass.

In most parts of Britain, autumn leaves are now at their most spectacular. Beeches are ablaze with orange and yellow and the few remaining limes that have leaves appear like pale parchment lamps when the sun shines through them. Cherry and gean are in every shade of purple and crimson. Sweet chestnut leaves flutter through the air like slender yellow fish, while the last prickly seed-cases plop to the ground: the grey squirrels quickly clean out the chestnuts. A rich, musty smell of leaves fills woods and gardens.

On the downs, spindle-trees are colourful, with purple leaves and bright pink berries splitting open to reveal orange seeds. Many flowers linger in skimpy patches: ragwort, scentless mayweed, yellow toadflax, ground ivy. The white grass of late summer has vanished and the autumn grass is thick and green again. Pygmy and common shrews are found dead on paths and lawns: the adults die each year of exhaustion, and only the young are left to get through the winter in the hedge-bottoms.

12 November – 18 November

Kingfisher families have broken up, and the members have resumed their solitary lives. Though they are such brilliantly coloured birds, they are well camouflaged in waterside bushes just now, their blue backs and orange breasts blending with the green banks and red bramble leaves behind them.

Loud screeches in town gardens indicate that jays have come in from the countryside. They are a kind of pink crow; when perched, they show a thin blue line above their flanks, but when one sees them from an upstairs window, flying below, they reveal a large patch of brilliant blue on their wings. There are blackbirds everywhere: the summer population has now been swelled by many migrants from central Europe.

Misty yellows and oranges envelop the countryside. Pale yellow maple leaves glow with a luminous intensity, oak leaves wither from the edges. Guelder roses are like red columns, with their leaves pink or crimson and their berries a transparent scarlet. The yellow flowers of wild turnip are still in bloom here and there: it is like charlock, but with pointed leaves that clasp the stem. The straggling seeds of old man's beard look like patches of dirty snow on the hedges.

Adders and grass snakes have gone into hibernation, coiled under wood piles or in abandoned birds' nests in the heather.

19 November – 25 November

Lapwings, or green plovers, are feeding in flocks on ploughland, many of them winter visitors from Scandinavia and Germany. Black-headed gulls often stand among them, each marking a lapwing like a footballer: when the lapwing finds a morsel of food, the gull chases it with harsh screams until the lapwing drops it. The plovers will feed by moonlight to avoid these attacks.

On quiet lakes, there are now many shovelers and gadwall. These are surface-feeding ducks, unlike the tufted ducks and pochards which dive for their food. The drake shovelers are like tricolour flags floating on the water, with their green heads, white breasts and red flanks; both sexes have beaks like large, black shoe-horns, with which they scoop up plant seeds and water-beetles. Gadwall swim about in pairs, and spend much time up-ending: one often sees two of their barred black-and-white sterns protruding from the water side by side.

Leaves are thick on the ground. Some, like lime-tree leaves, disintegrate quickly; others, especially plane-tree leaves, remain firm and intact until well into the winter. Last wasps are coming into houses for warmth, but only the new queens will survive. Hedgehogs are making nests of leaves and moss to hibernate in, usually choosing a hole in a bank; sometimes they will use an old wasps' nest.

The tiny muntjac deer now found wild in much of southern England bark like a dog at night, and in these last days of autumn they are sometimes glimpsed among the crumpling purple bracken.

26 November – 2 December

Winter visitors are now more conspicuous in the bird population. On the coast, there are small flocks of snow buntings: their sandy plumage merges with the background until they fly up, but then their white wings and dancing flight make them look like whirling snowflakes.

On the east coast, there are a few Lapland buntings from the far north of Europe: they run like mice among the grass and sea asters at the edge of the shore.

The first bramblings from the north have also arrived; they are rather like chaffinches, to which they are closely related, but have bright orange shoulders and a white rump. They do not follow such regular migration routes as most birds, but each year seek out the districts or countries where there is the best harvest of beech-mast.

Young magpies that have not yet got a territory for themselves are roosting in small flocks. The older birds stay in pairs all through the winter, and remain in their territories. In cold weather they store acorns or other food in holes in the ground; while they are digging a hole with their beak, they keep the food concealed in a pouch under their tongue.

Flowers still to be found include Oxford ragwort and herb-robert, with pink blossoms and leaves. Teasel plants stand tall, some as much as seven foot high: their spiky, purple seed-heads are defended like the flowers were by criss-crossing white swords. On alder trees, new purple catkins are growing among the black seed-cones. Weeping willows are still quite green, but the remaining leaves on the oak trees have a grey washed-out look. Grass is still very green everywhere, and glitters in the low sun and the strong wind.

3 December – 9 December

Starlings are roosting in vast flocks in small woods or on city buildings. If they are disturbed at sunset, the roar of voices ceases and they fly up, to wheel and criss-cross in the sky; the moment they settle, their mass chatter begins again. Many individuals return night after night to exactly the same twig or cornice. Black-headed gulls leave the fields at dusk to roost on reservoirs or lagoons; they glide in circles high in the sky, the whole ring of them slowly drifting in the direction they want to go.

Goldeneyes are among the winter duck now appearing on inland waters: both sexes have shining yellow eyes, and the drake has a white cheek patch on his glossy green head. They ride low on the water and look rather deliquescent and shapeless. Female tufted ducks also have conspicuous yellow eyes, but they sit more trimly on the water than the female goldeneyes, and are a darker brown.

On frosty mornings, the clumps of dead rosebay willow-herb are like shining feathers stuck in the ground. A few winged seeds still hang on the sycamores, but they are too chipped and water-logged to spin down as they do in autumn. On osiers, the thin, drooping yellow leaves look from a distance like hazel catkins that are full of pollen three months too early.

Water rats, or water voles, are still active: they are heard more often than they are seen, as they dive with a loud splash into the water. After that, they return to a hole in the bank, or swim away well beneath the surface.

10 December – 16 December

The main autumn migrations are over, and birds have little to do except eat. But with the days so short they have to look for food almost continuously. A cold night will use all their reserves of fat. Canada geese go foraging in large flocks from lake to lake; when they up-end to feed in the water, the white feathers under their tails rise into the air like broad sails. Herons appear at garden ponds: they wade up to their thighs in search of fish, or stalk along the muddy edge and dive headlong when they see their prey. On the coast, wintering greenshanks walk in the shallow water and kick at the sand to bring food to the surface. Among the dead leaves blackbirds clear neat circles of bare earth where they can get at insects and worms. Bullfinches come down to the ground to feed on nettle and dock seeds, and any dried-up blackberries they can find.

Tawny owls hunt till dawn for mice and roosting sparrows and can sometimes still be heard calling well after sunrise. The long, quavering hoot is the male's song; the commonly heard 'tu-whit-tu-whoo' is in fact usually a joint performance, the female making the sharp cry and the male hooting in reply.

Weeping willows are the greenest trees left. Brambles still have many purple leaves on them; bracken is brown and broken. But next year's buds are already noticeable on many trees. On horse-chestnuts, the buds are dark and sticky, aspen buds are plump and pink and on beeches the sharp buds show through the clinging orange leaves. On oak trees, marble galls or oak-apples are conspicuous, now dry and brown and deserted by the gall-wasps which grew in them as grubs: the small hole in each shows where the wasp came out.

17 December – 23 December

In strong winds, unusual bird calls in the treetops generally prove to be creaking branches. The loudest bird sounds high in the trees at present are the sharp cry of the great spotted woodpecker and the chattering of magpies.

Woodcock are lurking beneath the bracken and the bramble in many woods. They are most often seen when a dog flushes them: they rise quickly, bursting through the foliage, and zigzag away through the trees. At dusk they usually leave the woods to feed on earthworms in damp fields or ditches: they probe with the tips of their bills, then sink them deep when they detect a worm. A common sound at dusk just now is the 'chissick' call of pied wagtails as they come with looping flight into their communal roosts in laurels or reed-beds, sometimes from five or six miles away.

Wintering swans are back in Britain. The smaller Bewick's swans are concentrated in the Ouse Washes and at Slimbridge, while whooper swans are found, sometimes on quite small waters, throughout the northern part of Britain. Both species have yellow bills, in contrast to the orange bill of the mute swan; they are often best distinguished from each other by their calls, the Bewick flocks baying like a pack of hounds, the whoopers trumpeting in the way their name suggests.

In neglected city gardens, feverfew continues in flower here and there, often nestling against a gatepost; and gallant soldier, with its tiny white and yellow flowers, rampages in the flower beds. In the afternoon, swarms of winter gnats dance in the air in sheltered places: these gnats belong to the daddy-long-legs family, not the mosquito family, and do not bite.

24 December – 31 December

On moonlit nights, and by well-lit roads and motorways, some robins start singing at three in the morning. They are often mistaken for nightingales; but all the European nightingales are in Africa by now, and will not be back until mid-April.

Siskins have come south again from Scotland and are feeding in the alder trees. They have a very soft twitter that can easily be missed; you look up and notice one, and suddenly see that the whole tree is twinkling with them, the breasts of the males like gold in the low winter sunlight. Sometimes a whole line of them is hanging head forward on a branch, like a line of quotation marks. On pines and firs, tree-creepers probe for insects under the thin bark: they leave a shower of reddish-brown flakes falling beneath them as they climb the trunk. Along the coast, stonechats have established their winter territories around gorse bushes, and spend most of their time feeding quietly on the ground.

Japanese autumn cherries are in flower; thick clusters of pale orange keys still hang on the ash trees; silvery seed-pods linger on the laburnums. In the tops of lime trees, gigantic balls of mistletoe covered with plump white berries sway among the red buds and twigs. Spruce firs are covered with long orange cones; they are shallow-rooted trees, easily toppled by the winter gales, and sometimes fall in a line like dominoes. (Most Christmas trees are young spruces.) Earthworms tug the dead leaves into their holes, eat them, and leave the remains on the grass as worm-casts. Seven-spot ladybirds come out of tangled vegetation into the winter sunshine.

Index

124